ABOUT THE AUTHORS

MICHAEL PAULS and DANA FACAROS are professional travel writers. Over the past ten years they have lived in several countries concentrating mainly on the Mediterranean area. In Turkey they were, in their own words, "fortunate to have had experiences as diverse as participating in a dervish ceremony and being invited in for tea by Kurdish tr[illegible]dytes squatting in the remains of a 2000 year old underground cit[illegible]tion to this guide, their travel books include highly suc[illegible]he Greek Islands, Italian Islands and Spanish Isla[illegible]n and are at present based in Spain, resea[illegible]

CADOGAN GUIDES

Other titles in the Cadogan Guide series:

IRELAND
GREEK ISLANDS
THE SOUTH OF FRANCE
ITALIAN ISLANDS
THE CARIBBEAN

Forthcoming:

SPAIN
INDIA
SCOTLAND

CADOGAN GUIDES

TURKEY

MICHAEL PAULS & DANA FACAROS

Illustrations by Pauline Pears

Series Editors: Rachel Fielding and Janey Morris

CADOGAN BOOKS
LONDON

First published in 1986 by
Cadogan Books Ltd
16 Lower Marsh, London SE1
Reprinted 1987
ISBN 0–946313–36–9

Phototypeset in Ehrhardt on a Linotron 202
Printed and bound in Great Britain by Redwood Burn Ltd,
Trowbridge, Wiltshire

ACKNOWLEDGEMENTS

We would like to warmly thank Hasan Kocatürk, Assistant General Director of Information and Promotion of the Ministry of Culture and Tourism; Kamil Muren, Director of their National Tourist Office in New York, and Köksal Başaran of the Tourist Ministry for their kind assistance and insights into 'the whole bird'. We also owe a considerable debt of gratitude to the many provincial and local tourist offices throughout Turkey, and especially to Fuat Özdoğru of Diyarbakir, Zeki Selçuk of Van, and Leyla Ilova of the city tourist office in Bursa. Also special thanks to Wolfgang Feldmann and his photographic talents, to the Turkish Tourism Office in London for their kind assistance at the last minute and to Mrs Emine Türkece Connor for kindly checking our Turkish spelling.

CONTENTS

Part IX

The Black Sea *Page 231*

Anatolia

Part X

North-Western Anatolia

Part XI

South-Western Anatolia

LIST OF MAPS

INTRODUCTION

Suddenly Turkey is popular. As other fleshpots of Mediterranean tourism begin to burst at the seams with tour buses, jewellery shops, and hyperactive teenagers, people are beginning to see this ancient land as a new frontier. Lovely resorts and low prices make Turkey attractive to every vacationer, but there is more to it than broad beaches and a touch of the exotic conjured up in a puff of smoke from a traditional water pipe.

We will show you a Turkey with more classical ruins than Greece, and more monuments of Islam than Arabia. Its attractions range from the exaggerated and huge, like the decapitated stone kings of Mt Nemrut, to the exquisite and refined tilework in the Imperial mosques of Istanbul. You can ski in an alpine-style winter resort or bathe in a clean, warm Mediterranean sea in November; watch the dervishes whirl in December and greased wrestlers tussle in the spring. You can take in the renowned Biblical sites, from the Harran of Abraham to the Ephesus of St Paul, or go on a gourmet tour, sampling the ingenious dishes first prepared for the Ottoman Sultans.

In our travels through Turkey, from the Aegean coast to the Soviet Border, we have met every sort of traveller—carefree young backpackers and chic sophisticates, beachcombers and folklore scholars, Canadians, Iranians, and people from nearly every country in between. Some are regular visitors to Turkey, and of the first-timers almost all say they'll be back as soon as they can. Don't be surprised if you find yourself among them. Whatever you have heard or believed about Turkey, behind the enigmatic face it turns to the outside world, there is a land and a people whose unaffected charm and surprising hospitality will make your travels easy and pleasant.

You'll probably bring home some souvenirs—everyone who ever sets foot inside a Turkish bazaar does—and the low prices may make you stay longer than you intended. The best part of Turkey, though, is free—timeless images of landscapes untouched by the industrial revolution, goatherds and their charges wandering through the olive groves and ruined temples, women gossiping around the neighbourhood well in Istanbul, banana shaped dwellings carved from the rocks of Cappadocia, an amiable mystic demonstrating the 99 names of God inscribed on the human palm, hundreds of giggling, well-scrubbed schoolchildren in their black smocks snaking single file through a museum at a breathless pace, only pausing to ask you in earnest English 'Is Turkey beautiful?' It is indeed.

PLEASE NOTE

Every effort has been made to ensure the accuracy of the information in this book at the time of going to press. However, practical details such as opening hours, travel information, standards in hotels and restaurants and, in particular, prices are liable to change.

Prices in Turkey can be a very confusing subject. The country suffers from a chronically high rate of inflation (as much as 30%) but on the other hand, the Turkish lira is frequently devalued against Western currencies. As a result, the actual costs of your trip remain about the same—though the numbers are always changing! In this edition, prices are based on the rate current at time of writing, about 700 TL to the pound. Please bear in mind that, as Turkey becomes more popular, prices are subject to larger increases.

We intend to keep this book as up-to-date as possible in the coming years. Please write to us if there is anything you feel should be included in future editions.

Part I

GENERAL INFORMATION

Landscape in Western Anatolia

Getting to Turkey

By Air

British Airways has regular flights to Istanbul, as do the Turkish National Airlines, *Turk Hava Yollari* (THY) which links most European and Middle Eastern capitals with Istanbul. The lowest official fares start at £240 return with stringent booking conditions. Discounted tickets, however, are available from bucket shops* for scheduled flights on BA and THY: prices range from £180 (low season) to £210 (summer). The Sunquest agency in London (01 800 5455) consistently offers low fares, plus cheap seats on other airlines if the non-stop flights are full. There are no direct flights from North America to Turkey, though several airlines, including Pan Am, KLM, and Alitalia have connecting flights; typical fares average $1200 from New York. There are some, less frequent, direct international flights to Ankara.

As Turkey becomes more popular, **charter flights** become more frequent, especially to the coastal centres at Antalya, Dalaman (southwest coast), and Izmir. Fares from London are around £30 lower than discoun-

*Travel agencies specialising in cheap tickets.

TURKEY

Bulgaria
EDIRNE
Greece
Thrace
TEKIRDAĞ
Bosphorus
ZONGULDAK
KASTOMONU
ISTANBUL
IZMIT
ADAPAZARI
Sea of Marmara
Imroz I.
Lake Iznik
BOLU
KIZILIRMAK R.
Dardanelles
Koroğlu Mountains
Troy
Mt. Ida
BURSA
SAKARYA R.
ANKARA
BALIKESIR
ESKIŞEHIR
Mytilene
Pergamon
KÜTAHYA
Aegean
MANISA
GEDIZ R.
Chios
Salt Lake
Sea
AFYON
NEVŞEHIR
IZMIR
KUŞADASI
Ephesus
MENDERES R.
Lake Eğridir
Plain
Pamukkale
KONYA
of
Icaria
Samos
AYDIN
Lake Beyşehir
Mt Mycale
DENIZLI
BURDUR
ISPARTA
Konya
Lycian Mountains
BODRUM
Cos
Side
Taurus Mountains
ANTALYA
Rhodes
Cilicia
Mediterranean Sea
Cyprus

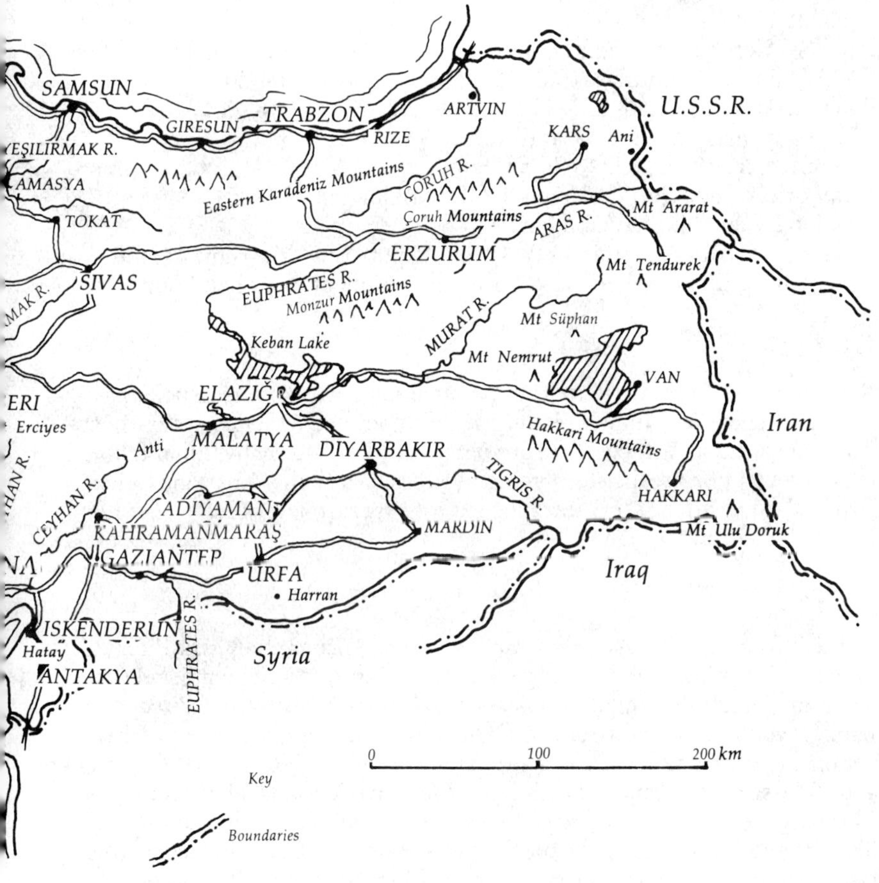

ack Sea
(Karadeniz)
SAMSUN
GIRESUN
TRABZON
RIZE
ARTVIN
KARS
Ani
U.S.S.R.
EŞILIRMAK R.
AMASYA
TOKAT
Eastern Karadeniz Mountains
ÇORUH R.
Çoruh Mountains
ARAS R.
Mt Ararat
ERZURUM
SIVAS
MAK R.
EUPHRATES R.
Monzur Mountains
Mt Tendurek
MURAT R.
Mt Süphan
Keban Lake
Mt Nemrut
VAN
ELAZIĞ
ERI
Erciyes
MALATYA
Hakkari Mountains
Iran
Anti
DIYARBAKIR
TIGRIS R.
HAKKARI
CEYHAN R.
ADIYAMAN
MARDIN
KAHRAMANMARAŞ
Mt Ulu Doruk
GAZIANTEP
URFA
Iraq
Harran
EUPHRATES R.
ISKENDERUN
Hatay
Syria
ANTAKYA
0
100
200 km
Key
Boundaries

ted prices on scheduled flights. Again, Sunquest can help. In the USA, contact either Unitravel (800–325–2222) or Am-Jet Amtravel (212–697–5332). Another alternative: if you don't mind a day or two in London, fly there on People Express and take a cheap ticket from there to Turkey.

ADDRESSES IN ISTANBUL

British Airways: Cumhuriyet Cad. 10, Elmadağ, tel. 48 42 35
British Caledonian Airways: Karavan, Cumhuriyet Cad. 131/3, Elmadağ, tel. 48 06 91
Pan Am: Cumhuriyet Cad., Hilton Hotel Arcade, Harbiye, tel. 47 45 30
TWA: Miltur, Cumhuriyet Cad. 135, Elmadağ, tel. 46 04 20
THY: Cumhuriyet Cad. 131, Harbiye, tel. 47 13 38 or 46 40 17
Mustafa Kemal Cad. 27, Aksaray, tel. 25 78 81
Hilton Hotel Arcade, tel. 48 39 55
Cumhuriyet Cad. Gezi Dükkânlari 2/7, Taksim, tel. 45 24 54
Hamidiye Cad. 28, Sirkeci, tel. 22 88 88
THY's terminal for Istanbul's Yeşilköy Airport is at Meşrutiyet Caddesi in Şişhane (Pera), tel. 45 42 08. Buses leave about every half hour.

By Train

Regular trains from Western Europe taking about 40 hours usually pass through Venice or Munich. Although the renovated Orient Express now goes only as far as Venice, there are other luxurious alternatives that follow the old route. For a real taste of golden Victoriana take the 'Nostalgic Orient Express' tour offered by Intraflug AG (Tagernstrasse 12a, CH–8127 Forch-Zurich, Switzerland).

By Sea

Turkish Maritime Lines runs a car ferry from Ancona, Italy and Pireaus, Greece, to Izmir about once a week between June and September. Libra Maritime Lines also runs a service several times a week from Pireaus to Izmir. If you're going by car, these ferries cut a considerable amount of driving off the trip. There are also car ferries from Haifa, Alexandria, Cyprus, and Odessa, and, year round, between the Greek island of Rhodes and Marmaris; in season there are passenger boats between Mytilini and Ayvalik, Kos and Bodrum, Samos and Kuşadasi and from Chios to Çeşme (the last two have some room for cars). Turkish Maritime Lines offers students a 15% reduction on international fares.

Addresses: Turkish Maritime Lines in London: Walford Maritime Ltd, Ibex House, 42/47 Minories, London EC3 N1AE, tel. 01 480 5621.
In Istanbul ring 44 02 07 for information; in Izmir, 21 00 94.

By Car

From London it's a good four-day 1900 mile drive to Istanbul. If that doesn't discourage you, the quickest route is through Ostend, Munich, Salzburg, Ljubliana, Belgrade, and Bulgaria; it is cheaper for British and American citizens to obtain a Bulgarian transit visa before leaving. Motorists have a choice of four points of entry from Europe: Ipsala and Kastanea-Pazarkule on the Greek border, or Kapikule and Aziziye on the Bulgarian frontier.

To bring your car into Turkey you'll need insurance that covers **both** European and Asian Turkey; a Turkish policy may be purchased at the border. The vehicle is noted on your passport and must be taken with you when you leave, or else be placed in the care of customs until you return to Turkey. The driver's best friend in Turkey is the **Turkish Automobile Club** (*Türk Turing ve Otomobil Kulübü*) which gives information on all aspects of driving in Turkey, as well as a repair service (free if you belong to your home auto club); see 'Turkish Topics' for the club's numerous other activities. An international driver's licence is not required, but is useful if you get into trouble.

Address: *Türk Turing ve Otomobil Kulübü,* Istanbul: Topkapi Gate, tel. 21 65 88, or in the city, Şişli Meydani 364, tel. 46 70 90.

By Bus

This is the cheapest way to get to Turkey, although there are no direct routes from London. The nearest departure point is Paris; take the Bosfor bus from the Gare Routière International, 8 Place du Stalingrad. Buses leave twice a week in the summer; tel. Paris 4 205 1210 for information.

Border formalities

Turkish customs officials generally don't even look in your baggage when entering the country. You are allowed to bring 2 cartons of cigarettes, 5 litres of alcohol, and a kilo of coffee, something you may want to consider if you can't live without it. Most places simply don't have coffee that isn't Turkish (thick, black, and served in lilliputian cups).

Important Note: When you enter Turkey you may be asked to pay an **entrance fee** (around TL10 500), this may be included in your ticket.

UK and US citizens do not require visas for visits up to three months, nor are any inoculations required. However, if you plan to go off into central or eastern Anatolia, you may want to have a tetanus booster, as well as a typhoid and cholera vaccine to be on the safe side; these dangers are not common but do still exist. If you plan to visit the Adana area, malaria tablets are another precaution.

The two things that can really get you into big trouble in Turkey are drugs and antiquities. Trying to leave the country with them, or even having them in your possession, almost always means a prison sentence. If you make a large purchase, like a carpet, make sure you keep your **currency exchange receipts** to get it out of the country without any hassle. Currency exchange receipts are also necessary to reconvert any extra Turkish lira to foreign currency when you leave. You are allowed to have $1000 worth of Turkish lira when you enter or leave Turkey.

Getting Around Turkey

By Air

Flying is the easiest way to get around Anatolia, and fares are on the whole less expensive than in Europe. All domestic flights are on the national carrier, THY; 10% discounts are available to families (if everyone has the *same last name*) and to students between the ages of 12 and 28. Children between 2 and 12 get a 50% discount, infants under 2, 90% and journalists, 50%.

Flights are more frequent between April and October and airport security is tight so make sure you get to the airport in good time.

From Istanbul you can fly direct to: Adana, Ankara, Antalya, Bursa, Dalaman, Diyarbakir, Gaziantep, Izmir, and Kayseri.

For many destinations in Anatolia you may have to go through Ankara. From here, there are direct flights to Elaziğ, Erzurum, Malatya, Trabzon, and Van. From Izmir there are direct flights to Antalya.

By Sea

Turkish Maritime Lines offers cruises of the Black Sea, the Aegean, and Mediterranean coasts. These large, slightly dilapidated floating hotels are very popular, and you should make reservations, especially for a cabin, in advance.

Address in Istanbul: (TML) Türkiye Denizcilik Işletmeleri, Rihtim Cadd., Karaköy, 440207. In London, contact Walford Lines Ltd, Ibex House, 42/47 Minories, London EC3 N1AE, tel. 01 480 5621.

In the summer there is one five-day cruise a week to the **Black Sea** from Istanbul to Sinop, Samsun, Giresun, Trabzon and back again.

There are two different two-week Aegean/Mediterranean cruises: one calls at Istanbul, Izmir, Datça, Marmaris, Finike, Antalya, Mersin, Alanya, Antalya, Fethiye, Bodrum, Kuşadasi, Izmir and Istanbul; the other at Istanbul, Izmir, Bodrum, Fethiye, Antalya, Alanya, Mersin, Antalya, Kaş, Marmaris, Güllük, Kuşadasi, Izmir, and Istanbul.

There is a year-round overnight car ferry from Istanbul to Izmir every four days in the summer, less frequently at other times; again, it's best to make reservations early.

There are frequent car ferries over the Dardanelles and Bosphorus, and two on the Marmara, daily between Kartal–Yalova; once a week Istanbul–Bandirma and Istanbul–Mudanya–Gemlik. Passenger boats on the Marmara link Istanbul with Bandirma, Avşa island Mudanya, Gemlik and Karabiga.

By Train

Turkish State railways (TCDD) has a rail network 5127 miles long. However, for the most part the trains are old and slow, and there's no reason you would ever need them; buses are much faster, much more convenient, and almost always cost less than half as much. If you have the time, and money, though it's fun to take the train, especially on overnight journeys. In Istanbul the starting point for all routes to Europe and the west is Sirkeci Station; all trains to Anatolia depart from Haydarpaşa Station in Asia.

Some of the more popular trains are night express trains between Ankara and Istanbul (the *Ankara Ekspresi* and the *Anadolu Ekspresi*) and the Ankara–Izmir express, all with sleeping cars.

In the provinces the train always seems to come in the dead of night; and for that one train a day there may well be eight timetables posted, all incomprehensible. A fairly accurate map of the nation's rail network is available from the Turkish Tourism office. A 20% reduction is available on return tickets; students get 10% off in addition.

By Bus

Unlike the trains, the coach companies in Turkey are all privately owned and are extremely competitive. Taking advantage of Turkey's ever improving highway system, they are wonderfully efficient and incredibly cheap. Fares are usually proportionate to distance (Istanbul–Mardin, for example, about TL 8000 for 1470 kilometres, Trabzon to Erzurum, TL 1950 for 310 kilometres. All the buses are made by Mercedez-Benz and are quite comfortable, though some companies keep them in better shape than others.

There's something of a carnival atmosphere in the average bus garage, nowhere more so than in Istanbul. The foundations have been laid for the city's new garage, which may or may not ever be built. Until then, you must use the two great temporary stations outside the city walls—one, the **Trakya Otogari** for European destinations, and the other **Anadolu Otogari** for Asia.

In practice, the division isn't so cut and dried. All you do is show up, and before you know it, a bus agent will have you on a vehicle to your destination. It's worth your while to do a little shopping around; another company may have an earlier, faster or more direct bus. If it's a long trip, you may even want to look at the buses first. Prices are controlled so you won't find a better bargain.

One problem on the buses is that the windows don't open, so on hot days try to get a seat directly behind a roof vent. Some companies, as a point of honour, seat foreigners in the front. On steep mountainous routes this is a dubious privilege as one can only do as the signs over the driver advise, 'Trust in Allah'. Stops for tea and snacks are frequent and most buses carry cold bottled water, free on request from the conductor.

By Car

Apart from Istanbul where traffic is a law unto itself, a car is the best way to see the country, especially its many archaeological sites. Most of the main routes along the coasts have been finished, improved, and widened, and traffic is usually light. Almost all signs have been converted to conform with the international highway code, and towns are clearly signposted (blue), as are archaeological sites (yellow). Petrol, thanks to the Iraqis, is cheaper than in most of Europe, and the Tourist Office's free map is very helpful, updated annually to show all new stretches of asphalt.

Be careful: Turkey's accident rate is disproportionately high. Night driving is best avoided, simply because you can't see many of the hazards, such as sharp winding roads, cattle and sheep crossing, drag racing tractors, slow buses or oil trucks racing to petrol stations that all close at 10 pm. According to the highway code passing is on the left, but in practice, in city or country, you will be overtaken on either side (or both at the same time). The busiest stretches of highway are on the E5 between Edirne and Istanbul (the **Londra Asfalti,** the mere mention of which makes normal people turn pale) and from Istanbul to Ankara. Auto club repair trucks are available to those in need. In the winter the mountain roads in the east are often impassable.

In the cities, especially Istanbul, parking can be a real headache (No Parking: *Park Yapilmaz*); the Turks park on the pavements as they have special permits to do so. If your car has foreign plates, you may park anywhere as the police won't ticket you. Traffic lights, even in Istanbul are rare, and rarely heeded; street signs anywhere are rare.

Renting a car in the major centres can be done with credit cards; plastic money has yet to reach the outlying provinces, and in general the further east you go, the more decrepit your Renault or Fiat-Murat will be. If you hire from one of the large international firms on the coast, there is usually no charge for dropping the car off at another point.

If you are involved in an accident, you must wait at the scene to make a police report. If you have a breakdown or need a repair, every town has a street or quarter given over to mechanics, each specialising in a certain repair. In Istanbul it is in the Dolapdere neighbourhood in the centre of Beyoğlu; in other cities, there are little car repair compounds that hardly ever close on the outskirts. Spare parts are likely to be your chief problem, especially outside the big cities. Bring a kit with you. Turkish mechanics, on the other hand, are very experienced and if they can't fix the problem, they can probably get your car going so you can get to the next big city.

Most of the filling stations are along the main highways: you'll find B.P., Mobil and Shell and the Turkish company, *Petrol Ofisi* at the sign of the wolf, and *Türkpetrol*, at the sign of the tipped cap. Outside the major tourist areas, there is only regular at the pumps. The price varies from one place to another, depending on how far the fuel has to be transported.

Road Signs. Common ones are: *DUR* (Stop), *YAVAŞ* (Slow), *DIKKAT* (Caution), *TEHLIKE* (Danger), *GIRILMEZ* (No Entry), *TEK ISTIKAMET* (One Way), *YASAK BÖLGE* (Military area, ie. no photographs).

Taxis

These are fairly ubiquitous and by European standards, very cheap. In Istanbul, Ankara, and Izmir they are metered; in other places they generally have fixed rates; you can agree on a price before setting out. Turkish taxi drivers are usually honest, but don't be surprised if it costs more to ride in a vintage '55 Chevy than a new car; it is allowed because the former consume more petrol.

If you haven't a car, taxis are the best alternative for seeing many of the outlying archaeological sites; in many places, the drivers do it regularly and have set prices, for a half or a whole day or for individual excursions. To cut costs, you can often share the taxi fare with other travellers. For a half day trip to a site like Ani or Boğazköy, TL 7000 is a fair price. Tipping, once unheard of, is now widespread.

Dolmuş taxis (from the Turkish for 'stuffed') run certain routes in and between cities and towns. These are very inexpensive and can be distinguished by the little sign in the corner of the windscreen stating the destination. You just wait for a suitable one, and pile in. The car is often a shiny old American bathtub with tons of chrome, or it could be a minibus, and your fellow passengers—a woman with a giant potted geranium, a man with a chicken on his lap—will welcome you aboard in the grand old spirit of dolmuş conviviality. Using them is an excellent way of meeting the locals, and you can get off wherever you like on the route.

Getting around Turkish cities

This is usually easy. Most are compact and easy to explore on foot. The others (except Istanbul) have grown up on a linear plan, with all the main points of interest spread out along one or two main routes, served by dolmuş. City buses are very very cheap, but you almost always need a ticket before you board. These are sold at the main stops, at little stands. One major problem in towns of all sizes is the lack of street signs, but almost every local tourist office can provide you with a map, often hand drawn, of the vicinity, which does help.

Historical sites

Those near villages can often be visited without the cost of a taxi, by taking a minibus from your base to the village and walking (a place good for a town in 500 BC is often just as good in the 1980s, so they're rarely more than a mile or two). However, **be sure you have transport back**. The minibus that brought you often returns at noon the next day, and in the village itself there won't be anything remotely resembling food or lodging. If you do get stuck somewhere, hitching a ride back is your best bet (and a safe, and good way of seeing the country if you're footloose and carefree). Buses will almost always stop for you anywhere along the road, if there's room (for some reason the chances are better if you're a foreign tourist than a hardworking Anatolian farmer).

Yachts

Chartering a yacht or sailing your own along the coast of Turkey is becoming more popular every year. Prices for the former are still quite reasonable compared with other Mediterranean countries: the Tourist Office, has lists of agents and charterers with whom you can reserve a boat (bare or with crew) before setting out; outside July and August you can usually get a yacht on the spot in the major ports—Antalya, Marmaris, Bodrum or Kuşadasi. One of the most memorable ways of spending a holiday in Turkey is to float along the delightful pine-forested coast, in and out of a hundred picturesque coves dotted with the remains of ancient cities, dining every evening off the day's catch. This is what the Turks call 'The Blue Voyage' which specifically is along the southwest coast between Bodrum and Antalya (see the section on the Lycian Coast). From Fethiye, for example, boat hire ranges from TL 18 000 to TL 90 000 per day depending on the size of the boat and the amenities.

If you have your own yacht, official ports of entry are Istanbul, Bandirma, Çanakkale, Ayvalik, Güllük, Alanya, Antalya, Bodrum, Çesme, Fethiye, Kaş Kuşadasi, Datça, Akçay, Izmir, Anamur, Silifke, Mersin and Iskenderun. On arriving in Turkey the captain must fill out a Transit Log. If you leave Turkish waters for seven days or less, you can leave the Transit Log with port authorities and reuse it on your return. Foreign yachts may remain in Turkey for up to two years for maintenance and winter berthing.

Maps and Publications

As mentioned above, the free map distributed by the Turkish Tourism Office is quite good and up-to-date; for minor roads, the Auto Club's map is good. Maps sold in your home country are often out of date or inaccurate. Beware the Turkish habit of putting all provincial capitals in large type; sometimes these have only a few thousand inhabitants (like Bilecik) while an insignificant looking dot may have a population of 100 000 (like Tarsus).

Turkish Tourism and Information Offices abroad

United Kingdom: First Floor, 170/173, Piccadilly, London W1 VDD, tel. 01–734 8681 Telex: 8954905 TTIOFC G

United States: 821 United Nations Plaza, New York, NY 10017, tel. 212–687–2194 Telex: 426428

Where to Stay in Turkey

The Turkish Tourism and Information office puts out an annual list, with prices, of the hotels, motels, pensions, holiday villages, and camp sites regulated by the Tourism Ministry. If you plan to do any extensive travelling in the country, try very hard to get one; demand often exceeds supply and they stop giving them out. Many fine establishments fall through the cracks of the Tourist Office's mysterious criteria, and their ratings are sometimes misleading; having a restaurant automatically leads to a higher rating. The booklet is especially useful if you're going east, where the hotels, while clean, offer only the bare necessities; at least one hotel in a small town will have a shower in the room but that's about it. Unless the hotel has 'continuous hot water', take your shower early in the morning or in the evening when the hot water's turned on. In smaller hotels and pensions you may have to ask for it to be turned on at the desk. Hotels at the very bottom of the scale provide little more than a bed and plastic slippers; you have to supply your own towel, soap, and toilet paper. Note that even the unclassified hotels are regulated, not by the Tourism Ministry, but by the municipal authorities, who fix their prices and will listen to any complaints; the chances of being ripped off are very slight. Most proprietors of cheap hotels in outlandish places go to great lengths to provide pleasant accommodation.

At the opposite end of the scale are the four Club Méditerranée holiday villages (at Kuşadasi, Foça, Kaş, and Kemer) and two international chain hotels in Istanbul. There are several Turkish chains, almost all along the west coast and Antalya region: *Turban* (which also operates several yacht marinas and camp sites—get their latest booklet from the Tourism Office), *Tusan* (mainly motels on the outskirts of the most popular towns), and *Etap* (in Ankara, and Istanbul—usually expensive and dull). Again, mainly on the coasts, there are several Turkish holiday villages (*tatil köyü*) that are quite nice and very good for families; in listings they are rated TK 1 or TK 2. In Turkey's rapidly growing winter sport centres, there are a number of Alpine-style chalets classified as *Oberj* (auberge). *Pansiyons* (pensions) rated 1 or 2, though again many are unclassified, are inexpensive, simple, and used mainly by Turkish families on holiday. Rooms in private houses are almost non-existent, except in the large tourist centres.

The staff in Turkish hotels, like the Turks in general, are extremely friendly and helpful. They may not shine shoes (this being the exclusive province of the *boyaci,* shoeshine boys or men, who may be found almost everywhere with their artistically embellished brass boxes), but are willing to handle almost any other difficulty that may arise: giving directions, finding taxis, making reservations and handling laundry (*çamaşir*). If you get a room that is dirty, or the lock or lights don't work, don't hesitate to complain or demand another one.

In this book, we have included only establishments open all year (unless otherwise stated) and hotels that do not have mandatory pension; we have left out several fine hotels on the coast because of this. Hotel restaurants, even in Turkey, the land of wonderful cuisine, are, in general, overpriced and dull, though we've put in several exceptions.

Ministry of Culture and Tourism Ratings

Hotels, motels, pensions and holiday villages that meet certain standards are given ratings: HL is a luxury hotel, H1 first class, H2 second class, and so on; there are two classes for motels, pensions, and holiday villages (these last rendered TK in Turkish). The following prices (in Turkish Lira) are current at writing,* note that at some establishments, usually in the higher categories there are additional service charge and tax, up to 18% of the total bill.

HOTELS AND PANSIYONS	SINGLE	DOUBLE
HL	12 000–39 000	26 500–57 500
H1	7500–17 000	10 000–26 500
H2	4000–14 500	6000–21 000
H3	4000–11 000	5000–14 500
H4	2000–6500	3000–7700
P (on govt. list 1 or 2)	2000–6000	3000–6500
Unlisted hotels and pansiyons	500–3000	1000–4000
MOTELS		
M1	3500–8000	6000–7200
M2	1000–3000	2000–4000
HOLIDAY VILLAGES		
TKA	7000–14 000	12 000–17 500
TKB	4000–8500	4500–11 000

Camp sites charge between 500–1000 TL a head for adults, half price for children, and something for the tent or camper (below 1500 TL).

All categories, as you see, cover a wide range. Of the extremes, the higher are usually in Istanbul, the lower in the eastern provincial cities. You may take the middle of these ranges as typical of prices. Many places have a 10% or 20% off-season discount; some reduce prices as much at 50%. As there still are not enough better quality hotels to meet demand, especially on the coast in the summer, make reservations in advance.

Youth Hostels

Youth hostels are rare: in Istanbul there are several unofficial ones and the official ones in the list below, for which you need either an International Youth Hostel Federation Card or an International Student Travel Conference (ISTC) card. All are open only from 1 July to 31 August.

Topkapi Atatürk Öğrenci Sitesi, on the Londra Asfalti, Cevizlibağ

*Please note that these prices are liable to increase by 30% or more so do check with the Tourist Office.

Durağı, Topkapi (Gate, not Palace), Istanbul, tel. 525 50 32. Bus 96/A or 93/A.

Kadirga Öğrenci Yurdu, at Cömertler Sokak 6, Kumkapi (near Sultanamet), Istanbul, tel. 528 24 80

Ortaköy Kiz Öğrenci Yurdu, at Palanga Caddesi 20, Ortaköy (near the Bosphorus Bridge), Istanbul, tel. 161 73 76. Bus 22, 22A, 25/C, or 30/C (women only.)

Cumhuriyet Öğrenci Yurdu, Cebeci, Ankara, tel. 19 36 34. Bus 17 or 21.

Atatürk Öğrenci Yurdu, 1886 Sokak, Inciralti, Izmir (on the beach west of the city; take a dolmuş or bus from the Konak terminal), tel. 15 29 80.

Camping

There are still too few official camp sites to meet demand. A large chain, Mokamp Kervansaray, has a number of organised sites for tents and campers along the most travelled routes; these often have swimming pools, restaurants, and tent rentals, as well as electricity and running water. Mokamps and other official camp sites are open from April or May to September or October. You can also camp outside official sites; if you do, the tourist office advises you to stay near a motel or service station to make use of the facilities.

OFFICIAL CAMP SITES IN TURKEY

ADANA: Raşit Ener Kampi, Girne Bulvari, on the Iskenderun road, tel. 119 04

ALANYA: Kervansaray Mokamp

ANKARA: Kervansaray Susuzköy Mokamp, Ankara–Istanbul road, tel. 43 13 66

BODRUM: Ayaz Kamp, Gümbet, tel. 1174

BURSA: Kervansaray Kumluk Mokamp, north of Bursa on the Bursa–Yalova road, tel. 139 95

ÇANAKKALE: Şen Mokamp, south on the Çanakkale–Izmir road in Kepezköyü village, tel. 1

ÇEŞME: U Kampi, tel. 21

EDIRNE: Kervansaray Ayşe Kadin Mokamp, tel. 1290

EMECIK (Datça): Aktur Kamping Tatilsitesi, tel. 106

FERDEMLI (Mersin): Kervansaray Kizkalesi Mokamp

FETHIYE: Deniz Kamp, Ölüdeniz, tel. 8–12

GÜMÜLDÜR (Izmir): Denizati Kampi, tel. 19–366

IPSALA: Kervansaray Ipsala Mokamp, on Istanbul road, tel. 38

ISTANBUL: Ataköy Mokamp, Sahil Yolu (road), tel. 572 49 61

Yeşilyurt Kamping, Sahil Yolu 2, Yeşilköy, tel. 573 84 08
Kervansaray Kartaltepe Mokamp, Çobançeşme, tel. 575 19 91
IZMIR: Kervansaray Inciralti Mokamp, Balçova beach, tel. 15 47 60
KEMER: Turban Kiziltepe Kamping (Antalya), tel. 1113
KIZILCAHAMAM: Yayla Mokamp (Ankara), on the Ankara–Istanbul road, tel. 7
KUŞADASI: Kervansaray Mokamp, Izmir–Kuşadasi road, tel. 1106 or 1087
NEVŞEHIR: Kervansaray Göreme Mokamp, Nevşehir–Ürgüp road, tel. 1428
ÖREN: Altin Kamp, Burhaniye, tel. 202 (on the Marmara)
ORTAHISAR: Paris Kamp, tel. 15–99
ÜÇHISAR: Koru Mokamp, tel. 2157
Lists of each area's unofficial camp sites can be obtained from the local tourist offices.

Eating in Turkey

People unfamiliar with Turkey are always pleasantly surprised when they discover Turkish cooking. The Turks themselves are fond of saying that there are three great cuisines in the world—Chinese, French, and Turkish. Whether or not you agree, eating is one of the main pleasures of visiting Turkey; there is an infinite variety of dishes, the freshest ingredients are common, and, on the whole, the diet of the Turk is a healthy one, based on fresh fruits and vegetables, grilled fish and meat, with many kinds of salad and yoghourt dishes.

Turks are especially fond of hot or cold hors d'oeuvres (*mezes*) of which they often eat several instead of a main course. The bread is delicious and plentiful. Where we look at bread as an accompaniment to meals, they look at their meals as something to go with their bread. The most popular dishes are based on lamb, aubergine (eggplant) and beans, found in the simplest lokantas, or tavernas. By Western European or American standards, prices are very low; if you're on a limited budget you can eat well for a dollar or so a night.

Although Turkish establishments call themselves either *lokanta* or *restoran*, the difference is that between an Italian *trattoria* and *ristorante*: some fancy places affect the name *lokanta* while some very simple places proudly call themselves *restoran*. In practice, there are two different types of eating places in Turkey: one with glass cases full of *mezes*, fish and various meat dishes cooked to order, where wine and beer are available, and someone probably speaks English or German (the price of a dinner will be from TL

2500 up); the other, where dishes already cooked are displayed on a steam table, and you point at what looks good (portions here are usually small, so don't be shy about choosing several). The latter type, where working Turks dine, are breathtakingly cheap, especially those with self service (*kafeterias*) but they almost never offer wine or beer. The first kind, though more pricey, are still inexpensive, and if you find some in the tourist centres with typical European prices, someone is making a pretty profit.

As well as *lokantas* and *restorans*, there are several types of restaurants that specialise in particular dishes.

Kebab salons offer a wide variety of grilled lamb from favourites like *şiş kebab* and *döner kebab* (a herbed lamb roll that cooks slowly as it rotates, served in slivers with melted butter or sauce on pitta bread) to specialities like *Adana kebab* (very spicy), *Kağit kebabi* (lamb and vegetables cooked in foil) or *Çöp kebab* (literally rubbish kekab, small pieces of beef on wooden spits cooked over charcoal), or *Iskender kebabi*, a mixed platter.

Pide salons are the Turkish approximation of pizza parlours; *pide* is a delicious flat bread, served with various toppings. *Lahmacun pide* has ground meat, tomatoes and onions, the delight of the Anatolian peasants. *Ramazan pide*, eaten during the holy month of fasting in lieu of bread, is plain with sesame seeds. Perhaps best is the Black Sea variety (*karadeniz peynirlisi*) with cheese, sausage, and so on. Many seaside restaurants serve only fish.

Işkembeci have only tripe, sweetbreads, brains, etc. The Turks claim tripe soup is the best cure for a hangover, which in part accounts for the popularity of the *Işkembeci*.

Börekci specialise in *börek*, a flaky pastry filled with cheese, herbs, or meat.

Muhallebici concentrate on milk puddings, yoghourts, sweets, and chicken soup.

Wherever you eat, the service will be somewhere between very good to wonderful, almost overwhelming. Service is almost always included in the bill, but it's good form to leave a tip, 10% or so, on the table.

Turkish wine is excellent (see **Turkish Topics**) as is the beer, the most popular drink in Turkey, and officially non-alcoholic. Raki, the favourite strong drink (50% proof) is distilled from raisins and flavoured with aniseed. Soft drinks are mediocre, though the fizzy bottled mineral water (ask for 'soda') is quite good and readily available. Fresh or bottled fruit juices may be found at snack stands—*büfes*—in all but the smallest villages. The white, milk-like drink you see everywhere is *ayran*, yoghourt and water whipped together. Turkish coffee (very sweet (*şekerli*), with a little sugar (*az şekerli*) or without sugar (*sekersiz*)) is good and thick, and sold in coffee houses.

Tea, however, is far more common. Grown on the Black Sea coast and sold by the State Monopoly, all Turks can afford it. As a guest, you will constantly be offered tea, and someone will appear with a tray and several glasses immediately. Ubiquitous as tea is, however, the old-fashioned tea houses are increasingly hard to find, with their beautiful gleaming samovars and *narghile* (water or 'hubble-bubble' pipes).

Pastry shops and some restaurants specialise in sweets, some with evocative names like *Hanim Göbeği* (Lady's Navel) and *Dilber Dudaği* (Lips of the Beloved), both served in syrup as is the better known *baklava* and shredded *kadayif.* Turkish pastry chefs produce a number of excellent cakes (often with chestnuts and hazelnuts), a large variety of *helva* (halva), good ice cream (*dondurma*) and of course Turkish delight (*lokum*), jellied squares flavoured with rose or mastic, coated with powdered sugar. Pistachios, almonds, chestnuts, and hazelnuts are often used, plain or in a number of exotic dishes; dried fruits and jams are excellent and plentiful; and fresh fruits in season are second to none. In many restaurants you can top off your meal with a fruit platter of plums, medlars cherries, strawberries, and every Turk's favourite, *karpuz* (watermelon). Cheeses are also very good, made from the milk of cows, sheep, or goats. Popular varieties found throughout Turkey include *tulum*, made in a skin, *beyaz* (soft white salted cheese), *mihaliç* (rich, unsalted, made from sheep's milk) and *kaşar* (hard).

Street food varies from place to place, although almost everywhere you can buy a *simit* (bread rings covered with sesame seeds), peeled cucumbers, fruit in season, fruit juice (sold from elaborate, jingling brass dispensers borne on the back), small kebabs, and nuts.

Listesi	lihs-teh-sih	**Menu**
Ekmek	ek-mek	bread
Su	Soo	water
Süt	s*eu*t	milk
Tuz	tooz	salt
Şeker	shek-ehr	sugar
Yoğurt	yo-oort	yoghourt
Tereyağ	te-re-yay	butter
Kahve	kah-veh	coffee
Kahve ala franga	. . . a-la frahn-ga	Western coffee (usually Nescafe)
Kizarmiş ekmek	kiz-ar-mish ek-mek	toast
Meyva suyu	may-va soo-yoo	fruit juice
Reçel	reh-chel	jam
Çay	chahy	tea

Oralet	or-a-let	orange-flavoured hot drink
Maden suyu	ma-dehn soo-yoo	mineral water
Turşu	toor-shoo	pickles
Zeytinyaği	zay-tin-ya-ih	olive oil
Sirke	shihr-keh	vinegar
Suyu	soo-yoo	juice
Salça	sahl-cha	sauce
Şarap (beyaz, kirmizi)	shar-ahp (beh-yaz, kihr-mih-zih)	wine (white, red)
Bira	bih-ra	beer
Buz	booz	ice
Limonata	lihm-o-nah-ta	lemonade
Kahvalti	kah-vahl-tih	breakfast
Öğle yemeği	*eu*-leh yeh-meh-ee	lunch
Akşam yemeği	ahk-shahm yeh-meh-ee	dinner
Garson	gar-son	waiter
Hesabi	he-sahb-ih	bill
Meze	meh-zeh	**Hors d'Oeuvres**
Fasulye	fah-sool-yeh	green beans (in olive oil)
Sigara Böreği	sih-gah-rah b*eu*r-ay-ee	cigarette-shaped borek, with cheese or meat
Cacik	jah-jik	ground cucumber, garlic, and yoghourt
Midye plakisi	mid-yeh plah-k*i*h-s*i*h	mussels cooked in olive oil
Kisir	k*i*h-s*i*hr	bulgar with onions, pepper, and parsley
Yalanci dolma	yahl-ahn-jih dohl-mah	stuffed vine leaves
Corba	chor-bah	**Soup**
Mercimek çorbasi	mehr-jih-mek chor-bah-sih	red lentil soup
Yayla çorbasi	yay-lah . . .	rice, yoghourt, egg yolks in broth
Işkembe çorbasi	ish-kem-beh . . .	tripe soup with egg sauce
Şehriye çorbasi	shehr-ee-yeh . . .	chicken noodle soup
Salata	sah-lah-tah	**Salads**
Tarama salatasi	tah-rah-mah- sah-lah-tah-s*i*h	roe with olive oil and lemon juice

Patlican salatasi	paht-l*i*h-jan . . .	mashed eggplant, olive oil, lemon juice, and mayonnaise
Çoban Salatasi	cho-bahn . . .	mixed vegetable salad
Beyin Salatasi	bey-ihn . . .	sheep's brain salad
Tarator salatasi	tah-rah-tohr . . .	sesame syrup, walnuts, and garlic
Et	et	**Meat**
Kuzu	koo-zoo	lamb
Kuzu kapamasi	koo-zoo kah-pah-mah-sih	grilled lamb cooked with vegetables
Haşlama	hahsh-lah-mah	leg of lamb with carrots and celery
Kuzu incik patlicanli	koo-zoo in-jik paht-l*i*h-jahn-l*i*h	lamb stew with eggplant
Et saç kavurma	et sahtch ka-voor-ma	thin slices of lamb, tomatoes, and peppers sauteed at the table
Siğir	s*i*h-*i*hr	beef
Biftek	bihf-tehk	beef steak
Papaz yahnisi	pah-pahz yah-n*i*h-s*i*h	beef, onions, and spices
Dana	dah-nah	veal
Kiyma	kee-mah	minced meat
Köfte	k*eu*f-teh	meatballs
Cizbiz	jiz-biz	grilled meatballs
Ciğer	jee-ehr	liver
Işkembe nohutlu	ish-kehm-beh noh-hoot-lu	tripe (with chickpeas)
Tavuk	tah-vook	chicken
Çerkez tavuğu	cher-kez tah-voo-oo	chicken in walnut sauce
Beğendili tavuk	beh-en-dih-lih tah-vook	chicken with mashed eggplant, milk, and cheese
Hindi	hin-dih	turkey
Balik	bah-l*i*k	**Fish**
Hamsi	hahm-sih	Anchovy
Iskorpit	ihs-kor-piht	Rock fish, Stone bass
Kalkan	kahl-kahn	Turbot

Barbunya	bahr-boon-yah	Red mullet
Kefal	keh-fahl	Grey mullet
Kiliç Baliği	kihl-itch bah-l*ı*h-*ı*h	Swordfish
Lüfer	l*eu*-fehr	Blue fish
Istavrit	is-tahv-riht	Mackerel
Karagöz	kahr-ah-g*eu*z	Sargus
Palamut	pahl-ah-moot	Bonito
Mercan	mehr-jahn	Pandora
Pisi	pih-sih	Brill
Dil	dihl	Sole
Pavurya	pah-voor-yah	Crab
Medye	mehd-yeh	Mussels
Istiridye	ihs-tihr-ihd-yeh	Oyster
Kalamar	kah-lah-mahr	Squid
Kerevit	kehr-ih-viht	Prawn
Kiliç şiş	kihl-itch shish	Swordfish kebabs
Barbunya Kağitta	bahr-boon-yah kah-it-ta	Red mullet in foil
Papaz Yahnisi	pah-pahz yah-n*ı*h-s*ı*h	Bonito in olive oil
Yumurta	yoo-moor-tah	eggs
Rafadan/haşlama	rah-fah-dahn/hahsh-lah-mah	boiled/poached
Omlet	ohm-let	omelette
Menemen	meh-neh-mehn	scrambled eggs with tomatoes, cheese and peppers
Pastirma	pahs-t*ı*hr-mah	Turkish pastrami, with lots of spice and garlic
Sucuk	soo-jook	Turkish sausage

Sebze	seh-bze	**Vegetables**
Biber	bee-behr	green pepper
Patlican	paht-l*ı*h-jan	eggplant (aubergine)
Domates	doh-mah-tes	tomatoes
Kabak	kah-bahk	zucchini, squash
Yaprak	yahp-rahk	vine leaves

(any of the above can be *dolmasi* (dohl-mah-s*ı*h) stuffed with rice and meat)

Enginar	en-gee-nahr	artichokes
Fasulye	fah-sool-yeh	beans
Bamya	bahm-yah	okra

Lahana	lah-han-ah	cabbage
Patates	pah-tah-tes	potatoes
Ispanak	*i*s-pahn-ahk	spinach
Soğan	so-ahn	onion
Bezelye	beh-zehl-yeh	peas
Havuç	hah-vooch	carrots
Kuşkonmaz	koosh-kahn-mahz	asparagus
Marul	mahr-ool	lettuce
Zeytin	zay-tihn	olives
Mantar	mahn-tahr	mushrooms
Nohut	no-hoot	chickpeas
Fava	fah-vah	broadbeans
Bamya Etli	bahm-yah et-lih	lady's fingers with beef
Imam Bayildi	ih-mahm bay-yil-dih	'the imam fainted'—eggplant stuffed with onions and garlic in olive oil
Pilav	pihl-ahv	rice
Iç pilav	itch pihl-ahv	rice with chopped liver, raisins and pine nuts
Bulgur Pilavi	bool-goor pihl-ah-vih	bulgar with onions and tomatoes
Firinda Makarna	fih-rin-dah mah-kahr-nah	baked macaroni, a bit like lasagna
Meyva	may-vah	**Fruit**
Ahududu	ah-hoo-doo-doo	raspberries
Armut	ahr-moot	pear
Çilek	chih-lek	strawberry
Elma	el-mah	apple
Erik	eh-rihk	plum
Incir	in-jeer	figs
Karpuz	kahr-pooz	watermelon
Kavun	kah-voon	melon
Kayisi	kah-y*i*h-s*i*h	apricot
Kiraz	kih-rahz	cherry
Muz	mooz	banana
Badem	bah-dem	walnuts
Şam fistiği	shahm fis-tee-yee	pistachios

Tatli	taht-l*ı*h	**Desserts/sweets**
Aşure	ah-shur-eh	pudding with beans, cereals, nuts, and raisins
Zerde	zehr-deh	sweet rice with saffron
Un Helvasi	oon hel-vah-sih	halvah made of flour and butter
Pasta	pah-stah	cake
Lokma	lohk-mah	round doughnuts in syrup
Kabak Tatlisi	kah-bak taht-l*ı*h-s*ı*h	slices of pumpkin in syrup
Dondurma	don-duhr-mah	ice cream
Çikolata	chik-o-lah-tah	chocolate
Peynir	pay-nihr	cheese
Krem karamel	krem kah-rah-mehl	caramel custard

Pudings	puh-dings	**Puddings**
Muhallebi	mu-hal-le-bih	milk pudding
Sütlaç	s*eu*t-lahtch	rice pudding
Tavuk Göğsü	tah-vook g*eu*-s*eu*	milk pudding with chicken breasts

Communications, Money, Health and other concerns

Money

The national currency is the Turkish lira (TL), which comes in bank notes of 10 000, 5000, 1000, 500, 100, 50, 20, and 10, and coins of 5, 10, and 50 lira. The Turks do not like coins, and you'll find yourself carrying wads of small notes for change. Major international credit cards as yet are only honoured in major tourist establishments. Traveller's cheques and Euro-cheques are easily cashed in any bank. Having money sent from abroad to a bank is very complicated, and it's wise to start the process two weeks or so at least before you need the money. Banking hours in Turkey are 8.30 to 12 and 1.30 to 5, Monday–Friday.

Post Offices

These are easy to find by their yellow PTT signs. Larger ones have telephones (see below) and poste restante (general delivery) services. To make sure letters reach the central post office, have them addressed care of Poste restante/*Merkez Postanesi* before the name of the town. Large central post offices in the major cities are open 24 hours a day; others as late as 11.30 pm. Smaller branches close at 6 pm.

PTTs almost always have **telephones,** which handle local or international calls. In the post office you buy telephone tokens (*jetons*), which usually work for local calls and, on occasion, calls elsewhere in Turkey, if you can get the required tokens in the slot fast enough. Technically in many places you can also make an international call this way, but you will save yourself time and exasperation if you let the man at the post office make it for you. You give him the number and sit down and wait. If you're in a hurry, you can make a long-distance call *acele* (rush) or even faster, *yildirim* (lightning), which cost respectively twice and four times as much as a 'normal' call. If you think you're up to calling direct, the price will be the same as *yildirim*. For a long-distance call within Turkey, dial 09, then the city code, and the number. For international calls dial 99, then the country code, city code (omitting any noughts before the city code) and your number. Note that Turkey is 3 hours ahead of Greenwich Mean Time and 7 hours ahead of Eastern Standard Time (New York), an hour less in the summertime.

Official Holidays

Both banks and post offices are closed on the following **Official Holidays:**
1 January: New Year's Day
23 April: National Independence—Children's Day
19 May: Atatürk commemoration—Youth and Sports Day
30 August: Republic Day
29 October: Victory Day

Embassies and Consulates in Turkey

ANKARA
Australian Embassy, Nenehatun Cad. 83, Gaziomanpaşa, tel. 39 27 50
British Embassy, Şehit Ersan Cad. 46/A, Çankaya, tel. 27 43 10
Canadian Embassy, Nenehatun Cad. 75, Gaziomanpaşa, tel. 27 58 03
USA: Atatürk Bul. 110, tel. 26 54 70

ISTANBUL
British Consulate, Tepebaşi, Meşrutiyet Cad. 34, tel. 14 47 540
USA Consulate, Meşrutiyet Cad. 104, tel. 14 36 200

IZMIR
British Consulate, Necatibey Bal. 19/4, tel. 14 54 70
USA Consulate, Atatürk Cad. 386, tel. 13 21 35

Health

In most towns in Turkey there is a doctor who speaks English or French; in Istanbul and Izmir there are also American hospitals. Consider taking out a traveller's health insurance policy before leaving; they are usually quite reasonable, but make sure your policy is valid for both the European and Asian sections of Turkey (if that's where you'll be) before buying. For minor problems—if you can make yourself understood—consult a chemist (druggist). Free assistance is available in walk-in clinics in the national hospitals as well. The Turks themselves are quite fond of herbal remedies; for diarrhoea, they recommend the 'India nut'. Tap water is not always safe to drink; bottled water, however, is inexpensive, and you may want to stick to it rather than have the discomfort of new, if harmless, bacteria in your system.

Electricity

Electricity is 220 volts in Anatolia and most of Thrace, except for a few 110 volt areas in Istanbul. In your hotel, there will be a notice telling you which they have. Some outlets have two prongs, some three, so if you must be plugged in, come with adapters and converters.

Museums, Sports, Festivals, Geography

Museums

Most museums in Turkey date from the early years of the Republic. To Atatürk, recreating an interest and pride in Turkey's great civilisations of the past was an important part of nation-building, and his government fostered the creation of archaeological collections and the restoration of old buildings throughout the country.

Today, besides the great museums of Istanbul and Ankara, almost every town of any size has its own. Don't assume they aren't worth visiting; even the most obscure often have surprises even for the jaded culture tourist.

Almost all are government owned. Hours vary slightly, but most are closed for an hour or so at noon, and all are closed on Mondays. Note that almost all the ruins and castles of Turkey, in fact all the outdoor sites of any archaeological or antiquarian interest are maintained by the government as 'open air museums' to which the same closing times apply. There may or may not be an admission charge, and the person on duty may or may not feel like collecting it; in any case the sum involved is insignificant.

In Istanbul some museums are exceptions to the usual closing days.

Topkapi Palace: open Mondays, closed Tuesdays
Military Museum: closed Monday and Tuesday
Municipal Museum: closed the 5th of every month and at holidays
Naval Museum: closed Mondays and Tuesdays
Dolmabahçe Palace: closed Mondays and Saturdays
Mosaic Museum: closed Mondays and Tuesdays
Beylerbey Palace: closed Mondays and Saturdays
Göksu Palace: closed Mondays and Saturdays

Sports and Recreation

WATER SPORTS

These are the primary summer activity. An increasing number of places along the Mediterranean and Aegean coasts hire out yachts and sailing boats of all sizes.

Windsurfing is just catching on at the larger resorts. Restrictions on underwater **diving** have recently been lifted, and there are now schools in Çeşme, Kuşadasi and Bodrum; all divers, however, must refrain from taking any ancient souvenirs from the deep. The only places where pollution may be a problem are near the main shipping harbours (the Gulf of Izmir and the beaches on the Marmara near Istanbul are unfortunately quite dirty).

The sea along the south coast is warm enough to swim in from April to November. The Black Sea coast, with its frequent winter rains and colder climate, is only warm enough in the summer. In July and August the Aegean coast is often plagued by the meltemi wind from the north, making rough seas.

Fishing for sport requires no licence; **hunters,** however, can only go out in organised groups sponsored by a travel agent. Wild boar hunts in the autumn are organised in Muğla province (Marmaris) and in the Taurus mountains. Write to the Union of Travel Agencies, Cumhuriyet Cad. 187, Elmadağ, Istanbul, for a list of sponsors.

MOUNTAIN CLIMBING

This is another fair weather sport. The tourist office has a list of mountain excursions for both beginners and experts; you can also write to the Turkish

Mountaineering Club, or the Dağcilik Federasyonu, BTGM, Ulus Işhani, A-Blok Ulus-Ankara.

Several other activities, well developed elsewhere, are just being discovered in Turkey. **White water rafting** enthusiasts have sent out rave reviews about the river Çoruh at Bayburt. Excursions to Turkey's numerous and often dazzling **caves** are organised by the cave exploring club (Bümak-Boğaziçi Üniversitesi Mağara Araştirma Kulübü) in Istanbul.

WINTER SPORTS

Winter sports, often with accommodation in Swiss chalets, are growing in Turkey. For a real adventure, and if you're in top condition, fly out to Erzurum's Palandöken ski centre, where the courses are long and you are guaranteed plenty of snow, best between December and April. Equally snowy and far away but less challenging is Sarikamiş at Kars. Beautiful and easily accessible is Bursa's Uludağ, with slopes of all degrees of difficulty, as well as Turkey's most sophisticated facilities. Just north of Antalya, you can ski in the Beydaği mountains at Saklikent; in March and April you can ski in the morning and swim in the Mediterranean in the afternoon. A fine, all round winter resort is at Kartalkaya near Bolu, between Istanbul and Ankara. At Erciyes on the high plateau near Kayseri, there is a small resort with a long season—from November to May.

If you're in the right place at the right time (see 'Festivals') you may be able to see three of the Turks' homegrown sports. Although football has more of a following, **wrestling** is still considered the national sport, and contests take place throughout the summer. Edirne is the greased wrestling capital of Turkey and hosts the most famous tournament. **Camel wrestling** (*Deve Güreşi*) pits camel against camel in a slow clumsy-elegant ritual in which one beast establishes its dominance; they are separated before doing each other any harm. This is most common along the Aegean coast in December and January, especially in Selçuk. To see **Cirit** ('javelins') a rather dangerous but exhilarating sport featuring galloping horsemen hurling blunted wooden javelins at opponents, you have to head out east to Erzurum where it's still played from time to time—contact the Erzurum riding club (*Atlispor*) for information on matches.

Less strenuous activities include lounging around a **spa** (there are famous ones in Bursa, Yalova, and Gönen, all easily accessible by sea from Istanbul; also at Ilica near Izmir, Pamukkale, and Hüdayi, in Afyon Province), playing *tavla* (backgammon) in the coffee houses and of course, a **Turkish bath** (*hamam*).

Almost every town has a *hamam*, either with separate facilities for men and women, or open to men and women on alternate days. The Turkish bath is a direct descendant of the Roman bath, adopted by the Byzantines and then the Ottomans; it is a wonderfully sensuous ritual, especially if you have a chance to luxuriate in one of the historic *hamams* in Istanbul: the 18th century Çağaloğlu Hamami, on Hilal-i Ahmer Cad. 34, near the Blue Mosque; the 16th century Galatasaray Hamami, at Suterazi Sok. 24 in Beyoğlu; or the 19th century Pangalti Hamami, on Dolapdere Cad. 224 in Pangalti; or in Edirne, the beautiful 16th century Sokollu Mehmet Paşa Hamami.

The *halvet* is the hot room where you perspire; the *göbektaşi* is the hot stone slab on which the bath attendant rubs you down. This they tend to do with great enthusiasm, either with a glove that removes dead skin or even by walking across your back; if it hurts you can always call out '*yavaş yavaş*' (slowly, slowly.) Be sure to tip the bath attendant when you leave.

Turkish Festivals

The two major national festivals in Turkey follow Ramazan (see **Historical Outline**), and thus the time changes from year to year. The first, **Şeker Bayrami,** or Ramazan feast, lasts for three and a half days and comes directly after the month-long fast. Shops are stocked with sweets for the children; the general mood is light and carefree. More important is the four-and-a-half-day **Kurban Bayrami** (Feast of the Holy Sacrifice), about a month after Ramazan. It is a time of visiting, giving gifts to children, and feasting. Traditionally, a sheep or lamb is bought and sacrificed on the day the festivities culminate, in imitation of Abraham's sacrifice of Ishmael, who takes the place of Isaac in the Mohammedan version. Both are bad times to travel; buses, trains, and aeroplanes are crowded with people going to visit relatives.

Other annual festivities are listed below. If you're in the vicinity, it would be a shame to miss one; the Turks will probably go out of their way to treat you as a special guest. Indeed, the summer festivals in the major tourist centres along the coast are put on to entertain visitors with displays of folklore, music, and dancing.

JANUARY
Sarayköy camel fights, Denizli, Aydin, and Selçuk

FEBRUARY
2nd week: Kel Aynak Festival, Birecik.

MARCH
Traditional Troubadours Festival, Erzurum.
End of month: Ski Festival, Erzurum.

APRIL
Last week: Atatürk University Folklore and Music Festival, Erzurum
Last weekend: Sultan Hisar Nyssa Festival, Aydin
Last week April, First week May: Tulip Festival, Istanbul
Mid April: Historical and Traditional Mesir Festival, Manisa

MAY
First week: Snake Friday, Mardin
Spring festival, Sinop
International Ephesus Festival, Selçuk
Spring festivities, Iznik and Bursa
Kirkağaç Pine festivities, Manisa
Yunus Emre Culture and Arts Week, Eskişehir
Doyduk Festival/Kov Kalesi Festival, Gümüşhane
Mid-May: Spring Day, Ordu
Silifke Music and Folklore Festival
Aksu Festival, Giresun
Last Sunday: Rose Festival, Konya
Last week: Marmaris Festival
Pergamum Festival, Bergama
Mesir Festival, Manisa

JUNE
First week: International Mediterranean Festival, Izmir
Tekirdağ Cherry Festival
Cherry Festival, Isparta
Second week: Kirkpinar Festival and Greased Wrestling, Edirne
Enez Fish Festival (Thrace)
Kastabala Culture and Arts Festival, Osmaniye
Third Week: Tea Festival, Rize
Bursa Keles Kocayayla Festivities
Last week: Saint-Pierre Mass, Antakya
Develi Seyrani Festivities, Kayseri
Nasrettin Hoca Festivities, Eskişehir
Kafkasör Bullfights, Artvin
Mid-June to mid-July: International Istanbul Music and Arts Festival

JULY
First week: Amasra Tourism Festival
Arhavi Tea Festival
Şarköy Wine Festival, near Tekirdağ
Zeybeks Day, Kütahya
Yarimca Sports and Folklore Festival, near Izmit
Akçakoca Sea Festival

Uluborlu Greased Wrestling
Javelin Competitions and Rahvan Horse races, Konya (weekends)
Mid-July: Bolu-Abant Festivities
Ceramics Festival
Traditional Circumcision Feast, Kütahya
Apricot Festival, Malatya
Hazelnut Festival, Ordu
Van Tourism and Culture Festival
Çatalzeytin, Ginolu Festival, Kastamonu
Şarkikaraağaç Halvah Festivities, Isparta
International Bursa Festival
Gerede, Köroğlu, and Esentepe Festivities
Adiyaman Nemrut Festival
Last week July: Datça Knidos Festival
Foça Water sports, Music and Folklore Festival
Dereçine Black Cherry Festival, near Afyon
Sultandaği Black Cherry Festival, near Afyon
Babaeski Agriculture Festival, near Kirklareli

AUGUST
First week: Veli Baba Memorial Day, Isparta
Sinop Festival
Mid-August: Çanakkale Troya Festival
Haci Bektaş Remembrance Day and Ceremonies, Nevşehir
August 15: Assumption of the Virgin, Selçuk
End August: Gözne Wrestling Festival, near Mersin
Burdur and Insuyu Festival
Izmir International Fair (through mid-September)

SEPTEMBER
First week: Bodrum Festival
Çal Wine Harvest Festival, near Denizli
Kirşehir Ahi Evran Crafts and Folklore Festival
Çankiri Honey Festival
Gölcük, Ihsaniye Apple Growers competition
Kuşadasi Tourism Festival
Çamlidere Uluçdaği Festival, near Ankara
Elmali Yeşilyayla Wrestling Matches, near Antalya
Mid-September: Iznik Grape Festival
Cappadocia Wine Harvest Festival, in Ürgüp and Göreme
Feke traditional Karacaoğlan Festival
Adana Arts and Culture Festival
Elmadaği Honey and Wool Festival

Germencik Fig Festival
Karakucak Wrestling Festival
Ayvalik Tourism Festival
Aydin Arts Festival
Last week: Konya Culinary Contest
Mersin Textile and Fashion Fair
Pigeon Competition, Konya
Weekends in September: Kizilcahamam Soğuksu Festival
Mahmudiye Autumn Horse Races

OCTOBER
First week: Seben Apple Festival
Antalya Film Festival
Mid-October: Şuhut Karadilli Wrestling Festival, near Afyon
Turkish Troubadour Week, Konya
Pervari Honey Festival, near Siirt
Last week October: Bağkonak Sugözü Festivities, near Isparta

NOVEMBER
First week: Karaelmas Coal Festivities, Zonguldak

DECEMBER
All month: Camel Wrestling, Aydin province
First week: St Nicholas festival, Demre, near Antalya
December 14–17: Mevlâna Remembrance Day and Ceremonies, Konya

Geography and climate

Turkey is more or less a rectangle, 400 miles wide (from north to south) and almost 1000 miles long (east to west), at once in Europe and Asia and the Middle East. The variety of both its climate and topography tend to surprising extremes. The great Anatolian plateau is an extension of the vast Himalaya–Alpine range that rises gradually as you head east, culminating in the majestic Mt Ararat (*Ağri dağ*) 16 786 feet high; at these lofty altitudes the climate is very harsh, the mercury dipping below freezing every day in the winter, when many towns are snowbound. On the other hand, the south coast enjoys a longer bathing season than any other place along the northern Mediterranean.

Although there are several extensive plains (around Konya, and in south-eastern Anatolia), you are never far from mountains. Both the Mediterranean and Black Sea coasts are bordered by tall mountain ranges. Thus, Turkey has many lakes, most famous of which is Lake Van in the east. The Taurus Mountains stretching along the southern coast are the largest chain in the country with many lakes as they sweep upwards in an arch towards Malatya, where they become the Antitaurus mountains and the roof of Turkey. From here the country's major rivers flow: the Tigris (*Dicle*), the Euphrates (*Firat*), the Halys (*Kizilirmak*) and the Yeşilirmak. Another river famous in antiquity, the Maeander (*Menderes*) flows from the Taurus Mountains to the Aegean, its annual floods creating the country's most fertile valley. The Black Sea coast, the rainiest and most humid area in Turkey, is always green; in vivid contrast, southeast Anatolia is so hot and dry that stepping out in the sun can make you feel burnt to a cinder. The south Aegean coast has the country's most agreeable climate, while Istanbul, the Marmara region, and Thrace often get snow in the winter and long gloomy spells.

Average daily temperatures

	Jan 15		April 15		July 15		Oct 15	
	°C	°F	°C	°F	°C	°F	°C	°F
Istanbul	5	41	12.2	54	22.8	73	16.1	61
Izmir	8.9	48	16.1	61	27.8	82	16.1	61
Antalya	11.1	52	16.1	61	27.8	82	20	68
Ankara	7.2	45	12.2	54	22.8	73	16.1	61
Trabzon	0	32	11.1	52	22.8	73	13.3	56
Erzurum	–8.9	16	5	41	18.9	66	8.9	48

Part II

HISTORY

Troglodyte dwellings in Göreme

Historical Outline

The Turks, in their tourist literature and in the archaeological exhibitions they send round to the world's museums, like to bill their country as the 'Land of Civilisations'. Unlike other nations of the Mediterranean, such as Italy or Greece, Turkey's present inhabitants are relative latecomers, and the 7000 years of history before their arrival witnessed an incredible pageant of peoples and cultures. If we learned in school that early history belonged almost entirely to Egypt and the Fertile Crescent, it is only because chance led the archaeologists there first. The mountains and plains of Anatolia, which in recent decades have seen more digging and theorising than perhaps any corner of the globe, can now also stake their claim as one of the birthplaces of civilisation.

Ancient History to 2500 BC

Discoveries in the Karain Cave and other sites around Antalya have taken Turkey's history back as far as Neanderthal man, but the really exciting event has been the recent excavation of an accomplished and artistic culture, 9000 years old, at **Çatal Höyük** near Konya, a peaceful, matriarchal town that lived on agriculture and the obsidian trade. It eventually grew into a city of some 32 acres, the oldest truly urban culture ever discovered. Its chubby goddesses and bull-horn shrines, along with the rest of its remarkable artworks, can be seen at the Ankara Museum. The latest levels of the excavations begin to show evidence of fire and strife, and we can take Çatal Höyük's end, in about 5500 BC, as the beginning of the first dark age. The neolithic cultures that replaced it, as at **Mersin** and **Hacilar**, near Burdur, were not nearly as sophisticated.

2500 BC–1180 BC The Bronze Age

After its great beginnings Anatolian civilisation entered a period of little interest, falling behind Egypt and Mesopotamia. Revival came with the **Hattian culture**, another recent discovery, about which little is yet known. The Hatti people flourished in central Anatolia c. 2500–2000 BC, caused their neighbours little trouble, and created some of the finest works of art of their age. At this time, a separate Bronze Age culture began to develop around **Troy**, more closely related to the peoples of the Aegean than to those of Anatolia.

Around 2000 BC, a new nation arrived from Thrace, the **Hittites**, a warrior aristocracy (as the later Turks were to be) who imposed themselves on the Hatti and founded a great capital at **Hattusas**. They introduced writing to Asia Minor by learning the Assyrian cuneiform and later developing their own hieroglyphics to fit their Indo-European tongue. They also gave Anatolia its first empire, a Bronze Age superpower that contended with Egypt for the mastery of the Middle East after King Mursilis I captured Aleppo and Babylon c.1590 BC. About 1180, just as the Hittites had reached the peak of their political and artistic accomplishment, their empire came to a sudden end at the hands of unknown invaders from the west. This period of migrations and catastrophes, which also witnessed the fall of Troy, sent Asia Minor into another dark age.

1180–546 BC: New Nations in Anatolia

Political and cultural unity in Anatolia died with the fall of the Hittites, and for centuries to come the region was divided among a number of new peoples, many of whom had migrated into the region only after the Hittite collapse.

Urartians

During the Hittite empire, a confederation of two peoples, forming the

ANCIENT REGIONS AND TOWNS OF ASIA MINOR

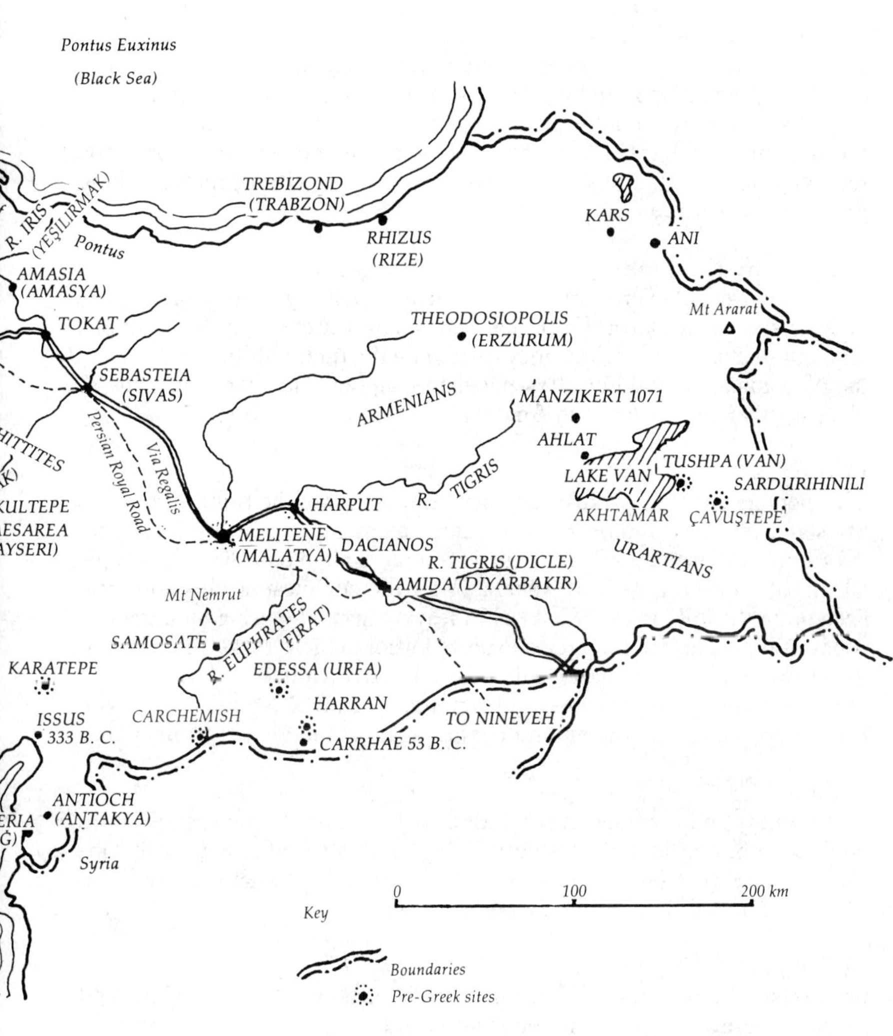

Pontus Euxinus
(Black Sea)
R. IRIS (YEŞILIRMAK)
Pontus
TREBIZOND (TRABZON)
RHIZUS (RIZE)
KARS
ANI
AMASIA (AMASYA)
TOKAT
THEODOSIOPOLIS (ERZURUM)
Mt Ararat
SEBASTEIA (SIVAS)
ARMENIANS
MANZIKERT 1071
AHLAT
Persian Royal Road
Via Regalis
HITTITES
LAKE VAN
TUSHPA (VAN)
SARDURIHINILI
R. TIGRIS
KULTEPE
HARPUT
AKHTAMAR
ÇAVUŞTEPE
MELITENE (MALATYA)
DACIANOS
URARTIANS
R. TIGRIS (DICLE)
AMIDA (DIYARBAKIR)
Mt Nemrut
R. EUPHRATES (FIRAT)
SAMOSATE
KARATEPE
EDESSA (URFA)
HARRAN
CARCHEMISH
TO NINEVEH
ISSUS 333 B. C.
CARRHAE 53 B. C.
ANTIOCH (ANTAKYA)
Syria
0
100
200 km
Key
Boundaries
Pre-Greek sites

'Hurri-Mitanni state', survived precariously as a buffer between the Hittites and Assyria. As successor to the Hurrians, a related people, the Urartians, appeared in the region around Lake Van in the twelfth century BC. They called themselves the Biainili, but as the Urartians (as they are known in the Assyrian chronicles) they gave their name to Mount Ararat. An Urartian state gradually coalesced, reaching its greatest extent under King Sarduri II, c. 750 BC, extending from the Black Sea to the Caspian. The Assyrian King Tiglath-Pileser III soon cut them down to size, though, and the Scythians finished them off in 609 BC. Urartian stone reliefs and metal work, recently recovered in a number of sites around Lake Van, at its best equals anything produced in that age.

Late Hittite Kingdoms

These survived all over south-eastern Anatolia, usually as Assyrian dependencies such as Malatya, Kahramanmaraş, and Carchemish, for example. Though politically powerless, they carried on the traditions of Hittite art, in the occasionally grand but often peculiar sculpture that takes the pride of place in so many museums in Anatolia.

Phrygians

This people, talented in music and art, grew up out of the ruins of the Hittite state; its little empire, ruled by kings alternately named 'Midas' and 'Gordius', flourished until the Lydians conquered it in 650 BC. Their capital was at Gordium, west of Ankara. After the conquest, a Phrygian state lived on in the hills south of Eskişehir, leaving many imposing monuments. A pastoral people, the Phrygians exported wool to the Greeks and diverted themselves with their orgiastic cult of Cybele and their music. They claimed to have invented the panpipes, and Marsyas, the mythological flautist who had the bad judgement to enter a contest against Apollo, was a Phrygian.

Lydians

The wealthy and commercially minded Lydians lived to the east of Izmir, but in their heyday in the sixth century BC they controlled an empire that included a vast area of western Anatolia. In 546 BC, the Persians under Cyrus put an end to Lydia as an independent power.

Lycians

On the southwest coast of Anatolia, the Lycians, like the Phrygians and Lydians, were a native people speaking an Indo-European dialect and were later Hellenised by the Greeks. Although mentioned by Homer, their relative inacessibility and reputation for fierceness kept them out of the mainstream of history; their most remarkable accomplishments were the lovely rock tombs they carved into cliffs all over Turkey's southwestern coasts.

None of these states was destined to last long. The aggressive and brutal Assyrian Empire (860–612 BC) kept Anatolia in constant turmoil. Even worse, tribes of mounted warriors from across the Caucasian mountains were constantly marauding through Anatolia. The **Cimmerians** learned cavalry tactics from the Scythians; in the seventh century BC, they occupied most of the eastern half of the peninsula. The **Medes** (c. 620–549 BC) who founded the first great Persian empire, destroyed the Assyrians and the Cimmerians, and succeeded to both their domains.

546 BC–334 BC Greeks and Persians

The Achaemenid kings of Persia, who replaced the Medes in 549 BC, created a world empire for themselves within two generations. After Cyrus' conquest of Lydia had given them undisputed control of the whole of Anatolia, the Persians found themselves confronted with Greece at the height of its classical age. The Greek city states had colonised these coasts centuries before. Their traditions dated the first arrivals to the 'mixed multitudes' of people set loose by the fall of Troy—an echo of the twelfth century dark age. Over the centuries, the Greeks prospered in Aeolia, Lycia, and Pamphylia along the coast, but their greatest success, **Ionia**, became, in the classical age, the tail that wagged the dog, as the city of Miletus became the centre not only of the sea trade but of Greek culture as well. Philosophy and art flourished as never before, and Ionia's partisans among the scholars and aesthetes of our own day claim for it a level of civilisation unmatched before or sincc.

334 BC–AD 300 Hellenistic and Roman Eras

Except for a brief period of freedom after the Greek defeat of Xerxes at Plataea in 479 BC, the Greek towns lived as satrapies of the Persian King of Kings. As in the rest of Anatolia, Persian rule was usually just, unoppressive, and quite conducive to the growth of culture. It was not to last. Alexander the Great crossed the Hellespont to snatch Anatolia in 334 BC; on his way turning Persia's empire into Alexander's. The change was profound. In the decades that followed, as Alexander's generals and their descendants fought over the scraps of the empire, Anatolia became thoroughly Hellenised. Trade and the growth of new cities such as Pergamon and Antioch gave the region new wealth and power. Even though successor states like Pergamon, the Seleucid Kingdom of Greek Syria, and the Kingdom of Pontus along the Black Sea made political unity an impossibility, Hellenistic Anatolia had become one of the centres of western civilisation.

One unusual event of the time was the invasion in 275 BC of the **Galatians**, Celts really, who installed themselves right in the centre of the peninsula. Their red hair and freckled descendants can still be seen on the streets of Ankara and in many other Turkish towns today. **Roman** control came gradually, a province at a time from the second century BC to the first AD. Under Roman rule Anatolia enjoyed the greatest prosperity it has ever known. Commerce and the arts flourished, and cities like Ephesus, Smyrna (Izmir) and Antioch (Antakya) each counted over five hundred thousand inhabitants.

AD 300–1071 The Byzantine Empire

The founding of Constantinople in the fourth century AD, and the division of the empire into halves seemed to confirm Asia Minor in its central role. While the West receded into barbarism, successful Eastern Emperors like Theodosius the Great (379–95), Justinian (527–65) and Heraclius (610–41) effected the successful transition of the state into the theocratic Christian Byzantine Empire, while keeping Avars, Alans, Persians, and Slavs at bay. For most of Anatolia, however, this period witnessed a gradual but irreversible decline, as Byzantine misgovernment and overtaxation slowly strangled the economies of the cities and the great landowners pushed the majority of the country people into serfdom. Beginning in the 7th century, the incredibly destructive Moslem Arab armies added the finishing touches. Trade died, and the coastal cities withered and disappeared; after a millennium and a half of sophisticated civilised life, Asia Minor had been destroyed.

Throughout the eighth century, the Byzantines had been preoccupied with the Iconoclastic struggles, in which disputes over the desirability of painted icons demonstrated a tremendous confusion of religious, economic, and political conflicts. Attacks from the surrounding Arabs, Bulgarians, and Russians brought them to their senses and under emperors Basil I (867–86), Basil II, 'the Bulgar-slayer' (976–1025), and Nicephorus Phocas, the 'Pale Death of the Saracen' (963–9), Byzantium brought about a brilliant cultural revival and a level of political stability. This was a little relief to devastated Anatolia; by now the Byzantines had come to look upon Greece and the Balkans as the centre of their empire.

However, their success encouraged a similar flowering of civilisation in **Armenia**. The Armenians had always been around, among the plains and mountains of Eastern Anatolia. Under their king Tigranes the Great, c. 85 BC, they had managed a short–lived empire; later, reduced to the status of a Roman client state, they became the first nation to officially embrace Christianity (in the third century). Now, in the ninth and tenth centuries, under kings such as Ashot the Great (c. AD 860) and Gagik I (AD 990–1020), the

Armenians kept their borders clear and commenced a cultural renaissance of their own that produced some of the finest medieval Christian architecture and art in their capital of Ani and around Lake Van.

1071–1243 The Selcuks lead the Turkish Invasion

In the emptiest of Asia's empty spaces, north of Manchuria, the Chinese chroniclers note a 'hill shaped like a helmet' that is the ancestral home of the '*Tu-kueh*'—the Turks; they first appear in history c. 500 BC, making trouble for the Chinese emperors. In about AD 800, a confederation of tribes called the Oğuz was gradually heading towards Europe. By AD 900, many of the tribes had become Moslem, mounted warrior clans that helped the central Asian states as they infiltrated, just as the various 'barbarians' had done in Rome. Though not the first Turks to find their way into the desolated cockpit of Asia Minor, the Selcuks, under their chief Alp Arslan, were the first to do it in style, gobbling up the hapless Armenians and ending Byzantine pretensions to Anatolia once and for all with a resounding victory at Manzikert, north of Lake Van, in 1071. They called their state, centred at Konya, the Sultanate of Rum—to the peoples of distant Asia, Rome was still a magic name. As soon as they settled down, the Selcuks transformed themselves with amazing speed into gifted rulers and patrons of the arts. At the height of their power, under the early 13th century Sultan Alâeddin Keykubad, they were the strongest and most civilised state of the eastern Mediterranean; their architecture, seen in the schools and mosques of Konya and so many other Anatolian cities, marks not only the beginning of Turkish art but one of its greatest achievements.

The Selcuks, unfortunately, were only the first wave of a huge migration from central Asia. As well as the many other Turkish tribes who set up petty emirates across Anatolia, the **Mongols** came, putting an end to the Sultanate of Rum at the battle of Kösedağ in 1243 and, once more, returning Turkey—for now we may call it that—to anarchy.

Even before 1243, the Selcuks were beset on all sides, not only by Turks, but also by the **Crusader States** founded by the Franks in the twelfth century. The greatest of these in Anatolia, the County of Edessa (Urfa), survived for over a century, and orders such as the Knights of St John controlled much of the southern coast throughout the Middle Ages. The Crusaders soon learned to leave the Selcuks alone, and not wishing to tackle the other Moslem nations either, decided to go after the heretics in Constantinople. A new Crusade in 1204, serving the ends of Venice and the Pope, took advantage of the absent Byzantine army to storm and sack the city for the first time, humbling its pride, violating most of the women, and carrying off every bit of its 900 years of accumulated treasure.

The Byzantine empire ends here. Although a government in exile was set up at Iznik (Nicaea) from which Emperor Michael Paleologos chased out the Italians and reclaimed the city in 1261, it was an impoverished, enfeebled Constantinople that survived until 1453 behind its impregnable walls. In 1359, Emperor John Paleologos gave in and became a tribute-paying vassal to his son-in-law, Sultan Orhan, leader of a new and growing Turkish tribe, the Osmanli, or **Ottomans**.

1300–1453 The Coming of the Ottomans

According to legend, these Turks were riding across Anatolia when they chanced upon a battle being fought on the plain beneath them. Under their chief, Ertuğrul, they chivalrously decided to join the losing side, and soon turned their defeat into victory. The victors turned out to be the Selcuks, who rewarded their new allies with lands in western Anatolia. In about 1300, Sultan Osman laid the foundations of the state and dynasty that was to bear his name. Equally talented in war and government and virtuous to an extreme, Osman made his little state a power in the region. All his successors were girded with his sword in place of a coronation, and the cry that went up was not, 'Long live the Sultan,' but 'May he be as good as Osman!'

Orhan (1324–59), his son, conquered Bursa in 1326 and made it his capital. His marriage to a Byzantine princess was not a rare case; by the fourteenth century Greeks and Turks had come to know each other very well. Many Greeks had converted to Islam, and most of the rest, considering their alternatives, saw the Moslems as a lesser evil than the schismatics of Europe and their hated Pope. Orhan, an able and liberal ruler, increased the Ottomans prestige as he widened their boundaries. Early in his reign, a group of adventurers called the Catalan Grand Company, paid to defend Constantinople, had ferried Orhan's army across the Bosphorus to help. The Ottomans took one look at Europe and decided they wanted to keep it; Orhan conquered Thrace, and his son Murat I (1359–89) added Serbia, Bulgaria, and Macedonia.

The Turks, in transition from their days as nomadic warriors to an imperial aristocracy, still suffered from a shortage of women, and consequently, a shortage of Turks for so small a state with such big ambitions. They solved this problem ingeniously with the *devşirme*, a harvest of 5% of the infant boys from captured Christian provinces (first-born sons were excluded). All were educated and brought up as Moslems; the best became the Sultan's generals and *vezirs* (ministers), while the rougher were enrolled in the Janissaries (*yeniceri*, or 'new troops'), a corps of highly trained soldiers that were to become the terror of Europe. The Janissaries were kept under the control of the Bektaşi dervishes, from whom they inherited an unusual tradition of rituals and titles based on the eating of soup. To show their displeasure with a Sultan, for example, they would turn their large kettle upside down and refuse to eat. In later years, as the Janissaries became a law unto themselves, they did this whenever they felt like deposing a Sultan. As long as discipline was maintained, they were the finest fighting force in the world.

For Beyazit I (1389–1403), they destroyed the flower of French chivalry at Nicopolis in 1396, finally damping the crusading urge. Beyazit, a young hothead, addicted to battle even more than to wine, met his destiny in the person of Tamerlane in 1403. The invincible Mongol destroyed the Ottoman force at Ankara and took Beyazit prisoner, and then mysteriously turned around and went back east. Mehmet I (1413–21) and Murat II (1421–51) picked up the pieces and carefully rebuilt, finding time in 1444 to win undisputed control of the Balkans at the Battle of Varna, after which the head of King Ladislas of Poland and Hungary ended up on the top of a pike in Bursa.

1453—The Capture of Constantinople

Almost from the beginning, this had been the Ottoman goal. Several earlier attempts against the city had failed, and it was left to Mehmet II (1451–81) to win the prize. Mehmet, perhaps the most remarkable of the Sultans, was a poet and scholar who had mastered six languages and, unthinkable for a Moslem, had his portrait painted by Gentile Bellini. He saw himself as a man of destiny, sent to fulfil Mohammed's prophecy about the capture of the city, and went about the task methodically. By 1453, he was ready with an enormous army, the biggest cannons in the world and a fleet. Inside the city, whose population had dwindled from over a million to under fifty thousand, an Italian *condottiere* named Giustiniani led 8000 Greeks and mercenaries for the defence. In spite of the odds, they held out for two months. The tide turned with Mehmet's brilliant trick of dragging his ships over land, around the famous Byzantine chain across the Golden Horn, to the exposed side of the city. On 23 May, Giustiniani died and the disheartened mercenaries fled. The few Greeks remaining beat back a furious attack, but in their excitement left open a postern gate; some Turks found it, and the empire breathed its last. Mehmet ordered that the usual three days' pillage should spare all the buildings; he walked in awe through the Aya Sofia and the long abandoned palaces, and remembered a bit of Persian poetry:

> The spider weaves the curtain in the Palace of the Caesars,
> The night-owl keeps the watch in the Tower of Afrasiyab.

To the Turks, Mehmet is *Fatih*, the Conqueror. He knew what the city meant, and rebuilt it as fast as resources allowed. In 1461 he added the Empire of Trebizond to his conquests, the last free Greek state, founded by refugee noblemen after the sack of 1204.

1454–1700 The Height of the Ottoman State

Mehmet's son, Beyazit II 'the Mystic' (1481–1512), seldom disrupted his reading for further conquests, but Selim I (1512–20), made up for him by swallowing up Egypt (thus gaining the Caliphate) and much of Mesopotamia. *Yavuz* Selim, as the Turks call him, is really an honorific meaning 'the Formidable', but historians like to call him Selim the Grim for his frequent massacres of Shiite heretics and his habit of beheading his Grand Vezirs at an average of one a year. His son, Süleyman the Magnificent (1520–66), presided over the glorious noonday of the Ottoman state; under him the Empire reached its greatest extent with the conquest of Hungary and North Africa. His title comes courtesy of his close allies, the French; to his own people he was 'the Lawgiver' for his thorough reforms of the legal code and commercial regulations.

Unfortunately, he also began the Empire's slow decline. The trading concessions he granted to Francis I were the first step in the Ottomans' loss of control of their own economy. From his weakness for his scheming harem–favourite Roxelana, he brought the harem into the palace itself and inaugurated the period of palace intrigue that was eventually to ruin the state. The Sultans that followed show clearly how far the decay had already penetrated. Selim the Sot (1566–74), and Ibrahim the Mad (1640–8), lead the parade of wastrels, drunkards, sex perverts, and imbeciles that decorated the latter-day Ottoman throne. Directly upon Süleyman's death the real power had passed to the Janissaries, the eunuchs and the ladies in the endlessly changing factions in the harem. Osman II (1618–22), who wanted reform, was murdered; his successors until 1832 were virtual prisoners of the Janissary guard.

In the *Divan* (cabinet), meanwhile, an unusual dynasty of Grand Vezirs of Albanian descent, the Köprülü family, did their best to hold the leaderless state together throughout the seventeenth century. By the eighteenth, decadence had progressed so far that the European powers had to keep the Ottoman corpse propped on its throne in order to keep the Russians from occupying the straits.

1700–1914 The Empire Crumbles

For three centuries, the Russians kept the pressure on with forty-three declared wars while, in the nineteenth century, some of the Empire's captive nations, the Greeks, Serbians, Bulgarians and Egyptians, successfully gained their independence. Attempts to reform were too few and too late. Under Mahmut II (1808–39), the Janissaries were massacred in what the Turks call the 'Auspicious Event' but the Empire was too far behind the Europeans militarily and technologically for it to make much difference. Mahmut's successors, Abdül Mecit I (1839–61), and Abdül Aziz (1861–76), proved too stupid and indifferent to keep his reforms going, and the paranoid Abdül Hamid (1876–1909), sold his nation to European economic interests while ruthlessly stamping out any progressive thinking at home.

Despite his efforts, underground efforts to bring Turkey out of its political nightmare continued, especially among circles in the army. Finally, in 1909, the Committee for Union and Progress, called 'Young Turks' in the Western newspapers, deposed the hated Abdül Hamid and established a constitutional monarchy dominated by the Committee's head, Enver Paşa.

World War I

Before the Young Turks had a chance to make any significant changes, the war intervened, and Turkey found itself fighting on the side of its closest ally and commercial partner, Germany. Turkish armies with their German advisors beat the British and French at Gallipoli in 1916, but elsewhere, against the Russians and the Arab–British forces under General Allenby, they made little account of themselves. After the 1918 armistice a totally exhausted and impotent Empire submitted to the 1920 Treaty of Sèvres which called for the virtual partition of Turkey. The British occupied the straits, the French the important port of Iskenderun, and a Greek army invaded Anatolia. Old, silly Mehmet VI, the last of the Sultans, sat in his palace and wondered what would happen next.

1919—The Turkish Revolution

What did happen was astounding. Throughout the Ottoman Empire, as under the Byzantines, Anatolia had been a surprisingly neglected backwater of the Empire, which saw its heartland more as Thrace and the Balkans. Even more surprising is the fact that to be called a 'Turk' was something of an insult among the aristocratic Ottomans; the patient Turkish peasants and townsmen of Anatolia had to put up with as much scorn and as little help as any minority of the Empire. Now, for the first time, Anatolia was to make a stand. Opposition to the Sèvres treaty centred around a brilliant, difficult general, Mustafa Kemal, with a miliary reputation earned at Gallipoli and a head full of nationalist ideas. He escaped from the intrigues of Istanbul on May 19, 1919, and landed at Samsun with the force of a Napoleon returning from Elba. Nationalist congresses were soon held at Sivas and Erzurum, and a provisional government set up for the deliverance of the nation.

Somehow a new army was created. Under Kemal's leadership the Turks chased out the French and Russians and decisively defeated the Greeks at the two battles of Inönü in January–March 1921. Retreating before the nationalists, the Greeks burnt and pillaged their way to the coast; by September 1922, the country was clear of all foreign troops. A republic was declared one year later, with Mustafa Kemal as its first president and Ankara, right in the middle of Anatolia, as its capital.

1922 to The Present: The Westernisation of Turkey

Few nations have ever had the will or unity to effect as many reforms as the Turks did in the 20s and 30s, trying desperately to make up for so many centuries of lost time. Mustafa Kemal's republic was to be thoroughly secular, and to accomplish this, the Caliphate was abolished, education and marriage secularised, the wearing of the fez banned. Turkey adopted the Christian calendar and made Sunday the day of rest. The language was also reformed. Arabic and Persian words were rooted out, and the Roman alphabet replaced the Arabic.

As the simplest way of Westernising its institutions, Turkey simply adopted the entire Swiss Legal Code, almost word for word. Women acquired equal rights. International time and measures were adopted, and the government worked with its meagre resources to improve industry and communications. To crown it, the President decreed that every Turk should have a Western-style surname. Mustafa Kemal's was chosen for him by the nation—Atatürk, 'father of the Turks'.

It was only his moral authority as the nation's hero that enabled the changes to be accepted with so much enthusiasm and so little resistance. In politics, Atatürk began what has become a modern Turkish tradition by establishing a dictatorship to make reforms, while constantly and sincerely telling his people that their first aspiration must be democracy. After his death in 1938, his right-hand man from the War of Independence, Gen. Ismet Inönü, took over with a pledge to bring democracy. World War II, in which the Turks remained neutral, postponed the experiment, but free elections in 1949 resulted in the victory of the opposition Democratic Party and its leader Adnan Menderes. The Democrats' misgovernment and their attempt to create a one-party state resulted in an army coup in 1960, after which Menderes was executed.

The army is Atatürk's true heir, and it has always seen itself as the guardian of the nation. Turkey must be the only nation in the world where the army intervenes to uphold democracy rather than subvert it. Twice since 1960, in 1971 and 1980, they have tossed out governments incapable of dealing with extremists of both left and right. After all three coups, they restored democracy within three years. Still, democracy in Turkey is as yet in its experimental stage. Until now the Turks have never had a chance to practise it, but today, not only the army, but the nation as a whole is devoted to the idea.

Turkey Today

Modern Turkey stands between the developed and developing countries in most respects. Its statistics are kept down by millions of Anatolian farmers, only just now working their way out of primeval poverty; some stay on the land, others migrate to Istanbul, Ankara, or the cities of Western Europe (they joke that West Berlin has become the 68th Turkish province). Their fertility is startling; the fifty million Turks today have one of the highest rates of population growth in the world. Despite this and other drawbacks—high inflation and a creaky and bureaucratic government among them, the Turks are determined to push their way into the developed world, their aim is Common Market membership in the 1990s. Booming tourism, textile exports, huge deals in construction with the OPEC nations, and a new government, elected in 1983 with a strong commitment to governmental and economic reform, can only help.

The Turkish people

The word for guest in Turkish is *misafir*, and to the Turks it is almost sacred. Wherever you go, you'll be offered a glass of tea; for many people, Turkish hospitality is almost overwhelming. Yet one never has the feeling that it derives from a sense of religious obligation, rather from a warm and spontaneous friendliness and concern for their fellow man. Coupled with this, especially in the small village, is a keen curiosity about the foreigner. In Eastern Anatolia the good farmer may just stop and stare at you; it's a bit unnerving but they mean no harm. Anyone, especially the school children, who knows a few phrases of English will want to try them out on you ('Is Turkey beautiful? Yes?') The country women are shier. If they're in a group (you'll see them coming and going from the fields in large trailers pulled by jaunty tractors), they may smile. Otherwise, they probably won't address you, unless you're a woman on your own. Then they open up and are even more friendly than the men. Turks dote on children and if you take them with you, they'll spoil them horribly. '*Maşallah, maşallah*!' they'll say, patting them on the head and giving them more sweets and fruit than they could eat in a year. '*Maşallah*' means 'God Willing'; children are too precious to receive any more direct compliments. That might incur divine jealousy.

As well as warmth and hospitality, the other central characteristic of the Turks is their intense nationalism and pride. This is the heritage of the Great Atatürk. When Turkey was still referred to as 'The Sick Man of Europe' he boosted his countrymen's morale with slogans that you still see everywhere, even inscribed on hillsides in giant white letters '*NE MUTLU TÜRKÜM DIYENE*' ('How lucky for a man to call himself a Turk!') and '*BIZ BIZE BENZERIZ*' ('We resemble ourselves'). Speak disparagingly of Turkey at your own risk, although you'll find plenty of sympathy on many subjects, from telephones to traffic conditions in Istanbul, Atatürk himself is the one really taboo subject, unles you want to pay his memory a compliment. It's also bad form to say 'Constantinople' instead of Istanbul, or imply that Turkey is not a member of the Western community. Turks are easily insulted. They are also quite modest and conservative socially; wearing your bikini in the village and becoming noisy and drunk are provocative.

While travelling with children in Turkey poses no special problem (except that disposable nappies (diapers) and baby foods are hard to come by in many places, and many children dislike the milk served in cafés), a woman travelling on her own, or with a girlfriend, may have to contend with stares, personal questions and some typical Mediterranean male annoyances. The Turks, especially off the well travelled tourist routes, are simply not used to seeing women on their own. But don't be afraid to go. It is rare for a man to try to force you into something you don't want. Turks may make the women sit in the back of the mosque, but they have a respect for their rights and dignity that could be an example to many men elsewhere.

Religion

According to the last census, 99.04% of Turkey's population are Moslem, but there are no figures on how many actually practise their religion seriously. During the 1930s, when Turkey was hell-bent on reform and secularism, religion became unfashionable, at least in the cities. Today, Turkey like many of its neighbours, is having a modest Islamic revival. The current prime minister is a *haci* (the title for someone who has made the pilgrimage to Mecca) and in many towns mosques that were once almost empty for Friday prayers are now almost full. Atatürk's revolution was thorough, however, and there is little room for extremists.

In the *hadis*, the collection of traditions and stories from the days of Mohammed that serves as a commentary on the Koran, it is recorded that the angel Gabriel, disguised as a Bedouin, confronted the Prophet on the road one day and demanded to know the practices of the true belief. Mohammed's five answers satisfied the angel, and, as the 'five pillars of Islam', they continue to guide Moslems today, a solid foundation for the simplest of the world's great religions.

One of the pillars is the professing of the simple formula 'There is no god but Allah and Mohammed is his prophet.' This is painted or inscribed in elegant Arabic calligraphy all over the mosques of Turkey. Another pillar is the pilgrimage to Mecca, for all who are able. Giving alms for the poor is a third, begging is frowned upon and the mendicant dervishes and kalenders having been outlawed since 1925, this duty is performed discreetly. Moslems are also expected to keep a total fast during the daylight hours of Ramazan, the holy month of the Moslem calendar. In public, at least, the fast is well observed. During Ramazan a mood of peaceful contemplation occupies the faithful. Much of the time on radio and television is given over to religious programmes, and every evening at sunset in many towns a cannon booms out the signal that the fast has ended. Mosques are often gaily decorated with coloured lights, nowhere more so than in Istanbul where Koranic messages are spelled out in strings of lights between the minarets of the great Imperial mosques.

The most conspicuous of the five pillars is the obligation of saying prayers five times a day, at hours proclaimed by the muezzins from the minaret balconies. It is permitted to perform these anywhere, and although Moslems usually go to the mosques for the midday Friday prayers, there is no mass or ritual in the Christian sense. In the main, Islam avoids ritual and ceremony. The imam (priest) is present merely to lead the prayers, and the formulaic discourse he declaims afterwards is hardly a sermon.

The architecture of the mosques serves to illustrate the simplicity of Islam. Most are large halls furnished only with the *mimber* (a pulpit), and the *mihrab* (the niche in the wall facing Mecca), that concentrates the thoughts and prayers of the faith like a lens. Unlike other Moslem countries, you are allowed inside a Turkish mosque during prayer time. Don't forget to leave your shoes at the door, dress sensibly (no shorts, short skirts, or bared arms and shoulders) and don't make a nuisance of yourself, but by all means don't feel unwelcome, either. Moslems themselves enjoy coming to the mosque for meditation and quiet, and they are pleased to share them with you. To miss the interiors of the Ottoman mosques of Bursa and Istanbul and the Selcuk 'Great Mosques' of the cities of Anatolia, would be to miss much of the finest in Turkish art and architecture.

One Islamic ceremony you may encounter, which accompanies the rite of circumcision, is a small parade with a bravely smiling nine-year-old in a costume, crown and cape. Most weddings in Turkey are civil and the ballyhoo and decorated cars differ little from those in other lands; the busy marriage chapel next to Istanbul's city hall is a good place to watch them.

As for the other 0.96% of the Turks, most are Greek or Armenian Christians or Jews, and most live in Istanbul. Six hundred years of peaceful coexistence between Greeks and Turks ended with the 1920 war and the 'exchange of populations' agreed on by the governments afterwards. Some Jacobite Syrian Christians still live around Mardin. Finally, if in a distant corner of Anatolia you should happen on a procession bearing a bronze cock or a black snake, you'll know you've found the *Yezidis*, the 'peacock angel cult', a centuries-old offshoot of Islam, whose followers are reported to be devil worshippers. These rites are understandably secret, but the Yezidis dominate scores of villages in Turkey and Iraq, with a branch office, we hear, in London.

Part III

TURKISH TOPICS

The Muradiye Waterfall, Van

Alexander the Great

Before moving on to Egypt, Persia, and India, Alexander polished off the Persian King Darius's satrapies in Asia Minor for practice. With some 40 000 men, including 5000 cavalry, he crossed the Hellespont in the spring of 334 BC, sacrificing a bull to Poseidon in mid-passage. After visiting Troy, and paying homage to his Homeric heroes, he and his men were immediately confronted by an army commanded by the Persian *satraps* (governors) of Phrygia and Ionia. At the river Granicus, they boldly stormed across the water into the Persian lines and routed them, setting the tone for the rest of the campaign.

Then the Macedonians marched down the Aegean coast, taking Sardis, Ephesus, and Miletus. In Ephesus he threw out the pro-Persian aristocracy and restored democratic institutions, and, by so doing, made himself popular with all the Greeks of Asia Minor not in the Great King's pay. Taking auguries at Miletus, Alexander saw an eagle flying towards the shore, and took it to mean he would conquer the Persians by land, not by sea. Accordingly, he sent his Greek navy home—he couldn't afford it—and marched across the Mediterranean coast to take the Persians' naval bases away. Termessus refused an alliance, and survived when Alexander decided it wasn't worth a siege. Perge, Aspendos, and Side were brought into the line, and then the Macedonian force split up, the great central Parmenio taking half the force to reduce the Cilician coast while Alexander headed north to chase the Persians out of Phrygia. Here, as recorded by his chronicler Arrian, he cut with his sword the famous Gordian knot. The two forces met again at Tarsus, where the always fragile Alexander took ill from a swim in the cold river Cydnus. He recovered just in time to meet Darius, the Great King himself, at Issus near today's Iskenderun. The Macedonian victory, at a disadvantage of perhaps five to one, opened the way for the conquest of Persia and Egypt.

Atatürk

People in the west who are unacquainted with Turkish history have probably never heard of him, but in Turkey his face is everywhere: in statues, in the portraits that adorn all public places and most businesses, on coins and banknotes, on banners and even in neon lights. The best ones try to emphasise his sharp features to make him into a kind of mythological hero; instead he comes out looking like the Wizard of Oz.

At first he was just Mustafa, a sullen, red-haired, blue-eyed boy from Salonika. His house there still stands, next to the Turkish consulate, and woe to the Greeks if they ever knock it down, as they threaten to whenever they feel the urge to Turk-baiting. A teacher who recognised his abilities gave him the name Kemal, meaning 'perfection'; by the time he was helping whip the British at Gallipoli, he had become General Mustafa Kemal Paşa. Atatürk, or 'father of the Turks' was the surname he assumed by general acclaim during his campaign to westernise Turkish names in the 1930s.

Cults of personality were all too common in those days, and we might easily dismiss Atatürk as just another strongman. On the contrary, he has earned a place among the very few great statesmen this century has produced. One of the famous photos of Atatürk shows him in European formal attire, demonstrating Roman letters to a crowd of his earnest but probably bewildered countrymen. It wasn't just what a modern politician would call a 'photo opportunity'; he did it hundreds of times all over Turkey. He took his job seriously and after so many centuries of decay, the job couldn't have been done any other way.

Atatürk found his people in decay and despair, gave them back their self-respect and prevailed against their enemies; he effected the quickest and most complete change in customs, manners and institutions that any nation has ever undergone. In foreign policy, his slogan was 'Peace at home, peace in the world', and Turkey, a responsible member of the international community, has done its best to live up to it.

Banks

As visitors to Turkey soon notice, there are more signs advertising banks than anything else in the country. Banks are the major force in the economy—more so than in most countries—but the largest are state-owned, the heritage of 'Kemalism' very much influenced by the corporatist ideas learned in the 1920s. Some banks have interesting stories. Sümerbank really isn't a bank at all so much as an enormous state-managed textile cooperative; its outlets are the Turks' version of J C Penny's. The nation's religious foundations run the Türkiye Vakiflar Bankasi which devotes its profits to the rehabilitation of historic buildings.

The Best of Everything

To make your planning easier, here is a brief list of what we consider the best places to go for whatever aspect of Turkish life and history you find interesting:

SITES

Neolithic sites: none, surprisingly. Museum: Ankara, Istanbul (Museum of the Ancient Orient).

Hittite sites: Boğazköy, Alacahöyük, Koratepe. Museum: Ankara.

Phrygian sites: hills south of Seyitgazi, Gordion. Museums: Ankara, Afyon.

Urartian sites: Çavuştepe. Museums: Van, Ankara.

Greek and Hellenistic sites: Pergamon, Priene, Didyma, Heraclaea. Museums: Istanbul, Selçuk.

Roman-era sites: Ephesus, Side, Perge, Aizanoi, Aspendos, Aphrodisias. Museums: Selçuk, Istanbul, Antalya, Antakya (mosaics).

Byzantine architecture: Istanbul, Trabzon, Sumela; **Painting and mosaics:** St Saviour in Chora and the Aya Sofia, Istanbul; Aya Sofia in Trabzon; rock churches of Cappadocia.

Selçuk art and architecture: Konya, Erzurum, Divriği, Kayseri, Sivas.

Ottoman architecture: Bursa, Istanbul, Edirne.

Architecture of other Turkish emirates: Diyarbakir, Urfa, Niğde.

Armenian art and architecture: Ani, Akhtamar, Kars.

Islamic relics and holy places: Topkapi Saray, Istanbul; Mevlevi Museum, Konya; Eyüp; Urfa; Hacibektaş.

Christian holy places: House of the Virgin Mary and Basilica and grave of

St John, Ephesus; Christianity's oldest church, Antakya; St Nicholas Church, Demre; Mt Ararat; Harran (native town of Abraham).

TURKISH FOLKLORE AND CRAFTS MUSEUMS
Ankara (Ethnographic museum), Istanbul (Turkish and Islamic Arts museum), Bursa and Kayseri.

CURIOSITIES
Pagan temples of Soğdamar; Mt Nemrut; underground cities and cave cities of Cappadocia; Pamukkale.

CASTLES
Rumeli Hisar (on the Bosphorus), Bodrum, Korykos, Anamur, Ankara, Hoşap, Bayburt, Alanya, several in Adana province.

BEST SCENIC ROADS
Silifke–Alanya (Cilician coast); Trabzon to Gümüşhane over the Zigana Pass; Van to Bitlis along the Lake Van shore; Fethiye to Antalya (Lycian coast); Sivas to Amasya through the Yeşilirmak valley; Van to Hakkari; Edremit to Bergama.

EXCURSIONS
The Bosphorus ferry; Lake Van ferry; funicular up Mt Uludağ (Bursa); 'Blue Voyage' along the Lycian coast (see **Getting Around Turkey: By Sea** p. 6).

FINEST CITIES
Bursa, Antalya, Urfa, Erzurum, Istanbul, Diyarbakir, Konya.

BEACHES
Around Alanya and Antalya, Samandağ, Fethiye; various secluded spots along the Cilicia and Hatay coasts; the Bodrum and Çeşme peninsulas, Gulf of Edremit.

East and west

William Butler Yeats, in his murky meditation, *A Vision*, wrote of east and west eternally contending. He saw them as alternately fertilising each other with new cultures in successive ages. However you choose to interpret this aspect of the world's secret history, it undoubtedly exists, and Turkey is its battleground. Alexander the Great carried Greek culture and philosophy eastwards through it, and his successors brought back the Persian concept of the divine ruler, without which the cult of the deified Roman emperors could not have been. Christianity began its conquests in Asia Minor, in a score of towns and churches mentioned in the New Testament from the Sufi poets, the Crusaders adopted the cult of chivalry; the troubadours, alchemy and many themes found in medieval literature owe their beginnings to Islamic culture. Today, the Republic of Atatürk heads the incursion of our secular, mercantile culture into the Middle East.

In poetry, it all begins with the Trojan War, and evocations of Homer fill the pages of Turkey's history. Like Alexander, Mehmet the Conqueror took time to visit Troy after 1453. He declared that by taking Constantinople he had avenged the 'peoples of Asia' on the Greeks. On his entry into the city after the conquest, Mehmet, according to tradition, knocked off with his sword one of the serpent heads of the old bronze column that stood in the Hippodrome. This monument had been brought to the city by Constantine the Great who had looted it from Delphi. There is no way Mehmet could have known that it commemorated the victory of the Greeks over the Persians at Plataea in 479 BC—almost 2000 years before.

Gecekondu

Under Turkish law, the authorities may remove no squatter's shack if the roof can be raised in one night. As country people flocked to Istanbul and Ankara in the 1960s and 70s in search of modern life and good jobs, the outskirts of these and other cities filled with *gecekondu* (overnight) neighbourhoods. These are the outward manifestation of Turkey's continuing social revolution. Most by now have grown into real neighbourhoods with real houses, as their hard-working inhabitants gradually make their way into urban society. Turkish planners once looked upon them as their greatest problem; now, by the curious and immutable laws of urban economics, it seems their resourceful, upwardly-mobile people may be one of the nation's great resources.

Hats

On the whole, Turks are, and always have been, sharp dressers. What is unusual, though, is the way in which matters of dress manage so frequently to insinuate themselves into matters of state: hats, for example.

Most of us have heard of Atatürk's famous Hat Law of 1925, outlawing the wearing of the fez, the conical felt hat with a tassel that Egyptians call a *tarboosh*. Here, what the Father of the Turks had in mind was to do away with one conspicuous symbol of pious reaction, and in public, he always wore a fedora or smart cloth cap to set an example. Ironically, though, the fez itself had been introduced during the nineteenth century *Tanzimat* reforms for the same purpose: to replace the then disreputable old Turkish turban.

Hats in politics go back much further. As far back as the 1460s, Mehmet the Conqueror was enacting a hat law, governing the colours of turbans that could be worn at court: green for vezirs, red for chamberlains, white for muftis, red, yellow or black for everyone else except infidels, who weren't allowed a turban at all. Mehmet followed this up with a shoe ordinance: black for Greeks, blue for Jews, violet for Armenians, and so on.

The *Hat Law* of 1925 accomplished its purpose in a roundabout way. Today most Turks have given up and don't wear any hat at all, except for the Kurds with their inevitable flat grey caps. Meanwhile, street hawkers go on selling fezes to tourists in front of the Aya Sofia every day.

Jason and the Argonauts

So many and tangled are the influences and sources of this cycle of myths that its origin can hardly be found. Homer only mentions Jason once, indirectly, and the earliest versions of the tale have Jason sailing not to the Black Sea, but up the Adriatic in search of the Golden Fleece.

Pelias, the usurper of the throne of Iolcus, would have murdered the infant heir Jason, but his mother took him secretly to Mount Pelion, where he was raised by Chiron the Centaur. When Jason arrived to regain his kingdom, Pelias promised to relinquish it on completion of this quest: the fleece had belonged to a flying golden ram sent by Zeus to rescue an ancestor, Phrixus, from execution; it carried him to Colchis, the farthest eastern land known to the Greeks. Jason accepted the job, and got Argus the Thespian to build him the famous Argo. The list of companions he collected included heroes from all over the Greek world: Heracles, Castor and Polydeuces, Mopsus the Lapith—who later founded so many cities on Asia Minor's southern shore—Atalanta the speedy virgin, even Orpheus the poet.

After dallying with the women of Lemnos (who had murdered their husbands) and repopulating the island, the Argonauts sailed through the Hellespont. Heracles' beloved squire Hylas disappeared on the coast of the Marmara near Bursa, and Heracles, who had just defeated Jason in a rowing contest, was marooned there by the captain as he searched for Hylas. At Salmydessus in Eastern Thrace the Argonauts chased off the Harpies that were plaguing King Phineus, and received, in return, advice on how to navigate the Symplegades, the 'clashing rocks' (probably ice floes that floated down from Russian rivers), that destroyed all ships attempting to pass the Bosphorus.

Along the Black Sea, they stopped at Mariandyne (somewhere near Akçakoca). Had Heracles still been with them, he could have shown them here the opening into Hades, from which he had dragged the captured dog Cerberus out on his twelfth labour. At Sinope they picked up new crew members, and from there they passed into the lands of the iron-smelting

Chalybians, the Amazons, and the promiscuous Mosynoecians. Soon afterwards, they crossed the Soviet border (Colchus lay north of modern Batum) where destiny and Medea awaited them. Their journey had as yet only begun.

One source of the tale was the Greek voyages of exploration in the Black Sea c. 1000 BC. The fall of Troy had, probably, opened up this new trade route to them, and they went in search of amber, iron, and furs from the east. Every Greek city in classical times wanted its trading sites there justified, and no doubt a few of them paid off the early poets to make sure their heroes were included among the Argo's crew.

The best version of the tale comes in the poem, third century BC, by Apollonius of Rhodes—the *Argonautica*, of which there are several good translations in English.

Media

Turks love reading newspapers, and they are big business, with most of the large dailies being distributed nationally. It's hard to tell whether Turkish papers are bad, but they certainly look bad. The tremendous success of the colour scandal sheets, like *Tan* and *Bulvar*, with their soft-core porn and crime sizzlers, is dragging the whole industry into perdition.

Indeed, the traveller in Turkey gets the impression the country is being buried alive under a vast avalanche of breasts and buttocks. We leave it to the sociologists to discuss what effect this is having on this very conservative society. *Hürriyet*, *Milliyet*, and *Cumhuriyet* are three of the respectable dailies; they bring politics out into the open, without censorship, and scramble for circulation as best they can. For the tourist, there's the admirable *Turkish Daily News*, in English, printed in Ankara, an invaluable source of education on Turkish life and politics. It's available in the big cities and occasionally turns up elsewhere. Foreign papers will only be found in Istanbul, Ankara, and occasionally in some resorts.

If you have a radio, the Third Programme of the *TRT* (Turkish Radio and Television) gives the news in English, French, and German several times a day in various places on the FM band. Turkish radio can be entertaining, with a mixture of Turkish and western classical music, good home-grown jazz, and wild musichall entertainments that are funny, even if you can't make out a word. Television, with one state-run channel (recently changed over to colour) is predictably awful, offering mainly masterfully-dubbed versions of the very worst American shows and movies. Local shows are often on the level of a favourite game show called *Yes or No*, where an emcee in a loud suit accosts members of the audience and makes them engage in conversation; if they can avoid saying either of those little words for a minute they win a small prize. If you frequent the coffee houses and *lokantas*, you'll be subjected to Turkish TV often enough. Even though it's still a novelty in parts of the country, you'll notice the Turks only look up from their food when the commercials come on.

Mevlâna

Islam has no saints, but Celâleddin Rumi, poet and Sufi mystic of Konya, approaches as nearly to that exalted state as is allowed. For westerners who have never been able to take Islam seriously, he is the man to know. Born on 30 September 1207 in Balkh, Afghanistan, Celâleddin and his family—his father Bahaeddin Veled was a renowned scholar—fled before the Mongol invasions to Anatolia, where they took refuge in the Selcuk capital, then in its heyday under Sultan Alâeddin Keykubad. Here he remained as a teacher in the city's mosques, withdrawing more and more into his meditations and his poetry until his death on 17 December 1273. The Mevlevi order of dervishes, the 'whirling dervishes' he founded was tremendously influential throughout the Middle East, and the hereditary line of its sheikhs, descended from the Mevlâna (literally 'our master'), even intermarried with the Ottoman Sultans during the reign of Beyazit I.

Few poets in the world have been more prolific. His greatest work, a subtly arranged medley of lyric poetry, mysticism and anecdotes called the *Mesnevi* (or *Mathnavi*), runs to some 25 000 couplets (longer than the *Faerie Queene*, the longest poem in English), and there are 44 000 more couplets in the anthology called the *Divan of Shems-i Tabriz*. The title of a third work *Fihi-Ma-Fih*, 'in it what's in it', clearly expresses the Sufi informality and disdain of dogmas and church establishments. All were written in Persian (good translations of selections exist, notably by Professors Nicholson and Arberry).

The Mevlâna's poetry has been described as an ocean; vast and boundless, encompassing all the systems and creeds of lesser men within it. In truth there is no readily discernible philosophy in his work that does not state the obvious; the Mevlâna wanted it to appeal to all men at all levels. The unity of God and of creation is a recurring theme, consistent with Islam and the teaching of the Sufis. It is the revelation of divine love that sets his work apart, and the spiritual allegory of the 'lover' and the 'beloved', the soul and its dissolution into the infinite, is the core of his thought. On this rarefied plane of understanding, the claims of the various religions seem mere games of language, and issues such as predestination or free will simply cease to be relevant.

As for the whirling dervishes, the Mevlâna and his followers believed as much in music and dance as forms of spiritual expression as they did in poetry. The *sema*, the ritual dance still performed annually in Konya on the anniversary of the Mevlâna's death, is his teaching of the abandonment of the self set into motion. The dervishes' tall hats represent their own gravestones, the jackets, which they shed, their graves. As the dancers spin around the floor, symbolically reflecting at once the movements of the cosmos and the soul's search for God, the dancers themselves attain a controlled mystic communion. With one hand raised and the other extended towards the ground, they '...take from God and give to man, keeping nothing for themselves...'.

Mimar Sinan

Not all Christian boys pressed into the Janissary corps ended up as soldiers. One young Greek, born about 1489, worked his way up through the military engineering branch to become the head architect of the Ottoman state. At the age of 59, Sinan built his first mosque, the Şehzade in Istanbul, for Sultan Süleyman the Magnificent. It was the beginning of a brilliant collaboration that created scores of mosques, schools, bridges and fortifications—the launching of the Ottoman Imperial style, as well as its greatest achievements. For the Turks, his profession became a title; they call him *Mimar* Sinan—Sinan the Architect.

It would have been impossible for one man to have accomplished the tremendous output with which Sinan is credited, several hundred buildings in all. Like Michelangelo and other Renaissance artists who attached their names to everything that came out of the workshop, even if all the details had been handled by students, Sinan must really be thought of as head of a huge public works collective. All these works (most are in Istanbul) are distinctive and gracefully proportioned, but those that most clearly bear the stamp of the master are the Selimiye in Edirne, the little Sokollu Mehmet Paşa Mosque, and the great Süleymaniye in Istanbul.

Music

Music is an important part of the Turks' cultural heritage and still a national passion. Western travellers unsympathetic to it have given Turkish music a bad name, calling it monotonous; even if you don't go out of your way to find it, you'll hear enough of it on radios and in buses to get accustomed to it and make up your own mind. What you hear most of, unfortunately, is something called *şarki*—'oriental' or 'arabesque', a noxious Arab-influenced pop style. Irritating as it is, the vocal strength and feeling of the performers, especially the women, makes western popular music sound like a nursery school pageant.

Western classical music came into fashion with Atatürk, though the last Sultans had cultivated opera and kept large dance orchestras. Today it is quite popular, and several Turkish singers and musicians have made names for themselves abroad. The Turks have their own classical tradition, however, and you hear what they call *sanat müziği*, 'art music', anywhere, even in night clubs. At first, this was heavily influenced by the Mevlevi dervishes; its main instrument is the lute (our word comes from the Arabic *al ud*). The lutes hanging in Turkish music shop windows differ in no respect from those in medieval tapestries and illuminations; the Crusaders brought them back from Anatolia. To this the Mevlevis in their own music add the *ney*, a ghostly, reedy flute. Both types of music are governed by modes (*makams*), like ancient Greek music. Their subtleties will require all your attention and good will.

The real treat, however, is Turkish folk music, which Bela Bartok said was the richest he had ever experienced. The *aşiks*, rural troubadours who improvise to a stringed instrument called the *saz*, can still be found (there may be one seated next to you on a bus) and folk music and dancing are still practised widely (the Black Sea and Aegean coasts, Konya, Kars, and Silifke are especially known for them). Wild dances for men like the Aegean *zeybek* and the *horon* of the northeast are its most spectacular manifestation, along with popular mainly improvised dances like the *çiftetelli*, traditionally performed at weddings. Besides the *saz* and lute, other instruments are the clarinet and accordion, a two-headed drum called the *davul*, the *kanun*, a 78-stringed dulcimer related to the Hungarian cimbalom, the *kaval* (shepherd's pipes), *kemençe* (a tiny violin played like a cello) and the *cura*, a sort of zither that has been traced back to the Hittites.

Finally, there's the inimitable *Mehter* music played by the Janissaries under the walls of Vienna and a thousand other towns to dishearten the defenders. With the aid of enormous drums carted around in their own wagons, the 66-piece Mehter bands made grand and gloriously noisy music. Though its art and melodiousness were probably lost on the besieged garrisons, Mehter is the ancestor of all our military music and marching bands; it has also found its way into western music through the Turkish bagatelles of Mozart, Beethoven, and Weber.

Nasreddin Hoca

This fellow, the clever-foolish country priest (*hoca*) who goes under the name of Goha in the Arabian Nights tales, is the classic comic figure of Turkish folklore. Outwitting himself as often as the Emperor Tamerlane, at whose court he is supposed to have lived, the Hoca's adventures are still current among all Turks and his tomb can be seen in Akşehir. He is very much a creation of the Sufis, the mystics of Islam who condense volumes of theology into such tales. One famous story has the Hoca walking with a friend discussing the completeness of creation. The Hoca considers that it would have been better if horses had wings; thus, they would be much more helpful to mankind. Just then some pigeon droppings fall on the Hoca's turban. He reflects, 'Allah knows best!'.

Patlican

This means 'aubergine' (eggplant). Take a moment to consider the Turkish aubergine; the Turks have considered it closely and most of them have some almost every day. It is said there are over a hundred ways of cooking them known to Turkish cooks, and you'll get your share of them in plain restaurants or fancy. Have a look when you pass the stands in the market; the Turkish aubergine is unlike any in the world, perfect in form and of a heartbreaking shade of violet. Give credit for this to the Anatolian farmer, one of the most careful and loving tillers of the soil in the world. Wherever nature permits, he turns his difficult land into little gardens, and all the produce he sends to market is infinitely better than you get elsewhere.

Turkey is one of the few nations to be self sufficient in agriculture. From tea along the Black Sea coast to bananas along the Mediterranean, everything a Turk could desire grows well somewhere in the country; everything except coffee, and they're experimenting with that now.

Photography

Turkey is wonderland for photographers, with some reservations. Look out for military or prohibited zones; the government can be touchy about them and they aren't always obvious. All the land around the ancient Phrygian site of Gordion is one, for example, and all harbours. Some important sites, like the Hittite reliefs at Karatepe, and many museums, prohibit cameras at the request of the archaeologists. These busy scientists will make you wait until their monographs are in print before you may photograph them. Finally, don't make a nuisance of yourself by waving your camera at picturesque country people in traditional clothes; they may well be good Moslems who find the depicting of the human form offensive. (If you see women wearing the *çarşaf* (veil), in cities, by the way, they're probably Iranian tourists who won't like it either.)

Police

These come in all shapes and sizes. Besides the regular police you may encounter the *Trafik Polisi*, who either clear up traffic jams or create them in the cities, and molest bus and truck drivers at rural intersections to make sure papers are in order and the weight limits observed. In the country, the peace is kept by the *jandarmas*, a force much like the famous Mexican *federales*; their green fatigues and rifles are a leftover from the old days when they had mountain bandits to chase. Finally, there are the *military police* in full army gear with a red stripe on the helmet with the letters AS.IZ. They were much in evidence in the troubles of the 1970s, but now their only job is to stand around post offices waiting for AWOL soldiers. In Istanbul, there is a *tourist police*.

Crime in Turkey is still rare, except perhaps for pickpocketing in the larger cities; there are almost no robberies. In some of the older traditional cities, like Kayseri, you may be treated to the night-watch interminably tootling its whistles up and down the streets, an old custom that is dying out.

Shopping

Customs men in most countries are on to this. 'And what did *you* buy in Turkey?' they ask. There are so many pretty things, and prices are so low that everyone goes home with something. Carpet merchants think you're only there to see them. They'll entice you into their shop somehow, bring lots of tea, and maybe you'll buy something. Carpets come in all shapes and sizes, from hand-made silk with four-figure prices to machine-made *kilims*, thin colourful cotton rugs that serve the Turks as coverings for floors, walls, beds, or furniture. Tourist towns are not the place to look for good buys, but try the bazaars of any out-of-the-way Anatolian city. You can bargain if you're up to it, but don't expect a markdown of more than 15%. Bargaining is not a battle of wits, but a little social ritual. You may only do it for large purchases although in some circumstances it works for foreigners paying taxis and even for rooms in the cheaper hotels. Avoid theatricals; if you don't like a price turn your eyes up to heaven, say 'thanks', and pretend to go.

Clothes of all kinds are good and very cheap; a trip to Turkey may be your opportunity to outfit your children for the next ten years. Jewellery, leather, and copperware are traditional favourites; antique shops do exist, especially in the newer parts of Istanbul, and they're good places to look for such orientalia as water pipes, mother-of-pearl inlaid *hamam* slippers, or Karagöz puppets. Museum gift shop trinkets are rare but look in Ankara's or Van's. There are some local specialities, such as meerschaum from Eskişehir and tiles and porcelain from Kütahya, the heirs of a centuries-old craft industry. The backstreets of Anatolian bazaars are full of surprises. Ask a tailor to make you up a pair of *şalvar*, the traditional baggy trousers for men or women, and he'll do it in an afternoon for about £4, and you'll be a fashion sensation at home.

Tekel

The Turkish State Monopoly manufactures all the tobacco and alcohol, although there are plans to turn it over to private industry. The cigarettes, all brands named after Turkish cities, are cheap and good. They also make cigars, impossible to find outside the cities. The national drink is *raki*, almost the same as Greek ouzo though not as good. The monopoly makes three different kinds of varying degrees of toxicity as well as brandy (*kanyak*) and a very good vodka.

Turkey, the world's sixth largest producer of wine, turns out some fine varieties, mostly on the dry side. The more prestigious labels—Kavaklidere, Buzbağ—for example, are quite good, but you can do just as well with many of the very inexpensive varieties available in any little shop or kiosk. Try any of the various kinds of Doluca. Tekel used to make a good beer, but the big European breweries are pushing them out of the market with their advertising campaigns. As a result, Turks are now drinking more beer than wine. The biggest seller, Efes, is made by Pilsener Urquell of Czechoslovakia.

Toilets

Conveniences in varying states of decomposition will be found in petrol stations, bus depots, etc. The best ones will be in mosques—just ask for the tuvalet or WC (pronounced 'veh-veh-jeh'); French-style holes in the floor await you in many of the cheaper hotels—but almost never in the government-listed establishments. The use of toilet paper is not a universally accepted custom (that's what the little taps are for); seasoned travellers carry their own.

TTOK

This stands for the Türkiye Turing ve Otomobil Kurumu—the Auto Club. This is certainly one of the nation's remarkable institutions. Even if you aren't driving, you will cross their path many times; as well as their services to motorists, like the mobile repair service on the Edirne–Ankara road, the TTOK under its director Çelik Gülersoy, a legend in his own time, has become the country's major force in promoting tourism, and also in historical preservation.

Everywhere you go in Istanbul, you will be drinking in their cafes, enjoying the lovely parks and old houses they've repaired, reading their guide books and maps, and using their tourist information services. They put up most of the area's road signs and park benches, and even operate hotels. Everything they do is first-rate, and you'll see them referred to often in this book.

Tulips

The Great Tulip Speculation of the seventeenth century is one of the oddities of European history. In Germany, France, and Holland these flowers briefly became an obsession pursued with the kind of fervour we now devote only to gold bullion and commodity futures. Some exotic varieties' bulbs actually brought more than their weight in gold; great financial houses and canny opportunists rose and fell with the fortunes of their favourite blooms, and tulip quotes filled coffee house conversation as stock market closings do today. The Turks can take all the credit. Tulips, like cherries, pizza, parchment, and angora wool are among Anatolia's contributions to civilisation.

A century later, it was the Turks' turn to get silly over tulips. What Ottoman historians call the 'Tulip Period' is generally associated with the reign of Ahmet III (1703–20). Here the Sultans and their court reached their most Chinese extreme of abstraction and contrived refinement, while their empire careered into decay. With their wedding cake turbans, layers of silk and brocades, and turned-up slippers, the bizarrely decorous Ottomans made a picture that fascinated contemporary Europe. Night garden parties among the tulips were the rage, illuminated by candles on the backs of wandering turtles.

Tulip art—for the Sultan interested himself in little else—can best be seen in the lovely tiled chambers of the Topkapi harem. If you want to see what started all the hubbub, there are wild tulips in the national parks around Ankara and Yozgat.

Tuğra

On many old Ottoman buildings, such as the Sublime Porte in Istanbul, you will see an unusual symbol, made of Arabic characters in a scroll of concentric loops. The *Tuğra* was the mark of the Ottoman Empire from the early days. It originated with Murat I, who like his predecessors was illiterate and signed documents with his thumbprint. An entire wall of tuğras, removed after 1920 from public buildings, can be seen in the garden of the Topkapi Saray.

Yok

This is one of the essential words to know. Its meaning approximates 'There's none', but it is used much more commonly than 'no' (*hayir*). It is a sentence from which there is no appeal. If a Turk is at all inclined to help you out, he will exhaust all possibilities before intoning the fatal 'yok'. Its positive counterpart is *var* 'There is', always a cheering note in Turkey though when you do get it, it may not be what you expect.

Yürüks

These are Turkish nomads, who migrate with their herds from valleys and coastal plains up to the *yaylas* (highland pastures in the mountains) every summer and back again in the autumn. Their numbers are decreasing but around such places as the Taurus Mountains and Lake Van, big sheep and cattle areas with large *yürük* populations, you see their tents everywhere in the summer. Their migrations are no longer so picturesque; that dilapidated truck packed full of cows and suitcases that hurtles past you on the highway is likely to be a *yürük* express.

Part IV

ISTANBUL

The Blue Mosque, Istanbul

Background

Just to vex the Turks, the Greeks still insist on calling it Constantinople, and print it that way on all their maps. The Ottomans never really meant to change the name; they probably thought of themselves as the successors of the Romans, just as the Byzantines had, and they did their best to keep Constantine's column in good repair. But through centuries of trade and diplomacy with the Greeks, they had often heard this fabulous remnant of antiquity referred to as 'Stin poli' or 'in the city'. Turkish has no prepositions, and to their ears it must have sounded like one word.

The name stuck; and what could be better for such a place than to be called, simply, The City. To the Turks, the Mongols, and other peoples of distant Asia, this was a kind of half-mythical land of dreams, known more through poets than historians or travellers, just as Cathay and the Indies were for medieval Europeans. All these Asian peoples migrated west to the 'Land of Rome' and its golden capital, and one day made it their own.

For sixteen centuries, Istanbul was the metropolis of the Eastern Medi-

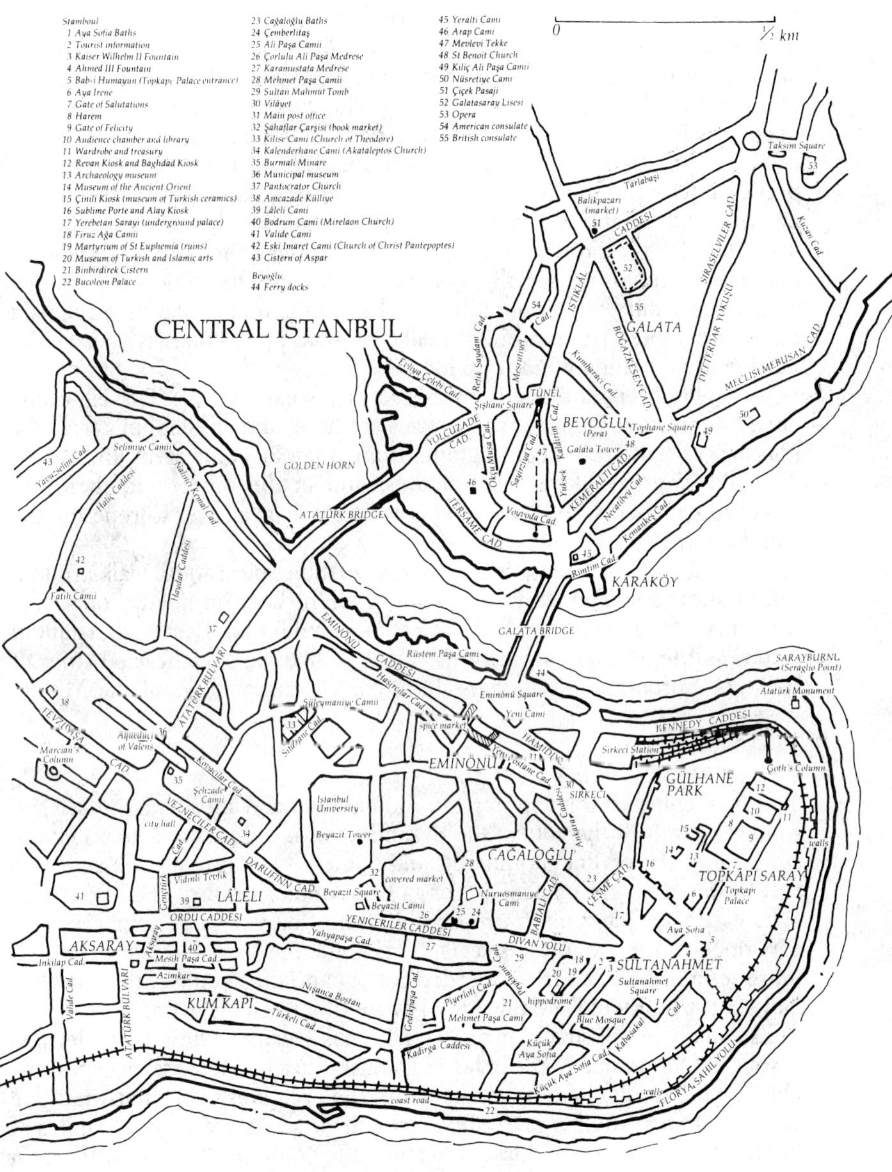
CENTRAL ISTANBUL
Stamboul
1 Aya Sofia Baths
2 Tourist information
3 Kaiser Wilhelm II Fountain
4 Ahmed III Fountain
5 Bab-i Humayun (Topkapı Palace entrance)
6 Aya Irene
7 Gate of Salutations
8 Harem
9 Gate of Felicity
10 Audience chamber and library
11 Wardrobe and treasury
12 Revan Kiosk and Baghdad Kiosk
13 Archaeology museum
14 Museum of the Ancient Orient
15 Çinili Kiosk (museum of Turkish ceramics)
16 Sublime Porte and Alay Kiosk
17 Yerebetan Sarayı (underground palace)
18 Firuz Ağa Camii
19 Martyrium of St Euphemia (ruins)
20 Museum of Turkish and Islamic arts
21 Binbirdirek Cistern
22 Bucoleon Palace
23 Cağaloğlu Baths
24 Çemberlitaş
25 Ali Paşa Camii
26 Çorlulu Ali Paşa Medrese
27 Karamustafa Medrese
28 Mehmet Paşa Camii
29 Sultan Mahmut Tomb
30 Vilâyet
31 Main post office
32 Şahaflar Çarşısı (book market)
33 Kilise Camii (Church of Theodore)
34 Kalenderhane Camii (Akataleptos Church)
35 Burmalı Minare
36 Municipal museum
37 Pantocrator Church
38 Amcazade Külliye
39 Lâleli Camii
40 Bodrum Camii (Mirelaon Church)
41 Valide Camii
42 Eski Imaret Camii (Church of Christ Pantepoptes)
43 Cistern of Aspar
Beyoğlu
44 Ferry docks
45 Yeralti Camii
46 Arap Camii
47 Mevlevi Tekke
48 St Benoit Church
49 Kiliç Ali Paşa Camii
50 Nüsretiye Camii
51 Çiçek Pasajı
52 Galatasaray Lisesi
53 Opera
54 American consulate
55 British consulate
0
½ km

terranean. The Byzantines had a word for their legitimate heirs to the throne, those sons of Emperors born in the famous Purple Chamber of the palace; it was *Porphyrogenitus*, or 'born to the purple'. This we can take as a title for the city itself, whose location astride both the land and sea routes between east and west guaranteed its long rule. There is a sinister aspect to this. Istanbul, both under the Byzantines and the Ottomans, was the most predatory city the world has ever known, sucking the economic life blood out of hundreds of provinces—even entire nations. For a long time, its matchless fortifications protected, even encouraged the kind of decadence that nature and history usually root out of societies. Only now is the city just waking up from the terrible Ottoman hangover; it can take its place as a modern commercial emporium, realising what a blessing it is to have the burden of governing lifted from its shoulders.

Its new burden, and one it gladly accepts, is carrying the Turkish economy; one third of the nation's factories are here, and of Istanbul's five million people half are recent migrants from Anatolia come to try their luck. The old diversity of peoples remains, and in the other half, there are Greeks, Armenians, and Jews, as well as others from all over Europe and the Middle East.

Istanbul will not disappoint. It is inexhaustible, pleasant to walk around, full of surprises. You could take your old aunt here on holiday or have a Bohemian dream vacation, live like a tycoon or a tramp. Best of all, Istanbul is **accessible,** in every sense of the word, unlike the cold-hearted cities of Western Europe or the unknowable flyspeck metropolises of the Middle East.

THE STREETS OF ISTANBUL

You may come to this city for the monuments and museums, to see the Sultan's jewels or the gold of the Byzantine mosaics, or simply to watch the sunset over the skyline of minarets and domes. The fantasies you entertain may be out of the Arabian Nights or an Eric Ambler spy thriller of the 1930s. Whatever your particular purpose, take care that you keep your eyes and ears open to the life in the streets. This is the real Istanbul, for which the mosques and palaces are merely decoration, and the people of the city have had centuries to cultivate this life of Istanbul into an art form.

Especially in the small things, Istanbul has sacrificed little to modernity. If your hotel is in one of the older residential districts, like Aksaray or Sultanahmet, you are likely to be awakened to the cry, 'Nefis ... simit, simit...' exquisite *simits*, and the man who carries these sesame-encrusted circles of bread on a stick or in a glass box may differ only in dress from those in sixteenth-century prints. If you were a Stamboullu, you would drop down a basket on a long rope for one. After the simit man comes the tinker's rattling empty cart, and his long unintelligible cries seem less a plea for trade, than an eternal rambling monologue on God's unfairness to tinkers.

Of course there are **street markets;** some of the old quarters are named after the day of the week on which they would occur. In Istanbul though, in the Middle-Eastern manner every street is an actual or potential market. Some have permanent sites: by Galata Bridge each morning, housewives and stray cats circle around tired fishermen, angling for their share of the day's catch, while, opposite, in the narrow maze of streets climbing to the Covered Bazaar, the metal doors bang open to reveal thousands of tiny shops, segregated into streets according to their trade: an avenue of baby clothes, a street of copper pots, a cul-de-sac of used Korans. However, more money changes hands on the bridge itself perhaps than in a large department store. On Galata Bridge, on any given day you may spend a few lira on socks, wind-up monkeys, copies of the Turkish Highway Code, contraband blue jeans, clothes hangers, pastel panties, aubergines (eggplants), sets of wrenches (English or metric), bicycle mirrors, hamsters, or portraits of Mehmet the Conqueror.

To all these, add the shoeshine boys; young apprentices with cheap wooden boxes and old paint tins to sit on, and dignified professionals with dozens of cut-glass bottles in gold-plated cases, embellished with scenes of Mecca, and autographed pictures of overripe chanteuses. Sellers of sherbet, ayran, unidentifiable pastries, and even water, abound. The fellows with the jingling sacks and packs of untaxed Marlboros are on the lowest rung of Turkish organised crime; you choose a number, pick a numbered token from the sack, and if you click, the Marlboros are yours. You can try your hand at shooting with the young men who have invested their capital in an air rifle and target, or patronise the poorest of all, those whose business consists of a single rusted bathroom scale, waiting to weigh all comers—perhaps ten people a day, when business is good.

As background, add the beggars (more than in Paris, fewer than in Philadelphia), military policemen, hosts of shabby-genteel cats and pigeons, farmers on donkeys, sleek 1949 Chrysler dolmuş cabs—still with their original half-ton of chrome, tourists from Iran and Indiana, seven hills, 1300 minarets, gypsies, ferryboats, Roman cisterns, and the best art nouveau buildings east of Palma de Mallorca.

A few older neighbourhoods have no monopoly on all this; it is the everyday ambience the Stamboullu takes for granted, varying in degree from the venerable precincts of Eminönü and Sultanahmet to the newer streets around Taksim Square and those on the Asian side. Try not to be too influenced by pre-conceptions. Istanbul is not especially dirty or dilapidated; ironically, these two qualities are concentrated around the main street of the new town, Istiklâl Caddesi. After a walk down it, you may have a strange urge to have a bath. The old town is the real surprise. Following Turkish rather than European idea of town planning, there are lots of trees, and the houses are as spread out as land values permit. Many of the outlying districts are really suburbs within the Theodosian walls, or better, aggregations of villages.

ORIENTATION

A brief orientation will help much in sorting out the complexities of the layout. Note that there are three parts. On the European side, the triangular peninsula south of the estuary of the Golden Horn is **Stamboul,** the old town—formerly Constantinople and Byzantium—which rises like Rome on seven hills, surrounded by the largely intact Byzantine walls; most of the sights—the Aya Sofia, Topkapi Palace, the Covered Market, Sülemaniye and the Blue Mosque—are concentrated within the square mile of its tip. We mention this only because you may not notice. Whether you're walking or in a cab, the impenetrable maze of meandering streets makes them all appear to be in different parts of the city. Take time to study the map before you set out.

Two bridges span the **Golden Horn:** the Atatürk and the famous Galata, connecting old Istanbul with **Beyoğlu,** the 'European quarter' ever since Italian merchants colonised it in the latter days of Byzantium. Its outer fringes have been fashionable for two centuries now. Galata Bridge, and the Eminönü Square behind it in the old town, are the nearest thing Istanbul has to a centre; the busy comings and goings here were a feature of Istanbul life before there was a bridge, going back to the days of the Byzantines.

The ferryboats depart from Galata Bridge and some of the places they go to are the districts of the Asian shore, **Kadiköy, Haydarpaşa** and others. The Bosphorus protects them, and has kept them quiet residential suburbs for centuries. Up the Bosphorus, Istanbul's metropolitan area has absorbed the picturesque villages on both sides, almost as far as the Black Sea.

THE SEVEN HILLS

Constantine the Great very consciously meant to make his foundation the New Rome; that was its name, at first, until the Emperor's vanity overcame him. Like the old Rome, it had a golden milestone, a Senate house, and a Forum; to govern it, Constantine divided it up into fourteen wards, just as Rome had been, and most importantly for Imperial continuity, he declared that it had seven hills; finding some of these requires an effort of the imagination.

Only these three reach any height: the **First Hill** where the Topkapi Palace and Aya Sofia are; the **Fifth Hill** along the Golden Horn with the Fener and the Selimiye Mosque; and the **Third Hill,** crowned by the Süleymaniye. None of the others will strain your legs: the **Second Hill,** roughly north of the Burnt Column; the **Fourth Hill,** around the Fatih Mosque; the **Sixth Hill** at the Topkapi Gate, the centre of the land walls; and the **Seventh Hill,** in the southwest corner of the city.

Old Istanbul (Stamboul)

SULTANAHMET SQUARE

Most visitors, however, begin their tours of Istanbul in the old city in **Sultanahmet Square,** the lovely garden of fountains and flowers between Aya Sofia and the Blue Mosque. A pavilion housing a very helpful **Tourist Information Centre** [2]* is here, near the **Kaiser Wilhelm II Fountain** [3] (a small gift from Sultan Abdul Hamid's big brother in Berlin, in the days when Germany was the declining Ottoman Empire's greatest ally). The low buildings along the southern edge, the **Aya Sofia Baths** [1], are among the few that survived the modern reconstruction of the square when acres of Ottoman buildings were cleared.

If you could have stood here in Byzantine times, however, you would have been in the city's grand ceremonial square, the **Augusteion.** Just to the left of Aya Sofia, the main street of the city entered through the Bronze Gate. A tall column bearing a golden statue of Justinian stood in front of the church, and near it, the golden milestone from which all distances in the Empire were measured. The baths of Zeuxippos, a domed structure probably not unlike the modern Turkish hamam, occupied the western edge of the square and next to this, the bulk of the Hippodrome could be seen behind the towers of St Stephens. The south edge fronted the Senate House, where the last remnant of the Roman Republic survived as a rubber-stamp council almost until the end of Byzantium. In this square the emperors could be seen at their accessions, and on the feast days of the Church. After the sack of 1204, when the Crusaders looted the square of its gold and ornaments, the area drifted gradually into ruin. Already the emperors had moved to the Blachernae Palace in the suburbs, and the restored empire after 1261 lacked the resources even to keep up the Aya Sofia. One traveller of the fourteenth century wrote of finding the great church eerily empty, its doors lying on the ground.

AYA SOFIA

You may feel the same, and may hear the ghostly echo of Justinian's 'Solomon, I have surpassed thee!', as you walk under the dome of the denuded church, once glowing with golden mosaics and chandeliers, a golden altar and iconostasis; now it is just chilly, dark and old. Since 1933, the Aya Sofia has been a museum, and lacks even the prayer rugs and mihrab to relieve the tremendous desolation. Even so, in its present state, the lack of orna-

* Numbers in [ ] refer to map of Central Istanbul on p. 65.

mentation perhaps makes the beauty and audacity of the architecture easier to appreciate. Undoubtedly this is the greatest dome in Christendom, though St Peter's in Rome and St Paul's in London are larger. In the sixth century, nothing like the Aya Sofia had ever been built, or even imagined, and, even today, the impression it makes cannot be experienced anywhere else.

The original Aya Sofia, which the Byzantines called simply the Great Church, was built by Theodosius II in 415, on the site of an even earlier church built under Constantine the Great. Theodosius' Aya Sofia burned during the street battles of the Nike Revolt. To provide a symbol for his dreams of imperial grandeur, and to a certain extent to justify them, Justinian determined to rebuild as quickly and as large as possible. The cornerstone of his new church was laid exactly forty days after the suppression of the revolt.

Building Aya Sofia

This seemed to give very little time for proper plans to be drawn up; the two men chosen to design the church were not really architects. Not long before, the Emperor had decreed an end to the Athenian Academy, the centre of learning of the classical world, and the last stronghold of philosophy untainted by the Gospels. In doing so, he put two of the greatest mathematicians of the age, Anthemius of Tralles (modern Aydin) and Isidore of Miletus, out of work. Between them, they did the job in only five years. The Imperial Treasury had been strained to the limit, but the new Great Church was consecrated in solemn ceremony on the 26th December, 537, St Stephen's Day.

The difficulties in the construction were manifold and understandable; no architect alive had experience of a task of such magnitude. Improvisation was a daily necessity. The four massive piers on which the entire structure is hung have stones held together not with any mortar, but with molten lead. The distinctive shape of Aya Sofia's capitals is no mere design conceit such as those of the classical Greeks; it is absolutely necessary to the structure. The 'impost capital' as it is called, had already been invented to give proper support to arches and vaults, but here it was perfected.

One of the problems was reconciling the strengths and weaknesses of so many different varieties of stone. Just as the Emperor spared no expense in getting in the best architects and workmen, every variety of stone in the empire is represented here: green marble from the Peloponnese, yellow from Libya, rose from Phrygia and Lydia, great slabs of porphyry that were floated down the Nile from upper Egypt. Ancient buildings were looted for tall columns; of those in the galleries, the red are from the Temple of the Sun in Baalbek, the green probably from the Artemision of Ephesus.

In the Church

One enters just as a Byzantine commoner would, through side gates in the outer porch (the exonarthex). The centre gate was for the Emperor alone, and it continues through a long thin hall to the narthex. Here, where the Emperor passed into the church itself, one of the surviving gold mosaics portrays Emperor Leo IV kneeling before a seated Christ. Below, on the brass lintel, the Holy Spirit descends with a book, open to the words, 'The Lord said, "I am the door of the sheep: By me if any man enter in ... he shall find pasture"'. An empty throne stands concealed behind.

One of the first things Atatürk did after converting Aya Sofia to a museum was to arrange for the restoration of the mosaics. The work was done over the next two decades by the Byzantine Institute, a private organisation in Boston. Justinian's church had none, mosaics were a later fashion, and those that remain—of the estimated four acres—date mostly from the ninth century or later, after the defeat of the Iconoclasts.

You, of course, may usurp the Emperor's privilege and walk right in. The central gate opens at the rear of the great nave, and as you approach the centre you realise the particular architectural problem Anthemius and Isidore faced, and their brilliant solution. From preference, and for reasons of grace and symmetry, with a little bit of geometric mysticism mixed in as well, the Emperor desired a central plan, symmetrical on two axes. The forms of Byzantine ritual, however, made necessary a basilica-plan church with a long nave. To accomplish this, Anthemius flanked his dome with two semi-domes along the axis of the nave and enclosed the space under the arches with solid walls full of windows. Underneath these, the mass is distributed down to the ground through a network of smaller semi-domes (exedrae), vaults and columns, thus opening to the light a space six times the area of the dome. This conquest of gravity is the magic of Aya Sofia. Contemporary chroniclers tell of visitors and citizens afraid to enter lest all collapse, or becoming dizzy trying to look at the top of the dome, 181 feet above the floor. The Byzantines always spoke of this dome as being suspended from heaven by a golden chain.

Details in the interior are few; little survived the Iconoclasts, the Crusaders, and the Turks. The bronze doors of the narthex are original, and the monograms of Justinian and Theodora can be seen on many of the capitals. The largest mosaic, on the apse above the place where the altar stood, is a portrait of the Virgin Mary with the infant Jesus, and below it, figures of the Archangels Michael and Gabriel can be made out. In place of the altar, only the Moslem *mihrab* and *mimber* fill the void, along with the raised loge built for the prayers of the Sultans. The four huge medallions painted with verses of the Koran, removed by Atatürk, have recently been replaced as a gesture to the Moslem fundamentalists. Above them, four sinister Byzantine seraphs stare down from the pendentives.

The Moslems, like the Greeks, segregated their women, putting them upstairs in the spacious galleries around the nave, making them climb about fifty feet of ramps to get there. It's worth the walk, for the view and for the best of the remaining mosaics. In the centre of the galleries, at the far end of the church, two green columns from Ephesus mark the place where the Empresses worshipped. The ladies, in fact, had only the **North Gallery**; the **South Gallery** was reserved for the rest of the Imperial family; the lovely screen that partitioned it off was given by the Turks the fanciful title 'Gates of Heaven and Hell'. A celebrated series of the thirteenth-century mosaics, one of the last improvements to the church under the Byzantines, can be seen around the gallery; Emperor John Comnenus and his family, Empress Zoe and her third husband (his face painted over that of number two) and Jesus with Mary, and John the Baptist. On the floor near this last one is a slab inscribed with the name Henrico Dandolo, the aged, bitter Duke of Venice who led the Sack of 1204. Surprisingly, the Greeks never disinterred him when they recaptured the city; the Turks did, within weeks of Mehmet's Conquest. This south gallery often served for the transaction of church business; two great General Church Councils, the second and the sixth, were held in it.

You may be disconcerted to see that very few of the columns of the galleries are actually in plumb. Some list at alarming angles, and the impression of a house of cards is inescapable. Even before Atatürk, the Turks kept a constant vigil over this fabulous patient, on and off the critical list for fourteen centuries. Anthemius and Isidore, for all their skill, could not make their church perfect. The dome, shallow enough now, was originally 20 feet lower, and had to be reconstructed when a forty-day series of earthquakes toppled it in 558. In the tenth century, the next thorough restoration kept the church closed for ten years. Again in the fourteenth century, a collapse seemed imminent; the emperors scraped the bottom of the treasury to construct the four colossal buttresses that so mar the exterior. No more money could be found to complete the repairs, and by the time of the Conquest, the church was no longer in use. Mehmet added more buttresses and the first minaret, and Mimar Sinan himself tore down much of the ruined old Imperial quarter to get stone for further strengthening. Seven thorough restorations since have accomplished the preservation of the mosaics and the reinforcement of the dome with steel; specialists are still on guard for any further signs of weakness. The galleries, they say, are in no danger, now.

The theology of the Moslems would, on the whole, have seemed almost acceptable to a man like Justinian, and, as fate would have it, the Moslems were to be the vehicle for preserving his symbol and his dream over the centuries. Justinian must surely have thought the building of his church would mark the advent of a new world age. His choice of men from the Academy to put it up was as much symbolic as practical. Here, the entire harvest of classical science and philosophy was to serve the ends of the Christian God. The Moslems, who already had taken their own deep draughts of Greek thought, felt entirely at home after 1453. More than any place in the Christian or Islamic worlds, this is the great house of monotheism, the place where human understanding and accomplishment were recognised as the Divine Wisdom, the 'Hagia Sofia', both faiths believed it to be.

Buildings outside Aya Sofia

The Moslems had more of a sense of humour than the Christians. In the **mausoleum** they built around Aya Sofia's garden were interred nearly all the worst of the worst Ottoman Sultans: Mustafa I, an imbecile and tool of the Janissaries, Ibraham the Mad, the ultimate libertine who picked off his subjects from the Topkapi walls for target practice, and Selim the Sot, whose honorific tells us all we need to know.

Behind the Aya Sofia, adjoining the walls of the Topkapi Saray, the indefatigable restorations of the Turkish Automobile Club have begun to rebuild an entire street of characteristic Ottoman wooden houses. This is only one part of their plan for beautifying the centre of old Stamboul. South of the Blue Mosque, they have a complex including shops in a restored medrese and the lovely wooden **Konak Hotel,** one of the best restored examples of Ottoman vernacular architecture in Istanbul.

Also behind the church, a famous monument of the Tulip Period can be seen as introduction to another aspect of Turkish architecture. The **Fountain of Ahmed III** [4], built in 1729, really a small pavilion, is covered with a wealth of green and blue tiles painted in floral motifs, and with verses of the Emperor who built it. Imagine it as it was before the tiles and gilt trim weathered, and you will see something distinctly Turkish, and also something of the super-refined and delicate sensibility of the Empire on the threshold of its decadence. There is much more of this behind the walls of Topkapi; the outer gate, the **Bab-i-Humayun** [5] stands only a few yards away.

THE BLUE MOSQUE (SULTAN AHMET CAMII)

Across the square from Aya Sofia, Sultan Ahmet in 1619 constructed the Sultanahmet, or the **Blue Mosque**—like a matching bookend—not so much to compete with the old church, as because all the other available sites already had big mosques on them. None of the city's other monuments has occasioned more argument among the critics; some claim it is the finest work of architecture in the city, while others say it is overdone and uninspired. Certainly there are no new departures in the plan; just another copy of the Aya Sofia, only more rigidly symmetrical than the others. The great dome, 70 feet across, stands on four semi-domes, each of these on three exedrae, and each of the exedrae on two arches. The main attraction here are the 21 043 blue Iznik tiles inside, painted predominantly with the blue arabesques that give the mosque its familiar name. Each one of these tiles set Ahmet back 18 *akçes*—twice the daily wage of a teacher in the palace school. The painted details on the ceiling that accompanied these are currently under restoration, and the mosque will soon be bluer than ever.

Ahmet was sure he was building for the ages, and with an arrogance possible only to a Commander of the Faithful, he had his architect, Mehmet Ağa, build six minarets instead of the two or four customary in Ottoman Imperial mosques. Previously, only the shrine of the Ka'aba in Mecca had been allowed six, and after a shrill chorus of protests from the divines of Islam, Ahmet was forced to send Mehmet Ağa down to Mecca to build a seventh. Don't forget this; knowing that the Blue Mosque is the one with six minarets may come in handy sometime when you're good and lost in old Stamboul. Also unusual in this mosque are the rows of great doors around the lovely courtyard—36 of them, all leading nowhere.

TOPKAPI SARAY

Immediately after the Conquest, Mehmet Fatih built his first palace on the hill north of Beyazit Square. In 1468, he began a summer palace on the beautiful and largely unoccupied hill at the tip of the peninsula, where the Golden Horn joins the Bosphorus. Later Sultans favoured the site, and Süleyman the Magnificent was the first to move here permanently. Most of the present buildings are from the eighteenth century; by then the Sultans had made themselves captives here, in this lovely soap-bubble of a world. Some of them spent more of their revenues here than in all the rest of the Empire.

The hill had been the acropolis of ancient Byzantium, with two theatres on its slopes overlooking the Bosphorus, several temples, a stadium and an arsenal and drill field called the *Strategion*. Just inside the Bab-i Humayun stood the little city's main square, the *Tetrastoon*. Not a trace of any of this remains, and we know surprisingly little of the use the quarter was put to after Constantine.

First Courtyard

The **Bab-i Humayun,** a simple stone gate, looks to have been more for defence than decoration, and it was. The many revolts and skirmishes of the Empire's decadent years put it to the test. Mahmud II hid here from his bloodthirsty Janissaries. Whatever the outcome, the gate would usually be adorned with the heads of the losers. Through it, one enters the **First Courtyard,** a large park. Two centuries ago, it was full of the palace outbuildings: the Imperial Mint, and, most importantly, the barracks of the Janissaries. From this spot this Praetorian Guard was able to keep a constant watch on its Sultans, standing between them and any hope of aid from the outside world. Mahmud demolished their buildings soon after their demise in the Auspicious Event.

In the same year Aya Sofia was completed, Justinian and Theodora also dedicated a smaller church, the **Aya Irene** [6], just behind it. The two churches shared a common sanctuary, but were cut off from each other when the Turks enclosed Aya Irene in the First Courtyard. Aya Irene, the Divine Peace, was never used as a mosque, its keys were given to the Janissaries, who following the precepts of the Bektaşi order of dervishes, were never allowed to enter a mosque. Instead, they used it as their arsenal, and kept it in surprisingly good shape over the centuries. The church is a basilica in form, but with a small dome and transepts, a very unusual plan for a Byzantine work. On the apse where the altar stood, a simple black and gold mosaic of a cross is believed to be original. The site is believed to have originally been occupied by a temple of Aphrodite; like the Aya Sofia, the church you see now replaced a work of Theodosius burned down in the Nike Riots. For a while under the Republic, Aya Irene was kept open as a military museum making use of the curiosities accumulated over the years by the Janissaries. When the present restoration is completed, it will become the new home of the **Mosaic Museum,** now in a small building just south of the Blue Mosque. The floor mosaics in the collection, excavated only in this century, were found near the Blue Mosque, and came from the palace of the Byzantine emperors.

Gate of Salutations

At the end of the First Courtyard stands another wall and the **Gate of Salutations** [7], the entrance to the official part of the Saray for which permission was required to enter; now it's where you buy the ticket. The medieval air of this gate, with its conical spires, is no accident. Süleyman was so taken with the castles and churches of Hungary when he campaigned there that he brought back Hungarian architects to build it for him. One of the customs of this gate was that no one except the Sultan himself might pass through it on horseback. The Head Gardener of the Saray had his office here; this is a good example of the Turkish fancy for euphemism, for the 'gardeners' were really armed guards who shared fully in the palace intrigues, and the 'Head Gardener', none other than the Sultan's Chief Executioner. The block, and the fountain in which he washed his blade, can be seen near this gate.

Second Courtyard: Court of the Divan and Harem

The next courtyard, the **Court of the Divan,** was divided between the highest council chamber of government and the palace kitchens; this arrangement would never seem silly to an Ottoman, for whom all real government was embodied in the person of the Sultan. For *divan*, understand the Sultan's cabinet; the vezirs met once a week in the Divan hall, under its tower on the left-hand side of the courtyard. The earlier Sultans would have been present at these meetings, where the affairs of the government were discussed. Süleyman introduced the screen to keep his vezirs honest; they could never know if he were behind it listening or not. His successors probably hardly went to the Divan at all.

The Divan is attached to the **Harem** [8], a group of buildings and courtyards one-sixth of the total area of the Saray. Süleyman began its construction when his favourite wife Roxelana, convinced him he could not live without her; as power devolved upon the ladies and their eunuchs, later Sultans expanded it into the labyrinthine complex we see today. After Abdul Mecit moved to the Dolmabahçe Palace in 1853, the surviving favourites of his predecessors lived on here, lonely and forgotten, some well into the twentieth century.

If you wish to visit the Harem—after the big jewels it's the most popular attraction in the Museum—stop beforehand at the booth by the Harem gate. Guided tours are given only at certain times and you may have some trouble getting in. Just inside the gate are the apartments of the eunuchs—the Black Eunuchs—who looked after the girls and more often after themselves. These ugly creatures (the Sultan's slavemaster picked out the ugliest, to avoid any chance of arousing passions among the ladies) with the silver tubes that assisted them in trips to the WC perched nattily in their tall turbans, became, in the latter days, a power unto themselves. Their chief, the Black Ağa, was after the Ağa of the Janissaries, the most useful ally any scheming lady could have.

The **Courtyard of the Sultan Valide** (the Sultan's mother) is adjacent to the eunuchs' quarter. Considering the bizarre issues of Harem politics—the steering of the right girls into the Sultan's bed, the manipulation, and sometimes, murder of prospective heirs—it becomes clear how only the greatest schemers of all could attain the glorious position of Sultan Valide. Their suite was usually the vortex of all palace intrigues. The next courtyard to the west housed the women slaves, again mostly blacks, and beyond them lay the damp, chilly, unadorned quarters of the beauties themselves, brought from all over the Empire to lead wretchedly dull lives here, chaste as any nuns except for the few who managed to catch a Sultan's fancy. Even these were left only with a thank-you, a small present, and the fervent hope that they might conceive a male child.

Perhaps the greatest attraction of the harem quarters, now that you're thoroughly disillusioned, will be the rooms of the northern half of the Harem, the chambers where the Sultans came for their pleasures. Several of these, the **Dining Room of Ahmet II;** the **Bedroom of Murat III,** and the **Library of Ahmed I,** for example, are adorned with some of the most beautiful painted tiles to be found anywhere in Turkey. Their designs of fruits and flowers may have violated Moslem taboos against images, but then few imams or members of the Ulema, the Moslem hierarchy were ever invited in to see them.

Carriage Room and Palace Kitchens

After the Harem there are two more sections of the museum you may wish to visit before passing through to the third courtyard. The **Carriage Room,** once the Sultan's stables, is full of the various conveyances of the nineteenth-century rulers, who apparently were as fond of fancy phaetons and landaus as modern third world autocrats are of shiny new cars. The **Palace Kitchens,** across the courtyard, a work of Sinan's, were ready, at the Sultan's command, to whip up almost anything for a party of from one to five thousand. There are some of the largest soup pots ever constructed on this planet, and a tedious infinity of silver and china from the nineteenth century. The Sultans accumulated these as presents from foreign rulers, in greater numbers than even a dinner of 5000 could require. The collection of **Chinese porcelain** is world-famous and priceless, note especially the Celadon ware, a favourite of potentates everywhere, since it was reputed to change colour in the presence of poison.

The Third Courtyard

The third courtyard itself is a wonderful park of plane trees and poplars. Visitors are often surprised to see how open and airy old Turkish palaces are. A love of nature, the necessity of having more than a bit of green around, was something the Ottomans never lost, even in their years of decay. They copied the form of the Saray—three successive courtyards of increasingly greater isolation—from the Byzantine Imperial Palace that once stood nearby (curiously the Hittite palace at Boğazköy also had the same plan). However, where the Byzantines probably had small, paved squares in the classical mode, the Turks built gardens like this, squeezing their buildings into thin quadrangles between them and the forested slopes of the Topkapi hill, for a view of trees on both sides.

To match this setting, the Turks evolved an architectural style very different from the grey mathematics of their mosques; this style was a unique eighteenth-century concoction of distinctive, very oriental shapes and forms, limited perhaps to the Topkapi and the now vanished gardens and palaces that once lined the Golden Horn and the Marmara shores. One of the finest examples is in this courtyard: the **Gate of Felicity** [9], the entrance to the *Selamlik*, the Sultan's Quarters. Very few outsiders were ever allowed the privilege of using this gate. On ceremonial occasions, such as an accession to the throne, the Bayram festival, or the commissioning of a new general, the Sultan would meet the assemblage seated directly under it, on the same portable bejewelled throne that went with him on campaigns. The Chief White Eunuch had his rooms here in the buildings around the gate, from which he and his fellow castrati oversaw the smooth operation of the *Selamlik*.

The **Audience Chamber** [10], a pretty parlour just inside the gate, served for the Sultan's meetings with his Grand Vezir and foreign ambassadors. Its ambience is thoroughly Turkish; perhaps for the Sultans it recalled the tents of their nomadic ancestors. The coloured tiles and lovely hearth were added to **Mehmet Fatih's** original building by **Ahmet III,** but the baroque ceiling came much later. This Ahmet also built the **Library** next door, a marvellous small pavilion with lots of glass and window seats, to be envied by all serious readers. Before the seventeenth-century fire that damaged much of the *Selamlik*, this space was occupied by the Great Hall, a building that housed the *Enderun*, the school for pages where the Christian children collected in the *devşirme* round up were converted into the ministers and generals of the empire. Before the decline, it had a reputation as the finest school in Europe, counting all the great Turkish poets and scholars among its instructors.

Treasures of the Sultans

Most of the fabulous treasures of the Sultans, the gold and jewels and the holy relics, are exhibited in the halls around the third courtyard. The spirit of the Topkapi was never to throw anything away, and one result is that costumes of every Sultan after Mehmet Fatih can be seen in the **Wardrobe** [11], from the gaily coloured flower-printed robes of Mehmet to the dreary European monkey-suit of Abdul Hamid. Osman II, most tragic of the Sultans, is represented by the blood-splattered caftan in which he was murdered.

It may prove difficult to get excited over the riches of the **Treasury** next door, simply because it's hard to convince oneself that they're all real. The four rooms of bejewelled vessels and weapons, coffee sets and cabinets, as well as famous gems like the 86-carat Spoon Diamond, make up the richest hoard in the world; particularly if you include the additional warehouse-full they haven't room to display. Other stars of the collection include the Emerald Dagger, made famous by the film *Topkapi*, and a golden casket supposedly containing the head of John the Baptist.

At the far end of the courtyard, the collection of **Miniatures** displays examples of another very Turkish art form; it seems the first portraitists of Islam felt guilty about breaking Mohammed's law, and so made their paintings very, very small. One two-volume set of these, the *Hünername*, or 'Book of Talents' ranks among the greatest works of Turkish painting and calligraphy. The celebrated **clock collection** occupies the next room. Byzantine historians often wrote of their Emperors' love of mechanical contraptions, like the famous golden tree full of singing birds, and like them, the Ottoman Sultans were better pleased by no gifts other than clocks and music boxes. Again, those on display are only a small part of the whole collection.

When Selim I conquered Egypt, whose ruler at the time was the Caliph—the head of all Islam—that title fell to him and his successors. The later emperors' oriental inapproachability had not a little to do with the fact that now they were Commander of the Faithful and the Shadow of God on Earth. In token of this great office, the Sherif of Mecca sent Selim the keys to the Kaa'ba, and here at Topkapi they remain in the **Hirka-i Saadet,** the hall of holy relics to which Moslems make pilgrimages, now that the public is allowed to see them (it's located near the clock collection). Under a great silver dome added by Murat IV are Mohammed's sword, bow, and standard, and the famous cloak he once bestowed on a poet who converted to Islam. Other relics include the Prophet's seal, a broken tooth, a cast of his footprint, hairs from his beard, and a letter he sent with an embassy to the Copts of Egypt—a bullying letter, full of threats. The sword of Osman, symbol of the Ottoman state, is also kept here.

Sultan's Residence

Next to this chamber, a fourth and final gate connects with the residence of the Sultan, this a group of individual pavilions around a courtyard, all with the best views of the Bosphorus and the Golden Horn. Two of these, the **Revan Kiosk** and the **Baghdad Kiosk** [12], must be accounted among the very greatest works of Turkish architecture for the simple magnificence of their form and decoration. Murat IV built them both, to commemorate his conquests of Baghdad and Jerevan, now in Soviet Armenia, and here he drank himself to death in the increasing revels of the last years of his reign. Among the marble terraces and roses of the Revan Kiosk is a marble fountain of three basins that approaches perfection more nearly than any other work of art in all the halls of the Saray.

To leave Topkapi, you must retrace your steps to the First Courtyard; from here instead of returning through the Bab-i Humayun, you can take the other route, around Aya Irene and down a shady cobbled lane towards the Gülhane Park and the Imperial museums.

THE IMPERIAL MUSEUMS

Hamdi Bey, by the standards of the late nineteenth century, was one very unusual Turk. A painter by trade, his knowledge of the ancient Greeks got him a job under Sultan Abdul Hamid looking after the Empire's antiquities. So well did he perform his duties, and with such panache, that he revolutionised the affairs of archaeology and museum-keeping, not only in Turkey but in the rest of Europe as well. Not only did he write the first law anywhere governing the export of antiquities, but he also made patriots of all the nations under Ottoman control work hard to keep their own archaeological discoveries from being shanghaied to the new **Archaeology Museum** [13] that he had talked Abdul Hamid into building. More often than not, they didn't succeed. Among the many excavations he oversaw was the one that uncovered the famous **Alexander sarcophagus** in Sidon. During the lengthy process of transporting this block of several tons to Istanbul, Hamdi Bey literally bound himself to it to impress upon the sailors that they had better take good care of it. On one later occasion, the Sultan proposed presenting the sarcophagus to the visiting Kaiser Wilhelm II. Hamdi Bey had the effrontery to inform the Sultan that this would only be accomplished by dragging it over his dead body and the Kaiser went home empty-handed.

Archaeology Museum

The collection he and his successors piled up in this tasteful eclectic building—the very image of what his generation thought a museum should look like—is one of the greatest in Europe. Sarcophagi were Hamdi Bey's speciality, and there's not enough room for them all; many more line the square in front of the museum. The Alexander sarcophagus, not *of* Alexander, but decorated with scenes from his conquests, is perhaps more bombast than art, but it's considered one of the finest examples of late Roman sculpture. Two other sarcophagi, one Hamdi Bey called 'des Pleureuses', and the other, a barn-roofed Lycian model, are in the same room, along with a famous bust of Alexander.

Some of the museum's other attractions include bronze pedestals that once supported various statues in the Hippodrome carved with scenes from the games; coats of arms of various states and knightly orders, some from the old walls of Galata; Egyptian works, Greek and Roman bronzes, the famous statue of a young man called the Ephebos of Tralles, a mosaic of Orpheus and the wild animals, and a remarkable 12-foot statue of the Phoenician god, Bes—the Greeks know him as the 'Cypriot Hercules'—toying with a lion.

Museum of the Ancient Orient

Across a small square from the Archaeology Museum, the government has more recently created the **Museum of the Ancient Orient** [14], an equally impressive cache of pre-classical finds from Turkey and the Middle East. Some of its best works are from Babylon; the city's Ishtar Gate is largely reconstructed here with its glazed reliefs. In the Assyrian Room are reliefs from the palace of Assurbanipal; nearby, two 3600-year-old copulating Kassites (from Northern Mesopotamia) may well be the world's oldest erotic art.

In the Assyrian room the museum has assembled a collection of 'interesting documents' from ancient civilisations, with translations: love poems and tables of astronomical events in Assyrian cuneiform, laws and penalties for various crimes ('2/3 mina of silver for cutting off someone's nose with a copper knife'), and the King of Lagash describing his struggles against his own government bureaucracy. The Treaty of Kadesh is here, an agreement of 1269 BC between the Pharaoh and the Hittite King Hattusilis, found in the state archives at Boğazköy, the oldest treaty ever discovered.

Museum of Turkish Ceramics (Çinili Kiosk)

The third building in the square is the **Çinili Kiosk** [15], an exquisite small palace built by Mehmet Fatih in 1472, as part of the original Topkapi Saray. Its painted tiles show the lingering influence of the Selcuks in their design. Fittingly, the Kiosk now houses a museum of Turkish ceramics from Selcuk times up to the present.

SUBLIME PORTE AND GÜLHANE PARK

Continuing down towards Gülhane Park from the Kiosk will take you to the north gate of the Saray, none other than the **Sublime Porte** [16] that became a figure of speech representing the Ottoman government during the nineteenth century. Built into the Topkapi walls here is the **Alay Kiosk,** the Saray's window on the outside world where the Sultan would review his troops and be seen by the people—on very rare occasions. **Gülhane Park,** a part of the Saray, was converted to a public garden in 1913. This lovely oasis, with a pond and woebegone zoo, stretches all the way to Sarayburnu, Seraglio Point. Here, Istanbul keeps its **Atatürk Monument,** perhaps the only one in Turkey not on a main square. Across the road just under the walls of the Sultan's quarters of the Saray, you can see the stump of a granite column that is the oldest monument in the city, the **Goth's Column** commemorating the victory of the Romans over the invading Goths in AD 269.

Yerebatan Sarayi

Returning to Sultanahmet Square down Alemdar Caddesi, you come to a main street in the Cağaloğlu district, Hilali Ahmer Caddesi; here just off the square an unprepossessing little shed leads you in to the **Yerebatan Sarayi** [17]. No one has yet proposed old Constantinople's water supply for associate membership in the Wonders of the Ancient World, but this perhaps is only because this network of underground cisterns is so little known. The 'Underground Palace' as the Turks call it, is a great hall 230 by 460 feet, supported by ranks of columns and vaults. Though the largest, it's only one of several in the city. Two more have recently been discovered near the Aya Irene, and it is possible that some others remain unknown. By the sixteenth century, though the old aqueducts were still in use, these reservoirs had been quite forgotten. A French antiquarian named Petrus Gyllius spent weeks looking for this one in 1545, until he had the good fortune to find a resident of the quarter who had a trap door in his house. Down in the cistern, this gentleman kept a boat and used it daily to catch fish, which he sold to his puzzled neighbours. No one even suspected the cistern existed, even though the wells of their houses led directly into it.

Each of the 40-foot columns—there are over 300 of them—has a capital to bear the arches, and some of these are carved as if they had been part of a church, instead of a reservoir. Justinian, who is responsible for most of these works, here was forced to demolish an old basilica that stood above it, and simply re-used the capitals.

THE HIPPODROME

In Byzantine times, the site of the Blue Mosque held the Golden Hall, the outermost building of Justinian's palace where the throne was kept and the affairs of government transacted. A private corridor connected this part of the palace with the *Kathisma*, or Imperial box of the **Hippodrome,** which once stood just to the west. No stadium, ancient or modern, was ever so famous in its time, or played such an important role in its city's public life. Much more went on here than just chariot races and the athletic events. Emperors celebrated their victories here, and executed their enemies. Even the games should not be taken as simple entertainment; during the Roman period, they had evolved into a strange sort of mystic communion between the Emperor, who of course picked up the bill, and his people. Everything about the games became a symbol, reflecting some aspect of the politics of the day.

Factions

Septimus Severus, who also built the Circus Maximus in Rome, began construction of the Hippodrome in 203, but it remained unfinished until the reign of Constantine. Subsequent emperors improved and enlarged it, and by the time of Justinian it was nearly a third of a mile long, with seats for 100 000. Much has been made of the Hippodrome factions, the Blues and

Greens, that caused so much trouble in the sixth century. It would be giving the Byzantines more credit for decadence than even they deserved to suppose that the course of the empire was governed by militant sports fans. Originally, there were four factions; the Reds and Whites later merging into the others. They were nothing less than the organised *demes* or tribes traditional in any Greek city. They had both military and civilian functions; it was they who built the city walls, and their leaders received salaries as officers of the state. Gradually they came to identify with socio-economic divisions within the city (exactly how the historians can't tell), but when the Blues and Greens joined forces in the Nike Revolt, they were fighting for the city's liberty, and their own, against Imperial absolutism and all its aggression abroad, its cops and spies, and its unbearable taxes. They lost when Byzantine General Belisarius, at the head of an army of Goths and Alans—the Greeks could not be trusted—surrounded the rebels in the Hippodrome and massacred them all—60 000 of them if contemporary sources are to be believed.

The Crusaders in 1204 thoroughly wasted the Hippodrome, and as the restored Empire had little spare money to spend on games, the great stadium gradually fell into ruin. Under the Turks, most of its stones found their way into new building projects, but the Sultans always left the surviving monuments alone, and kept the ground clear for practising their game of *cirit*, a form of polo. From this, the square where the Hippodrome once stood came to be known as the *At Meydan*, Horse Square, and this name is still sometimes heard. In the late 1960s, the square became something of a hippie encampment, until Turkish patience finally ran out. Now, unfortunately, it is the best place in Istanbul **not** to sit and have your shoes shined, swarming as it is with the most persistent street hawkers and carpet-shop commission agents in all Turkey.

The Hippodrome today

The present square, though it follows the contours of the Hippodrome's field, is less than half as big. Its centre line can be traced through the three surviving columns. This line was the *spina*; the Byzantines liked to call it the 'Axis of the Empire'. Originally its two ends were marked by golden columns representing the sun and the moon—the symbolism of the games was astronomical as well as political. These were the pylons around which the charioteers raced, and, between the two columns, the *spina* had an almost unbroken line of monuments; the Crusaders carried away or wrecked most of these, most famously the bronze horses of Lysippus that now adorn St Mark's in Venice. The three that remain were too heavy to move.

In the case of the first, the **Column of Constantine Porphyrogenitus,** the crusaders had to settle for melting down the bronze plates that covered it. The second monument the **Serpentine Column,** a twisted stump of bronze, retains little of beauty or interest to remind us of its fascinating history; from faint inscriptions on its base, it has been determined that this column was the monument dedicated by the united Greek cities to celebrate their victory over the Persians at Plataea in 479 BC. After transporting the column in joyous ceremonies through all the towns that shared in the victory, it was erected at the Temple of Apollo at Delphi, where it stood, until Constantine the Great stole it to embellish his capital. Before it toppled, sometime around 1700, the column had the form of three intertwined serpents, their heads supporting the legs of a great golden tripod dedicated to Apollo.

The third monument, the **Obelisk of Theodosius**, was acquired by that emperor in 390 especially for the Hippodrome; an obelisk was something no stadium could be without. This one came from Heliopolis, and the hieroglyphic inscriptions on its sides record the victories of the mighty Pharaoh Thutmose III. Like most of the Egyptian obelisks that have found their way to the world's capitals, this one is in surprisingly good shape for its 3400 years; all the hieroglyphs still stand out clearly.

The marble base on which the obelisk was raised has been called one of the finest works of fourth-century sculpture; its reliefs portray Theodosius and his family in the *Kathisma*, viewing the games, the Emperor with a wreath in his hand ready to crown the victor. Another relief shows the transporting of the obelisk, and the inscriptions on the sides, in both Greek and Latin verse, recall the difficulties of erecting the heavy stone and the praise due to Proclus the prefect for accomplishing it. The wells in which these three monuments are sunk will give you an idea how much the level of the land has risen since the Hippodrome was last in use. A group of British officers on leave excavated the bases of the three monuments during the Crimean War.

Firuz Ağa Camii

North of the Hippodrome, going back near Kaiser Wilhelm's Fountain, stands a small mosque that is one of the oldest in Istanbul. The **Firuz Ağa Camii** [18], built in 1491, has nothing of the grandeur of later imperial mosques, but its architecture definitely points towards them, in a transition from the old, plain Ottoman style whose masterpieces you can see in Bursa. Five times a day, a real *müezzin* climbs up the short minaret to give the call to prayer. The big mosques usually have only loudspeakers, but with the renaissance of Moslem piety in Turkey, many mosques have gone back to the old-fashioned way. The unexcavated ruins near this mosque belonged to a nobleman's palace, converted in the seventh century to the **Martyrium of St Euphemia** [19].

West of the Hippodrome

Just across the street from the monuments of the Hippodrome, the palace of Ibrahim Paşa, a Grand Vezir first favoured, then executed by Süleyman the Magnificent, has recently been restored to house the **Museum of Turkish and Islamic Arts** [20], with a well arranged collection of ceramic and brass works, carpets and carved lecterns, some dating from the first centuries of Islam.

All of this area west of the Hippodrome is built over another of Justinian's underground cisterns, though the entrance is difficult to find. From Divan Yolu, the main street of the city, head three blocks south on Klodfarer Caddesi to a playground where bits of a large retaining wall are visible. Here you'll find the entrance to the **Binbirdirek Cistern** [21]—the 'thousand and one columns', the name a familiar Turkish hyperbole. This one, though smaller than the Yerebatan Saray, is dry, and you can explore its entire extent. In Byzantine records it was known as the Cistern of Philoxenes.

SULTANAHMET DISTRICT

In Istanbul, the Blue Mosque is more commonly referred to as the Sultan Ahmet Camii, after its builder, and in this form, the mosque has given its name to the quarter west and south of it, one of the most interesting old residential neighbourhoods of the city. Some parts of the **Sultanahmet** near the Marmara shore, with street after street of characteristic Ottoman wooden houses, do not even have a modern water supply, and the women of the district can be seen gossiping around the corner *çeşme* (fountain), just as they are pictured in engravings of centuries ago.

The plumbing was probably better when this part of the town was the **Palace of the Byzantine Emperors.** Since no excavations have ever been made, it's impossible to tell much about the layout. The palace began to decay already in the twelfth century, when Alexius Comnenus abandoned it for Blachernae out by the city walls. From contemporary accounts we can expect there were plenty of golden domes and towers, and that its three divisions, the Chalce, the Daphne and the 'Sacred Palace' covered an area not much smaller than the Topkapi Saray. All that is left is a small court, believed to have been part of the stables, that housed the Mosaic Museum before its removal to the Aya Irene, and a section of the sea walls to the west where Justinian built his **Bucoleon** [22], the seaside pavilion. The area between the Blue Mosque and the Marmara, apparently, was devoted to the Imperial polo grounds. Throughout the history of the empire, polo was the top snob sport, and most of the emperors, not too debilitated by their lifestyles, indulged in it.

KÜÇÜK AYA SOFIA

If you follow the twisting sidestreets south of the Hippodrome, where you can see the stone walls that supported the closed end of the stadium above the slope, with luck you will find the **Küçük** ('little') **Aya Sofia,** the name the Turks give to the sixth-century church of St Sergius and St Bacchus. Emperor Justinian's first major building project in his capital, modelled after the famous Church of S Vitale in Ravenna begun the year before, can be looked at as an experiment on the way to the big Aya Sofia, with its semi-domes, exedrae, and two levels of arcades around the central space. Its plan, like that of S Vitale, is square with an octagon of piers and columns inside it, supporting a dome just small enough to avoid the need for pendentives. Many of the capitals are finely carved, and like those of Aya Sofia they bear the monograms of Justinian and Theodora. Some vine motifs can be seen in playful allusion to Bacchus, who with his comrade Sergius was the first Christian soldier in the Roman legions to suffer martyrdom. Sergius and Bacchus were the patrons of soldiers, and especially meaningful to Justinian, preoccupied in the early years of his reign with one war after another. As an adjunct of the Imperial palace, Küçük Aya Sofia was given the role of erstwhile Catholic Church, where embassies from the Pope were allowed to say Mass according their own usages. Pope Gregory the Great, before his election, was long the papal legate to Byzantium, and he must have prayed here often.

THE DIVAN YOLU

On your way back to the Divan Yolu, try to find Kadirga Sokak and the **Mehmet Paşa Camii** built in 1571 for one of the famous Sokollu Grand Vezirs. This small mosque, along with its courtyard, porticoes, and school complex, is one of the most beautiful of all the works of Sinan, though few people trouble to see it in its out-of-the-way location.

The Divan Yolu was and is the main street of Istanbul. Though today it changes its name every few blocks—to Yeniçeriler Caddesi, then Veznecil-er Caddesi after Beyazit Square—in Byzantine days, the whole stretch as far as the Adrianople Gate was known as the *Mese* (the Middle) lined with arcades on one side, and then on both, where it passed through the choicer districts. **Cağaloğlu,** the area north of Divan Yolu, takes its name from the **Cağaloğlu Baths** [23] on Hilal-i Ahmer Caddesi, built in the eighteenth century and still popular. This is one of the prettier parts of old Stamboul, mostly nineteenth-century buildings interspersed with fine mosques and institutions endowed by the Sultans and their courtiers.

Çemberlitaş [24], the 'bound monument' further up Divan Yolu, commemorates the very beginnings of the Byzantine Empire. The Column of Constantine, as it was called, was the first monument erected by that emperor on his re-founding of the city; with the modesty for which his house was so renowned, Constantine had a golden statue of himself bolted on top. The Forum of Constantine, of which the small square you see today is the only remnant, was the business centre of the city, and the monument served as the site for many public festivals, including the annual ceremony on the anniversary of the foundation. A storm in the eleventh century brought the old Emperor down to earth, and the golden cross with which Manuel Comnenus replaced it did not survive long under the Turks. The Sultans left the column standing, though, contributing the bronze bands that have held it together since the fires of the eighteenth century; from these, the scorched monument took on its other popular name the 'Burnt Column'.

The mosque across the street is the **Ali Paşa Camii** [25], built in 1497 by a Vezir of Bayezit II, and the larger one behind it, the **Nuruosmaniye Camii,** the 'light of Osman' is one of the better examples of the Turkish Baroque. By the eighteenth century, the religious architecture of the Ottomans had lost all the momentum built up in its earlier inspirations. The result, an attempt to maintain the form, while prettifying it in a bastard half-Italian, half-Persian style, seem sensible enough here, but the greatest horrors were still to come.

Some of the other buildings along the Divan Yolu are worth a mention: west of Çemberlitaş, is an additional complex of three separate schools of architecture, the **Sinanpaşa Mosque** (1595), **Çorlulu Ali Paşa Medrese** [26] (1711), and the **Karamustafa of Merzifon Medrese** [27] (1690); east of Çemberlitaş, the **Çemberlitaş Hamam** (1593), and the **Türbe of Sultan Mahmut** (1839), containing the sarcophagi of most of the nineteenth-century Sultans. The **Mehmet Paşa Camii** [28], some blocks north near the Nuruosmaniye, is the oldest in Istanbul, built just ten years after the Ottoman Conquest.

Sirkeci and Eminönü

One of the main thoroughfares of **Cağaloğlu** is Babiali Caddesi; if you follow it north to where it becomes Ankara Caddesi, passing the most conspicuous of Istanbul's consulates—the Iranian—and the provincial government house, the **Vilâyet** [30], you'll end up in the **Sirkeci** quarter, a twilight zone of cheap hotels and night clubs around the ornate Victorian **Sirkeci Station** (1885). Foreign companies built the first railway into Istanbul, and they and Sultan Abdul Hamid are responsible for the greatest act of municipal vandalism in the city since the Sack of 1204: for the tracks, they destroyed the entire Marmara shore and many of the gardens and woods of the Topkapi hill.

Eminönü, the area just west of Sirkeci along the Golden Horn, was in the last century the business district of old Stamboul, as opposed to the European-dominated Beyoğlu across the Golden Horn. Its streets are still lively, its property values the highest in the city, and if you must pass through to visit the monumental Main Post Office [31], take time to admire this and the many other outlandish works of c. 1910, eclectic architecture. Two of the best art nouveau works, grimy fantasies with cast iron flowers on their balconies and pseudo-Ottoman painted tiles, are the small business block on the square opposite the Post Office, and the **Büyük Vakif Han,** an enormous landmark just two blocks away, in the direction of **Eminönü Square,** old Stamboul's window on the Golden Horn. From the square, the famous **Galata Bridge** crosses over to Beyoğlu, carrying the life of the city with it back and forth.

Just after the Conquest, Mehmet's army engineers built the first bridge here, of boats lashed together and covered with planks. One of the succeeding Sultans, the Turks say, invited Leonardo da Vinci to design a permanent structure, but he declined, and none was constructed until 1845. The present, like its companion **Atatürk Bridge** further up the Golden Horn, is a floating metal drawbridge. Caissons could only have been planted into the mud bottom with great difficulty, and so this unusual method was adopted. German engineers built it in 1912. Both bridges are only opened in the early morning hours to allow long lines of ships to pass in and out. In the days of the Sultans, they were also opened at the least sign of trouble in the city, to prevent insurrection from spreading.

The docks on either side, from which you can catch ferry boats to Asia, the Bosphorus, or the Prince's Islands, once were the busiest part of the commercial waterfront. Old travellers always remarked how close the city's life was to the life of the sea; any trip through town was likely to involve elbowing your way past deck hands and stevedores, and staring into the cannons of the ships-of-the-line. Today, besides the creaky ferries, the maritime experience is limited to the informal fish market on the Beyoğlu side, and the cafes on the lower deck of the bridge, where you can sit and sample the notorious aromas of the Golden Horn. All this lies in the shadow of one of the great Imperial mosques, the **Yeni Cami.**

YENI CAMI AND SPICE MARKET

This mosque, a landmark more for its location than for any special virtue of its architecture, was begun by a Sultan Valide (mother) named Safiye, a wife of Murat III, in 1597. Three different architects had a hand in the work, which was often interrupted, and only finished in 1663. Of the original *Külliye* of foundations, only two fountains and the Sultan Valide's *türbe* remain, along with the **Spice Market,** whose rents still go to the upkeep of the mosque. Most of the locals call this market the *Misir Çarşisi*, the 'Egyptian market', since most of the herbs and concoctions traditionally sold here came from the banks of the Nile. Today, in the long, L-shaped hall, a smaller version of the Covered Bazaar, you may purchase anything from jewellery to electric tin-openers, but at a few of the old stands, it's still fun to guess just what the hundreds of items displayed in barrels, bags, and jars could possibly be. 'Spices' to the Turks, as to the rest of Europe, once meant not only herbs for cooking, but also drugs, dyes, preservatives, cosmetics and any other useful substance that grows. One of the biggest sellers today, for example, is *kina*, or henna, for the ladies' hair.

The yard between the market and the Yeni Cami, where seeds, bulbs, and garden tools are sold, is also the traditional home of the city's **scribes,** the placid gentlemen with typewriters on little stands, who compose letters for the unlettered and fill in government forms for the bewildered. Perhaps it is a sign of progress that their numbers are decreasing.

RÜSTEM PAŞA CAMII

As seen from the bridge or from Beyoğlu, the Yeni Cami stands in the shadow of the great Süleymaniye, on the heights to the southwest. Between the two, the little mosque called **Rüstem Paşa Camii** is hardly even noticed. A closer look will reveal one of Sinan's most elegant works, built in 1550 for Süleyman's Grand Vezir. The real surprise, though, is within; the mosque is almost entirely covered with the very best Iznik tiles, in a spectacular variety of colours and patterns. For all these Ottoman creations, it will never do to ask where the funds came from. Rüstem Paşa was a son-in-law of Süleyman the Magnificent and Roxelana, and the Sultan's favourite, in her endless intrigues, determined to make him Grand Vezir. To accomplish this, all she had to do was to convince Suleyman to have his old friend, the Vezir Ibrahim, murdered. She had little trouble; Ibrahim was soon strangled by the palace mutes, and Rüstem distinguished himself by inaugurating the practice of putting government offices up for sale, an Ottoman tradition ever after.

THE COVERED BAZAAR

It seems likely that Constantinople had some kind of market on this spot; over one of the arches of this vast and rambling structure, a Byzantine eagle can be made out clearly. Long before the days of shopping malls, covered markets like this were an eastern tradition, not only for convenience but to discourage burglars. No one disputes Istanbul's claim that theirs is the largest in the world. Since Mehmet Fatih built the two *bedestens*, or strong houses, in the 1460s, street after street of shops, covered with simple barrel vaults and skylights, have grown up around them, always well maintained and promptly rebuilt after such disasters as the earthquake of 1896 or the fire of 1954. Today, the *Kapali Çarşi*, as it is called, is a city unto itself, with several thousand shops, a mosque, a school, even its own post office and police station.

It isn't just for tourists—far from it. Though you'll see plenty of trinkets and little signs proclaiming the owner's proficiency in English or German, the Covered Bazaar has its more prosaic side, as the purveyor of all manner of goods, from diamonds to dust pans to the Stamboullu; note that Mehmet built it before embarking on either his mosque or his Topkapi palace. The market was the key to bringing the half-abandoned city back to life. Even today, despite the advent of industrialism and high finance in Turkey, what goes on here, and in the seemingly endless maze of wholesalers, warehouses, and workshops to the north of it, still carries some weight in the nation's economy.

This mighty citadel of the independent businessman also stands ready to give any perceptive visitor some advanced lessons in a free market economy. The location of shops, for example, will tell you all about everyone's profit margins; the jewellers will be found in the centre and around the entrances, of course, while the dealers in raw leather or children's mittens are tucked away in low-rent alleys where you'll never find them. Most of the street names tell what trades were followed long ago—for example, the Fezmaker's Street or the Avenue of the Slippers—though the locations gradually change with the years. Atatürk put the fezmakers out of business long ago, and now their street sells mostly blue jeans. Other names are more colourful, like the Louse Bazaar. You may wander its broad avenues and dim cul-de-sacs, recently renovated and cleared of their ugly thicket of electric signs, and look for bargains to your heart's content. Don't miss the **Iç Bedesten** at the centre, devoted to copper and rare antiques; they glitter in Mehmet's dim hall like the treasure in the cave of the Forty Thieves.

Stamboul's market district really stretches as far as the Golden Horn, and the Kapali Çarşi is only its glamorous retail end. Many of the surrounding streets, like those inside, have a particular function. One of the most interesting is the **Sahaflar Çarşisi** [32], the old Bookseller's Market, just outside the Beyazit Square entrance to the Covered Market. This lovely courtyard full of tiny shops, with its fountain and large population of cats, is believed to have been around in one form or another since Byzantine times. North of the Covered Market, around Uzunçarşi Caddesi, are a number of old *hans*, no longer performing their old functions as merchant hotels, but still buzzing with porters and handcarts, the whirr of old machinery, and the decorous transactions made over tea.

BEYAZIT SQUARE AND BEYAZIT CAMII

An old story relates how when Beyazit II was building the mosque that bears his name, the oldest of the Ottoman Imperial mosques still standing, a pious old woman offered a pair of pigeons—Turks are fond of pigeons—for the courtyard and gardens. Their descendants rule **Beyazit Square** today, and you'll earn some credit in Allah's bank of grace for spending a few liras on them; someone will always be there to sell you a plate of seeds. The square, entirely redone several years ago by some berserk minimalist architect, has become an outstanding piece of urban design with few admirers apart from the pigeons, who seem happier than ever even if there are fewer trees. This is what the critics would call an architectural square, a vast expanse of grey granite blocks on different levels; it is a veritable symphony in grey, between the pavement, the pigeons, and the subtle variety of grey tones in the **Beyazit Camii,** the grand and beautiful mosque the square was designed to show off.

Whether or not this was the mosque that set the pattern for later Imperial foundations we cannot tell. The mosque of Beyazit's father Mehmet, the original Fatih Camii was destroyed in an earthquake. Its architect was a Greek named Christodoulos, and the Beyazit Camii, completed in 1504, is the work of his sons. They built their mosque after the plan of the Aya Sofia, only without the upper gallery, and endowed it with a particularly fine courtyard and fountain.

ISTANBUL UNIVERSITY

Across the square, the monumental gateway in some sort of Persian Rococo is the entrance to **Istanbul University.** The date over the arch, the Roman numerals 1453, is a sorry deception. That was the year of the Conquest, but the University was not founded until 1845, as part of the reforms of Abdul Mecit. Since Atatürk, the University has expanded greatly, taking over the buildings of the old *Seraskeriat*, the War Ministry, in the large park behind the gate. If you want to meet the students, the open-air cafe behind the Beyazit Camii is full of them.

For one of the best possible views of Istanbul, try the 200-foot **Beyazit Tower** on the campus. Mehmet II built it in 1823 as a watchtower for fires (or insurrections); it is the tallest structure in old Stamboul. Along Yeniceriler Caddesi, on the south side of the square, the recently excavated ruins lying about belong to the **Forum of Theodosius**—Beyazit Square's ancestor on this site.

SÜLEYMANIYE CAMII

Mimar Sinan, in the last years of his life, is supposed to have said that the Selimiye in Edirne was his favourite among all his scores of mosques; the great architect chose to live, however, near his **Süleymaniye** (1557), and nearby also is his tomb. If you have the chance to visit only one of the Imperial mosques, your time would be best spent here. No features of the construction are unique or original; the same elements of the classic design will be found in the same places. The building's only excuse for existing is perfection. Just as a mathematician can sometimes look at a complex equation and understand it by what seems to be intuition, so, when we look at the Süleymaniye we have no need of measurement or analysis to know that each proportion and line is nothing either more or less than right. The outstanding features are subtle: the excellent stone porticoes on either side, the courtyard and the smooth plain hierarchy of domes, to which we could add the surviving stained glass, the work of a legendary artist called Ibrahim the Drunkard.

No mosque in Istanbul, and certainly not the Aya Sofia, has such a feeling of openness within. For a moment, it's easy to forget the reality of columns, arches, and vaults and imagine the Süleymaniye as a great stone tent, hung on the four square solid piers at the corners of the dome. Just as Süleyman's reign marked the high noon of the Ottoman state, so does this mosque that Sinan built for him, declare the zenith of his nation's art. Time was to show that neither had much more to give.

Almost alone among the Imperial mosques, the Süleymaniye retains almost all of its *külliye* (or complex) of religious and educational institutions. As the grandest *külliye* ever built by the Ottomans, and an integral part of Sinan's perfect composition, no one has dared tamper. The eight low buildings, with over 200 domes between them, have all recently been restored, and several are creatively re-used, one as a library, and another as a clinic to benefit the people of the neighbourhood, just as their builders intended. In the courtyard of the mosque, you can see the separate *türbes* of Süleyman and Roxelana, both done in fine Iznik tiles. A smaller tomb, at the narrow angle of a street in the northernmost corner of the complex, is that of Sinan himself.

Just west of the Süleymaniye, in a small courtyard off Kirazli Mescit Sokak, stands the small Kilise Camii [33], formerly the **Church of St Theodorus;** though much was rebuilt in the twelfth century, the foundation and much of the structure are from the fifth, making this the oldest religious structure in Istanbul.

From Beyazit Square west along Vezneciler Caddesi

Returning to Beyazit Square, and continuing west along Vezneciler Caddesi, still following the route of the old *Mese*, we pass reminders of the Ottoman or Byzantine eras on almost every block. The **Kalenderhane Cami** [34], at the corner of the Büyük Reşit Paşa Caddesi, where six streets meet, was originally the church of the Akataleptos Monastery; thirteenth-century frescoes have recently been discovered inside. A *kalender* was a kind of dervish, and it appears the function of this and many other monasteries changed little after the Conquest.

ŞEHZADE CAMII

Many consider the **Şehzade Camii** (1548), two blocks further east, to be one of the finest of the Ottoman mosques, but its lofty dome conceals a great crime—also, perhaps, the secret of the decline of the Ottoman Empire. Süleyman the Magnificent had a son named Mustafa by one of his concubines, an intelligent and virtuous young man who gave every promise of being an excellent soldier and ruler. All that stood between him and a brilliant reign was the unfortunate matter of his mother's name not being Roxelana. The Sultan's favourite had sons of her own, younger than Mustafa, and she was determined to do anything to see them one day on the throne. She had already driven Süleyman to murder once, in the case of the Grand Vezir Ibrahim, and now, on the evidence of forged letters that suggested that Mustafa was planning to stage a revolt, she persuaded the Sultan to do him in.

Mustafa, called back from the province he was governing, went unsuspectingly to his doom; it is said Süleyman watched from behind a curtain while the mutes and the bowstring went to work—spilling royal blood was an unthinkable crime, and a garroting with a bowstring was the custom for such necessities. Roxelana, ironically, never lived to enjoy the power of a Sultan Valide, but her son Selim II, called the Sot, was to reign for eight years, as the first dissolute Ottoman, before succumbing to cirrhosis. It is said Süleyman built the Şehzade Camii, the 'Prince's Mosque' out of remorse. Sinan used the opportunity to experiment, bestowing upon his mosque one of the most unusual exteriors to be seen in Istanbul, with plenty of Persian—and Moorish—inspired detail on the minarets, domes, and windows. Later Turkish architects were to draw on these, especially during the Baroque era, but Sinan himself returned to his accustomed austerity just in time to design the Süleymaniye.

Just behind the Şehzade a small mosque, the **Burmali Minare** [35], was built by an Egyptian paşa two years after its larger neighbour was completed. The name refers to the 'twisted' minaret, unique in the city. All this area around the intersection of the *Mese*—called Şehzadebaşi along this stretch—and Atatürk Boulevard, was developed into a park as part of Istanbul's first ambitious planning scheme in the 1940s. Across the street, the steel and glass City Hall was its centrepiece, and broad **Atatürk Bulvari** designed for cars, its major improvement. Amazingly, this is the first street in 1600 years ever laid out to directly connect the Marmara and the Golden Horn.

AQUEDUCT OF VALENS

The park was opened up partly to expose the **Aqueduct of Valens,** supported by an arcade over a half mile in length between the Third and Fourth

Hills, and nearly 60 feet tall where it passes over Atatürk Caddesi. The fourth-century emperor Valens really only expanded and repaired an older aqueduct, but the popular name credits it to him even though most of what you see was constructed by, of course, Mimar Sinan, who rebuilt the city's water supply for Sultan Süleyman. The aqueduct was in use well into the twentieth century; today you can follow its crumbled end into a street of car mechanics in the Fatih district. In its shadow, next to the boulevard, the early seventeenth-century Gazanfer Ağa Medrese was restored in the 1940s as Istanbul's **Municipal Museum** [36], a good idea that no one has carried forward in all the years since. The present humble and dusty collection includes maps and views of the city, expropriated relics from the dervish orders, Imperial firmans directed to the city, portraits, Karagöz puppets, and other bric-à-brac.

CHURCH OF THE PANTOCRATOR

A walk a few blocks north along Atatürk Caddesi will take you past the Zevrek Kilise Camii, once the **Church of the Pantocrator** [37], built in 1124, its history intertwined with that of the Empire in its last centuries. John Comnenus, 'Good John', who presided over the last spell of peace and prosperity for Byzantium, built it, and he is buried here along with his Hungarian wife Irene, a great patroness of the arts. During the occupation of the Crusaders it became a Catholic church, the seat of the Venetian Bishop Morosini; ironically, later it was to be the Church of Gennadius, the prelate who worked so fervently in the 1460s to avert the proposed union of the churches, Constantinople's last hope for aid from the west against the Ottomans. Mehmet rewarded Gennadius after the Conquest by making him the first Patriarch under the new dispensation. The monastery of which this church was a part has completely disappeared; the retaining walls of the huge cistern that served it and the neighbourhood are all that is left.

After passing Atatürk Caddesi, the old *Mese* changes its name one last time, to Fevzi Paşa Caddesi. The *külliye* here, a fine example of Turkish architecture, is the 1698 **Amcazade** [38], built by one of the Grand Vezirs of the Köprülü family. Two blocks south of Fevzi Paşa, the most complete surviving Roman monument in Istanbul stands on a quiet street of apartment blocks; the **Column of Marcian,** built c. AD 450. The tall granite shaft, surmounted by a Corinthian column and a much-effaced winged symbol, once bore a gold statue of this vain emperor, an intriguer with no real successes to commemorate.

Traces of the reliefs on the base can be made out.

LÂLELI DISTRICT AND AKSARAY

From Marcian across Atatürk Bulvari, the neighbourhood south and east, behind the city hall, is called **Lâleli,** named after the **Lâleli** (tulip) **Cami** [39] on busy Ordu Caddesi, a famous work of the Turkish baroque, built under Mustafa III in 1760. The high stone platform on which the mosque stands now contains a little bazaar of shops added in the 1950s. Long ago, before Laleli was even built, it was the central hashish and opium den of Istanbul, a distinction it seems also to have had under the Byzantines. Murat IV, a tremendous drunkard, closed it down for the good of the nation. Across Ordu Caddesi, **Aksaray** is a bustling, thoroughly modern district packed with hotels and a large Arab and Persian influence. Here, tucked away on **Mesilipaşa Caddesi,** is the Bodrum Cami, originally the church of the **Mirelaon Convent** [40], rebuilt and renovated so often since the sixth century that no one knows to whom to credit it.

The Lâleli Cami may be the place where Turkish Baroque went over the edge, but the indescribable **Valide Cami** [41], on Aksaray square, must be the supreme example of the preciousness of a decadent nation carried to its wildest extreme. The Turks were as eclectic as anyone in 1870, and the idea here was to invent Turkish Gothic.

Fatih district

North of Laleli, **Fatih,** the quarter named after Mehmet the Conqueror and the great complex of religious buildings he erected at its centre, is enormous, home to over a hundred thousand of Stamboul's working people; plain and honest, it has survived both urban decay and creeping modernity. When Mehmet built his **Fatih Cami** here in 1463, this Fourth Hill was one of the choicer districts of the city. Here stood the Church of the Holy Apostles, the church second in size and importance only to Aya Sofia. Mehmet demolished it, one of the few instances of wanton destruction of Christian buildings on the part of the Turks. Eighteen of its columns can be seen in the mosque's courtyard. It should not be too hard to imagine how the Holy Apostles looked; St Mark's in Venice was modelled on it.

Mehmet's mosque, which we know had two equal domes in the fashion of the earlier Ottoman mosques of Bursa, was shaken down by an earthquake in 1766. The reigning Sultan Mustafa III, had it rebuilt even bigger in the classical style, but the result is just another uninspired copy from the same mould. The *külliye*, an enormous complex elevated on a platform that turns a vast blank face towards Fevzi Paşa Caddesi, is even larger than that of the Süleymaniye; its institutions and foundations still provide important services for the people of the Fatih. Yet another small, inconspicuous Byzantine building survives a few blocks to the north, the twelfth-century **Church of Christ Pantepoptes** [42] built by Alexis I Comnenus. Now it's the Eski Imaret Cami.

Outlying Areas to the West

EXOKIONION

On the map (pp. 98–99), you can follow a line of avenues—Haliç, Caddesi, Akdeniz Caddesi, and Kizil Elma Caddesi among others—starting at the Golden Horn and winding an irregular course behind the Fatih complex and across the peninsula. These generally follow the line of the original long vanished walls of Constantinople, paced off by Constantine himself after a vision showed him how best to defend the city. Even after the Theodosian walls were built further west, this area beyond the older line had the legal status of an extra-mural district, and during the various conflicts over church dogma, heretics were allowed to hold religious services here. The Greeks called this wide swath of land between Constantines' and Theodosius' Walls the *Exokionion*. Today it is home to hundreds of thousands of Stamboul's poorer residents, in a disorganised conglomeration of villages and market gardens, with some dense concentrations of flats, all up and down the Fifth, Sixth, and Seventh Hills.

With the help of the dolmuş and minibus, those with a real interest in tracking down the wealth of Ottoman and Byzantine monuments here can start their expeditions. Doing it properly will require some walking, and in some cases, climbing around the Fifth Hill in particular, the only one of the seven that truly deserves the name. Your troubles will be rewarded by an endless supply of curiosities past and present, as well as insights into the working life of the more prosaic corners of the fantastical city.

The neighbourhood directly north of the Fatih, along Darüşşafaka Caddesi, gets the travelling market on Wednesdays, and the day *Çarşamba* in Turkish, has given the quarter its name. From here Yavuz Selim Caddesi ascends the Fifth hill to the **Sultan Selim Camii,** or Selimiye, begun by the conqueror of Egypt but not completed until 1522, in the reign of his son Suleyman. Behind this austere and beautiful mosque, Selim built his *türbe* in its garden. From here, you can look out over the rooftops of one of Stamboul's oddest neighbourhoods, a pretty sunken village built around crags of antique masonry at the bottom of the **Cistern of Aspar** [43], a fifth-century addition to Constantinople's water supply.

FENER QUARTER

Progressing any further will require a stout heart and shoes, for the streets that introduce you to the quarter of the **Fener** are the steepest and roughest in all Istanbul. The old ladies storm up and down like mountain goats, and the children play vertical tag, but you may be hard pressed. The Fener takes its name from the old Phanar (lighthouse) Gate, a part of the Theodosian walls along the Golden Horn. After the Conquest it became the district allotted to the Greeks, and some live here to this day. Since 1923, however, most have either returned to Greece or moved to newer parts of the city across the Golden Horn.

The Fener today, with its melancholy, half-empty streets, wrapped in the silence of the tomb, stands in sharp contrast to the past centuries. Even after the Conquest, the talents of the Greeks in the arts and in commerce, and the natural disinclination of the Ottoman elite to earn an honest living, ensured that the more accomplished of the infidels would find many doors open to them. Throughout the Empire, the Greeks controlled shipping, finance, and many of the trades, and provided the Sultans with most of their officials and tax collectors. The capital of this conspicuous and favoured community was here, and on many of the streets near the Golden Horn you will see the ruins of great houses, and even some fashionable late nineteenth-century blocks of flats, to testify to the wealth and influence the Phanar—as it was then called—once enjoyed. The stranglehold they maintained over the Empire's economy, and thus over the Sultans themselves, was notorious; the monopolies they effectively held in many fields contributed as much to the economic decline of the Empire, as the incompetence of the government, and so great were their exactions from the subject peoples that 'Phanariot' became a term of opprobrium used by Slavs, Turks, and Arabs alike.

Most historians have chosen to present the struggle of the Byzantines and Ottomans as an apocalyptic battle of two faiths, both incapable of either understanding or showing any sympathy at all for each other. On the contrary, the Greeks and Turks had known each other for so long before 1453—five centuries of alliances, intermarriages, and scholarly discussion—that when the end came for Byzantium, the transition was accomplished with a minimum of hysteria. After the pillage Mehmet had promised his troops, life for the Greeks gradually returned to normal, and even improved, as the Sultan's efforts to re-establish trade began to pay off. In the Phanar, the heirs of the once-great Byzantine families, the Paleologues, the Comneni, and the rest, were reported still to be around as late as the 1900s.

The Patriarchate

One of the first acts of Mehmet after the Conquest was to co-opt the Greek church by naming Gennadius Patriarch, as much a servant of the Sultan as was the Sheikh ul-Islam, and meant to act as an intermediary between the Greeks and the Ottoman state. Gennadius' successors live on in the **Greek Orthodox Patriarchate** [a]* on a steep hill just above the Golden Horn. Old St George's Church, where the Patriarchs sat on the throne of St John Chrysostom, burned down in 1941, and the centre of the complex is now a

* Letters in [ ] refer to map of Istanbul on pp. 98–99.

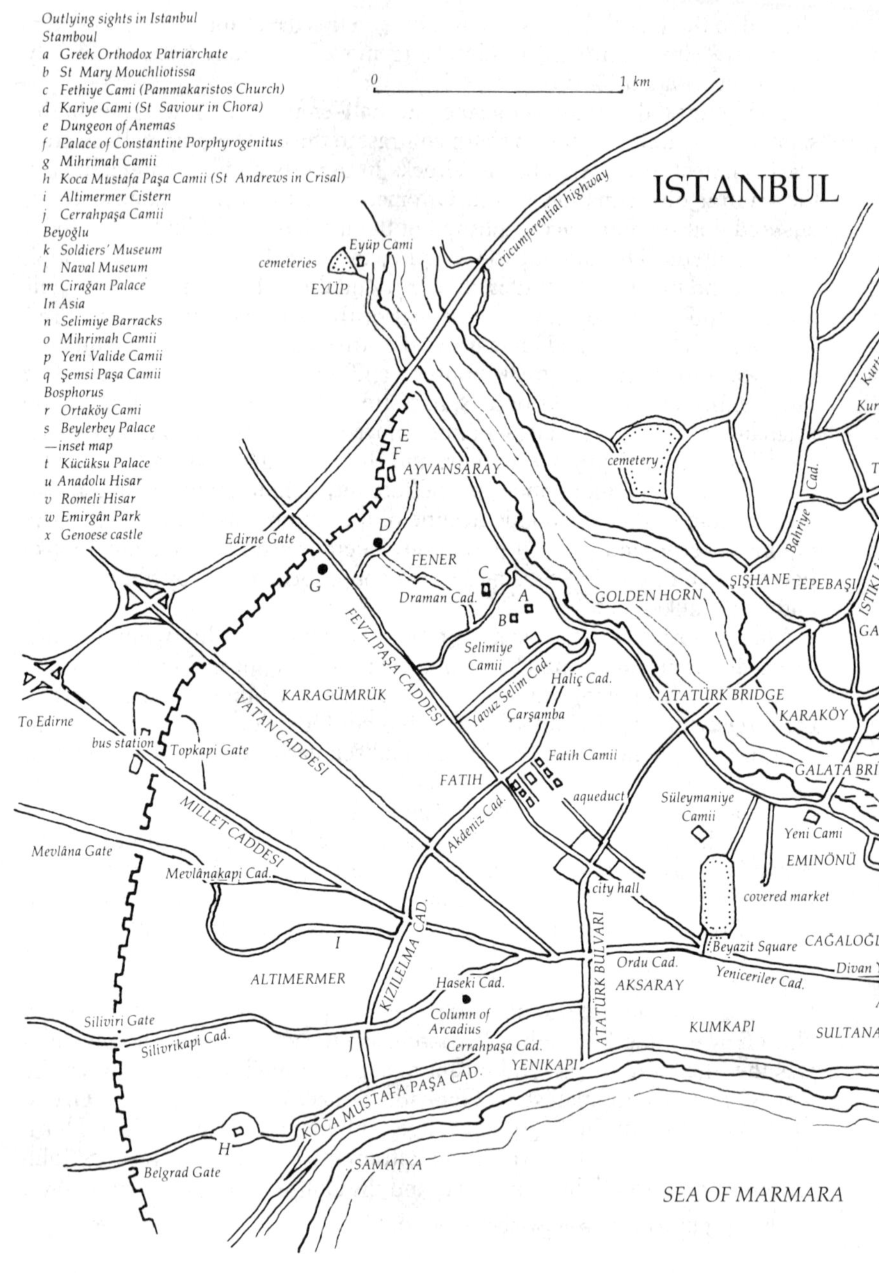

Outlying sights in Istanbul
Stamboul
a Greek Orthodox Patriarchate
b St Mary Mouchliotissa
c Fethiye Cami (Pammakaristos Church)
d Kariye Cami (St Saviour in Chora)
e Dungeon of Anemas
f Palace of Constantine Porphyrogenitus
g Mihrimah Camii
h Koca Mustafa Paşa Camii (St Andrews in Crisal)
i Altimermer Cistern
j Cerrahpaşa Camii
Beyoğlu
k Soldiers' Museum
l Naval Museum
m Cirağan Palace
In Asia
n Selimiye Barracks
o Mihrimah Camii
p Yeni Valide Camii
q Şemsi Paşa Camii
Bosphorus
r Ortaköy Cami
s Beylerbey Palace
—inset map
t Kücüksu Palace
u Anadolu Hisar
v Romeli Hisar
w Emirgân Park
x Genoese castle
0
1 km
ISTANBUL
cricumferential highway
Eyüp Cami
cemeteries
EYÜP
cemetery
E
F
AYVANSARAY
D
Edirne Gate
G
FENER
C
Draman Cad.
A
B
GOLDEN HORN
ŞIŞHANE
TEPEBAŞI
Bahriye Cad.
Selimiye Camii
Yavuz Selim Cad.
Haliç Cad.
FEVZI PAŞA CADDESI
KARAGÜMRÜK
VATAN CADDESI
Çarşamba
ATATÜRK BRIDGE
KARAKÖY
To Edirne
bus station
Topkapi Gate
Fatih Camii
FATIH
GALATA BRID
aqueduct
Süleymaniye Camii
Akdeniz Cad.
MILLET CADDESI
Yeni Cami
EMINÖNÜ
Mevlâna Gate
Mevlânakapi Cad.
city hall
covered market
KIZILELMA CAD.
I
ATATÜRK BULVARI
Beyazit Square
CAĞALOĞLU
Ordu Cad.
Yeniceriler Cad.
ALTIMERMER
Haseki Cad.
AKSARAY
Column of Arcadius
Siliviri Gate
Silivrikapi Cad.
J
Cerrahpaşa Cad.
KUMKAPI
YENIKAPI
KOCA MUSTAFA PAŞA CAD.
H
SAMATYA
Belgrad Gate
SEA OF MARMARA

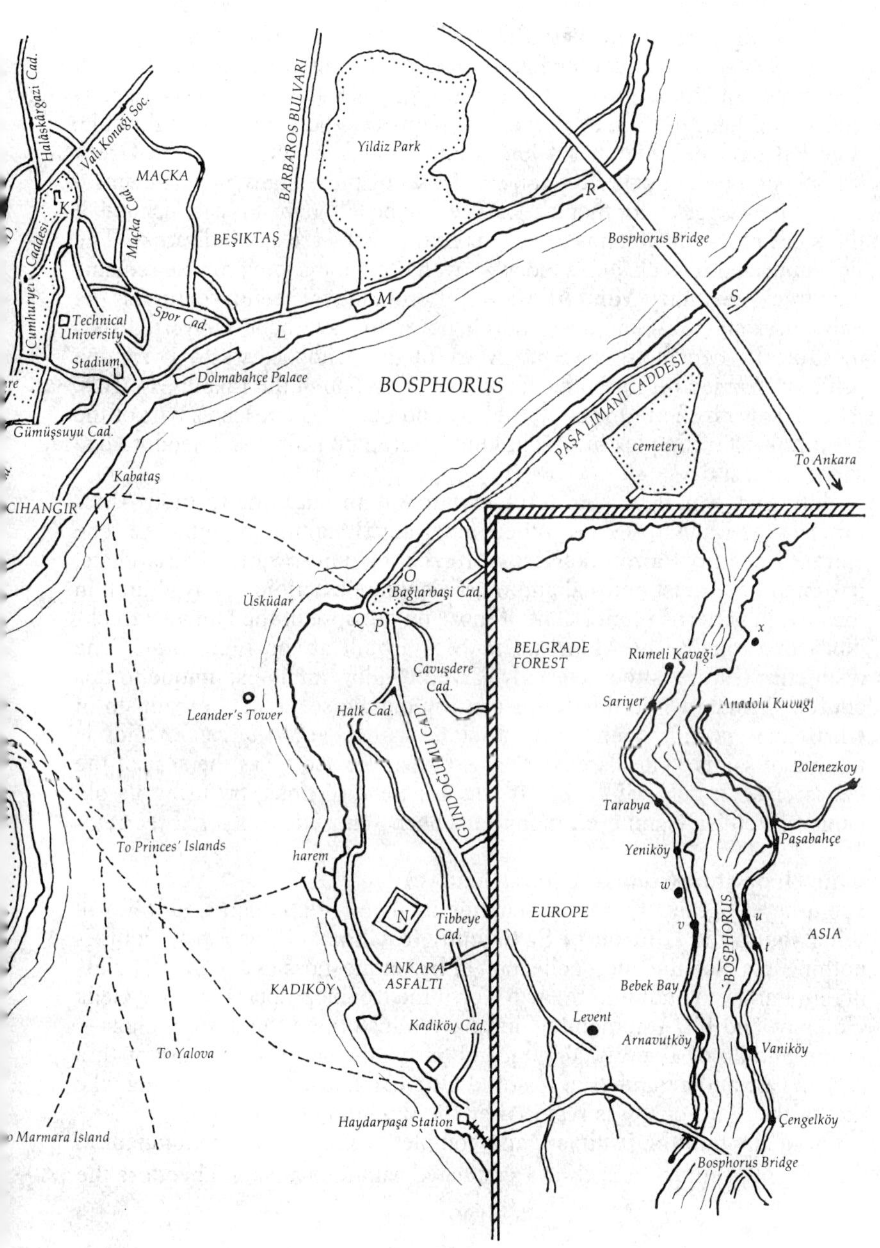

Halâskârgazi Cad.
Vali Konaği Soc.
MAÇKA
Maçka Cad.
K
Cumhuryet Caddesi
BEŞIKTAŞ
BARBAROS BULVARI
Yildiz Park
R
Bosphorus Bridge
M
S
Technical University
Spor Cad.
L
Stadium
Dolmabahçe Palace
BOSPHORUS
PAŞA LIMANI CADDESI
cemetery
To Ankara
Gümüşsuyu Cad.
Kabataş
CIHANGIR
O
Bağlarbaşi Cad.
Üsküdar
Q
P
BELGRADE FOREST
Rumeli Kavaği
x
Çavuşdere Cad.
Sariyer
Anadolu Kuvaği
Leander's Tower
Halk Cad.
GUNDOGUMU CAD.
Polenezkoy
Tarabya
Paşabahçe
To Princes' Islands
harem
Yeniköy
w
N
Tibbeye Cad.
EUROPE
BOSPHORUS
u
v
ASIA
t
ANKARA ASFALTI
KADIKÖY
Bebek Bay
Levent
Kadiköy Cad.
Arnavutköy
Vaniköy
To Yalova
Haydarpaşa Station
Çengelköy
Marmara Island
Bosphorus Bridge

huge tower—incredibly enough done in Victorian-Gothic, built in the 1880s.

The main gate of the Patriarchate has not been opened since Easter Sunday 1821. On that day the Patriarch Gregory, implicated in the Hetairist conspiracy of the Phanariot Greeks working for their nation's independence, was hanged from it; all those with business here enter from the side. The Patriarchate today has a lonely and forlorn air about it. The Greek school, supported by the Republic, as it was by the Sultans, appears almost empty. Few Greeks, for that matter, seem to be left in the neighbourhood, if the faces of the inhabitants and signs in the shops are any indication. The tiny, unpretentious chapel, a block away, has great meaning for the remaining Greeks: **St Mary Mouchliotissa** [b], from the thirteenth century, is the only surviving pre-Conquest church never to have been converted to a mosque. Its benefactress, 'Saint Mary of the Mongols' was a Byzantine princess married off for political reasons to a Khan of the Ilhanli Mongols. After his death she returned to the city and built this church as part of the great monastic complex in which, long before, the Empress Theodora had spent her last days.

With luck, you'll be able to pick your way through the tortuous lanes towards the walls to see two other important Byzantine monuments. The eleventh-century **Pammakaristos Church** [c], quite near the Patriarchate, has one of the most unusual and most elaborate exteriors of any church in the city, in patterns reminiscent of those on the apse of the famous Greek-Norman cathedral of Monreale in Sicily, built at the same time. One distinctive feature is the delicately carved window mullions, unique to this church. Inside, a fine thirteenth-century mosaic scene of the baptism of Christ has recently been restored, along with a large number of mosaic figures of saints. The Pammakaristos ('most blessed') was the seat of the Patriarchate from 1456–1586. If you ask for directions, try using its old name of Fethiye Cami even though it's been a museum for some years.

Church of St Saviour in Chora (Kariye)

From here, Fethiye Caddesi, changing its name to Draman Caddesi, will bring you to the **Church of St Saviour in Chora** [d], or *Kariye*. This is nothing less than the finest collection of Byzantine mosaics and mural painting in Turkey. You'll find the trip worth the trouble, especially since Çelik Gülersoy and his Automobile Club have transformed the surroundings—in the middle of a very shabby neighbourhood—into a small oasis with a garden cafe and a number of restored Ottoman houses. The art inside, like that of the Aya Sofia, was restored by the Byzantine Institute.

Originally built by Justinian, and completely rebuilt by the Comneni in the eleventh century, it is always associated with the name of Theodore the

Logothete, a high official in the late fourteenth century who fell victim to political intrigue and ended his days as a poor monk in the church he had restored and beautified. In the latter days of the Empire, when the Aya Sofia was falling into decay and the emperors had moved to the Blachernae Palace nearby, the Chora became the city's fashionable church, where the Imperial family usually attended services. An icon of the Virgin kept here, one of those supposedly painted by St Luke, was credited with saving Constantinople from the siege of Murat II in 1428; the Turk's final attack failed shortly after the icon was carried solemnly around the walls.

Architecturally, little in the Chora is outstanding; the major attraction is its wealth of frescoes. Byzantine painting has always been undervalued by the critics, their eyes dazzled by the gold of the less expressive, less articulate mosaics. The restoration of the frescoes in the **Paraecclesion,** or mortuary chapel of the Chora, as well as those in other late Byzantine churches like the Aya Sofia in Trabzon, has already gone a long way towards correcting this. In these paintings, it is easy to see the influence and the inspiration without which the Italian Renaissance would not have been possible.

Of these, the greatest perhaps is the spectacular version of the **Last Judgement,** in which Jesus raised the dead over a shower of broken locks and keys; Adam and Eve are shown redeemed, along with the unbaptised kings and prophets of the Old Testament. The remainder portray various biblical scenes, the Burning Bush and Jacob wrestling with the angel, as well as a whole catalogue of Orthodox saints and some unusual trompe-l'oeil borders. Theodore the Logothete himself appears in one of the mosaics, presenting his rebuilt church to Christ. A figure of the Christ Pantocrator and other mosaics with scenes from his life, and portraits of apostles and saints cover the outer and inner narthexes; unfortunately few have survived in the nave of the church.

THEODOSIAN WALLS

The **Theodosian Walls** can be seen just a few blocks west of the Chora, in their own right, they are among the greatest monuments of Istanbul. No city has ever had better; without them, the Byzantine capital could easily have succumbed on scores of occasions to Huns, Avars, Bulgarians, Russians, Arabs, Goths or Turks; with them, even in its darkest and most decadent moments, the Empire was able to maintain itself as the bulwark of Christendom, and the heir of Rome.

Fully seventeen miles in length, the walls stand almost intact between the Golden Horn and the Marmara, but in fragments along the shores. The inland walls, the easiest to attack, are the most impressive. Anthemius, Theodosius's prefect, made them invulnerable by doubling them, with a raised inner wall looking down over and protecting the outer, and a deep ditch in front of that. For most of their length, you can walk between them or even on them. Where the wall meets the Golden Horn, two towers stand as remnants of the **Dungeon of Anemas** [e] where the Byzantines kept unsuccessful schemers and political prisoners. These walls are actually not part of the original work, but a long loop added around the **Palace of Blachernae,** the huge suburban garden palace of the late emperors. Very little of it remains; the palace encompassed all of what is now the green district called **Ayvansaray,** its houses and gardens betraying occasional traces of an old wall or bit of carved stone. The **Palace of Constantine Porphyrogenitus** [f] adjacent to the Blachernae still stands, a stony pile, literally a shell of what it once was, without roof, floors, or even its marble façade.

Edirne Gate

Just inside the **Edirne Kapi,** the old Adrianople Gate, is another fine mosque built by Sinan for Süleyman the Magnificent, the **Mihrimah Camii** [g] (1562), named after the Sultan's favourite daughter. The section of the walls to the south, in the dangerous spot depressed by the valley of the Lycus stream, saw much of the heaviest fighting during the Siege of 1453. Here Mehmet's cannons pounded away relentlessly for days. Giustiniani, the Italian commander, was wounded then, and although the wall was not breached, his loss greatly disheartened the defenders and contributed much to the fall. The postern gate of Charisius, the one accidently left open that caused the defeat, is just north of the Mihrimah. The tallest of the towers is at the old Roman Gate, now the **Topkapi** ('cannon gate') the major entrance to the city by road.

Marmara Shore and South-western parts of Stamboul

On the Marmara shore, the **Marble Tower** at the end of the inland walls was a famous Byzantine landmark. Just to the north, all the Emperors, on their accessions or their triumphs, entered at the **Golden Gate.** Most of its legendary embellishments are long gone, but the Crusaders could not remove the marble triumphal arch at the centre of the gate, built to commemorate Theodosius' victory over the pretender Maximus in 391. To its four towers, the Turks of Mehmet II added three more and an inner wall, creating the **Yedikule** (seven towers) **Castle,** recently restored. Here Osman II was murdered by the Janissaries; later Sultans used it for incarcerating foreign ambassadors when the mood struck them.

The south-western parts of Stamboul have little to offer. Byzantine churches like those of the monastic complex at Studion, the largest in the city, and the Peribleptos Monastery have long ago been battered out of recognition by earthquakes and subsequent rebuildings. One church, that of **St**

Andreas in Crisal [h], is still substantially intact as the **Koca Mustafa Paşa Camii.** Many Armenians live in this area, and their mostly nineteenth-century churches are still in use, including the Armenian Patriarchy in Sarapnel Sokak near the Marmara end of the Atatürk Bulvari. The largest of all open cisterns, the **Altimermer** [i], may be seen in the quarter of the same name, and the 1593 **Cerrahpaşa Camii** [j] has the most interest among the area's mosques. Better than these, take yourself to Vatan Caddesi, one of the broad empty boulevards driven through Stamboul in the 1940s, and see the ancient metropolis from the top of a Ferris wheel in the little amusement park there.

EYÜP

Once upon a time, the Golden Horn was the most beloved of all the embellishments of Istanbul. From Eminönü Square all the way up the estuary, both banks were lined with *yalis*, the wooden mansions of the paşas, set among gardens and groves of plane trees and cypresses. Marble quays brightened the shores, and the only boats to be seen were pleasure craft and water taxis.

Then in the 19th century Abdul the Damned—Abdul Hamid II, the Sultan not even the Turks will speak kindly of—let in the foreign syndicates and industrialists and, in no time at all, the Horn became a seamy polluted waterfront, the black sewer of Istanbul.

Just beyond the inland walls at Ayvansaray, the little village of **Eyüp** was, before Abdul Hamid, a rare jewel of the waterway. Set on a height, enjoying the best view of the domes and minarets of the city, Eyüp was a garden suburb of lovely modest houses, favoured by the most influential artists and public men of the Ottoman Empire. Also, it was a holy place, a traditional spot for pilgrims to stop on the way to Mecca. Today, surrounded by factories and *gecekondu*, Eyüp has become a poor district and somewhat bedraggled, but still tries its best to keep its head above the miasma.

Although it is believed the spot has been holy ground since ancient times, Eyüp acquired its sanctity for Moslems during the Siege of 1453, when Mehmet or one of his vezirs had a dream directing him to the unmarked grave of Eba-Eyüp-el Ensari, the Standard Bearer of the Prophet Mohammed, who had died here during the first Arab attack on Constantinople in the seventh century. Eyüp—the name is the Arabic form of Job—was found just where the dream had promised. Mehmet built a *türbe* and mosque, and when an earthquake knocked it down in 1800, Sultan Selim III replaced it with the **Eyüp Cami** you see today. It was here that the Sultans, upon their accessions, were girded with the sword of Osman, which served them in place of a crown as the symbol of sovereignty.

All around, between the blocks of small shops selling Korans and a strange assortment of Islamic trinkets, the living village shares the space with acres of beautiful cemeteries, their marble headstones laid out in walled gardens, with names like the Pavilion of Idris and the Valley of the Nightingale.

Beyoğlu

BACKGROUND

In Byzantine times, there was no bridge over the Golden Horn—there was no reason to cross it. The little settlement on the opposite shore called Sycae never played much of a role in the life of the city. Galata, the port of Beyoğlu on the tip of the Golden Horn, began as a Genoese trading colony in the ninth century. As the Italian control of trade routes strengthened, Constantinople's economic power declined, and by the fourteenth century, Galata was a large and prosperous town; such trade as passed through the Bosphorus landed here, not at the impoverished capital.

Italians had long played a role in the city, not only the Genoese, but Pisans, Venetians, and Amalfitani. At one point in the twelfth century, some 60 000 of them were reported to be living within the walls. Their commercial arrogance, not to mention their heretical Christianity, infuriated the Greeks, and in 1180, a mob—among whom we may guess were many of the Italians' debtors—massacred thousands. Diverting the Fourth Crusade to sack Constantinople was the Italians' way of returning the favour.

When the Greek emperors returned in 1261, Galata began to build walls against the possibility of another such debt moratorium. The restored empire, weak as it was, became entirely dependent on the Genoese. The Genoese nonchalantly declared their neutrality during the Siege of 1453, and kept some of their privileges under the Turks for long as Genoa remained a maritime power. Under Ottoman rule, Galata maintained its role as a foreign compound; the Genoese were gradually replaced by the French and others, who were granted their first commercial privileges, or 'capitulations', by Süleyman the Magnificent in 1525.

Life in Stamboul was perhaps too unsettling for the ambassadors of the European powers, and they soon began to construct large embassy compounds on the lovely hills of **Pera** (Beyoğlu) above Galata. Fashion and influence followed, and enough money flowed into the capitulations to build Galata and Pera into the real centre of the city. As the Turks and their government became increasingly impotent and irrelevant, eventually even the Sultan joined the migration, building a new palace, the Dolmabahçe, on the Bosphorus in the 1850s. Most of the recent growth of the city has occurred on the Beyoğlu side of the Golden Horn. While in many places you can still look out over open countryside from the Theodosian walls of

Stamboul, new districts have spread for miles northwards from Pera; today even the villages along the Bosphorus are considered part of the metropolitan area.

Fashion has certainly left Galata and Pera behind. These streets were once legendary throughout the world for their scenes of ostentatious wealth mixed with age-old grime and squalor, their Levantine mix of a hundred nationalities and languages, their excesses and their intrigues. The advent of Atatürk's republic simply let all the air of out of them, and now they display a kind of decayed grandeur that only cities like Naples and Palermo, or certain parts of New York can approach. Even now that money and the cultural diversity are mostly gone, Pera and Galata are too set in their ways to change, still the natural habitat of The Maltese Falcon characters, Joel Cairo and Caspar Gutman, immune to urban renewal, a world unto itself.

GALATA/KARAKÖY

Coming across the Galata Bridge, you meet first the grey mess of warehouses, work shops and office blocks of **Karaköy**, the modern name for Galata. If the gritty surroundings suit you, walk around; Istanbul's oldest Catholic church, and other peculiar relics of Galata's past are tucked away in corners where it will take you some effort to find them. Just a block east of the bridge, the **Yeralti Cami** [45], 'underground mosque', originally occupied the cellar of a defence tower believed to have been built by the Romans. The more conventional mosque building over it was added in the 1750s. To the west, off Tersane Caddesi, the **Arap Cami** [46] started as a Byzantine church, and was rebuilt as a Dominican chapel in the early fourteenth century; in 1492 Bayezit II converted it into a mosque for Arab refugees expelled from Spain.

Voyvoda Caddesi takes its name from the redoubtable fifteenth-century Voyvode of Transylvania, Vlad Dracul, stalwart enemy of the Turk and inventor of a hundred novel ways of disposing of captives and indiscreet ambassadors. His metamorphosis into the blood-sucking Count Dracula at the hands of novelist Bram Stoker is well known. The Turks say they caught him and stuck his head on a pike; somewhere along this street it is supposed to be buried. The Rumanians, and most of the historians, maintain Vlad was never defeated. Come around some night and look.

The **Galata Tower,** the most conspicuous symbol of the quarter, the centre of its skyline as seen from the Stamboul side, was built in 1350 as part of the Genoese fortifications. Under the Ottomans, it was put into service as a fire tower. Recently restored, it has a restaurant on the top floor with a fine view of the city. Nearby, on Galip Dede Caddesi, the **Museum of Divan Literature** [47] is really the subtle Turkish republican way of preserving Istanbul's Mevlevi House, the *tekke* of the whirling dervishes, after the order's dissolution in 1925. While the *tekke* began here as early as the 1490s, most of what you see here are the contributions of the nineteenth-century Sultans, traditionally the friends of the Mevlevis.

KEMERALTI CADDESI

As a perfect counterpoint to the dervish house, Istanbul has long kept its **red-light district** in a compound of shabby blocks off Kemeralti Caddesi, guarded by a policeman at the front gate (to keep out unlicensed females). Kemeraltai continues westwards, past the fifteenth-century **St Benoit Church** [48], tucked awkwardly between two warehouses. Long the church of Pera's French community, St Benoit holds the remains of Ferenc Rakoczy, the eighteenth-century Hungarian patriot who fought, not the Turks, but the Hapsburgs of Austria and ended his life in exile in Turkey after the defeat of his revolutionary army.

Kemeralti ends at **Tophane Square;** the name commemorates the first Turkish cannon foundry built here in the early nineteenth century by Sultan Selim III. The **Kiliç Ali Paşa Camii** [49] here is a noteworthy late work of Sinan and the larger mosque to the west, the 1826 **Nüsretiye Cami** [50] was completed just as Mehmut II won his death struggle with the Janissaries, hence its name 'Victory Mosque'.

THE TÜNEL

No trip to Istanbul would be complete without a ride on the world's shortest underground, the **Tünel,** which will take you from the environs of Galata Bridge some 600 yards up the modest slope to Istiklâl Caddesi. The motives for building this little inclined railway in 1877 are unclear; some say its original purpose was to move livestock through to Istanbul avoiding the crowded streets of Pera. From Tünel Square, where it ends, you may start up Istiklâl or go back to **Şişhane Square,** one of the unusual, overlooked corners of the city. Some nineteenth-century interests invested a lot in this frilly, cobbled Italianate plaza with its radiating avenues and overdressed buildings. It's come down in the world now, but buildings like the old City Hall, by a high-society Italian architect named Barbarini, are fun to look at. Turkish Airline's city terminal is here, and Şişhane may be your introduction to Istanbul.

ISTIKLÂL CADDESI

Istiklâl Caddesi was once known as the **Grand Rue de Pera** where the ambassadors rubbed elbows with the city's commercial élite. In the nineteenth century it became heavily built up with European-style apartment and business blocks. Most of these are now empty above the first floor, but the street is still Istanbul's shopping and entertainment centre. All that sounds simple and innocuous, perhaps, but this boulevard of broken dreams has an atmosphere unlike any other. Its extreme narrowness, bad air and grime, and the half-decayed state of its once-elegant establishments all contribute to the effect. Another essential ingredient is the art nouveau architecture of many of the buildings, their balconies dripping cast-iron vines and flowers over the tawdry street scenes below; one of the best is at no 479 (more good ones are on Kemeralti Caddesi and the other streets in Pera). Finally, add the old embassies, now reduced to the status of the world's fanciest consulates. Many of the embassy compounds included churches; today you'll need to peek behind the shops into their quiet courtyards to find them: two especially fine ones, both Italian, are the Church of S Maria Draperis (1783) and S Antonio di Padua (1725) at nos 431 and 331 respectively.

Istiklâl is full of arcades—*pasaji*, in Turkish—dim covered alleys or grand follies like the **Avrupa Pasaji,** serving a wide variety of purposes. Most famous is the one devoted to beer, the **Çiçek Pasaji** [51], or 'flower arcade', four-feet wide and lined with crowded cafes and stand-up joints with sawdust on the floor. The most colourful clientele in Istanbul bellies up for big glasses of brew, providing the city's cheapest and best floor show. Behind it, Istanbul's liveliest street market, the **Balikpazari** ('fish market') covers a maze of streets. The building in which parts of the Çiçek Pasaji are located is itself part of the Istiklal scenery, a florid, incredible pile with iron letters proclaiming CITY OF PERA on the cornice, now a burned-out, empty shell. Across the street, the school behind the big gates is the **Galatasaray Lisesi** [52], once the most prestigious in the Empire, where instruction was carried on, naturally, in French.

TAKSIM SQUARE

When Istaklâl finally gives out, it leaves you stranded in **Taksim Square,** the centre of Beyoğlu, a dull place full of cars where the dilapidation of Pera fades into the well-painted concrete of the newer areas. The **Opera** [53], a bland block of glass and stone, was completed in 1962 as the showpiece of the city's cultural life. Grand opera has had a home in Istanbul since Donizetti Paşa, brother of the famous composer, conducted the Palace Symphony in the 1840s. On the northern fringes of Taksim, really more a large park than a square, the city's two fancy chain hotels, a Hilton and Sheraton, loom above the trees. Both are isolated, self-contained compounds, seemingly the last survivals of the days of capitulations and trading colonies.

SOLDIERS' MUSEUM

The modern neighbourhoods beyond, Harbiye, Şişli, and Macka, are bright and busy, but there is little to see. If you're anywhere near, though, stop in at the **Soldiers' Museum** [k] (Askeri Müzesi), housed in an old barracks in the hillside park a half mile north of Taksim. The Janissaries, like the Sultans, never threw anything away, and the vast hoard of souvenirs and curiosities they piled up on their tours of Europe and Asia, and saved in the Aya Irene Church armoury made this natural museum collection: crusaders' swords, Byzantine battle flags, Tamerlane's coat of-mail, flags of the '16 historical Turkish Empires' (including Tamerlane's and Attila the Hun's), the famous chain the Byzantines used to close off the Golden Horn, a whole hall of wax dummies of the Sultans and Janissaries—the whole crazy hierarchy from the Ağas, the Makers of Soup and Water Carriers, down to the dwarfs, the *soytari* who as their card explains 'do funny things for Sultan', and a table-and-chair set made entirely out of rifles, a gift of Kaiser Wilhelm. If you come at 3 pm, you'll be treated to one of the best shows in Istanbul, a performance of the **Mehter Band** in all its glorious cacaphony. The early Ottoman armies marched to this music, the precursor of all band music in Europe.

DOLMABAHÇE PALACE

At the end of the park, where it descends towards the Bosphorus, your view of the water will be blocked by the **Dolmabahçe Palace** (1852). No better monument to the spirit of the later Ottomans could be imagined. Abdül Mecit, the reforming Sultan of the Crimean War, was acutely aware of, and sensitive to, the growing backwardness of his nation, compared to the rest of Europe. To restore Turkey to its place in the sun, he emptied his treasury—literally putting the Ottoman Empire into receivership—not on armies, or railroads, or factories, but on this preposterous Versailles, all marble and only about half a block shorter than the Tünel. Here Abdül Mecit could receive ambassadors in a proper frock coat, hold grand balls, even indulging in a waltz or two himself, or treat his guests to a private performance of Donizetti Paşa's orchestra. The Empire was now officially up-to-date.

Take the tour; you've never seen anything like it before. More bad taste is concentrated in this one building than in Napoleon's Tomb, the Great Hall of the Soviets and the Vittorio Emanuele Memorial all combined, with still enough left over to balance all the funeral homes in Los Angeles. All the gold and silk and crystal are real, of course. No particular style predominates; probably early on it occurred to the architects and decorators that the Sultan only desired that they lay it on thick. Czar Nicholas sent polar-bear rugs, and a present of elephant tusks came from the governor of the Hejaz. The British, though, knew what the Ottomans really liked; Queen Victoria sent him the biggest chandelier in the world.

The Dolmabahçe has lots of clocks, and they've all been stopped at 9.05, the hour that Atatürk died here on 10 November, 1938. To his credit, the Turkish leader occupied only a small room on his visits here; he converted the rest into a conference centre and exhibition hall. Today, the city uses it to put up whatever kings, sheikhs, and presidents happen to visit.

BEŞIKTAŞ AND YILDIZ PARK

Beşiktaş, the neighbourhood at the end of the palace further up the Bosphorus, begins the fashionable quarters of the modern city. Where its main street, Barbaros Bulvari, meets the Bosphorus, Turkey's **Naval Museum** [l] wants to remind you that the Ottoman state was, in the early sixteenth century, the leading sea power of Europe. The **Tomb of Barbarossa,** just outside, honours the brutal Greek-born corsair who, in the service of Süleyman the Magnificent, made that pre-eminence possible. Eleven years after Abdül Mecit built Dolmabahçe in 1852, his successor Abdül Aziz grew tired of it and built a new one a half mile up the Bosphorus. **Çirağan Palace** [m] is only a third as large; presumably that was all the great powers and their Ottoman Debt Commission would allow. A fire in 1910 left only the four enormous exterior walls standing, and Çirağan has been a ghostly shell ever since; plans are to rebuild it as a luxury hotel.

In another thirteen years, Abdül Aziz was gone—deposed for his reckless extravagance—and his successor Abdül Hamid, finding the treasury even emptier, could only build the small pavilions in **Yildiz Park.** These were left to rot after the deposition of the Sultans, but recently the Automobile Club has restored both the buildings and the grounds to their original appearance, adding open-air cafes and terraces with a view over the Bosphorus. Altogether the park is one of the most beautiful in Turkey, and the restoration of the **Malta Kiosk** has won an architectural award.

Istanbul in Asia

In truth, the Asian side is older. The Delphic oracle had told Byzas the navigator to settle 'opposite the land of the blind'; when his Argive expedition arrived at the Golden Horn, they found a colony of Megarans already established near what is today the suburbs of **Kadiköy.** Byzas knew who the blind were; the advantages of the European side for building a city were plain. In the Roman and Byzantine eras, Kadiköy was the sizeable town of Chalcedon, the site of many councils of the early church. The emperors never favoured Chalcedon; on the contrary, they sealed its fate when they took most of the stone from its walls to build their own aqueducts after various sieges. Chalcedon dwindled to nothing in the last days of the Empire, and the Turks took the rest of its stones for their own projects; columns from its famous Church of St Euphemia can be seen in the courtyard of the Süleymaniye.

From the kiosks of the Topkapi Palace, or any other place with a good view of the Bosphorus, Kadiköy's two huge landmarks will be seen; the **Haydarpaşa Station** with its squat towers built by the Germans, the terminal for all Turkey's Asian rail routes, and the **Selimiye Barracks** [n], a part of the military reforms of Selim III; this was the home of the Ottoman new model army the reformers hoped would replace the Janissaries—until the Janissaries ordered it disbanded. Florence Nightingale did her work during the Crimean War at the Selimiye hospital. The landing at **Harem,** near the barracks, is one of two places you may reach by ferries from Galata Bridge; **Üsküdar,** a large suburb a mile to the north may be reached from Kabataş. Under the Byzantines, Üsküdar was called Chrysopolis, the 'city of gold.'

On the ferry, you will pass **Leander's Tower,** a landmark in the Bosphorus since Byzantine times, with its lighthouse and customs house.

Three large and beautiful mosques decorate the open space around Üsküdar landing. Sinan built the **Mihrimah Camii** [o] (1547), which, like the other Mihrimah, was built in honour of Süleyman's favourite daughter. Standing opposite it, there is the eighteenth-century **Yeni Valide Camii** [p], built by Ahmet III, and, above it on the hills, another work of Sinan, the **Şemsi Paşa Camii** [q].

The Bosphorus

Even if you have only a little time in Istanbul, you will probably want to invest some of it on a trip up this lovely waterway. No industry or over-development has harmed the famous scenery of wooded hills, villages, and the wooden summer houses of the Ottoman era called *yalis*; without putting on airs, these shores are the most civilised corner, perhaps, in all Turkey. Roads follow both the European (*Rumeli*) and Asian (*Anadolu*) sides, but the best way to see the Bosphorus is by boat. Regular ferries from Galata Bridge traverse its length, most taking a zig-zag course up and down the straits and giving you the chance for a fine fish dinner in one of the villages before your return.

THE BOSPHORUS BRIDGE

Just as you leave the built-up areas of the city, you will pass the **Bosphorus Bridge,** a new symbol of Istanbul often seen on souvenirs and brochures these days. It's the fourth largest suspension bridge in the world, the longest in Europe, and the only one to link two continents. It was completed in time for the fiftieth anniversary of the Republic, and the Turks like to think of it as an emblem of the great progress they have made. Now they're planning a second bridge; the tolls have already paid for this one.

Two symbols of the bad old days are underneath the bridge: the 1854

Ortaköy Cami [r], on the European side, a mosque with Corinthian columns, looks even more like a '20s American movie-palace than the others of its ilk; on the Asian side Sultan Abdül Aziz found the money for yet another marble pile, the **Beylerbey Palace** [s].

Napoleon III's wife, the Empress Eugénie, spent a few weeks here in the 1860s, and she must have felt right at home. The Beylerbey's other famous occupant was Sultan Abdül Hamid, who was allowed to stay on here by the Young Turks after they deposed him. Abdül the Damned lived out his life here in a simple room with simple furniture; he brought none of his wives or servants with him—just his cat, the only one he trusted. On the hills above Beylerbey, Turkey's tallest structure, the TRT television tower, stands atop **Çamlica Hill,** a popular resort in the old days, with a wonderful prospect of the city and the straits. There are cafes and carriage rides, part of the recent rehabilitation and re-landscaping of the hill by the Automobile Club.

ARNAVUTKÖY AND THE RUMELI HISAR

Back on the European side, **Arnavutköy,** the 'Albanian village' is the prettiest town along the Bosphorus, with tall elegant nineteenth-century houses built right up to the water's edge. A little further on, the straits open up into **Bebek ('baby') Bay.** The little palace across the way, a cupcake compared to the over-frosted wedding cakes down the straits, is the **Küçüksu Palace** [t] built by Abdül Mecit. This is often called the Palace of the Sweet Waters of Asia, for the lovely stream that flows down from Çamlica. In Ottoman times, the rivers that led into the Golden Horn were called the 'Sweet Waters of Europe'.

Just after Bebek Bay, the straits close to their narrowest point, guarded by two Turkish castles, antedating the Conquest. Sultan Beyazit I built the **Anadolu Hisar** [u] in 1393 to choke off Constantinople's Black Sea trade. Across the straits, Mehmet tightened the grip with the **Rumeli Hisar** [v] in 1452. It's difficult to believe the latter could have had any military purpose; draped languidly over the slopes, with its neat crenellations and perfect round towers, the Rumeli Hisar is the most picturesque castle imaginable. Once it had wooden towers inside, but these have been cleared out and, instead of old cannons and dust, the castle is filled with flowers and trees, and also has an open-air theatre where plays and concerts are presented in the summer.

From Emirgân to the Kavaği

Emirgân [w], on the European side, was a garden-palace compound the Sultans used for captured or exiled potentates in their care. The grounds and pavilions have been restored—by the Automobile Club, of course—most notably, the lovely **Yellow Pavilion,** an outstanding example of the

Rumeli Hisar and the Bosphorus

Turkish talent for fairy-tale architecture. An annual Tulip Festival is held here in May. All the land west of this section of the Bosphorus is Istanbul's famous and beautiful suburban park **Belgrade Forest,** originally a hunting preserve of the Ottomans. The name comes from the Serbian prisoners-of-war that the Sultans settled here; they and their descendants formed a tight little community charged with the responsibility of keeping up Istanbul's aqueducts and reservoirs, until the paranoid Abdül Hamid had them expelled for fear they would poison the water supply.

The oldest surviving wooden *yali* can be seen at **Kanlica** on the Asian side, hanging gracefully out over the water. A few miles north, in the hills above Çubuklu you can see a very different kind of house, the **Hidiv Kasri,** an art nouveau palace of an exiled Khedive of Egypt, now restored with a restaurant and tea salon. From nearby Pasabahçe, you can get to **Polonezköy,** some eight kilometres to the east. This weekend resort, famous for food and scenery, has been, as its name implies, a thoroughly Polish village since 1842, when refugees from the freedom struggles against Russia settled here. The land was a present from the Sultan, in return for the Poles' services in the Crimean War. (Having a common enemy in the eighteenth and nineteenth centuries, the Poles and the Turks were quite close, and devotees of Polish culture will be interested in the **Adam Mickiewicz Museum** on Tatlibadem Sokak in Beyoğlu, the home in exile of Poland's greatest poet.)

Some lovely towns on the European shore are **Yeniköy,** where a small Greek church overlooks the waterfront, **Tarabya,** a quite ritzy corner of the Bosphorus with a yacht harbour, and **Sariyer,** where cafes and fishing boats crowd each other along the tree-lined waterfront. The last two towns the ferry visits, **Rumeli Kavaği** and **Anadolu Kavaği,** a pair of perfect book-ends on either side of the Bosphorus, quiet and pleasant, well beyond the bounds of Istanbul's suburbs. Beyond these, much of the land is given over to the military; it's very discreet and you'll never see them, but these straits are well guarded now, just as they always have been, as testified by several ruined fortifications, including the **Genoese Castle** [x] north of Anadolu Kavaği.

At the end of the straits, where the Symplegades, the clashing rocks of Greek mythology, were defeated by Jason and the Argonauts, all is quiet and still; two old lighthouses the Anadolu Fener, and the Rumeli Fener, wait to guide all ships into the channel.

THE PRINCES ISLANDS

There are nine of these in the Sea of Marmara, and the ferry from the Galata Bridge calls at the four largest, inhabited islands—**Kinali, Burgaz, Heybeli** and **Büyük Ada.** The first two are inhabited mainly by Armenians who commute to jobs in Istanbul, while the last two, especially Büyük Ada ('Big Island'), have long been favoured as summer retreats from the city, with their lovely pine groves, often dramatic cliffs dropping into a clean azure sea, lanes plied by horse-drawn carriages instead of cars, and colourful flower gardens.

Their name seems to derive, not from any son of the Sultan, but from the fact that from the earliest days of Byzantium up until the fifteenth century, they were a place of royal exile, as well as a popular spot for monasteries and, occasionally, pirates' nests. A few ruined churches and monastic buildings remain, but far more impressive, especially on Büyük Ada, are the grand old wooden summer houses, in all their pastel, 'gingerbread' Victorian-Gothic splendour. Another advantage of taking a trip out to the islands is the twilit return 'sailing to Byzantium', when the great domes and minarets of the Imperial mosques glow in the rosy dusk, creating one of the most rarefied and poetic city scapes in the world.

Getting Around

Many travellers take one look at Istanbul's medieval street plan on a map and surrender to despair, a feeling that is confirmed after the first attempt at reaching a destination on foot ends in utter bewilderment.

It isn't really so bad; as in most old cities, remember that the streets are laid out to make sense to your eyes, more than to be read on a map. After walking a while through old Istanbul, you'll learn to orient yourself to the major landmarks. Public transport in all forms, is surprisingly inexpensive.

BY BUS

You'll need tickets beforehand, and you buy books of them in any of the main centres; more conveniently, men in the street will sell tickets to you for a few pennies extra. Very soon, we've been given to understand, the IETT will publish a map of its routes, but until then, you're on your own. Start at one of the big stations, and ask at the ticket booth for the bus to your destination. The main bus stations are at Aksaray; Beyazit Square; Eminönü, near Sirkeci Station; Taksim Square; and on the Asian side, Harem, near Haydarpaşa Station. Tickets are approximately TL 50. Buses will usually be crowded.

BY TAXI

All the taxis have meters now, and you'll have no trouble finding one on any major street. Don't be surprised if the drivers seem to be going a little out of the way; they stick resolutely to the main thoroughfares to avoid traffic jams; again, they are quite inexpensive—and invaluable when you get hopelessly lost. If you're staying in a small hotel or in an out-of-the-way street, be sure to write the name down, as well as any nearby main streets or landmarks; the drivers often don't know the city as well as they might—especially when you try to pronounce your destination in Turkish.

DOLMUŞ

If you want to know which American cars of the last forty years were the best built, examine the dolmuş lines of Istanbul. At least two thirds will be '49 Chryslers, '55–56 Chevys or '51–57 Plymouths and Dodges. There are no Fords. The Dolmuş is a communal taxi, getting into one is easy; just wait near one of the red, white, and black dolmuş signs, see if the roof-sign of the car goes anywhere near your destination, and pile in. In many parts of the town, they're simpler to use than the buses, and equally inexpensive.

BY MINIBUS

These work much like the dolmuş, and operate mostly from the city walls, going down the main streets; few penetrate further in than Beyazit Square. Like the dolmuş they have destination signs. Don't mistake Topkapi Gate for Topkapi Palace.

BY BOAT

Ferries for all points depart either from the Galata Bridge, or the Kabataş landing near Dolmabahçe Palace. Cruises up the **Bosphorus** depart from the Stamboul side of the bridge, usually twice a day; you can get off where you please, or stop for lunch and catch the boat on the return trip, from any of its stops along the straits.

Ferry-boats to the Asian side depart every hour or so from Galata Bridge (from the last docks on the right, going towards Sirkeci Station), and from Kabataş for Üsküdar. Other boats for **Kadiköy-Haydarpaşa** station leave from the Beyoğlu side of the bridge.

For the **Princes' Islands,** several boats a day (more in the summer and at weekends) leave from both Galata and Kabataş landings, some are express, getting to Büyük Ada in about an hour; others call at all four islands and several Asian ports as well. Note that you only pay for the trip *to* the islands—the return fare is included in the price. From the dock to the left of the Galata Bridge on the Stamboul side, a boat leaves every half hour to go up the **Golden Horn** to Eyüp and beyond.

Other boats leave from the docks near Tophane Square for **Marmara Island** (5 hours) and **Avşa Island** (6 hours), in the Marmara, and for **Mudanya,** the port of Bursa; there are also boats from Kabataş to **Yalova,** across the Marmara. Ticket booths are clearly marked; in most cases you cannot buy tickets in advance. Don't expect to find timetables posted, or any sort of system; just go and ask.

Tourist Information

The government Tourist Ministry has offices in a pavilion on Sultanahmet Square (tel. 522 4903); in the Hilton compound in Taksim Square (tel. 140 6300); and occasionally at the Yeşilköy Airport (tel. 573 7399)

The **Turkish Automobile Club** has an office at 364 Şişli Meydani north of Taksim Square, and a big centre for motorists just outside Topkapi Gate, along the Londra Asfalti, the main road to Europe. In addition, if you have troubles you can tell them to the **tourist police** in the *Karakol* (police station) on Alemdar Caddesi, near the Topkapi Palace.

MAPS AND PUBLICATIONS

All the usual rules for Turkish cities apply here; there are no street signs, streets are known by different names to different people, and many people know nothing of the city outside their own neighbourhood. If you plan to do any detailed sightseeing, you'll want a good map; of the several available, the best are published by the **Turkish Automobile Club** (available at their offices) and by **Keskin Colour** (from hotels, newsstands, and shops in the tourist centres).

Unfortunately, there are no regular publications in English to tell you what's going on in the nightclubs and theatres, but an annual called *Spot on Istanbul*, with entertaining details on every aspect of life in the city, is available at many bookshops and airline offices. Though expensive, it's indispensable for anyone planning a long stay. English language bookshops with books about Turkey can be found along **Istiklâl Caddesi,** just north of the Tünel: *Haşet*, *Sander* and *ABC*.

Where to Stay

The subject is inexhaustible; besides the ones you'll find listed in the official tourist literature, there are literally hundreds of unclassified establishments.

MORE LUXURIOUS

For those who like their hotels modern, spotless, comfortable and international, there's the **Sheraton Oteli** (tel. 148 90 00) on Taksim Square, the tallest building in Istanbul, with a swimming pool, as well as television, air conditioning, refrigerators in every room, and a baby-sitting service; singles in season are 46 000 TL, doubles 58 000 TL. The **Hilton Oteli,** on Cumhuriyet Cad. (tel. 146 70 50) has the same facilities, as well as tennis courts, for 42 000 TL a single, 52 000 TL a double.

Far more convenient for the sights, and affording a lavish view over the Golden Horn, is the magnificent **Pera Palace** at Meşrutiyet Caddesi 98/100 (tel. 145 22 30). The Pera Palace is the city's most famous hotel, a great Edwardian pile that has changed little over the years, and has provided the setting for several novels about the city. Its bar is legendary, its restaurant excellent. Rates are 40 000 TL for a single with bath, 65 000 TL for a double. In the same area, is the only slightly less plush **Grand Hotel de Londres** (Büyük Londra) at Meşrutiyet Caddesi, Tepebaşi (tel. 145 06 70), with the same view and some of the luxury (though no restaurant), originally built as the home of a wealthy Italian family in the 1800s. Rates here are approximately 10 000 TL a single, and from 12 500 TL in low season, to a maximum of 18 000 TL in high for a double.

Another mansion recently turned hotel—this time a wooden Ottoman home—has been done up elegantly by the Auto Club. This, the **Yeşil Konak** (tel. 511 1150 and 528 67 64) is conveniently located between the Aya Sofia and the Blue Mosque, and has a quiet garden; rates are 25 000 TL for a single, 41 000 TL for a double. Some time soon, in the same spirit, the old Ottoman houses behind the Aya Sofia will be open as guesthouses for tourists.

REASONABLY PRICED

There are many other reasonably priced hotels in Stamboul, especially in the Aksaray and Laleli quarters; quiet Gençtürk Caddesi has a whole string of small hotels, like the **Hotel München** at no 55 (tel. 526 53 43) where every room has a private bath, and water is brought in to alleviate the common problem of low water pressure in the city. The friendly staff speak English (but not German). Singles are 5250 TL, doubles 7070 TL; Turkish breakfast available.

LESS EXPENSIVE AND YOUTH HOSTELS

In the same area, but less expensive is the **Hotel Klodfarer,** Klodfarer Caddesi 22, (tel. 528 48 50) with clean rooms and bath en suite; 3000 TL for a single, 4500 TL for a double. Istanbul's youth hostels are also in the same area: the **Yücel Hotel** at 6 Caferiye Sok, (tel. 522 45 01) complete with a Turkish bath for women; beds are around 500 TL. The larger IYHF **International youth hostel** is in Aksaray, at 63 Cerrahpaşa Caddesi, (tel. 543 00 08) open July–September; 700 TL for a bed.

OUTSIDE ISTANBUL

Outside Istanbul, the best beach hotel on the Bosphorus is the modern **Büyük Tarabya,** on Kefeliköy Caddesi in Tarabaya (tel. 162 10 00), with a sauna, restaurant, etc.; rates are 34 150 TL for a single, 47 000 TL for a double, both with bath.

Near the airport, on the beach at Yesilköy, is the **Çinar** at Fener Mevkii (tel. 573 29 10), another luxury hotel with refrigerators, TV, sauna, and baby-sitting service, with singles for 28 500 TL and doubles 40 000 TL. More charming, though, is the **Yeşilköy Pansiyon,** a nineteenth century villa, with a fine restaurant and promixity to the beaches.

Of the **Princes Islands,** only Büyuk Ada has any accommodation, and the best of these is the cosy **Villa Rifat** at Yilmaztürk Caddesi 80 (tel. 351 60 68), open May-September, its six rooms, all doubles with bath at 2250 TL.

Eating out

Eating in Istanbul is a pure delight, nor is it surprising that the great metropolis has attracted the best of the country's chefs; many places still serve old Turkish specialities, almost impossible to find elsewhere in the country. The old classic restaurants of Istanbul still offer a good introduction to the wonderful world of Turkish cuisine.

Konyali, on Ankara Caddesi 223 (with a branch in the Topkapi Saray) and **Pandelis,** above the Spice Market are excellent, but expensive: expect to pay 9000 TL for a meal. Less expensive but also very good is **Borsa,** Yali

Köşkü Caddesi 60–62, in Sirkeci: 7500 TL, approximately. Other good bets for delectable Turkish cuisine in Beyoğlu include **Haci Baba** at Istiklâl Caddesi 49: moderate, 7000 TL; **Arzu,** Meyve Sokat 18, near Cumhuriyet Caddesi: also moderate; and **Yuva,** Recep Pasa Caddesi 23, just off Taksim Square: inexpensive, at around 3000 TL.

Puddings and pastry dishes are old Turkish specialities. One shop that specialised in the former, the **Pudding Shop** at Divanyolu Caddesi 6, next to Aya Sofia, became in the 1960s the international rendezvous of young travellers in Istanbul and is still going strong; it's inexpensive (500–600 TL), has many other dishes besides puddings, and a rarity in Turkey, Nescafe. Other *Muhallebici*—pudding shops—are **Lalê,** Istiklâl Caddesi 71, and **Saray,** Istiklâl Caddesi 102 just a shade more expensive. *Börek* (filled pastry) is the speciality at **Harbiye,** Cumhuriyet Caddesi 265. Black Sea style pizza (*Karadeniz Peynirlisi*) is the speciality at **Şimşek Pide,** on Taksim Caddesi 8 (pizzas are around 500 TL). For kebabs, try **Çavuşoğlu,** at Şair Fitnat Sokak, 4/11, in Lâleli; **Bey,** Meşelik Sokak 5, Taksim; or **Murat,** at Ordu Caddesi 212, in Lâleli; the last two are quite moderately priced (around 1500 TL for a meal).

OTHER NATIONALITIES

French and Italian restaurants are quite popular, especially in Beyoğlu. For French, try **Motorest** on Dolmabahçe Caddesi 117 (8000 TL); for Italian, **Ristorante Italiano,** at Cumhuriyet Caddesi 6 (6000 TL); and for both, **Yekta,** at Vali Konaği Caddesi 39. '

One of the most famous eateries in Istanbul is Russian, **Rejans** (favourite of Atatürk's), at Olivo Çikmazi 15, Galatasaray (prices are reasonable—4000 TL).

For Chinese, try the **Green House China,** in the Hilton Hotel.

For the unusual, get yourself one of the four tables at the **Sadrazam Mahmudun Yeri,** at Iskele Caddesi (where an excellent meal is around 5000 TL); **Sütlüce,** with its famous pilaf served Ottoman style (2000–4000 TL) or, **Çimen,** at Kişla Caddesi 116, Gaziosmanpaşa, where you can get a whole lamb roasted on a spit (for a normal portion 3000 TL); trendy **Merih Şarap Mahzeni,** at Kuruçeşme Caddesi 25, in Arnavutköy, is a Byzantine wine cellar, with food and cheeses as well (expensive).

Outside town, there's always the enormous **Beyti** at Orman Sokat 93, near the airport with its heliport, three kitchens, and the much imitated *Beyti kebab* (but reasonably-priced, at around 5000 TL for a full meal).

On the **Asian side** the views of Istanbul are often as good as the food. A good choice for both are **Huzur,** at Iskele Caddesi 20, in Salacak (7000 TL); **Yeditepe,** at Nakkaştepe (Kuzguncuk) (9000 TL); and **Aşşrom II,** Büyük Çamlica Caddesi 28, Çamlica (5000–7000 TL).

On the Bosphorus, Abdullah, in Emirgân, is the most famous (8000–10 000 TL), and **Telli Baba,** at Telli Baba mevkii has the best views of the strait, as well as good fish (7000 TL).

On Büyük Ada in the Princes Islands, try **Milano,** on the waterfront, for its fish as well (5000–7000 TL).

Part V

THRACE

Troops during the Campaign in Gallipoli

Thrace, or European Turkey, has long held a special place in Turkish dreams and aspirations. The tribes out of the East called it Rumelia, the land of Rome that they had heard so much of and so ardently sought. Although it comprises only three per cent of Turkish territory, modern Turks, from Atatürk to the current government, pin their hopes on it being an especially magnetic chunk of real estate; they hope it is capable of pulling the rest of Turkey away from the insoluble squabbles of the Middle East into the Common Market and the democratic traditions of the west.

Historically, Thrace has been a battleground, the mainland route of conquerors bent on Europe or Asia. Xerxes came this way, and Alexander and the Romans, who went about their conquering more systematically, bisected it with a highway, the Via Egnatia (the modern Londra Asfalti) to speed their legions to and from the eastern marches. Many towns of Thrace's three provinces began life as Roman or Ottoman garrisons, and have known other armies as well, including Goths, Bulgars, Avars, Crusaders, Russians and Greeks. Battles that have changed history have taken

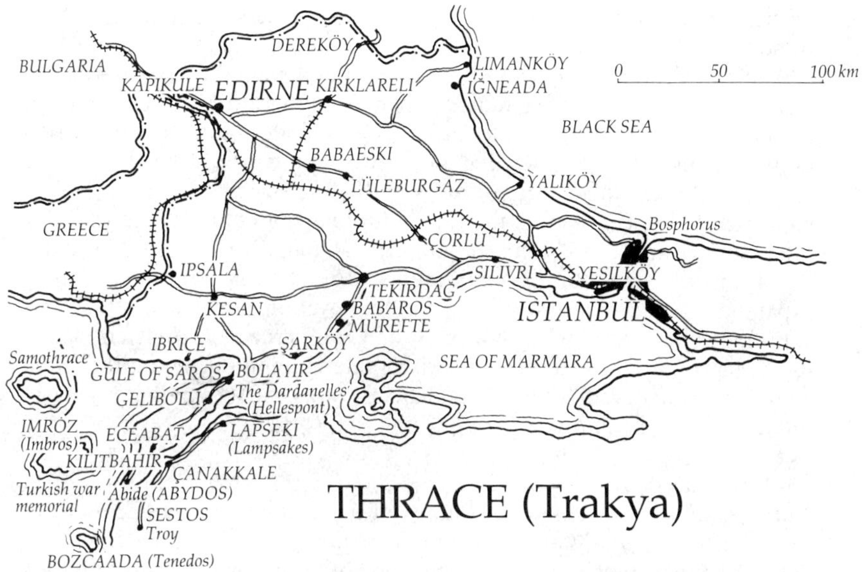

THRACE (Trakya)

place here, or off shore in the Dardanelles, from the days of Homer to World War I.

However, Thrace is a quiet, almost lonely place these days, with few monuments to show for the great events that have occurred on its soil. Most of the land is a rolling plain, emerald green in the spring, but hot and humid in the summer, and snow-blasted in the winter. For many visitors, its coasts are the main attraction; there are a few budding resorts on the Black Sea, and Marmara, as well as the congested Babylon of campsites and hotels, spawned by Istanbul immediately to its west.

Edirne

The one great exception is Thrace's largest town, **Edirne,** or Adrianople, close to both the Greek and Bulgarian frontiers. If you're driving from the north to Turkey, it's on the way; from Greece it's worth the detour from the main coastal route, for you won't find a better introduction to Turkey and the Islamic world. From Istanbul, it's a four-hour bus ride, and worth it, if you're at all interested in architecture—or greased wrestling, the one thing that keeps Edirne's juices flowing these days. Though the city once served as the Ottoman capital, like Bursa it has few modern industries to keep it growing and prosperous, and today looks more or less the same as it did a hundred years ago.

The Emperor Hadrian founded the town and named it after himself in AD 125. Almost exactly two hundred years later, his successor Constantine the Great fought a major battle nearby, a prelude to his capture of Byzantium; a thousand years after that Murat won it for the Ottomans. Since a capital of the Ottoman Empire in its early days was wherever the Sultan happened to be, Edirne was the capital for many of the following years, as the Ottomans waited for Constantinople to fall into their hands. If there was trouble in the east, the Sultan stayed in Bursa; if he was interested in expanding the boundaries of Rumelia, he stayed in Edirne. Although this shuttling about ended when Mehmet the Conqueror took Constantinople, the Sultans continued to bestow lavish Imperial monuments on their first European capital, until it reached the height of its beauty and importance in the late sixteenth century.

SELIMIYE MOSQUE

The crowning achievement of this age of building—itself set like a crown over Edirne—is the grand **Selimiye Mosque,** built by Mimar Sinan for Selim II. Sinan finished the mosque, which he personally considered his finest, in 1575, when he was over eighty years old. According to legend it has 999 windows and its dome is slightly larger than the Aya Sofia's; its four identical lofty minarets, each encircled with three carved balconies, were supposedly aligned to appear as a single one from the distance, to deceive enemy artillery. Unlike most mosques of its stature, the Selimiye is uncluttered with a large complex of religious foundations, and those it does have are all on one side, allowing impressive views of the mosque itself from three sides.

But it was in the interior that Sinan worked his best magic. The great dome hovers on eight massive piers, while on floor level the eye is drawn towards the exquisitely carved marble mimber and mihrab, the latter set back in an apse with walls adorned by Iznik tiles. An even lovelier display of tiles may be seen in the **Imperial loge;** if you weren't one of the lucky few to get into the harem of the Topkapi Saray, here's a chance to see what you missed: a masterpiece of Iznik tilework. Another feature worth noting is the loge's mihrab, perhaps the only one in Turkey with a window opening towards Mecca.

The medrese, in typical cloister style, now houses Edirne's **Museum of Turkish and Islamic Art** with items from the local *tekke* of whirling dervishes, calligraphy and charming photographs of great wrestlers from Edirne's past. A new **Archaeological and Ethnographic Museum,** with an excellent collection of costumes, kilims and carpet saddle bags, artifacts from ancient Trakya (Thrace) and ancient coins, is behind the Selimiye. The arcade of shops along the west flank of the mosque, the **Kavaflar Arasta** was built exclusively for Edirne's cobblers.

OTHER MOSQUES

Just below the Selimiye, off central **Cumhuriyet Meydani,** are two other Imperial mosques, offering an excellent opportunity to observe the development of the Classical Ottoman style. The **Eski Cami,** a plain, nine-domed square, was begun in 1402 by the three sons of Yildirim Beyazit after their father had met both Tamerlane and his Maker; during the next 11 years, as the mosque was erected, the three brothers fought for control of the Empire. The winner, and sole survivor, Mehmet I, had the honour of dedicating the mosque. One distinct feature of the Eski Cami are the great Arabic letters painted on the outer walls, giving the mosque a curiously primitive appearance.

The other mosque, the **Üç Şerefeli Cami,** was built in 1447 by Murat II; its name 'three balconies' derives from one of its minarets so adorned, which at 218 feet was the tallest the Ottomans ever built—until Sinan made the four minarets at the Selimiye ten feet higher. Üç Şerefeli, the last great imperial mosque, built prior to the capture of Constantinople, is covered with one large central dome and a clutch of smaller domes; inside, the architect achieved a surprising airiness. Although its other foundations are derelict, the mosque's **Sokurlu Hamam,** built by Sinan in the fifteenth century and one of Turkey's most elegant, has been restored and serves as a bath today. Sinan's finely restored **Rüstem Paşa Caravanserai** adjoining the Eski Cami, until recently also served its original function as a hotel; there are now plans to convert it into a municipal art gallery.

OTHER MONUMENTS

In the Cumhuriyet Meydani Atatürk has to share space with a peculiar statue of two wrestlers, each of whom has two faces, so the work has no 'back'. Also here are the two bazaars, the **Bedesten** and Sinan's **Ali Paşa Çarşi.** They are fun to visit, although their wares are mainly of the domestic variety for local consumption.

Besides these, Edirne contains literally hundreds of other Ottoman monuments and structures in its cobbled lanes. Especially interesting (and especially in danger of collapsing) are the great wooden Ottoman houses, typically unpainted, but adorned with folk motifs carved on the gables and balconies. Edirne is the only place where you see many of these houses outside Istanbul; a couple have been converted into rather shoddy pensions, in the back streets behind the Ali Paşa bazaar. When built, however, each had separate quarters for the men and the women.

Several other Imperial mosques lie on the outskirts of Edirne, mostly along the banks of the **Tunca,** a tributary of the Meriç (the Greek Ebros) that forms the border between Greece and Turkey. One, however, the **Muradiye** is a short walk from the Selimiye, up the Caddesi Mimar Sinan. Murat II founded the mosque in 1435 for the Mevlevi dervishes and decorated it with some fine Iznik tiles. Further north, a bridge built by Sinan crosses the Tunca for an islet called **Sarayiçi,** after the Edirne Sarayi, or Sultan's palace that once stood there. Nothing now remains.

Outskirts of Edirne

Sarayiçi today is the site of Edirne's annual **Greased Wrestling Tournament,** which takes place in the middle of June with great enthusiasm and festivities. The Turks call the tournament *Kirkpinar* ('forty springs'); according to tradition, the bouts began in the fourteenth century, when Suleyman Paşa, son of the second Ottoman Sultan, Orhan Gazi, brought his forty heroes to campaign in Europe. In between battles, they amused themselves by wrestling. Two, it seems, were wrestled to death and buried; by their tomb a spring appeared, which became known as the 'spring of the forty'.

The Kirkpinar tournament, which attracts thousands of spectators, begins with the contestants, dressed in their leather breeches, or *kispet,* oiling their skin with olive oil. Next the announcer or *cazgir* leads a prayer and introduces the pairs of wrestlers; part of the Turks' enjoyment of the matches is hearing the cazgir recite each wrestler's claim to fame and his best tricks. The actual bouts, which are freestyle, last only between three and five minutes, accompanied by horns and drums. Wrestlers from all over Turkey attend the event, and compete in four categories, classed by age and prowess. A grand champion (*Baş Pehlivan*) who retains the title for three years straight, is awarded the highest honour, the Golden Belt. One who won it around the turn of the century, *Koca Yusuf* ('Enormous Joe'), has become a legend in Edirne: he went on to challenge and defeat the greatest champions of Europe and the US, but was killed on his return voyage from America to Turkey when his ship sank, finally, as the Turks sigh, 'beaten by his own bad luck'.

MOSQUE OF BEYAZIT

Downstream of Sarayiçi, on the far bank of the Tunca, stands the **Mosque of Beyazit II,** (1484). Of all the Imperial mosques in Edirne, this has the greatest number of religious foundations attached to it, including a hospital and *Timarhane,* an insane asylum, both considered among the most progressive and well equipped of their day. The complex also included a medical school, two hospices, and baths. The six-arched **Beyazit Bridge,** built at the same time as the complex, connects it to Edirne. Several other fine Ottoman bridges span the Tunca and Meriç; one however, originally dates from the Byzantines, the **Gazimihal bridge,** on the highway to Bulgaria. Next to it is a mosque of the same name, built in 1421 by a Greek who converted to Islam. North of here, in an unmarked battlefield, Visigoth horsemen devasted Roman infantry in 378, the first major gain by Germanic tribes in the doomed Roman Empire.

THRACIAN VILLAGES

The Yildiz Mountains mark the boundary between Bulgaria and Turkey; local beauty spots in the area are at the frontier post of **Dereköy,** and at the Black Sea fishing village of **Iğneada** which are surrounded by forest scenery. Inland, each of a triangle of small towns in central Thrace has its Ottoman ornament; **Kirklareli** with its 1407 Hizir Bey Cami and old hamam; **Babaeski** with its Cedit Ali Paşa Mosque, built by Sinan; and **Lüleburgaz,** ancient Arcadiopolis, with another of Sinan's works, the **Mehmet Paşa Mosque** and its large collection of religious foundations, including baths and a soup kitchen.

Marmara Coast

Tekirdağ, ancient Bisanthe, is the largest town on Thrace's Marmara coast, and one with aspirations to becoming a resort, with nearby beaches at Kumbağ and Değirmenalti. Although mostly modern, Tekirdağ is spread attractively over the hills, and has two works by Sinan: the Covered Bazaar and **Rüstem Paşa Mosque.** On the seaside promenade stands one of the best Atatürk statues, depicting the father of his country, with his famous chalkboard and pointer, teaching two earnest citizens their vowels. A mile to the west of here, lived the Hungarian patriot, Prince Ferenc II Rakoczy, who spent a career leading his countrymen against the Hapsburgs in the Hungarian War of Independence; in 1717, the Ottomans granted him political asylum in Tekirdağ, where he lived until his death in 1735. The song Rakoczy's troops sang in battle, now known as the Rakoczy March, has roused Hungarian patriotism ever since; once, when Liszt played it as encore to a recital, it caused a riot. In 1932 the Hungarian government made the house into the **Rakoczy Museum,** containing Rakoczy's flag, documents, Hungarian weapons, and paintings from the era.

East of Tekirdağ there's a beach at **Marmara Ereğli;** to the west, the road to the Gelibolu peninsula passes through vineyards to other beaches at **Barbaros Mürefte** and **Şarköy.** On the narrowest neck of the peninsula, **Bolayir** overlooks both the Dardanelles and the Saros Gulf; here Süleyman Paşa, son of Orhan Gazi, and leader of the forty heroes who captured Gelibolu fortress in 1354—the Ottomans' first handful of Rumelia—is buried in a *türbe* at one end of the village. Next to him, is the grave of the nineteenth-century poet Namik Kemal, a native of Tekirdağ and leader of the movement to reform the Ottoman Empire at the end of the nineteenth century.

DARDANELLES

Gelibolu, the Turkish name for Gallipoli, is a pleasant fishing village, whose **Castle** has long guarded this entrance into the straits; the walls you see today date from the fourteenth century, when the Ottomans captured the town. One of the two Dardanelles ferries crosses here, to **Lapeski.** If you're driving, the road to Çanakkale along the Asian shore is more pleasant, but the peninsula route has more tales to tell: from Protosilaus, the first casualty of the Trojan war, to battles in the Crimean war, the First World War, and the Turkish War of Independence. Some nine miles south of Gelibolu, at the mouth of the stream Aegospotamos (modern **Ince Liman**), Lysander and his Spartans clobbered the Athenian fleet in 405 BC, in the decisive final battle of the Peloponnesian War.

A little further south stood **Sestos,** across the strait from ancient **Abydos.** Nothing remains of either of these but stories. Here in 480 BC, Xerxes' army, marching to invade Greece, crossed the strait on a bridge of boats while the Persian King of Kings himself watched from the heights of Abydos, sitting on the marble throne he had had carted along with him. Here lived the famous lovers, Hero, a priestess at Sestos, and Leander, a resident of Abydos; he would swim the strait every night to see his love, guided by her lamp. One night, however, a storm blew the lamp out, and Leander was lost and drowned; when his body was discovered the next morning, Hero flung herself into the sea and drowned herself, too. Romantic-minded travellers can make the swim as well, taking care to avoid the many steamers that ply the strait; Byron did it in 1810.

TIP OF PENINSULA

The car ferry crossing to Çanakkale departs from **Eceabat,** near a village called **Kilitbahir,** 'Sea Lock', located where the Dardanelles are at their narrowest and most defensible. The castle on the shore was constructed by Mehmet the Conqueror to cut off Constantinople before he besieged the capital, and here the Allies suffered their first setback at the hands of the Turks in the Gallipoli Campaign. From Eceabat to **Abide** at the very tip of the peninsula, the land is dotted with British, Commonwealth, and Turkish cemeteries and memorials erected by the combatants of the bitter World War I battle. The scenery is pleasant, and the chances are you'll have it mainly to yourself; but it's hard to avoid melancholy. Over a hundred-thousand young men and the hearts of those who loved them lie buried in this thin pine-clad strip of land.

GETTING AROUND

By Car: Edirne is linked to Istanbul by Highway E5, better known as the Londra Asfalti, a name that sends chills down the backs of old travellers, but really isn't bad at all until you get to the environs of Istanbul.

By Bus: Buses travel the route eight times a day (taking 3½ hours). Buses from Istanbul and Edirne go to Tekirdağ, and there is also a frequent service to Çanakkale via the Eceabat ferry.

By Train: You can also take the train to Istanbul, the last leg of the old Orient Express, which stops at Edirne, between Kapikule (on the Bulgarian frontier) and Istanbul, but it takes much longer and runs less frequently than the bus.

By Ferry: The two car ferries, Eceabat–Çanakkale and Gelibolu–Lapseki cross the Dardanelles every two hours, until midnight.

Both the train station to the south and the bus station to the east of Edirne are too far to walk with luggage, and you may want to take a taxi or dolmuş into the centre. Edirne has Bulgarian and Greek consulates to help with any border difficulties.

TOURIST INFORMATION

Talatpaşa Cad., near the square, Edirne, tel. (1811) 1490 5260. At Kapikule, on the Bulgarian frontier, tel. (1818) 10 19. At Ipsala, on the Greek border; at Tekirdağ, tel. (1861) 2083, near the Atatürk statue. In Kirklareli, Belediye Cad., Kizilay Işhani, tel. (1871) 16 62.

WHERE TO STAY

Edirne has a number of nondescript hotels and two on Talât Paşa Caddesi that are a cut above: the **Kervan Oteli** (H2), at no. 134 [tel. (1811) 1355–1167] with comfortable singles for 3000 TL, doubles for 4000 TL, and **Sultan Oteli** (H4), [tel. (1811) 1372–2156] where a single with bath is 5800 TL, a double 7500 TL. Both are open all year.

In Tekirdağ the new and modern **Yat Oteli** (H4), [tel. (1861) 1054–1746] has sea views: singles as low as 3800 TL without bath; doubles with bath 7500 TL.

Kumbağ beach to the east, has a number of pensions and motels, including the **Miltur Turistik** (M1), [tel. (1861) 2–101] open April to October, with swimming pool, tennis courts and other recreational offerings: a single here is 6500 TL, a double 9000 TL, both considerably reduced in the off-season. On the Gallipoli peninsula there is moderately-priced accommodation near the ferries.

There are three campsites near Edirne and one near Ipsala.

EATING OUT

In Edirne the restaurants are mostly simple, inexpensive lokantas; a good one is **Meriç,** on Karaağaç, where you'll pay about 2500 TL for a meal.

In Tekirdağ, try the spacious **Sahil Dörtler** near the waterfront, across from the tourist office, with fish and meat specialities averaging around 3000 TL.

Part VI

THE NORTH AEGEAN COAST: TROY TO IZMIR

The model of the Trojan Horse in Troy

After the great city of Istanbul, Turkey's Aegean coast has long been the country's main attraction, originally for scholars and philhellenes who came to stroll through the ruins of cities renowned in antiquity, and nowadays, for others who combine a tour of the archaeological sites with a seaside holiday. The climate is pleasant and Mediterranean, tempered by the sea in the summer and winter; olives and vineyards cover the fertile valleys and coastal plains. Mountains are never far away, nor are beaches, some in the throes of becoming major resorts, others quite deserted. Of all Turkey's regions, the Aegean coast has the best hotels and more sprout up every year.

Troy

From the time of Alexander the Great, many travellers have come expressly to see **Troy**. No place is so highly charged in the Western imagination; for two and a half millennia it has intrigued, inspired and become a metaphor.

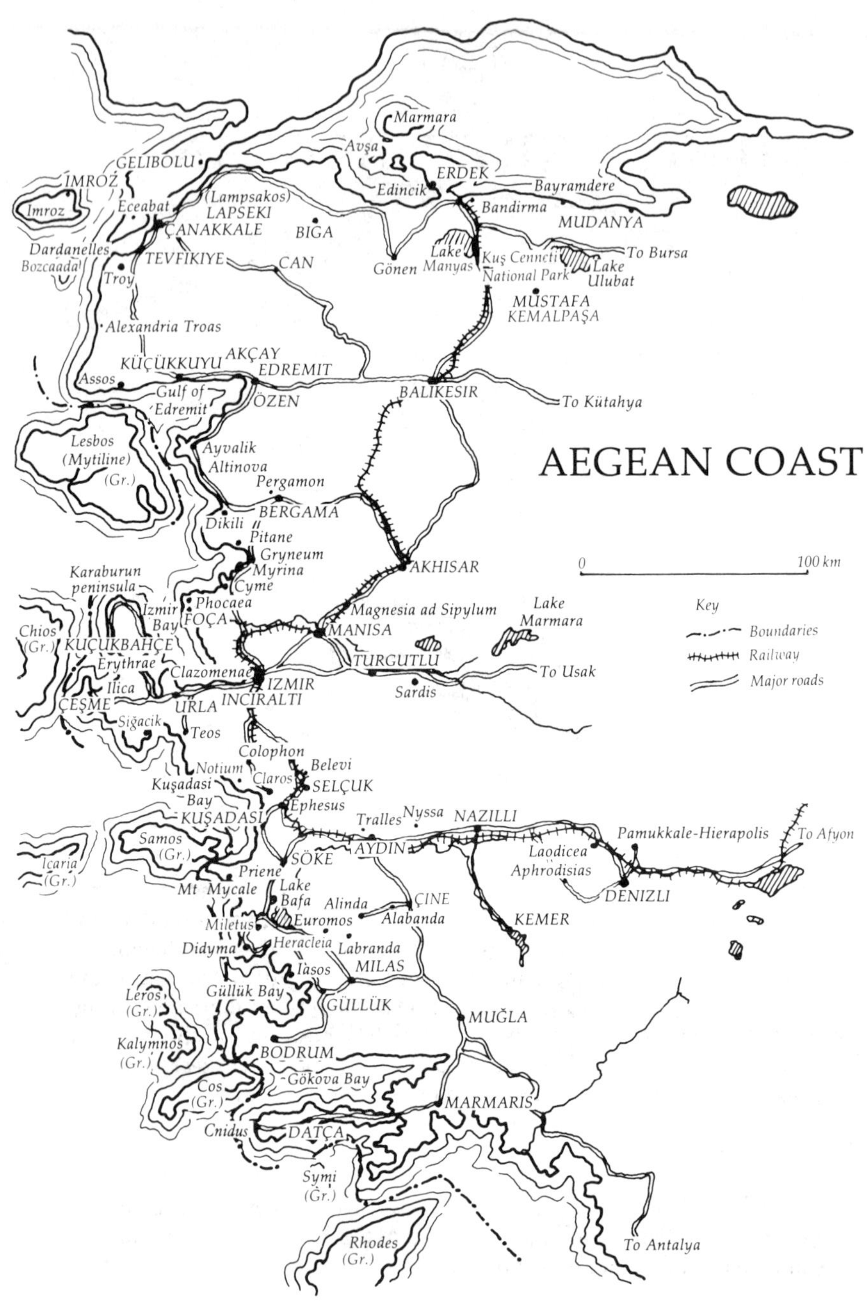
AEGEAN COAST
0
100 km
Key
Boundaries
Railway
Major roads
Marmara
Avşa
ERDEK
Edincik
Bayramdere
Bandirma
MUDANYA
GELIBOLU
IMROZ
Imroz
Eceabat
(Lampsakos)
LAPSEKI
ÇANAKKALE
BIGA
Dardanelles
Bozcaada
TEVFIKIYE
CAN
Gönen
Lake Manyas
Kuş Cenneti National Park
Lake Ulubat
To Bursa
Troy
MUSTAFA KEMALPAŞA
Alexandria Troas
AKÇAY
KÜÇÜKKUYU
EDREMIT
Assos
Gulf of Edremit
ÖZEN
BALIKESIR
To Kütahya
Lesbos (Mytiline) (Gr.)
Ayvalik
Altinova
Pergamon
BERGAMA
Dikili
Pitane
Gryneum
Myrina
Cyme
AKHISAR
Karaburun peninsula
Izmir Bay
Phocaea
FOÇA
Magnesia ad Sipylum
Lake Marmara
Chios (Gr.)
KUÇUKBAHÇE
MANISA
Erythrae
TURGUTLU
Clazomenae
IZMIR
To Usak
Ilica
Sardis
ÇEŞME
URLA
INCIRALTI
Siğacik
Teos
Colophon
Belevi
Notium
Claros
SELÇUK
Kuşadasi Bay
Ephesus
KUŞADASI
Tralles
Nyssa
NAZILLI
Pamukkale-Hierapolis
To Afyon
Samos (Gr.)
AYDIN
Laodicea
Icaria (Gr.)
SÖKE
Priene
Aphrodisias
Mt Mycale
Lake Bafa
ÇINE
DENIZLI
Alinda
Miletus
Euromos
Alabanda
KEMER
Heracleia
Didyma
Labranda
Iasos
MILAS
Leros (Gr.)
Güllük Bay
GÜLLÜK
MUĞLA
Kalymnos (Gr.)
BODRUM
Gökova Bay
Cos (Gr.)
MARMARIS
Cnidus
DATÇA
Symi (Gr.)
To Antalya
Rhodes (Gr.)

The tale of the Trojan War—the wrath of Achilles, the beauty of Helen, the death of Hector, the ploy of the wooden horse and the sack of the high walled city, the misfortunes that dogged the victors on their journeys home—all are stuff our culture was born of. Homer's *Iliad* and *Odyssey*, though they describe only two events in a great cycle of stories are the first if not the best works of Western literature. For the ancient Greeks, the *Iliad*'s account of the Olympian gods was the source of religious beliefs and many agree with Herodotus who looked on the Trojan War as the root, not least a mirror, of all later antagonisms between East and West.

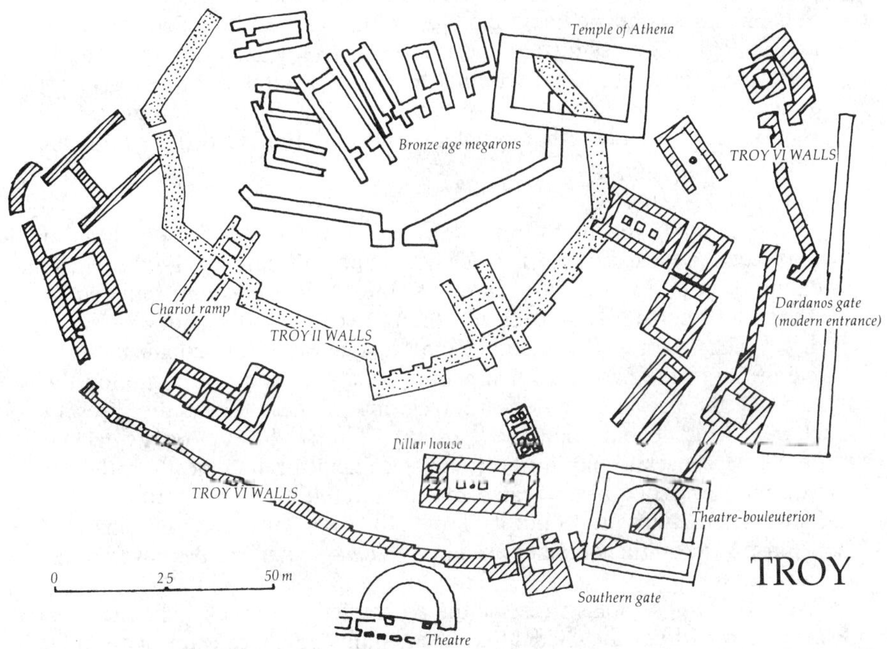

Few ancients doubted the veracity of the story of Troy and the war; Alexander was said to have actually exchanged some of his own armour for weapons from the Trojan War still hanging in Athena's temple. But by the sixth century AD the city was abandoned, its port silted up, the Anatolian dust thickening over it until the physical Troy vanished from all memory. Outwardly the site resembled a hill, which the Turks called Hisarlik, and travellers and scholars in later years argued over exactly where the city might have stood, if indeed it ever really existed. Byron was one of many who visited the Troad (the region around Troy), but one of very few who came away believing in it. In *Don Juan* he wrote

> ... I've stood upon Achilles' tomb,
> And heard Troy doubted; time will doubt of Rome.

Another believer was Heinrich Schliemann, a merchant who made a fortune from the California Gold Rush and the American Civil War. In 1868, forty-six years old and tired of his business career, he came to the Troad, where he met an Englishman named Frank Calvert, who had dug a trench in Hisarlik and showed Schliemann his finds: part of a Classical temple, and deeper down, signs of older civilisations, layered one on top of the other. Schliemann was hooked, and the former businessman became an amateur archaeologist, one destined to unearth not only Troy, but also Mycenae and Tiryns in a series of spectacular finds that electrified the world. Subsequent archaeologists, Schliemann's assistant Dörpfeld and the American Carl Blegen, have found further proof that Hisarlik is indeed the site of the ancient city of Troy.

RECENT THEORIES

As Calvert had brilliantly surmised, Schliemann found layer upon layer of civilisation in the excavations, which he numbered from Troy I—the oldest, dating back to 3600 BC—to Troy IX, the Hellenistic Ilion, founded by Alexander's general Lysimachus. Although Schliemann's main aim was to discover the Troy of Priam and Hector, he uncovered a fascinating chronicle of life in the past, in which people built, over and over again, on the ruins of the previous settlement. Was one of these Troys the Troy of Homer? Most scholars date the War to c. 1250 BC, just before the decline of the Mycenaean empire; Troy VII(a) coincides rather neatly with that date, and evidence has revealed that it suffered a terrible conflagration. However, the city preceding it, Troy VI(h), was far more imposing and better fits the epithets Homer used in the *Iliad*—but it was destroyed by an earthquake.

Turkish archaeologists resolve the contradiction by seeing the magnificent Troy VI(h) as the citadel that Agamemnon's Achaeans unsuccessfully besieged for ten years; rebuilt shoddily after the earthquake, it was then easily captured. The Wooden Horse, it follows, was an offering by the Achaeans to Poseidon, the sea god and earth-shaker, whose assistance was crucial in their sack of Troy. Others believe the *Iliad*, composed some 500 years after the traditional date of the war, recalls not one particular event but several Mycenaean raids on the Anatolian coast; or perhaps even recalls the last great twilight expedition, recited for latter-day kings by their bards to evoke the good old days.

In any event, no proof has ever been discovered in Troy that the Trojan

War took place, although many recent discoveries, especially in Miletus, show that the Mycenaean Greeks were in Asia Minor as early as the fifteenth century BC; in 1984 some of their tombs were discovered on an ancient beach at Besike Bay, one of the possible sites of Troy's long vanished harbour.

But what has kept the debates on the Trojan War in the headlines since Schliemann's discovery is the finding of references to Troy in the dead languages of Anatolia. In the 1920s, scholars read about the Ahhiyawans—probably the Achaeans—when translating the tablets from the Hittite archives at Boğazköy, dating to the 15th century BC. The archives also refer to a place called Wilusa, believed to be Homer's sacred Ilios, his other name for Troy. Then, in 1984, some very suggestive evidence turned up in Luvian—an ancient Indo-European language—possibly the language of the Trojans, referring to 'steep Wilusa' and men named Priya-muwas (Priam ?) and Paris. If you add the fact that some lines of the *Iliad* have been shown to be older than the traditional date of the Trojan War (1250 BC), the problem becomes even more complicated. Recent scholarly symposiums in England and America and Michael Wood's excellent BBC series on Troy have heightened interest in the question: Did the Trojan War take place as Homer recounts?

THE SITE

The Trojan horse is certainly still there or at least its modern Turkish descendant. It's the first thing you see at the site and the only thing most tourists take pictures of. For, in all honesty, the site itself is bewildering, 'a ruin of a ruin' as some call it, a victim of nineteenth century archaeology. The University of Cincinnati, the most recent archaeological team to work the site determined that Schliemann's original nine layers contained some 46 substrata. What you see as you walk through the excavations are fragments from each of the Troys. Most impressive, though, are the tall, finely built Mycenaean walls of Troy VI, among the most beautiful of the ancient world. They fit the Homeric descriptions of 'beetling' and 'steep', and at one point in the *Iliad* (Book XVI) Homer refers to their most unusual feature—angles or offsets that divide the wall into several sections. Here also are the foundations of a mighty bastion, perhaps Homer's 'great tower of Ilios'. Yet splendid as these walls still are, they are not of any great extent, this eminence was the citadel of Troy, not the city. The South Gate (Homer's Scaean gate?), facing the plain was the most important; the so-called **Pillar House** above it is the most popular candidate for Priam's Palace.

Near the entrance you can walk up to a section of the old Hisarlik mound, giving a view that evokes Homer perhaps even better than the old stones; for there, on a clear day is Mt Ida to the southeast, from which Zeus watched the war; to the west, on a **very** clear day you make out Mt Fingazi (Moon Mountain) on the island of Samothrace, where Poseidon sat. In the plain below wanders the Scamander River, whose god tried to drown Achilles for turning the water red with the blood of the Trojans. The two mounds near the river's mouth at Sigeion Point are by tradition the tombs of Achilles and his friend Patroclus, whose death at the hand of Hector finally roused Achilles from his sulking wrath to return to the battlefield. On most days, you are also aware of another Homeric epithet—'windy'. Much speculation has gone into determining the location of Troy's harbour, and where the 'beaked ships' of the Achaeans were beached for the duration of the war. Certainly much of what is dry land now was once a shallow bay or flood plain and marsh, if the Argives had to commute to the battlefield every day from any contemporary harbour, they would hardly have had time to fight.

THE CHARIOT RAMP

The path through the excavations leads past the ruins of the temple of Athena, last rebuilt by the Romans, to the great flagged chariot ramp. It was near here that Schliemann unearthed the controversial 'Jewels of Helen', the one really splendid treasure found on the site. In Schliemann's day the jewellery convinced many doubters that he had indeed discovered the Troy of Homer. (He couldn't resist smuggling them out of Turkey to adorn his wife at Athenian social gatherings!) Finally he gave the jewellery to the Berlin Museum, where it disappeared in 1945, by all accounts, pillaged by Soviet occupation forces. Both the 'Jewels of Helen' and the chariot ramp, however, date back to Troy II (2600–2300 BC), which, though a glorious city in its day, pre-dates the commonly accepted date of the Trojan war by a thousand years.

THE ROMANS

The other prominent remains belong to Troy VIII, the Greek Ilion (700–300 BC), and Troy IX (300 BC to fourth century AD), respectively, the Hellenistic and the Roman New Ilium. One can see a partially restored shrine, Roman theatre and bouleuterion. Neither of these cities were very large, though as the successors of Troy they enjoyed a certain renown. Julius Caesar like many modern visitors, was disappointed by the meagre ruins; Emperor Julian the Apostate was delighted to find that Christianity in AD 354 had not yet done away with sacrifices on Achilles' tomb. Yet it was the voice of the East that has had the last word. After conquering Constantinople, Mehmet II came to Troy and declared: 'It is to me that Allah has given to avenge this city and its people ... Indeed it was the Greeks who before devastated this city, and it is their descendants who after so many years have paid me the debt which their boundless pride had contracted—and often afterwards—towards us, the peoples of Asia.'

Around Troy

Troy, or *Truva* as the Turks call it, is 27 kilometres from **Çanakkale,** which most visitors use as a base for visiting the excavations. On the way you can stop at **Tevfikiye,** the only oasis of tackiness Troy has produced, with its 'House of Schliemann' and trinket shops; actually, the whole village was built of materials quarried from Schliemann's dig. There is a small museum on the site of Troy, and a new **museum** at Çanakkale that's more interesting, with its finds from the Dardanos Tumulus. This, dating from the fourth century BC was discovered 10 kilometres south of Çanakkale in 1959 and produced golden diadems, votive statuary, and the remains of a wooden harp.

Çanakkale

Çanakkale, at one of the Dardanelles' ferry crossings, is a pleasant provincial capital. Its name in Turkish means 'saucer castle'; the castle, one of several built by Mehmet the Conqueror to hem in Constantinople, still guards the Hellespont, and contains not only soldiers but a small **Soldiers' Museum**. There's a more interesting one across the strait in the giant pi-shaped **Turkish War Memorial,** dedicated to soldiers killed in Gallipoli and the civil war—displays range from buttons to jawbones. 'Saucer' recalls the town's old ceramics industry, which, though now defunct once produced florid Turkish art nouveau. Çanakkale was once a bustling international town, and signs of past grandeur still exist here and there, especially along the seaside promenade.

GETTING AROUND

Çanakkale is connected by bus to Istanbul, Bursa, Izmir, and Edirne; the ferryboat crosses the Dardanelles from Eceabat hourly between 6 am and midnight. The crossing takes 25 minutes and is ridiculously cheap. You can also cross via motor dolmuş from Kilitbahir. From Çanakkale's *otogar* frequent minibuses go to Troy and the neighbouring villages.

TOURIST INFORMATION

Iskele Meydan 67, by the port, tel. (1961) 1187.

WHERE TO STAY

In Çanakkale the most comfortable hotel is the **Truva,** tel. (1961) 1024, on the waterfront, with rates at 3500 TL for a single, 5050 TL a double, with bath. Near the clock tower there's the less expensive **Oteli Konak,** tel. (1961) 1150, with a private shower for 2700 TL, double for 3500 TL. If you're driving, you can get a good deal at the **Ida-Tur Moteli,** tel. (1961)

56–106, by the beach and with a swimming pool in nearby Küçükkuyu. Open all year, rates are 3000 TL for a single, 4000 for a double.

EATING OUT

There are a number of good fish restaurants near the castle. For both a good meal and a view, eat up at the **Yalova Liman** with its terrace (5000–7000 TL). Cheaper restaurants are scattered through Çanakkale.

South West Marmara Coast

Although the scenery along the south shore of the **Sea of Marmara** is quite beautiful and blessed with a number of beaches, it doesn't figure on many foreign visitors' itineraries; most of its ancient sites have little to show for themselves today; nothing remains of ancient Abydos or **Lampsakas** (modern **Lapseki,** the second ferry crossing), though to the east two famous battles of antiquity occurred: Alexander's first victory in Asia, in 334 BC over the Persians at the mouth of the river Granicus, and further east at **Edincik** (ancient Cyzicus), Alcibiades and the Athenians defeated the Spartans in the Peloponnesian War.

Erdek, with its fine scenery and beaches is the largest of the area's resorts, and is a good base for visiting **Kuş Cenneti** (Bird Paradise) **National Park,** a sanctuary for migratory waterfowl, especially pelicans, grey and white herons, and cormorants, who come to nest along the willow-shaded banks of Lake Manyas between February and October, then fly south to India and Africa in the winter. In all, 179 different species of birds have been seen in the sanctuary. Just west of here, at **Gönen** other airborne creatures—namely, tens of thousands of bats—have taken up residence in the Dereköy Caves. Gönen also has one of Turkeys major thermal spas for rheumatism.

Another beach, one of the few accessible by paved road, is north of Karacabey, at **Bayramdere. Mudanya,** a large port town, saw the signing of the armistice ending the Turkish war of independence in 1922.

The two inhabited islands in the Marmara—**Marmara** and **Avsa islands**—both have places to swim and pine groves, and are quiet resorts in the summer months. Less developed for tourism are the Aegean islands—mountainous **Imroz** (Homer's Imbros) and flat **Bozcaada** (ancient Tenedos). According to epic tradition, the Achaeans had a base on Tenedos; here they hid their ships, waiting for Odysseus to emerge from the belly of the wooden horse and signal that the sleeping Troy was theirs for the taking. Up until the fifteenth century Greeks living on the island would act as tour guides for foreigners seeking Troy. A fifth of the residents of Imroz are of Greek descent, and coexist on good terms with their fellow islanders.

GETTING AROUND

Towns on the south Marmara shore are easiest reached by bus between Bursa and Çanakkale. From Erdek minibuses serve the surrounding towns and beaches. Avsa and Marmara islands are served by boat from Istanbul, daily in the summer, and once a week in the winter. Çanakkale is the port for Imroz, and boats depart daily. For Bozcaada, boats depart from Odun Iskelesi on the mainland opposite.

TOURIST INFORMATION

Hükümet Caddesi 6/B, Erdek, tel. (1989) 113.

WHERE TO STAY

In Erdek, the **Gül Plaj Moteli** (M2) on Kumlu Yali Cad. 86, tel. (1989) 1053, is clean and on the beach, with singles for 4400 TL and doubles 5500 TL, with private bath (open June–September). There are many other hotels and pensions, though hardly any are open all year. Near the thermal baths in Gönen hotels are open all year, like the **Yildiz Oteli** (H2) on Banyolar Cad., tel. (1985) 1840–3, where in addition to the baths there's a sauna, Turkish hamam, and a pool. Tariffs are 6400 TL a single, 9000 TL a double. Marmara has one official hotel, the **Mermer Oteli,** tel. 21, open from July to August, at 2200 TL a single, 2600 for a double with bath, as does Avsa, with the **Çinar Oteli** tel. (1452) 360, open May–October, with refrigerator in each room; rates are 3500 TL a single, 4800 a double. Both islands have several unlisted pensions as well. On Imroz and Bozcaada, there are rooms to let in private houses.

EATING OUT

There are many small lokantas along the coast and on the islands, though many close in the winter. In Erdek, the **Tanova Lokatasi** serves good meat and fish dishes, though it's more expensive than most, with a fish dinner averaging 8000 TL.

The Troad

Alexandria Troas

South of Troy lie the ruins of the city that superseded it in Hellenistic times, **Alexandria Troas,** a few miles south of the sandy beach at **Geyikli;** in fact many early travellers to the Troad mistook it for Troy itself. The city was founded by Antigonus the One-Eyed at the end of the fourth century BC, but achieved its greatest glory after another of Alexander's generals, Lysimachus, killed Antigonus in battle and renamed it in memory of his old commander. He made it the main port in the Troad and one of the richest commercial centres on the entire coast. In Hadrian's time, Herodes Atticus, the Rockefeller of his day, endowed it with a monumental bath and aqueduct. Once prosperous, its position on the main sea route later brought about its demolition, as the builders of Istanbul's Imperial mosques dismantled it, block by block. Today the most impressive remains, besides the baths, are the great broken stones scattered on the beach.

Assos

South of Alexandria Troas, on the north shore of the lovely gulf of Edremit at **Behramkale,** is the most imposing site of ancient **Assos.** You reach it on a paved road from Ayvacik, crossing a charming fourteenth century Ottoman bridge, from which you can see the modern village, hugging the top of an extinct volcano, some 785 feet over the sea.

Some archaeologists believe the Hittite King Tudhaliyas IV established his colony of Ashachuva on the commanding height, in the thirteenth century BC, to keep an eye on the Mycenaeans troubling his western frontiers. The traditional date of the founding of Assos by Aeolians from Methymna, Lesbos, is around the first millennium BC. In ancient times the city was best known for its great archaic Doric temple of Athena (540 BC), that once crowned the very summit of the acropolis.

HISTORY

Assos passed through several hands—Persians, Athenians—a banker once governed it, and a eunuch. The latter was Hermias, a student of Plato at the Academy, one who had a chance to apply his teacher's theories of an ideal city-state to his own realm of the Troad and Lesbos. He invited other students of Plato to found a branch of the Academy in Assos, and for three years, Plato's greatest student, Aristotle, lived here, busy founding the sciences of biology and botany, and marrying Hermias' niece. Aristotle's own pupil, Alexander, later captured the city; after that it came under the kings of Pergamon. Several Crusaders' battles took place nearby, until the Ottomans captured Assos in AD 1330, and at once began to quarry the site to build a mosque and bridge over the Tuzla. The villagers of Behramkale took up the stones, when the Ottomans left off; one anonymous Turkish writer describes Behramkale as 'a rusty dagger piercing the walls of Assos'. Perhaps because of this Assos is one of the more dishevelled gardens of weeds along the coast; be prepared to scramble through the prickles to see the remains.

WALLS OF ASSOS

Most remarkable, especially in light of the quarrying on the site, are the **walls,** among the best preserved in the whole eastern Greek world. Stretching some two miles, they stand 46 feet high in places; features are excellently preserved gates, each done in a different style. They date back to the mid-fourth century BC, perhaps built under the rule of Hermias. Inner walls surround the acropolis and the **Temple of Athena.** Of this once magnificent structure little remains but the platform it once stood on, and a few decorative elements. Its Doric friezes are scattered in museums in Paris, Boston, and Istanbul. The view, however, of Lesbos and the Gulf of Edremit on one side and the valley of the Satnioeis on the other is worth the climb.

Other remains, all in the lower town, include two stoas of the agora (third century BC), an agora temple, a Hellenistic bouleuterion, gymnasium, and theatre. The most interesting thing about these are their similarities with the Pergamon style of architecture—the location of the temple in relation to the agora, and the unusual mix of Doric and Ionic orders in the decorative scheme. The gate was the main entrance to the city. Outside it, in the Hellenistic-Roman **necropolis** are numerous broken sarcophagi; Assos exported similar ones through the ancient world. If you're energetic you can hike down to the fine white pebble beach for a swim and a look at the remains of the ancient breakwater.

Gulf of Edremit

The **Gulf of Edremit** is one of the loveliest places in the whole of Turkey. Here are fine sandy beaches, writhing olive groves, dark pine forests, and pretty seaside villages, many sparkling white. To the east loom the bosky slopes of Mt Ida (*Kaz Dağ*) and in the gulf the emerald Alibey islets float in a crystal sea, with the shapely green outline of Lesbos as a backdrop. **Akçay** and **Özen** are two of the bigger resorts on the gulf; between them, the larger town of **Edremit,** the ancient Adramyttium, was sacked by Achilles in one of his raids along the coast. It was in Adramyttium that Achilles captured Chryseis, daughter of the priest of Apollo, and gave her as a prize to Agamemnon. The *Iliad* begins with Agamemnon's refusal to accept the father's ransom for the girl. Of all the resorts in the Gulf, **Ayvalik** is the prettiest with its many trees. Unlike many Turkish towns, it's sprawled out languidly along the shore affording wonderful views of the Gulf.

GETTING AROUND

Buses between Çanakkale and Izmir serve the coast well. For Ayvalik, which is a few kilometres from the main road, you may be let off and have to hitch the rest. From May–September, Greek and Turkish boats connect Ayvalik and the island of Lesbos 3 or 4 times a week; once a week in the off season. Assos (Behramkale) is reached by bus from Ayvalik.

TOURIST INFORMATION
In Edremit, Barbaros Meydani, tel. (6711) 113. In Ayvalik, Sahilboyu, Atatürk Cad. tel. (6631) 2122.

WHERE TO STAY
The new **Tüzün Oteli,** Orucreis Cad. 2, tel. (6711) 554 is open all year in Edremit and located on the beach. Rooms are 3500 TL for a single, 4500 TL a double. There are also many motels in Edremit and Akçay; a pleasant one on the beach in the latter is the **Öğe Moteli** on Oruçreis Cad., tel. (6711) 4, with a restaurant and motorboat for guest use; rates are 3200 TL a single, 4500 TL a double. There's also the **Turban Akçay holiday village** in Edremit, tel. (6711) 204 with many sports facilities, tennis, swimming pool, and water skiing and reductions for children. Singles are 3800 TL and 4800 TL for a double, with bath. In Ayvalik the **Ankara Oteli** at Sarimsakli, tel. (6631) 1195, is on the beach and good value for money, with reduced rates in the off season. Singles with bath are 4800 TL, doubles 6000 TL.

EATING OUT
This area of the coast is heaven for oyster eaters and many places specialise in the mollusc. One of the best restaurants is the **E Restoran** at Altinova, where a fish dinner runs around 4000–5000 TL. There are several little seaside restaurants on Ali Bey Ada.

Aeolia

Aeolia was famed in antiquity for the fertility of its soil, so fertile, it seems, that the early Greek colonists from Thessaly and Boetia spent all their labours tilling it, with little time left over for the intellectual pursuits and adventures that preoccupied the Ionians to the south. But it is here in Aeolia that we find **Pergamon,** a city that rivalled Athens and Alexandria as a cultural centre in its day.

Pergamon

Pergamon was not an Aeolian city, but rather a Hellenistic city state, a creation of Alexander's heirs. Although it was inhabited before the Hellenistic

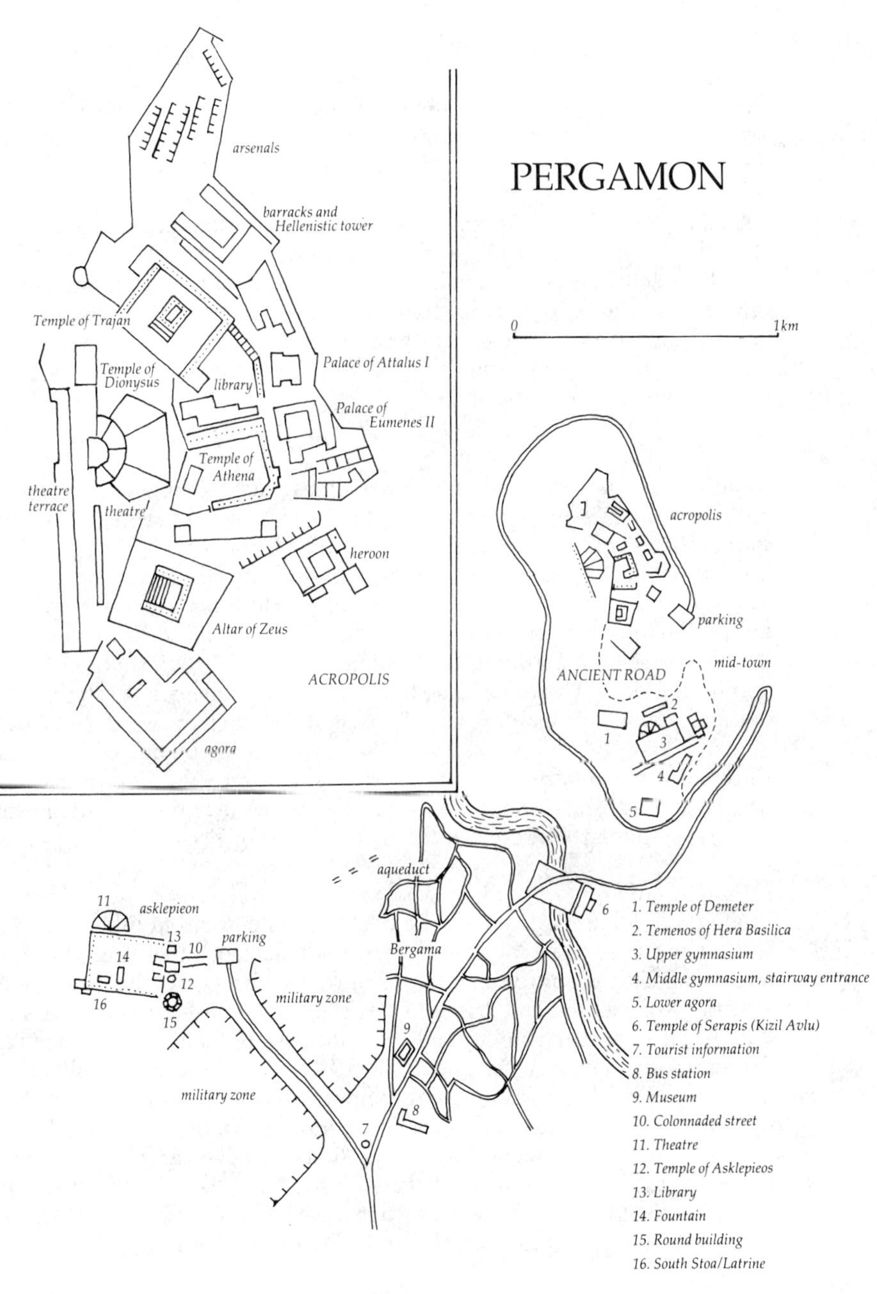
PERGAMON
0
1km
arsenals
barracks and Hellenistic tower
Temple of Trajan
Temple of Dionysus
library
Palace of Attalus I
Palace of Eumenes II
Temple of Athena
theatre terrace
theatre
heroon
Altar of Zeus
ACROPOLIS
agora
acropolis
parking
ANCIENT ROAD
mid-town
aqueduct
Bergama
asklepieon
parking
military zone
military zone
1. Temple of Demeter
2. Temenos of Hera Basilica
3. Upper gymnasium
4. Middle gymnasium, stairway entrance
5. Lower agora
6. Temple of Serapis (Kizil Avlu)
7. Tourist information
8. Bus station
9. Museum
10. Colonnaded street
11. Theatre
12. Temple of Asklepieos
13. Library
14. Fountain
15. Round building
16. South Stoa/Latrine

age, it was never very important—a minor Greek-Persian satrapy, first mentioned in 399 BC when Xenophon stopped here, after his famous march. Doubtless, had it been nearer the sea, it would have thrived much earlier, for few cities could boast such a splendid defensible site, a citadel 1300 feet above the surrounding plain, with streams flowing below on two sides. When Alexander's general, Lysimachus, came into a fabulous fortune—9000 talents—the spoils of war in the Troad, Pergamon seemed the perfect place to safeguard the treasure. When Lysimachus died without an heir in 281 BC, the man he set to watch over the loot, a certain Philetaerus, simply kept it, using the money to wine friends and build monuments in Pergamon. His adopted son Eumenes is the first of the famous Kings of Pergamon; Eumenes' adopted son, Attalus (ruled 241–197 BC) gave the rulers their dynastic title, the Attalids.

ATTALUS I

Attalus I was audacious and spent much of his reign fighting for more territory; most notably, he stood up to the bellicose Gauls of Galatia, who were running a kind of protection racket in Anatolia. Upon his refusal to pay, they came to collect, fierce and more numerous than the Pergamene defenders, who were reluctant to engage them in battle. However, Attalus ordered a sacrifice to the gods, and miracle!—plainly written on the victim's lungs was the word 'Victory'. Inspired, the Pergamenes soundly defeated the Gauls despite the odds. Only later was it discovered that the priest offering the sacrifice, or more probably Attalus himself, had written the word backwards in ink on his hand and pressed it on the entrails when no one was looking. But even if the augury was a cheat, Attalus had freed the western Greeks from a serious threat, and in honour of the victory over the barbarians, his successor, Eumenes II, erected the famous Altar of Zeus.

EUMENES II

Eumenes II ruled Pergamon at the height of its power and influence. But just as the city owed its initial prosperity to the luck of a treasure deposit, it owed its great rise in prestige to a second lucky break. Attalus had kindly sent the Romans the cult statue of Cybele, the Great Mother goddess of Asia when they asked for it, and in return the Romans, upon defeating Antiochus the Great at Magnesia (190 BC) gave Pergamon Antiochus' provinces of Asia Minor, stretching from the coast to Konya. Relations between Rome and Pergamon became even closer as Eumenes assisted Rome militarily against its enemies, including the most worrying, Hannibal, who ended up in Bithynia after his defeat at Zama, and according to tradition, died and was buried in Iznik. Eumenes' brother, Attalus II, continued his policy of helping Rome, especially in the subjugation of Greece.

ATTALUS III

But it was his nephew, Attalus III, who recognised the inevitable, and amazed the classical world by willing Pergamon to Rome when he died in 133 BC. Some accounted it a Roman trick, and perhaps, as a result, a body of stories has grown up, attesting to Attalus III's eccentricities, that he loved his mother so well that he took the title 'Philomater', that he was obsessed with poisonous plants, which he fed to condemned criminals to try out his cures, that he never went out in public except to work on his mother's tomb, where one day, in the heat, he fainted and died, only five years into his reign. Rome had no problem in accepting Attalus' bequest, and according to the terms of the will, left Pergamon a free city. This state of affairs lasted until 88 BC, when Mithradates came to 'liberate' the Greek states from Rome and ordered all Romans massacred, an order the Pergamenes carried out with great zeal. When Rome, in return, defeated Mithradates, Pergamon lost all its rights, and even, 40 years later, its greatest treasure, the famous library, which Antony gave to Cleopatra. This gift ended once and for all the rivalry between the libraries of Alexandria and Pergamon.

SITE

Pergamon was one of the most beautiful cities of the ancient Greeks; a masterpiece created from a combination of natural position, wealth, and talent. Its architects and sculptors were among the finest in the Hellenistic world, though to see the best of it you have to go to the Pergamum Museum in East Berlin. However, what remains of the ancient city in the modern town of Bergama is wonderfully evocative, second only to Ephesus in the extent of its remains.

ACROPOLIS

The majestic **acropolis** looms behind the modern town, from which there is a paved road to the top (it's a stiff walk, so you may want to spring for a taxi). Since 1878, the Germans have completed four major excavations in Pergamon, and currently a fifth is underway. One project in the works is the reconstruction of the columns of the **Temple of Trajan,** at the highest level of the acropolis; it is the only structure dating wholly from Roman times. Both Trajan and Hadrian were worshipped here; their two huge marble heads, found in the temple may now be seen in Berlin. Directly behind the temple stood the Hellenistic **barracks and tower,** perfectly located for the view over the plain. Adjoining the barracks to the south were the two **palaces,** peristyle mansions of the kings of Pergamon, of which not much remains, except some walls and cisterns. Water was always a headache in the citadel, and anyone caught polluting the reserves was severely punished.

LIBRARY

Southwest of the palaces stood the renowned two-storey **library,** begun by Attalus II, which at its height had some 200 000 volumes. Eumenes II in particular was obsessed with acquiring books, and made a special habit of borrowing and not returning. For books by Aristotle and Theophrastus he is said to have paid their weight in gold.

The Pergamene library became so great that it excited the jealousy of the Ptolemies in Egypt, whose library at Alexandria was its only serious rival. As a result Egypt banned the export of papyrus. All books at the time were written on long scrolls of this brittle stuff; but Eumenes, undeterred, offered a large reward to anyone who could come up with a replacement. A certain Crates of Smyrna recalled the old Ionian custom of writing on skins treated with lime and dried. This 'Pergamon paper' became known as parchment, and as it was too thick to roll up like papyrus, the codex, or modern paged book was invented. The library in Alexandria survived until the days of Caliph Omar, when it was used to stoke the fires in the baths.

THE THEATRE

A **temple of Athena** stood next to the library, of which little more than the foundations remain. The Athena of this temple was Athena Nickephoros, or 'she who grants victory' and it is thought that the original of the famous 'Dying Gaul' now in Rome once stood in its precincts. From the temple a narrow stair-passage descends to the **Greek Theatre.** It's not unusual to find ancient theatres carved into hillsides, offering spectators not only a view of the stage but a panoramic backdrop as well, but this is an extreme case; nowhere will you find a theatre so dizzyingly steep and dramatic, resembling nothing so much as an immense fan. Its eighty rows of seats could hold 10 000 spectators. A **temple of Dionysus,** the god of theatrical performances, stood off to the audience's right, closing one end of the long promenade of the **Theatre Terrace**; since the stage of the theatre was portable, it could be removed at the end of a performance to permit access to the terrace (where the post holes for the wooden set can still be seen). Architecturally, the Dionysus Temple (also known as the Caracalla) is considered a landmark—set up on a platform, closed on three sides, it is the prototype of many later temples in Rome.

ALTAR OF ZEUS

The great **Altar of Zeus** stood on another terrace, below the temple of Athena. Built during the age of Eumenes II, this was one of the outstanding monuments of the Hellenistic age, shaped like a horseshoe and covered with the famous high reliefs portraying a battle between the gods and the giants, symbolic of Pergamon's (or civilisation's) victory over the Gauls (or barbarism). These are in the Berlin Museum; all that remains on the acropolis are the foundations. To the south of the Altar, on a lower terrace, are the remains of the **Upper Agora** and its temple, in a mixture of Ionic and Doric orders, a common trait of Pergamene buildings. Carl Humann, the engineer who discovered the Altar of Zeus reliefs (incorporated in a Byzantine wall) is buried here.

MID-TOWN PERGAMON

Recently much of the **Ancient Road,** connecting upper Pergamon to the **mid-town area,** has been cleared. While the acropolis was reserved for the kings, nobility and officers, regular citizens lived in the mid-town, which also has several important public buildings. Mysteries, similar to those at Eleusis, took place in the **Temple of Demeter,** erected by Philetairos and later enlarged by the wife of Attalus II, Appolonis. The temple—with its pit for the blood of sacrifices, fountain, and rows of seats for spectators of the mysteries—has unusual archaic palm leaf capitals. Near here are three terraces, each with a gymnasium. Young men trained and studied in the upper gymnasium, which doubled as an auditorium for ceremonial occasions with its small theatre; the middle gymnasium was reserved for adolescent boys, and the third served as the children's playground. The **stairway entrance** connecting the lowest level to the second is one of the finest pieces of workmanship in all Pergamon, an early and very well preserved example of vault and arch construction.

The main street through the mid-town is impressively paved with massive blocks, worn by pedestrians and scored by chariot wheels. Along it are the ruins of shops and houses. Especially interesting here is the peristyle **House of Attalus,** a fair example of how the upper classes of Pergamon lived. Beyond the house in the **Lower Agora,** the famous head of Alexander, now in the Istanbul museum, was discovered.

REMAINS IN THE MODERN TOWN

Modern Bergama has engulfed lower Pergamon, with one monumental exception. The Turks call it *Kizil Avlu,* the Red Courtyard. This red brick mastodon originally served as a Temple of Serapis, or Osiris, an Egyptian god. According to legend, the thousands of bricks in the temple were relayed to the site from hand to hand in a great human chain, so they would neither be on earth or sky; indeed the whole temple is built over the Selinos stream, which still runs through the ancient tunnel below. Other underground chambers and tunnels had a religious significance. One of the temple's two massive towers now contains a mosque. The whole building was converted into a basilica by the early Christians. The Church of Pergamon was one of the seven churches of Asia addressed by St John in *Revelations*, the one that was singled out as possessing the 'throne of the Devil'.

What John meant by this has been disputed. Literalists point to the Altar of Zeus, others believe he meant the seat of Roman authority.

ASCLEPIEON

Also remaining in the modern town are a few arches of an aqueduct; if you walk up the maze of streets towards them you'll eventually find the short-cut to ancient Pergamon's **Asclepieon,** the sanctuary of healing. You can drive there by taking the road that branches off next to the tourist office, passing a large military base.

Pergamon had the most renowned Asclepieon in Greek Anatolia, and produced one of the best physicians of the ancient world, Galen (AD 131 to 201). Asclepieos was the god of healing, himself the son of Apollo; the 'doctors' were his priests, who cured the faithful with surprisingly modern methods—diet, baths, music and exercise in a lovely environment, combined with dream interpretation and auto-suggestion. Over the entrance of the sanctuary were inscribed the words 'By order of the gods Death may not enter here'.

The sanctuary in Pergamon pre-dates the kings of Pergamon and reached its greatest extent in the second century AD, when the Emperor Hadrian endowed it with most of the structures you see today. The **Sacred Way,** a wide colonnaded street that led to the Ascelpieon from the Roman town, still takes you to the entrance gate, or **Propylon,** of which only a few steps remain. Within is a circular open space, the main **temple of Zeus-Asclepieos,** at one time covered with a dome, modelled after the Pantheon in Rome. This gives onto the main grounds of the Asclepieon itself, encompassed by three long stoae; there, patients could sit in the shade or be sheltered from the rain. When bored, they could use the **library,** a square building north of the temple (the north is the best preserved). The sanctuary's **theatre,** off the end of the north portico could seat 3500 and is believed to have been used to entertain both patients and locals. A sacred spring flowed in to the **fountain** nearby that has marble steps. Such water was very important in the healing process; someone in the 1970s analysed it at the source and found it contained radioactive properties. There are two other fountains in the sanctuary, a sacred well near the entrance of the **Tunnel,** used for drinking, and carved in the rock pool near the west stoa, probably used for the frequently prescribed mud baths.

THE SACRED TUNNEL

The **Tunnel,** 266 feet long, leads from the centre of the sanctuary to a large mysterious structure of brick. Built in Roman times, this two-storey, excellently preserved **round building** is not referred to by any ancient writer—it may have been a treatment centre, added on to the original Asclepieon—rather like a modern hospital annexe, attesting to its great popularity. Some believe the tunnel itself was more than a passageway, but also played a part psychologically in the healing of patients.

The **south stoa** near here had to be supported on columns to attain the level of the rest of the sanctuary, producing a basement you can still walk through; at the far end is a luxurious marble **latrine** for men, and a small, less well-appointed one for the women. Much of the central area of the Asclepieon proper had shrines to the several gods of healing—Hygiea and Apollo among them, and incubation chambers, where patients slept, hoping for a dream from the god to guide them in their cure.

BERGAMA

Bergama itself is an old and attractive town, and has a fine little **Archaeology and Ethnographic Museum,** where there is a small model of the Altar of Zeus and some small finds from the site, including two statues of hermaphrodites. If you like the antique wedding dresses in the ethnographic room, you may be able to purchase one in the shops in town. Bergama is the only place where we've seen many for sale. Cruise ships call at **Dikili,** the port of ancient Pergamon and the nearest beach, which is safe for children.

Bergama to Izmir

Between Bergama and Izmir the coast is dotted with Aeolian cities, of which little remains beyond their names: **Pitane,** northernmost of the Confederacy, now modern *Çandarli*, has a picturesque thirteenth-century Venetian castle, the village's main attraction, next to the small beach. Beside the centre, stood **Gryneum** (*Temasalik Burnu*), once renowned for its temple and oracle of Apollo, of which only a mound in a field now remains; continuing south was **Myrina,** reputed to have been founded by the Queen of the Amazons, and beyond that, on the coast, the once great **Cyme,** both of which contributed most of the building material of modern Ali Ağa.

Phocaea

Phocaea, at modern **Eski Foça,** was the northernmost Ionian city, and unlike its Aeolian neighbours, a great seafaring city, boasting one of the best harbours in the area. The seafarers of Phocaea founded numerous colonies, most famously Marsalla (Marseilles) and Elea, in Italy. Again, almost everything that remained of ancient Phocaea went into the medieval castle on the shore. What does remain, oddly enough, is the so-called **Taş Kule**, a mysterious tomb, eighth century BC, believed to have been built by the Phrygians or Lycians. It lies on the road to Eski Foça, resembling an Art Deco petrol station of the 1930s more than anything else. Both Yeni and Eski Foça are pleasant villages with pleasant beaches, attracting the likes of the Club Méditerranée.

GETTING AROUND

Bergama is the transportation hub of the area, though if you go there on any but a direct bus you'll be left on the highway 7 kilometres from town and have to catch a minibus into town. (There is a direct one to Bergama every half hour.) To see the ruins in a day you'll do well to invest in two taxi trips: one up to the acropolis and one to the asclepieon. From Bergama's otogar there are minibuses every half hour to Dikili.

TOURIST INFORMATION

In Bergama, Zafer Mah. Izmir Cad. 54, on the main road into town, tel. (5411) 862. In Foça, Atatürk Mah. Ilçe Girişi, tel. (5431) 122.

WHERE TO STAY

Bergama is poorly served by hotels. The best in town is the **Park Oteli** (tel. (5411) 246, on the main street, where rates are 2000 TL for a double. Just outside town there's a shady campsite, and the **Tusan Bergama Moteli** on the Izmir road, tel. (5411) 1173, with plain, clean rooms at 3750 TL a single and 5000 TL a double. In Foça, the **Hanedan Oteli** is a pleasant, reasonably priced hotel near the beach, with a restaurant. Open all year, rates are 2800 TL a single, 3500 TL a double with baths.

EATING OUT

Bergama has numerous small, inexpensive lokantas, like the Kardeşler restaurant (1500 TL) near the taxi stand. There are waterfront restaurants at Dikili and Foça with delicious fish.

Izmir

HISTORY

Of all the ancient Greek cities on the coast of Asia Minor, only Izmir (old Smyrna) has survived as a city into modern times. Few can boast such a splendid situation, at the head of a long narrow gulf, spread out beneath the flat topped hill known as Mt Pagus by the Greeks, and more picturesquely, the Velvet Castle (*Kadifekale*) by the Turks. The Aeolians colonised it in the tenth century BC; surprisingly, they chose not the present site of the city but a small peninsula at the end of the gulf, called Bayrakli. One day while the entire city was out celebrating the Dionysia, the Ionians simply moved in and took over. According to ancient tradition, Ionian Smyrna was the birthplace of Homer, said to have been born on the banks of the river Meles (*Halkapinar Suyu*). Ancient Smyrna was plagued by the Lydians and never thrived until Alexander the Great, while hunting on Mt Pagus, dreamt that he should found a city there. The inhabitants on the peninsula moved, and the new Smyrna prospered and was eventually welcomed into the exclusive

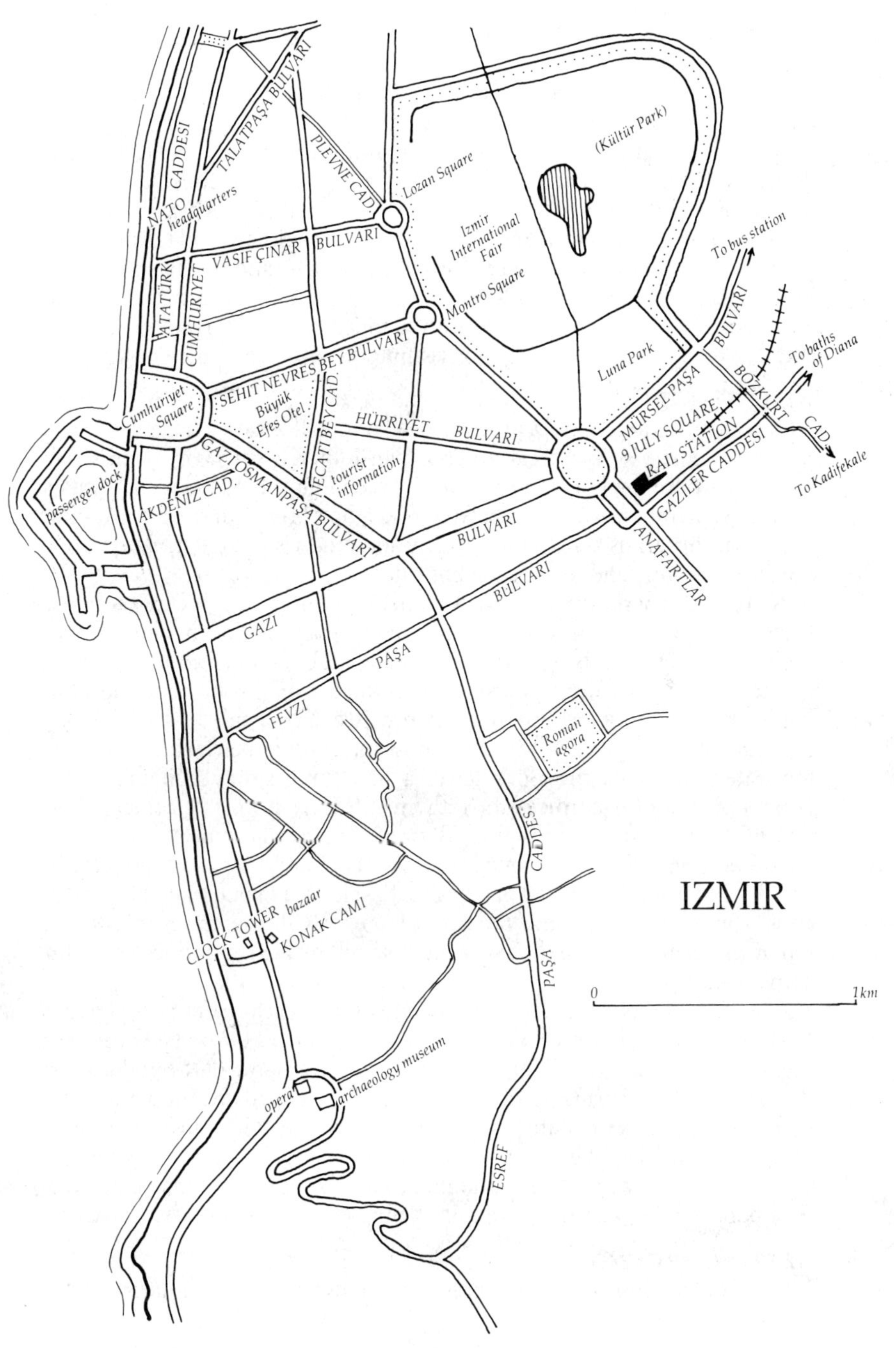
NATO CADDESI
TALATPAŞA BULVARI
NATO headquarters
PLEVNE CAD.
Lozan Square
(Kültür Park)
Izmir International Fair
VASIF ÇINAR BULVARI
Montro Square
To bus station
ATATÜRK
CUMHURIYET
SEHIT NEVRES BEY BULVARI
BULVARI
To baths of Diana
Luna Park
MÜRSEL PAŞA
BOZKURT CAD
Cumhuriyet Square
Büyük Efes Otel
NECATI BEY CAD.
HÜRRIYET BULVARI
9 JULY SQUARE
RAIL STATION
GAZI OSMANPAŞA BULVARI
tourist information
GAZILER CADDESI
To Kadifekale
passenger dock
AKDENIZ CAD.
BULVARI
ANAFARTLAR
BULVARI
GAZI
PAŞA
FEVZI
Roman agora
CADDES
IZMIR
bazaar
CLOCK TOWER
KONAK CAMI
PAŞA
0
1km
archaeology museum
opera
ESREF

confederacy of Ionian cities as its thirteenth member. Strabo and many other ancient authorities referred to the city's charms, and 'beautiful Smyrna' is a name that has stuck through the centuries, despite frequent disasters. Earthquakes and fires, the chief culprits, culminated in the catastrophe of 1922, when, after Atatürk's defeat of the Greek army and the mass exodus of Greek civilians from the city, it caught fire and burned to the ground. Thus perished the great Levantine Smyrna and from its ashes rose modern Izmir, the third largest city in Turkey and its busiest port. It is an important NATO headquarters with a touch of Mediterranean languor, and, for many people, the base for visiting the sites along the coast.

WHAT TO SEE

The points of interest of Izmir can be seen in half a day. The centre of the city is occupied by the great green expanse of **Kültürpark,** Izmir's fairgrounds, where the Izmir International Trade Fair is held from mid-August to mid-September, when it is hard to find a hotel room in the city. At other times Kültürpark is quiet, almost hauntingly so, visited for its garden outdoor restaurants, and its amusement rides.

Near Kültürpark, there's always a queue of horse-drawn carriages waiting to take you to Konak district, distinguished by its lovely **clock tower,** built in the nineteenth century by Sultan Abdul Hamid, and the small but ornate eighteenth-century mosque, **Konak Cami.** From here you enter Izmir's **bazaar district,** a maze of narrow streets and cul-de-sacs that predate the great fire, one of the city's most interesting quarters. South along the waterfront from the clock tower a new three-storey building houses Izmir's **archaeology museum,** with an extensive if unspectacular collection of artefacts from the region. Between the bazaar and Kültürpark are the excavations of the **Roman agora;** here there are two rows of colonnades and three statues discovered on the site: Poseidon, Demeter and half of Artemis. Almost directly above the agora looms Mt Pagus, the *Kadifekale*, on top of which are some of the fortifications built by the Byzantines and Ottomans.

The view of Izmir from the walls of one of the nearby cafes is vertiginous. East of the central city, on Gaziler Caddesi, the *Halkapinar Gölü* has been identified as the ancient **Baths of Diana,** where a statue of the goddess was discovered. This spring-fed pool, now on the grounds of the Izmir water company, supplies the entire city, and is believed by many to be the source of the ancient River Meles. A homeric Hymn refers to a pool of Artemis in the vicinity, and, according to tradition, Homer sat on its banks and wrote. The pool is still a charming oasis in the big city, and visitors are welcome.

GETTING AROUND

Izmir's Çiğli airport is frequently served by flights from Istanbul and

Ankara, as well as weekly direct THY flights from London, and numerous charters from abroad. The THY terminal is next to the Büyük Efes Hotel, and is connected by bus to the airport one hour before every flight. From Izmir's central Basmahane Station, at the head of Fevzi Paşa Bulvari, there are rail links with Aydin, Denizli, Konya, and Ankara. The main bus terminal (Yeni Garaj) is northwest of town in Halkapinar, on Şehitler Caddesi. It is linked with the central city by bus (no. 50) as well as taxi and dolmuş. From here you can go to Ephesus and Kuşadasi. Another terminal is by the sea in Konak; this primarily serves the towns and resorts on the Çeşme peninsula.

The Yeni Liman or Alsancak is the port for ferryboats and the Turkish Maritime Lines cruise boats; in Izmir their address is Atatürk Bulvari 125. Once a week from May until October they operate a car ferry between Izmir and Ancona, Italy, as well as frequent overnight ferries to Istanbul.

TOURIST INFORMATION

In Izmir, Gaziomanpaşa Bul. next to the Büyük Efes Hotel, tel. (51) 14 21 47. There's also a helpful office of the Auto Club at Atatürk Bulvari 370, in Alsancak, tel. (51) 21 71 49.

WHERE TO STAY

In Izmir the **Büyük Efes** is an institution, its enclosed garden occupying a large wedge of the city's most expensive real estate, on Cumhuriyet square. Although aging, it has all the amenities, from sauna to tennis courts, television and refrigerators, Turkish bath to swimming pool. Tel. (50) 14 43 00; rates are 19 600 TL a single, 29 400 a double. Less expensive, the **Anba Oteli** at Cumhuriyet Bul. 124, tel. (50) 14 43 80, is centrally located, air conditioned, and a good value with singles from 8400 TL and doubles at 10 500 TL, with a 25% discount in the off season.

A good place to look for inexpensive accommodation is along Gaziomanpaşa Bulvari and Gazi Bulvari; the best here is the **Babadan** at Gaziomanpaşa Bul. 45, tel. (50) 13 96 40, with singles for 5200 TL, doubles 6500, all with bath.

EATING OUT

In Izmir there are restaurants of every size and price. The fancy places to eat are along the waterfront, both ends of Atatürk Bulvari, where seafood is the speciality. Others are in Kültürpark, like the deluxe **Park Restoran,** where a delicious full course meal may cost 10 000 TL. For something different, there's a Chinese restaurant, the **Çin** on Necatibey Bul, near the park, with prices in the 5000 TL range. For less expensive restaurants, look around Konak and the market; for inexpensive fish try **Kazan** at Atatürk Bulvari 112 (5000 TL, more or less).

Manisa

East of Izmir is **Manisa,** ancient **Magnesia ad Sipylum,** the westernmost outpost of the Hittites; just east of Manisa, at Akpinar, there is a carved relief of the mother goddess **Cybele** on the side of the ancient Mt Sipylus. Mt Sipylus is closely identified in ancient mythology with Tantalus, and his sons Pelops and Broteas, and his daughter, Niobe. Broteas is credited with carving the Cybele; Pelops was chopped up in a soup at the banquet Tantalus prepared for the gods. The gods (except for Demeter, who ate a bit of shoulder) recognised the meat for what it was and punished Tantalus in Hades with eternal thirst and hunger, water and fruit always just out of reach (hence 'tantalise'). Zeus restored Pelops to life, with an ivory shoulder, and he went on to conquer southern Greece and give it his name—the Peloponnese. Niobe had seven daughters and seven sons, but was rash enough to boast that she was a better mother than Leto, who only had two children, Apollo and Artemis. These two stern archer gods then avenged their mother by slaying Niobe's fourteen. Niobe's grief was so great that Zeus took pity on her and turned her to stone. A natural rock formation southwest of Manisa is believed to be the one referred to by ancient writers; it lies along the road to Karaköy, near a picnic ground, one of the many scenic spots in the region.

Finds from Magnesia and Sardis can be seen in the **Manisa museum,** including a very good statue of a young girl from the Roman age and inscriptions from a synagogue discovered in Sardis in 1962. The museum is in the Medrese of the **Muradiye Cami,** a work of the great Mimar Sinan, notable for the tiles and goldwork in the interior. The fourteenth century **Ulu Cami,** half way up to the derelict Byzantine fortress on the ancient acropolis, has a Selçuk-style minaret, with coloured tiles and columns from an ancient temple. A third mosque, the 1522 **Sultan Cami,** built by the mother of Süleyman the Magnificent, is the most famous in Manisa, for here, at the end of May, the Mesir festival takes place. Mesir is a paste, a concoction of some forty-one ingredients and spices, which has a wide reputation as a cure-all, and is tossed in paper wrappers from the top of the minaret. According to popular belief, it only works if you scramble for it, and hundreds of people do so, every year.

Sart/Sardis

A little more than an hour east of Izmir is the twentieth-century village of Sart, built over the ruins of the ancient capital of Lydia, **Sardis**. Situated below the steep Mt Tmolus, dominating the fertile plain of the River Hermes (the *Gediz Nehri*) and located on the great Royal road of the Persian

Empire, Sardis from the seventh to the mid-sixth century BC was the world's richest city. A good part of its wealth was in gold washed down from the mountain by the river Pactolus, which the Lydians collected in sheepskins spread in the shallows, perhaps a source of the legend of the Golden Fleece.

The Lydians

The Greeks were fascinated by the Lydians, and their fame went as far as the Assyrians who called them the *Luddi* in their inscriptions. The Lydian race was a mixture of native Anatolian and western invader; their language was related to Phrygian and curiously, Etruscan (Herodotus writes that Etruria was a Lydian colony), and used many Greek letters. Besides building giant mounds for their deceased rulers, the Lydians were also notable for condoning prostitution; it was the way a good Lydian girl earned her marriage dowry.

There were three Lydian dynasties. At the end of the second, the Heraclid, the Lydians gained ascendency as Hittite power in the region declined. The Lydians last king was Candaules (700 BC), who, it is said, was so proud of his wife's beauty that he contrived that his trusted minister Gyges see her naked. The queen, however, saw the unwilling voyeur and the next day gave him a choice: either kill her husband and marry her, or die on the spot. Gyges chose the more pleasant alternative, and founded a new dynasty, the Mermnad that brought Sardis and Lydia, almost literally, a golden age. By the time of Croesus (563 to 546 BC), Sardis controlled the whole of Asia Minor, which Croesus was said to rule with a very benevolent hand. Lydia had been the first city in the world to mint coins, and Croesus the first to issue them in pure gold and pure silver. His reputation for wealth has come down to us, but did little to impress the visiting Athenian lawgiver Solon, who, after touring the fabulous treasuries, merely commented, 'No man can be reckoned happy until the end'.

In Croesus' reign, the Persians under King Cyrus menaced Lydia's borders. So Croesus asked the Delphic oracle whether or not he should attack. The oracle replied that if he crossed the River Halys he would destroy a great empire. Encouraged, he went ahead, only to meet defeat. Cyrus chased the Lydians back to Sardis, and after a two-week siege the city fell to the Persians. So it was Croesus' own empire that fell. Croesus was condemned to be burnt at the stake. 'Solon, Solon!' he groaned as the fire was lit, and Cyrus asked what he meant. Croesus told him what the Athenian had said and, moved, Cyrus ordered the king be saved.

Cyrus made Sardis the capital of a satrapy and, as such it was sacked when the Ionian cities revolted against the Persians in 499 BC. It recovered in the Hellenistic era, until the earthquake of AD 17 flattened it. Tiberius had it rebuilt, and it became a centre of early Christianity, one of the seven churches of Asia and an important bishopric under the Byzantines. In 1401, Tamerlane destroyed the city so thoroughly that it was never rebuilt; when excavations began in the early twentieth century, the archaeologists had to dig down thirty feet in places, so much had the soft rock of the acropolis silted down over the lower city.

SITE

One thing the excavators have discovered is that Sardis was at its largest under Croesus, and it takes some walking to see it all. The **Temple of Artemis,** most famous of ancient Sardis' monuments, is about a kilometre up the Pactolus valley; the sanctuary was founded in the fifth century BC, although the temple itself wasn't begun until the third. Its two Ionic capitals are some of the finest anywhere; thirteen others have been re-erected to give an idea of the temple's shape. In Roman times the temple was divided into two, half dedicated to the worship of Artemis, the other half to Faustina, wife of the Roman emperor Antoninus Pius. Along the road to the centre of Sardis, an altar to Cybele was discovered, as well as the workshops where the Lydians worked the gold they 'fleeced' from the river.

Equally impressive are the Roman gymnasium and baths from the second century AD, just off the highway; shops and a synagogue complete the complex with the **Marble Court** in the centre. Nearby, part of the Royal Road has been uncovered, and, most interestingly, what appears to be a prototype bazaar dating back to the seventh century BC, giving rise to the theory that Sardis was the first city to practise organised retail trade. Next to this, the **House of Bronzes** (sixth century AD) was perhaps the residence of the bishop of Sardis. If you're reasonably energetic you can walk up the **acropolis,** one of the most dramatic in Asia Minor, its sheerness accentuated by the dagger-shaped rock formations around it. However, the walk from the valley takes less than an hour; on top most of the surviving fortifications are Byzantine. Six miles north of Sardis are the Bin Tepe, or **Thousand Hills,** actually some 100 built by the artisans, merchants and prostitutes of Sardis the largest of which is the **Tomb of Alyattes** the father of Croesus. At threequarters of a mile in circumference and 260 feet high, it's the largest mound in Turkey.

Kemalpaşa

Between Sardis and Izmir, **Kemalpaşa** is the ancient town of Nymphaeum, where Andronicus I Comnenus built the **Palace of Nymphaeum** in 1184, the ruins of which are just outside town. In **Karabel,** on the main road south of Kemalpaşa, there is a second **Hittite relief,** this one of a large warrior; Herodotus referred to it, although, like all Greeks in the Classical era, he knew nothing of the Hittites, and assumed it was Egyptian.

Çeşme Peninsula

The peninsula west of Izmir has several popular beach resorts and thermal spas. **Inciralti** is the closest to Izmir and thus the most crowded; just to the south, the **Baths of Agamemnon,** in use since antiquity, are noted for relieving rheumatism. Further west, near **Urla** and another beach, a causeway leads out to an islet where once stood the ancient city of **Clazomenae**. The original causeway, constructed by Alexander the Great, can be seen just below the surface of the sea; otherwise little remains of this Ionian city that produced the great pre-Socratic philosopher Anaxagoras, the precursor of Plato, in the sixth century BC.

SIĞACIK

You can go south from Urla to Seferihisar and from there to **Siğacik,** the prettiest village on the peninsula, its old houses clustered around an old Genoese fortress and small port. Here, by the lovely white beach of **Akkum** stood the ancient **Teos,** an Ionian city, one of the wealthiest on the coast. Teos was the birthplace and home of the lyric love-poet Anacreon; it is also the site of a famous **temple of Dionysus.** This was built in the Hellenistic era, with an unusual trapezoidal enclosure. Some columns have been re-erected, and make a picturesque tableau in the olive grove. Nearby is the **theatre,** which, though in poor condition, offers the fabled view from its upper seats. Better preserved is the **Odeon,** with its eleven rows of seats, where concerts were performed.

ÇEŞME

At the far western end of the peninsula is **Çeşme** ('fountain'), named after its numerous hot springs. It is the westernmost town in Turkey, a distinction that has an added significance during Ramazan, when the pious Moslems of Çeşme have to wait longer than anyone else to eat supper. An attractive town, with red tile roofs, it is dominated by a large, sloping Genoese castle captured by Yildirim Beyazit in 1400. Two important naval battles took place off shore here: the decisive Roman defeat of Antiochus III in 190 BC, giving the Romans a free hand in Asia Minor and in 177, the destruction of the Ottoman fleet by the Russians. Çeşme faces the Greek island of Chios, much favoured by the Sultans for its mastic, some of which went through the **caravanserai,** built in 1529 by Süleyman the Magnificent in a U-shape; it's currently being restored.

AROUND ÇEŞME

The west coast of the peninsula is embellished with beaches, most popular being the great white sandy strand at **Ilica.** Others are at **Boyalik, Şifne** and **Ildiri.** The latter is near ancient **Erythrae,** a member of the Ionian Confederacy; unfortunately the site was well quarried in the nineteenth century, and little remains on the picturesque spot beyond some well-built walls and a ruined theatre. In ancient times Erythrae was famous for an archaic statue of Hercules which floated on a raft from Egypt to a point between Chios and Erythrae. Both wanted it, but the raft couldn't be budged until a blindman in Erythrae had a dream telling him the statue could only be towed away with a rope of women's hair. The women of Erythrae refused to part with their locks, but their Thracian slaves used theirs to make the rope that actually indeed pulled the raft to their city. The statue restored the blindman's sight, and in the sanctuary subsequently built for it, no women were allowed except Thracian. It's now impossible to tell which of the remains was Hercules' sanctuary, but a stream that tastes bitter still flows in the walls and, according to Pliny—a notorious story-teller—it causes hair to grow all over the body. Erythrae is on the eastern flank at the foot of the **Karaburun peninsula,** which is mountainous and scenic.

South of Çeşme, there are beaches at **Pirlanta, Tursite,** and more remote, at **Alaçati** and **Güvercinli.**

GETTING AROUND

Both Manisa and Sardis are connected to Izmir by rail and bus (1½ hours). There are frequent buses from Izmir's Konak bus station to Çeşme and the resorts on the peninsula. Between April and November there's usually one or two boats a week between Çeşme and the Greek island of Chios; in season they go every day and can take three or four cars.

TOURIST INFORMATION

In Manisa, Doğu Cad. 8, Eylül Işhani, tel. (5511) 2541. In Çeşme, at the harbour, tel. (5492) 1653.

WHERE TO STAY

In Çeşme there are a clutch of inexpensive, unlisted pensions and the moderate priced **Ertan Oteli** (H4) on Cumhuriyet Mey. 12, tel. (5492) 6795 near the beach, with singles for 4800 TL, doubles 6000 TL, all with bath. Around Çeşme the top beach resort hotel, popular with Americans is the Golden Dolphin, in Turkish the **Altinyunus Tatil Köyü** with 515 bungalows and nearly every possible recreational facility, including horse riding and water skiing and thermal baths. Tel. (5492) 1250; rates are 14 000 TL for a single, 32 000 TL for a double, with a 40% cut in the off season. In Ilica, among the many small hotels with thermal establishments is the elegant **Turban Çesme,** tel. (5492) 1240, open year round, with tennis and swimming pool. A single with a bath is 9375 TL, a double 12 500 TL, also with a considerable discount in the off season. There are camp grounds in the summer at Gümüldür (Denizati Kampi, tel. 19–366), at Balçova (tel. 15 47 60) and near Çeşme (V Kampi, tel. 21).

WHERE TO EAT

In Çeşme, there's the very good but expensive **Çalli** on Inkilâp Cad. (7000 TL); less expensive are **Durak** (7000 TL) and the cheap **Pide Salonu** in Ilica.

Part VII

THE SOUTH AEGEAN COAST: KUŞADASI TO MARMARIS

The Temple of Hadrian, Ephesus

This section of the coast encompasses most of ancient Ionia. If Greece was the cradle of western civilisation, then Ionia was the midwife. But the region is blessed with more than the remains of great cities and past glories. As Herodotus, a native of the region, wrote, the climate of Ionia is the fairest in the world, and it is endowed with a light filled Aegean beauty to complement the weather. Names like Kuşadasi, Bodrum, and Marmaris, only a few years ago sounding strange and exotic, now roll off the tongue of many a travel agent, yachtsman (the jagged coast is exceptionally well suited for sailing) and even the most timid package-tourist. Yet modern and trendy as the South Aegean coast has become, it is paradoxically the only place in Turkey where you're likely to see a camel or, in winter, that most exotic of Turkish sporting events, camel wrestling.

Kuşadasi Bay

Colophon

One Ionian city splendid in its own day, but almost forgotten now, is Colophon, most easily reached by heading directly south from Izmir; indeed, it was the people of Colophon who took ancient Smyrna from the Aeolians when the latter weren't looking. Colophon was renowned in antiquity for its horses and mighty cavalry, and for its fierce dogs trained to fight in battle; yet it was also one of two places in the ancient Greek world where dogs were sacrificed (Sparta was the other). Because its land was wonderfully fertile and its fleet powerful, it became so wealthy that the men wore kingly purple robes daily, drenched themselves with musk, and ate twelve-course meals. It is said lavish living made them soft, and Colophon was one of the first Greek cities to fall to the Lydians. In the Hellenistic age it became a backwater as Ephesus stole all the trade, and today little remains except a few scanty walls.

Notium and Claros

Notium nearby was the port of Colophon, and although mainly visited these days for its sandy beach, it has some well-preserved sections of wall, the foundations of a temple and stoa and a small theatre. What really makes the trip to the area worthwhile are the excavations at **Claros,** a 20-minute walk from Notium. Here stood the famous temple and oracle of Clarian Apollo, visited from as far away as Britain and southern Russia.

The valley of the temple is flooded every year, and over the ages, the temple disappeared in the mud. In the 1960s it was rediscovered and excavated by the French, though during the wet season good parts of it will be under water. The lower chamber, to which the priest would descend to drink the sacred water and utter the oracles, is all flooded, but you can make out the purposely disconcerting maze-like corridor that led to the *Adyton*, the sacred oracle chamber. The temple was built in the Doric style, surprisingly, because Doric was usually reserved for temples on heights, where it showed to better advantage. A sacred way led to the entrance from the monumental **Propylaea,** or gate. Around the temple, fragments of three colossal statues—of Apollo, Artemis, and their mother Leto—lie strewn about; Apollo's leg alone measures over ten feet. The **altar,** just east of the temple, is some 60 feet long, half dedicated to Apollo, and half to Dionysus, who, as in Delphi, took over the temple during the winter months, when the sun god went to frolic with the Hyperboreans. Near the temple there's a **sundial** dedicated to Dionysus and a smaller, **Ionic temple** dedicated to

Apollo's twin, Artemis, lies north west of the main temple.

Although the structures date from the Hellenistic age, Claros had been a sacred spot for hundreds of years before. The weary Leto (Apollo's mother) stopped here before giving birth as she fled the relentless jealousy of Hera; and here the famous Sibyl, Herophile, predicted that both Asia and Europe would be destroyed because of Helen.

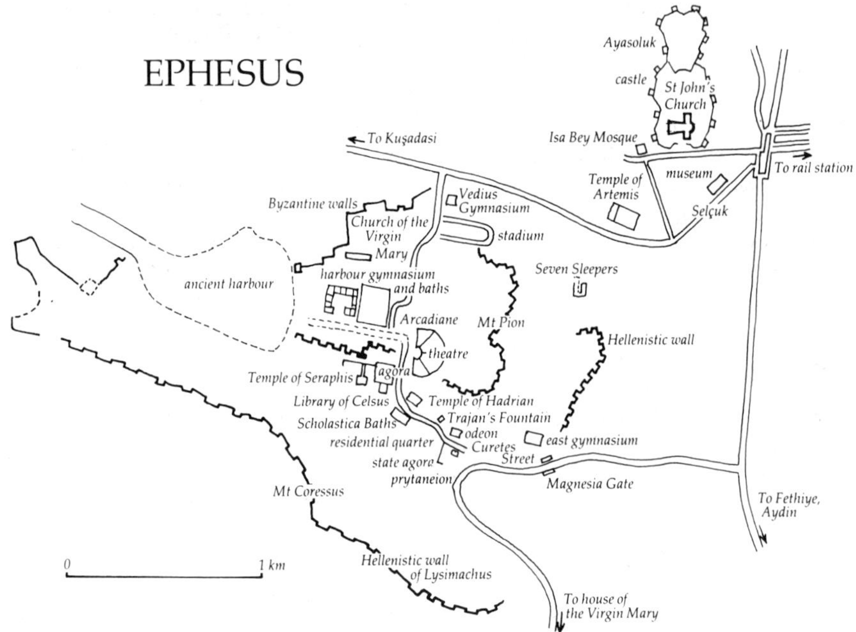

Ephesus

The main highway south of Izmir leads to Selçuk, successor of the great city of **Ephesus.** Of all the ancient cities of Turkey, Ephesus is the best preserved and most visited, in all ages, a destination of pilgrims. Aegean cruise ships often call at the pretty port of Kuşadasi, a short drive away.

HISTORY

Ephesus was first settled by the Lydians and Carians who worshipped the great Anatolian goddess Cybele. When the Ionians arrived, around the tenth century BC, they combined the ancient cult of Cybele with their own of Artemis, a syncretism that had unusual success, even though the Ephesian Artemis has little in common with usual depictions of the Virgin goddess of the chase; she is an oriental, mysterious, fertility figure, studded with breasts—or eggs, a common fertility figure. From the start the new cult was very popular, and the temple was the one constant in the city's history, for Ephesus itself moved no fewer than four times. The early Ionian settlement was on the slopes of Mt Pion (*Panayir Dağí*), above the theatre, and its harbour was near Selçuk. It prospered until Croesus, King of Lydia, conquered it in 550 BC. He destroyed the town and rebuilt it on the plain near the temple of Artemis. There it stayed until 301 BC, when Alexander's general, Lysimachus, who inherited this part of Asia Minor, saw that the River Cayster was silting up the port, and once more relocated the city, this time to the valley between Mt Pion and Mt Coressus.

Here Ephesus had its golden age, especially since Lysimachus removed the citizens of Colophon and Lebedos to populate the new settlement. In Roman times, it was the capital of Asia, the banking and trade centre of the east, and, with some 500 000 inhabitants, the largest city in Anatolia. In its heyday it boasted that it was four times chosen 'Neocorus' or 'temple warden'; four different Roman emperors had granted it permission to construct a temple for their own worship—a great honour. Yet Ephesus' prosperity was subject to one constant vexation: the silting up of its harbour. Several dredgings and other solutions were attempted, with only temporary success; today the sea is more than three miles from Ephesus.

ST PAUL

The city, while still in its prime, witnessed some of the events that marked the great change of religious belief, from the great goddess Artemis, to the new God of the Christians. The Apostle John converted many of the natives to Christianity even before St Paul came to live in the city. After three years, St Paul left memorably: the doctrine he preached attracted so many that the local silversmiths, who made cult figures of Artemis, felt their livelihoods threatened and started a riot. Soon the great theatre was packed with people shouting, 'Great is Artemis of the Ephesians!' The tumult was finally quelled, but St Paul left shortly afterwards. With the decline of Rome and the silting of its harbour, Ephesus dwindled, and in the sixth century the city was abandoned for a new site—modern Selcuk.

THE TEMPLE OF ARTEMIS

Most of what you see in Ephesus today is Roman, except for the melancholy remains of the **Temple of Artemis,** which are about a half mile from the excavations on the Kuşadasi–Selçuk road. This, one of the Seven Wonders of the Ancient World, now has only a single column standing on a ruined fundation, which, as it's below the water table, is often flooded; at the moment of writing a stork was sitting on the lone column. At least three temples have stood on the site. The original, built around the seventh century BC, was replaced in the sixth with a far grander edifice (most importantly, bigger than the temple of Hera, under construction on the nearby island of Samos). The temple measured 179 by 374 feet, larger than a football field, and four times the size of the Parthenon, surrounded by a forest of 129 columns. Amazingly the whole thing was made of marble, except for the wooden roof and inner architrave and in 356 BC, on the night of Alexander the Great's birth (or so they say) a mad arsonist in search of immortal fame burned the temple. It lay in ruins until Alexander himself came and offered to pay for its restoration. The Ephesians politely declined, with the excuse that one god should not build a temple to another. They then rebuilt it themselves on the same massive scale. Gigantic as it was, by the mid-nineteenth century, when British engineer J. T. Wood tried to find it, not a trace remained, so thoroughly had the marble quarriers and mud consumed it. For some nine years, Wood searched for the temple, until 1874 when an inscription discovered in Ephesus gave the directions to the Sacred Way, Wood excavated the Way and followed it to the great temple.

THE MAIN EXCAVATIONS

Excavations at Ephesus begun in 1895 by the Austrians continue to this day. On the road leading to the parking lot lies the vast **Gymnasium of Vedius,** built in AD 150 by a prominent citizen, Publius Vedius Antonius. In the Roman style, the structure combined both gymnasium and baths, the latter and the latrine being well preserved. Next to it is a partially excavated **stadium,** much quarried by the Selçuks for their castle. Across the road are the few remains of a temple, believed to date from the time of Croesus; south of this are some ruined Byzantine baths and the long, narrow **Church of Agia Maria,** built in the second century as a bank and market, and in the third converted into a church dedicated to the Virgin Mary—the first church anywhere to be consecrated to her. Here, in AD 431, the Emperor Theodosius II convened the Third Ecumenical Council that decided that Jesus was both the son of Mary and the Son of God and in 1967 Pope Paul VI celebrated mass in the church.

THE THEATRE

Beyond the parking lot and the ticket booth are the remains of the **Harbour Gymnasium and Baths,** the largest structure in Ephesus, only part of which has been uncovered so far; it included two palaestrae for exercises. Beside it runs the **Arcadiane,** the main street to the harbour, lined with colonnades, two stoas, paved with marble, and one of the few streets in antiquity with street lights. At the end of the street rises the majestic **theatre,** carved into the side of Mt Pion, originally built in the Hellenistic era and remodelled by the Romans under Claudius and Trajan. In classic Greek theatre, all the action took place in the orchestra, but by the Hellenistic age, the actors performed on a small stage set above the orchestra which was now relegated to the increasingly less important chorus. By Roman times, fashion had moved all the drama to the stage, which, in Ephesus, reached grand operatic proportions—three levels with an ornate façade, adorned with statues and columns. The theatre seats 24 000, and is used today during the annual Ephesus Festival. The top seats give a fine view of the city.

ALONG THE MARBLE ROAD

From the theatre, the **Marble Road,** with its deep cart ruts, was the main street of Ephesus. Following it will bring you to a first century **Doric stoa** and, the most elegant of Ephesus' buildings, the **Library of Celsus,** with its lovely white marble façade, fine carvings and statues. This was built in AD 110 by the Consul Gaius Julius Aquila as a temple-tomb for his father, Gaius Julius Celsus, whose unopened lead casket is still in its sarcophagus in the grave chamber. The reading room of the library had three floors; as in Pergamon, niches remain in the walls where the bookshelves once were. In Roman times the reading room burned, but the façade survived unharmed, and in the fifth century the depression around it was filled with water to make a reflecting pool. Behind the **Agora** (currently being restored) stood the **Temple of Serapis,** built in the second century, perhaps by the Egyptian residents of the city, though the god Serapis had a cult following among Greek and Roman alike, and was worshipped throughout the Mediterranean. Like the temple of Serapis in Pergamon, this one is massive; each of its eight monolithic columns weighed 57 tons.

STREET OF THE CURETES

At the library the street turns and becomes **Street of the Curetes.** According to the Ephesians, Artemis was born in the area, at a place called Ortygia; her mother, the goddess Leto pursued by Hera, was able to deliver her here thanks to the Curetes, the young men who frightened Hera away by banging on their shields. The Curetes are perhaps better known for guarding the cradle of the infant Zeus, where their banging kept his unpleasant father Cronos from hearing his cries. Their presence in Ephesus, and the fact that an order of priests in the Artemision were called the Curetes, indicates the primeval nature of the Ephesian Artemis.

The **Baths of Scholastica** (second century AD) were re-named after a Christian lady who remodelled them in the year 400. Her headless statue still presides over the entrance; inscriptions indicate the baths also served as the town brothel. Much of the stone Scholastica used for her remodelling came from the neighbouring **Temple of Hadrian,** which was partially destroyed in an earthquake. Part of it has been reconstructed, and with its four reliefs (the originals are in the museum) it is one of the most attractive monuments in the city. On the other side of Curetus street, on the slopes of

Bülbüldağ (Mountain of the nightingales), a large **residential quarter** has recently been excavated, bringing to light many well-appointed mansions of the Ephesian merchants.

You next come to the fountain of Trajan, or **Nymphaion.** A colossal statue of the emperor once stood over the fountain, and from what remains—his giant feet, one resting on the world—suggest this must have been a colossal work of dubious taste. The street continues past numerous small buildings, some reliefs and fountains, to Domitian Street leading to the ruined **Temple of Domitian** (first century AD) the first of the temples consecrated to imperial worship. Another huge statue stood within, but nowadays the walk to the temple's terrace is justified by the view. Little also has survived of the **Statte Agora** next to the temple. Adjoining the north stoa of the agora is the **Prytaneion,** or city hall, and the **Odeon,** which was probably used for government meetings rather than concerts. An eternal flame was kept burning in the Prytaneion and it was here that the two fine statues of Artemis in the museum were found, carefully buried perhaps by a secret worshipper to hide them from the Christians.

THE SEVEN SLEEPERS

The road goes on past a great fountain, another bath and the **East Gymnasium** (all second century AD) on its way to the ruined **Magnesian Gate,** one of the two main gates of the city built by Emperor Vespasian c. AD 75. The Sacred Way to the Temple of Artemis passed through here and around Mt Pion. Following the track, you pass a large, impressive early Christian cemetery that surrounds a church and the graves of the **Seven Sleepers.** The Seven Sleepers are a popular motif in Christian and Turkish folklore; here, in the mid-third century, there were seven young men of Ephesus who hid in a cave in the mountain; good Christians, they wanted to escape the mandatory imperial worship. They fell asleep, and when they woke, discovered that they had slept for 200 years. When they died they were buried here, and the church was built over them. The track continues to modern **Selçuk.** (Taking the track to the right from the Magnesian Gate leads to the **Walls of Lysimachus,** well preserved in many places.)

Selçuk

Selçuk has an exceptionally fine **archaeology museum.** Here are the two statues of Artemis, a dramatic tableau of Odysseus blinding the Cyclops, some lovely carved ivory furniture, erotic statuary from the brothel, and most surprising, a frieze from the altar of the Temple of Domitian in a style that can only be called Roman Art Deco.

Dominating Selçuk is the old acropolis of Ephesus, crowned by Justinian with the **Basilica of St John.** The Apostle John was said to have lived the last years of his life here and his burial spot is marked by a slab of marble.

The church was once covered with a large central dome and several smaller domes to form a cross. Today you enter through the **Gate of Persecution** (no one knows the origin of the name), and can see the baptistry, the apse with some surviving tenth-century frescoes in a shelter. Directly above the basilica towers the **Citadel of Ayasoluk,** with its Byzantine-Turkish fortifications, unfortunately usually closed to visitors. Just below the church stands one of the masterpieces of Selçuk Turkish architecture, the **Isa Bey Mosque,** built in 1375. Isa Bey was a prince of the Aydin Turks who ruled western Anatolia for a brief period in the fourteenth century, and his mosque was the first to be built with a courtyard, anticipating the later Ottoman style.

AROUND SELÇUK

Five miles southeast of Selçuk is the Panayia Kapulu, or the **House of the Blessed Virgin,** where Mary, who accompanied St John to Ephesus, is said to have died. While the site has long been associated with the Virgin, the house was unknown until 1891. The story of its discovery curiously parallels a common Middle Eastern folktale; in this case, a German woman called Catherine Emmerich, who had never been to Ephesus and who had been an invalid for twelve years, had a series of visions which enabled her to give exact directions to the house and a detailed description. In 1891, a search party found it exactly where and as she had described it; a brick house of the sixth century, its foundations dating back to the first. (Similarly, Mehmet Fatih discovered the grave of Mohammed's standard-bearer Eyüp near Istanbul, and this house has become a holy shrine, visited by Pope John Paul II.) The Virgin's tomb, according to Catherine Emmerich, is about a mile from the house, but has never been found.

Belevi

Ten miles north-east of Selçuk, on the Izmir road, in the village of **Belevi** are two unusual monumental tombs. One, known as the **Belevi Mausoleum** is just off the road; it stands on a massive square base carved from living rock, topped by a chamber of marble, surrounded by columns and sculpture; the sarcophagus, however, was hidden in the base in an effort to foil grave robbers (it is now in the Selçuk Museum). Many believe the man buried here was the Seleucid King Antiochus II who died in Ephesus in 246 BC, poisoned by his wife. The other tomb, a hilltop tumulus surrounded with a wall of fine masonry, also probably dates from the third century BC.

Kuşadasi

Kuşadasi in the early seventies was still a sleepy little port town; today it has become Turkey's slickest, and one of its most expensive tourist resorts, where seven or eight cruise ships call a day, and luxury yachts under many different flags bask in the marina. Kuşadasi means 'bird island' in Turkish; there's an offshore islet, called Pigeon Island, the site of a Genoese castle, with cafes and a garden dotted with pigeon houses. The caravanserai in the centre of the town is now a hotel and restaurant. There are beaches on either side of town.

In 1985 the forests above Kuşadasi and Ephesus were hit by a devastating forest fire but beautiful **Samsundağ National Park** on the peninsula 20 miles to the south was spared. The park encompasses the beautiful Mt Mycale (modern *Samsundağ*), its 4082 feet plunging down into the strait facing Samos; it has abundant wildlife, caves, beaches, springs, and a castle. There are campsites and picnic grounds and paths up the mountain (though visitors are advised not to go walking alone because of the bears).

GETTING AROUND

Kuşadasi is a port of the Turkish Maritime Lines cruises and is linked year round with the Greek island of Samos; in the summer as many as five boats make the crossing a day. Buses go to Selçuk (a kilometre from Ephesus) and Kuşadasi every hour from Izmir; between Kuşadasi and Selçuk there are minibuses every 20 minutes or so in season. There's also a typically slow rail connection between Izmir and Selçuk. To reach Colophon and Claros, take the bus from Izmir. Stylish fifties dolmuş line up by the Kervansaray hotel in Kuşadasi, linking the port to the nearest beach, Kadinlar. For Samsundağ National Park you must take a taxi.

TOURIST INFORMATION

Near the quay, Kuşadasi, tel. (6361) 1103. (Kuşadasi's Haşet Bookstore has an excellent selection of books about Turkey in English.) Selçuk: next to the Agora, tel. (5451) 328.

WHERE TO STAY

Kuşadasi has a wide range of accommodation in every category. For luxury, there's the elegant **Mehmet Paşa Kulüp Kervansaray** (open April–October), located in the centre of town in a 17th century caravanserai, with a beautiful garden restaurant in the courtyard. Tel. (6361) 2415, rates are 8500 TL for a single, 11 100 for a double. If you'd prefer something on the beach, the **Tusan Oteli,** south at 31'ler beach, tel. (6361) 1094 fits the bill and offers a wide range of recreational facilities. Open year round, singles are 11 200 TL, doubles 14 000 TL. In the town, and open year round is the new **Efe Oteli** at Guverçin Ada Cad. 37, tel. (6361) 2404, where a single with bath is 6500 TL, doubles 8400 TL. Most meticulously clean of the cheaper hotels is the **Neptun,** at Bezirgin Sok, tel. (6361) 1540, with fine views, where a single is around 2000 TL, and a double 2500 TL, with hot showers. There are 3 campsites within a kilometre or two of Kuşadasi: **Cennet Camping,** tel. (6361) 1500 and adjacent **Diana Mokamp** (6361) 1457 are on the Izmir road, as is **Önder Camping** (6361) 2413, furthest and the most pleasant. In Selçuk you can find many homes with rooms; just follow the little *pansiyon* signs. There's also the friendly **Kale Han Guest House** on Kalealti Sok, tel. (5451) 154, in a renovated stone inn; open all year, rates are 3750 TL a single, 5250 for a double.

EATING OUT

Kuşadasi has many excellent fish restaurants on the waterfront though they are expensive. Generally the further you go from the sea the less expensive places are. **Duyur Restaurant** next to the bus station is good value at 300 TL–500 TL for a full course meal. For döner kebab, the tastiest is at **ALP** on Teyyare Cad., where an order with all the trimmings is 400 TL. In Selçuk the **Hitit Restaurant** on the main street is good and reasonable (700 TL) as is the **Villa,** in a garden across from the market, with very spicy Adana kebabs, for 400 TL. The **Meryemana Restaurant** is next to the House of the Virgin Mary and serves average food at slightly higher than average prices.

The Maeander Valley

The cities of southern and eastern Ionia grew up around the Maeander (modern Menderes), the largest and most important river of western Asia Minor. Its often changing course gave us the word 'meander'; yet much as the river contributed to the fertility of the soil through its annual flooding, and to trade, it proved as much a curse as a blessing to Priene and Miletus, the two cities at its mouth. Like Ephesus, both were once on the coast, but the tons of silt the Maeander carried down to the sea each year filled up their harbours, and caused them to be abandoned. Today both are miles from the sea.

Priene

Priene was never a large city; estimates of its greatest size range from 4000 to 6000 free citizens. Nor did it play much of a role in the politics of the age. In late Roman times, as its harbour gradually became unusable, the city dwindled, and after the sixth century nothing more is heard of it. Even so, you may find its ruins more alive, more evocative of the ancient world than the other cities of Asia Minor. Despite its small size, Priene had a reputation as a city of talent and accomplishment. Its remains, largely excavated and quite well preserved, reveal a well-built and beautiful city, especially its residential quarters. Also, Priene's very lack of prosperity under the Romans make it, in one sense, unique. Unable to build on the scale of Ephesus, Priene changed little after the fourth century BC; outside Greece itself it remains the best example of a Hellenistic city.

Nothing remains of the original Priene, founded at the same time as the other Ionian cities. Its site on the Maeander hasn't even been found. By the fourth century, the advancing coastline made a new foundation necessary, and with the support of Athens, a new Priene was laid out on the slopes of Mt Mycale. Following the precepts of Hippodamus of Miletus, the famous town planner, the steep and difficult site was forced into a strict gridiron plan of narrow streets, with a broad central avenue connecting the major buildings and agoras. The plan has an elegant simplicity, but it's a matter for conjecture whether the Prieneans used it for art's sake or simply to make land surveys easier.

THE SITE

After a fair climb up from the parking lot, you enter Priene through the northwest gate. Continuing across this unexcavated portion of the town will bring you to one of the finest extant examples of a classical Greek **theatre.** Unlike the theatres elsewhere in Asia Minor, built under the Romans and intended as much for wild beast shows as for drama, this one is small and horseshoe-shaped, leaving more space for the orchestra and chorus, the centre of attention in a Greek play. The seats around the orchestra were for the nobles of the city, a kind of ancient dress circle. At the centre is an altar, dedicated to Dionysus. Also unlike later works, there is no elaborate stage building. The small colonnaded structure, the **proskenion,** dates from the second century BC. Originally, the three doors were used for the entrance of actors, and the spaces between them covered with painted boards for scenery. The roof of the proskenion, used for the deus ex machina, took more and more of the action as drama evolved; eventually it came to hold the action, and the proscenium became what we know as the stage.

Facing it, at the right hand end of the first row of seats, is a square stone base that held a water clock; as Greek theatres were also used for political meetings, and occasionally also for important trials, the water clock controlled the time allotted to each speaker.

Immediately below the theatre are the foundations of a Byzantine church and a gymnasium. Below these lies the **agora** and centre of the city. On its north side the **sacred stoa,** according to its inscriptions, was built as a gift of King Ariarthres VI of Cappadocia. The well preserved **bouleuterion** behind it has become one of the famous buildings of Greek Ionia thanks to a beautifully drawn reconstruction that appears in most books on Greek architecture. Even among the ruins, though, you can gain an insight into the public life of an ancient Greek democracy. A bouleuterion is a council house, where matters not crucial enough to submit to the citizen assembly were discussed. Speakers stood next to the altar that held the sacred fire, symbolising the purity and continuity of Priene's civic life. Their peers, in the seats on three sides, were close enough to look them in the eye. Next to the bouleuterion is the **prytaneion,** where committees delegated by the council dealt with routine city business.

THE TEMPLE OF ATHENA

The agora served as the central square of Priene, devoted to commercial and religious affairs as well as political. The small square just to the east was the city's food market while the sanctuary of Zeus Olympios, now gone, occupied the square's eastern face. Just to the northwest of the agora, stairs up from another stoa lead to the most important building of Priene, the **Temple of Athena.** Its architect, Pytheos, also designed the Mausoleum of Halicarnassus, one of the wonders of the ancient world. Pytheos himself, though, seems to have thought more of this temple; he wrote a book about it, a classic example of the Ionian order, that was used as a textbook by architects throughout the Mediterranean. Several of the columns have been re-erected, and it's not hard to imagine how the temple must have appeared, looming over the agora. Priene's most conspicuous landmark, it could be seen for miles around. Here, as in all the city's buildings, the predominating grey of the stone gives you a false impression of Priene. Under its weathered surface the stone is really a luminous cream-coloured marble from Mt Mycale. Almost everything was built from it, and the view of the city from the distance must have been dazzling.

An inscription on the temple relates that Alexander the Great financed the completion of the temple. For this, and for their liberation from the Persians, the Prieneans devoted a small shrine to him, in the company of the other gods. The **House of Alexander** is near the end of the central avenue, where it passes through the western gate. On the way, you go through the excavated residential district of Priene. The houses, four to a block, with central courtyards, are among the best preserved in Ionia, though the remaining walls are seldom very high. The finest ones are just a few squares west of the theatre.

If you're up to a little climbing, you may visit the other sites on the north and south sides of town. In the northern heights, not too far above the theatre, is the oldest temple in Priene, the **Sanctuary of Demeter and Kore** where the temenos wall, benches to hold votive statues, and the sacrificial pit can be seen. To the south, just below the agora at the city's walls, are the **gymnasium,** with its well preserved washrooms, where the water poured out of lion-headed spouts, and the **stadium.** Like the theatre, this is an example of the earlier Greek style, rather than one of the Roman extravaganzas. Seats are only on one side, and the course is a short and simple one-way track. There are remains of the starting gate near the entrance from the gymnasium, the Greeks started their runners as we do horses.

Miletus

Priene stood on the northern edge of the Latmian Gulf, the inlet now filled by the advancing delta of the Maeander. On the southern shore was **Miletus,** first among the Greek cities before the fifth century BC. Few cities have ever achieved such power and brilliance, with as little left to show for it. The river again is to blame. Of the original Miletus few traces remain; scholars still dispute its location. The present ruins date from the second foundation, after the old city had been completely destroyed by the Persians in 495 BC.

HISTORY

Miletus' origins are shadowy. Mythology credits an eponymous founder, a mortal son of Apollo who sailed from Crete; it is believed the Cretans in their heyday made the town into the greatest naval base of the Aegean. Another story has the Ionians seizing the town, killing all the Cretan men and marrying their wives. The Mycenaeans were here too, the ancient legends have been borne out by the recent discovery of Mycenaean tombs. In about 700 BC, Miletus really began to prosper, controlling the Aegean trade routes and sending out more colonies than any other Greek city—ninety of them, from Naukratis on the Nile delta to Sinope on the Black Sea.

With these accomplishments, Miletus must also be given much of the credit for the golden age of classical Greece. Thales, foremost among the Seven Sages, was a Milesian as were the early philosophers Anaximander and Anaximenes. Only after the sack by the Persians did Miletus begin to lose its cultural pre-eminence. Even before that, artists and philosophers had begun to drift off to the growing city of Athens. Yet when Miletus suffered its great defeat, there was so much sympathy between it and Athens that a play called 'The Fall of Miletus' caused the whole audience to burst into tears, for which the dramatist was fined 1000 drachmae.

Miletus was rebuilt immediately after its disaster, on a new site and with a new gridiron plan according to the precepts of its native son Hippodamus. Its arrangement of agoras and public buildings was a triumph of Greek urban design, but you can see that from the ruins. It is, in fact, likely to be the biggest archaeological disappointment of your trip. So thoroughly has the Maeander scrubbed away and silted over its ruins that little beside the theatre remains. It is now difficult to tell even where the coastline was, and the city that contributed so much to western civilisation has become a creepy desolation of muck and prickly weeds.

THE SITE

With a map from the small **museum,** a half mile south of the ruins, you can find some of the city. Miletus' great **theatre,** then as now the most conspicuous landmark, rises on a hillside above one of the city's five harbours, well preserved above the floods of the Maeander. The Roman theatre, with seats for 15 000, was built around the earlier work of the fourth century BC that seated only a third as many. The columns that marked the 'royal box' still stand. Scanty ruins of an agora and the stadium occupy the harbour's opposite shore. From this side of Miletus, you have a good view of the island of Lade, now a mere hill in the Maeander Plain. Here, in 495 BC the Persian navy destroyed the combined fleets of the Ionian cities and put an end to their rebellion. Miletus had been the leader of the revolt, and its destruction was assured. Ironically, the Persian garrison later took refuge here when Alexander the Great stormed the town.

Climbing over the hill on which the theatre was set takes you to the **city centre,** a network of stoas, avenues, and agoras around the narrow **Bay of Lions.** In wartime this harbour had special significance; it needed no fortifications on the shore, as a chain could easily be extended across it to protect both the town and the fleet. Some searching among the weeds reveals the two big stone lions that stood on either side of the harbour giving it its name. Inside the harbour, there is a large triangular base that once held a **monument of Augustus,** commemorating his victory over Cleopatra and Mark Antony at Actium in 31 BC.

Around the harbour, the only structures of interest are along the wide processional avenue; first, the **Temple of Apollo Delphinius,** with the foundations of a colonnaded sanctuary with statue bases and a curious circular temple. On the same side of the avenue are the **Capito Baths,** the **gymnasium,** a **nymphaion,** and a fifth-century **church.** If you wish to make any further explorations, follow the avenue south through the enormous **south agora;** beyond lies a fine fifteenth-century mosque, **Ilyas Bey Camii,** belonging to the nearby village of Yeniköy. The low hill beyond the city's southern walls called *Kalabak Tepe* is believed to be the acropolis of the original Miletus.

Medusa Head from the Frieze of the Temple, Didyma

Didyma

If Miletus disappoints, **Didyma** won't; Didyma, south of Miletus and in its territory, is only a temple and not a city. Yet few in western Asia Minor are so well preserved or impressive.

Didyma was a holy site before the Ionians ever arrived, and was believed to be the oldest oracle in Asia Minor. The Greeks rededicated the Anatolian cult to their own god Apollo and continued the oracle. When Croesus was considering his invasion of Persia, he wanted the advice of an oracle, but first decided to put three of them to the test. He sent ambassadors to ask each of them, on the same day 'What is King Croesus doing?' Delphi knew he was boiling a lamb and tortoise stew, Didyma failed utterly. When the Persians sacked Miletus they also destroyed the temple and its oracle, which was silent until the advent of Alexander the Great. Then the sacred spring suddenly flowed again, and the oracle declared Alexander to be the son of Zeus.

Seleucus I of Syria started to rebuild the temple on a massive scale; work continued for some five hundred years but was never finished. It is almost as large as the Artemission in Ephesus, encompassed by a double row of columns, some 120 in all. The cella, with its 70-foot walls, was too large to be roofed over, so the cult statue of Apollo was kept in a smaller temple behind the cella. Many columns have been re-erected by the excavators. Because the temple was never completed, some of the columns are unfluted, and many of the blocks still bear the masons' marks. Every five years the Didymeia—sports, drama, and music contests—were held at the sanctuary and the **stadium** next to it; names carved in the steps of the temple are those of spectators with reserved seats.

Lake Bafa and Heracleia

Near Didyma there are two beauty spots: **Altinkum** with fine sandy beaches on the tip of Didyma's peninsula, and a lake, **Bafa Gölu** on the main north–south highway, once part of the sea, cut off by the silting Maeander, its wonderfully blue waters now fresh. Overlooking the lake towers the looming jagged form of Mt Latmos where the beautiful shepherd Endymion lived, beloved by the moon goddess Selene and blessed by Zeus with perpetual youth.

Beneath the mountain stood **Heracleia,** a Carian city (the Carians, like the Lydians and Lycians, were a native people of Anatolia later Hellenised by the Greeks). Heracleia was never very important, but is a must for all romantics, who, for the full effect, must sail to it across the lake from the camp site on the shore (a new road also leads around the lake to the site). The ruins are impressive; especially the walls and defensive works built by Lysimachus in the third century BC that twist and clamber up the slopes of Mt Latmos. The setting gives the towers, gates, stairs, and parapets an other-worldly air.

In the city, the **Temple of Athena,** high on a bluff, dominates the other monuments, its cella walls intact. The **agora** behind the temple is also well preserved, especially its fine south wall. The theatre, nymphaeum, and bouleuterion have not held up so well, but in the southern part of Heracleia is an unusual temple identified as the **Sanctuary of Endymion,** partially cut into the rock, rounded in the back, with a row of columns in the front. The early Christians, who had several monasteries and hermitages in the area, venerated Endymion as a mystic saint, who spent his life on Mt Latmos meditating on the moon, seeking the name of God. When he finally learned it, he died and was laid to rest here. Once a year the Christians opened up his coffin, at which his bones were said to hum, trying to communicate the name of God. Further south, beyond the **Byzantine castle** is a **Carian necropolis,** the graves cut into the rock, some of them under the surface of the lake.

Myus and Magnesia ad Maeander

Up the Maeander from Lake Bafa are the scanty remains of an Ionian city,

Myus, lying between the north shore of the lake and the river, near the modern village of Avşar; it was chiefly notable for malaria and for having once been given away by Philip V of Macedon in exchange for the figs given him by **Magnesia ad Maeander,** which is up the river, between Söke and Ortaklar.

Like the other Magnesia (now Manisa), Magnesia ad Maeander was founded by settlers from Greek Magnesia. Under the Persians Magnesia itself was given away to their old enemy, Themistocles, hero of the Great Athenian victory over the Persians in 480 BC. Towards the end of his career Themistocles lost the favour of the Athenians and struck up a friendship with the Persian king Artaxerxes who gave him Magnesia (for his bread), Lampsacus (his wine) and **Myus** (food to go with his bread). Themistocles lived in Magnesia and is said to have committed suicide there by drinking bull's blood, while sacrificing at the **Temple of Artemis Leucophryene,** the only monument of Magnesia that has survived. The temple dates from the second century BC, after the goddess herself made a miraculous appearance in the city. Because of this, Magnesia was considered sacred, and had no walls.

Tralles (Aydin) and Nyssa

Continuing up the fertile Maeander valley, you come to the large town of **Aydin,** the descendent of ancient **Tralles,** which is just to the west. A military installation now occupies the site, and it can only be visited with special permission. Its chief claim to fame was its son Anthemius, mathematician and co-architect of the Aya Sofia. Twenty miles to the east, a sign directs you to ancient **Nyssa,** close to the main highway, near modern Sultanhisar. The city, in a lovely, picturesque gorge beneath Mt Messogis, was founded by Antiochus I in the third century BC; most of what we know about it comes from the geographer Strabo, who studied there. He calls it 'a double city', half of the year a torrential stream divides it in two. Remains to be seen are an excellently preserved **library,** a two-storey structure built by the Romans and the **theatre,** a Roman Imperial structure equipped for the staging of simulated sea battles. Strabo described the impressive vaulted **tunnel** that helped drain the spring torrents and supports the square in front of the theatre, a **Roman bridge** nearby also spans the gorge, as did the amphitheatre, or **stadium,** though the seats have been destroyed by flooding. On the other side of the torrent you can see a fine **bouleuterion** from the second century AD and the remains of the **agora.**

Aphrodisias

Aphrodisias, a lofty plateau below the slopes of Babadağ ('Mt Dad'), is a 70 kilometre detour south of the Maeander, but one that most people find worthwhile. This ancient city, dedicated to the goddess of love, is one of most exciting recent discoveries in Turkey. Excavations begun in 1961, by Dr Kenan T. Erim and the University of New York, partially financed by the National Geographic Society, have revealed monuments and statues of great beauty, owing their state of preservation, in part, to earthquakes in the Middle Ages that covered the city and its approaches.

The site was always sacred, perhaps as early as the Neolithic age; Aphrodite's predecessor may have been the eastern goddess Ishtar or Astarte; the Carians called the city Ninoe, their name for the goddess. By the Hellenistic age, 'Ninoe' had become 'Aphrodite'. History tells us little about Aphrodisias, except that the Romans preserved the sanctity of the great Temple of Aphrodite; the young Octavian was so impressed with it that he declared, 'I choose this city from among all those in Asia for myself...'. By the Middle Ages, the town was known simply as Caria, as it was the chief town in the province, and this was corrupted into Geyre, the name of the village at the site. From the quantity of excellent statuary found, made of the fine bluish marble from Babadağ, it has been concluded that a very creative school of sculpture existed here, adorning Aphrodisias itself and exporting many works throughout the Mediterranean; signatures on works elsewhere are now identified with the 'Aphrodisian school'. A small museum has recently opened on the site to house the statues.

THE SITE

Of the city, little more than a third has yet been excavated. The Temple of Aphrodite in the centre of the site was built in about 100 BC over a sanctuary at least 600 years older; 14 of its columns still stand. Hadrian built the **monumental gateway** that led into the temenos, or sanctuary area; south of it lie the **odeon,** which has a fine mosaic floor, and the **Bishop's residence,** this dating from the fifth century when the temple was converted into a church. South again is the **agora,** impressive even though it has yet to be excavated. The porticos in the north are in the Doric style, those in the south in the Ionic, the splendid columns set off by a poplar grove. Further south is the great **Portico of Tiberius** and the giant **Baths of Hadrian,** with their huge galleries, heated rooms, and palaestra. A smaller bath stood near the **theatre,** which has a seating capacity of 10 000, and is built into the side of a mound, or tell, of several Early Bronze age settlements. North of Aphrodite's temple is the **stadium,** perhaps the largest, and certainly one of the best preserved ever discovered. It stretches 865 feet from end to end and could seat 30 000; one side was enclosed for gladiatorial bouts.

Denizli

Returning to the main highway, the E24, you continue to **Laodicea,** chiefly remembered today as one of the Seven Churches of Asia addressed by John in *Revelations* and as the last residence of Cicero. At the head of the Maeander valley is the major market town of **Denizli** unremarkable except for two statues of chickens, the bird to whom the city owes its present prosperity, one in the centre of town and one in the roundabout on the road to Pamukkale.

The calcareous waterfalls of Pamukkale

Pamukkale

Pamukkale ('Cotton Castle') is one of the most enchanting and remarkable sights in the whole of Turkey. Although there are photographs of it all over the place, they hardly prepare you for the sight of the great dazzling white plateau, almost 400 feet high, rising in a curtain of stalagmites and shallow pools, giving one into another on hundreds of different levels, a fairyland of cotton white forms and pale blue water cascading gently down. This amazing confection was formed by nothing but the limestone-rich water issuing from the thermal springs of Cal Daği. If you have young children, frolicking in the glistening pools with the lovely green valley of the Maeander spread out far below, will very likely be the highlight of their holiday.

HIERAPOLIS

The charms of the place and its thermal springs also caught the eye of Eumenes II of Pergamon, who founded the Holy City, or **Hierapolis** on top of the plateau. Like Pergamon itself, the will of Attalos III bequeathed Hierapolis to Rome. An earthquake shattered it in AD 17, but it was quickly rebuilt and had its greatest prosperity in the second and third centuries. The Apostle Philip lived here and was martyred in the year AD 80, and in the Byzantine era, the church of St Philip dominated the town.

The great **Baths** near the parking area were constructed in the second century and are so well preserved that they now serve as a **museum,** displaying the fine marbles unearthed by the Italian excavators of the site; many of the statues come from the Aphrodisian school. At least three Roman Emperors visited Hïerapolis and bathed in the portion of the bath especially reserved for them.

Behind the bath stands a **temple of Apollo,** chief deity of the city, a **fountain,** and a small grotto believed to have been a sanctuary of Pluto, the god of the Underworld; a sign warns of poisonous vapours. The impressive and recently restored **theatre** dates from the second century AD, and is especially interesting for the fine reliefs of Artemis. Behind the theatre and outside the Roman wall is the **Martyrium of St Philip the Apostle,** of the fifth century. From the bath, the road leads to the other excavations: a **colonnaded street** erected by Domitian, a monumental **gate** of the same period, another **bath,** and stretching on for over a mile, the **necropolis** with a fascinating variety of tombs and sarcophagi dating from Hierapolis' foundation up into Christian times.

Many of the hotels in Pamukkale have their own thermal springs; one, the aptly named Turizm Hotel, captured the prize of the lot: the ancient **Sacred Pool.** The water is warm and slightly effervescent and a lovely garden surrounds the pool; for a small fee, non-residents can while away an afternoon in this dreamland.

GETTING AROUND

Söke is the transportation hub for the coastal area, with frequent minibus service to Priene and Didyma. There's no public transport to Miletus, though a Söke minibus goes to Yeniköy,.5 kilometres away. To reach Lake Bafa, take a bus from Söke to Bodrum and ask to be let off at the lake. From the campgrounds, you can take a boat to Heracleia.

Trains run frequently from Izmir and Selçuk to Aydin and Denizli; the overnight 'Pamukkale mototreni' connects Denizli with Istanbul and Ankara. Buses are twice an hour from Izmir to Selçuk to Denizli; from Denizili minibus-dolmuş go up to Pamukkale when they have a load of passengers. Minibuses also provide service to Aphrodisias from Nazilli, or you can take a direct bus from Izmir to Geyre, or Karacasu, a larger village 12 kilometres away, with dolmuş service to Geyre.

TOURIST INFORMATION

In Aydin, Aydin Il Halk Kültüphanesi Binasi, tel. (6311) 4145. In Denizli, next to the train station, tel. (621) 13393.

WHERE TO STAY

Söke is very dull; it is better to stay near Didyma on lovely Altinkum beach at the **Çamlik Pansiyon** (open May–September), tel. (6351) 58; its ten rooms are 2000 TL a single, 3500 TL a double. There are numerous other inexpensive pansiyons as well. On beautiful Lake Bafa there are three places to camp, the best of them, **Çerinin Camping**; it has a decent restaurant as well. If you're not camping, there's the **Turgut Motel** with doubles for 4000 TL. In Pamukkale you can either stay in the hotels on the top of the falls, or stay cheaply in the village below. On top you can stay around the Sacred Pool in the **Motel Turizm**, which is exactly as the name suggests, though the pool is beautiful and you can splash around in as much as you wish; rates are 5000 TL for a double. The **Tusan Motel** is right behind some of the nicest pools, tel. (local) 1, rates are 7500 TL for a double. Down in the village (a path leads down from the cliff) **Ali's Travellers Resthouse** (local) 52 is a famous institution, with everything from a campground to private rooms, a restaurant to a swimming pool. A single room at Ali's is 650 TL, a double 900 TL. There are many hotels in Denizli if Pamukkale is full, but otherwise there's no reason to stay there.

EATING OUT

Right below Priene, next to the waterfall is the **Şelale** restaurant, a wonderful oasis after clambering over the ruins in the sun, and you can eat for around 500 TL. There are many more restaurants and lokantas by Didyma, and several around Lake Bafa. In Pamukkale nearly all the restaurants are attached to the hotels and are somewhat overpriced—except for Ali's, which is one of the liveliest places in all Turkey, dinner runs around 400 TL.

Caria: Euromos to Bodrum

This section of the southwest coast once belonged to the Carians, yet another native people more or less Hellenised by the time history discovered them.

Small Carian cities

Euromos, the northernmost Carian city, is notable these days for its

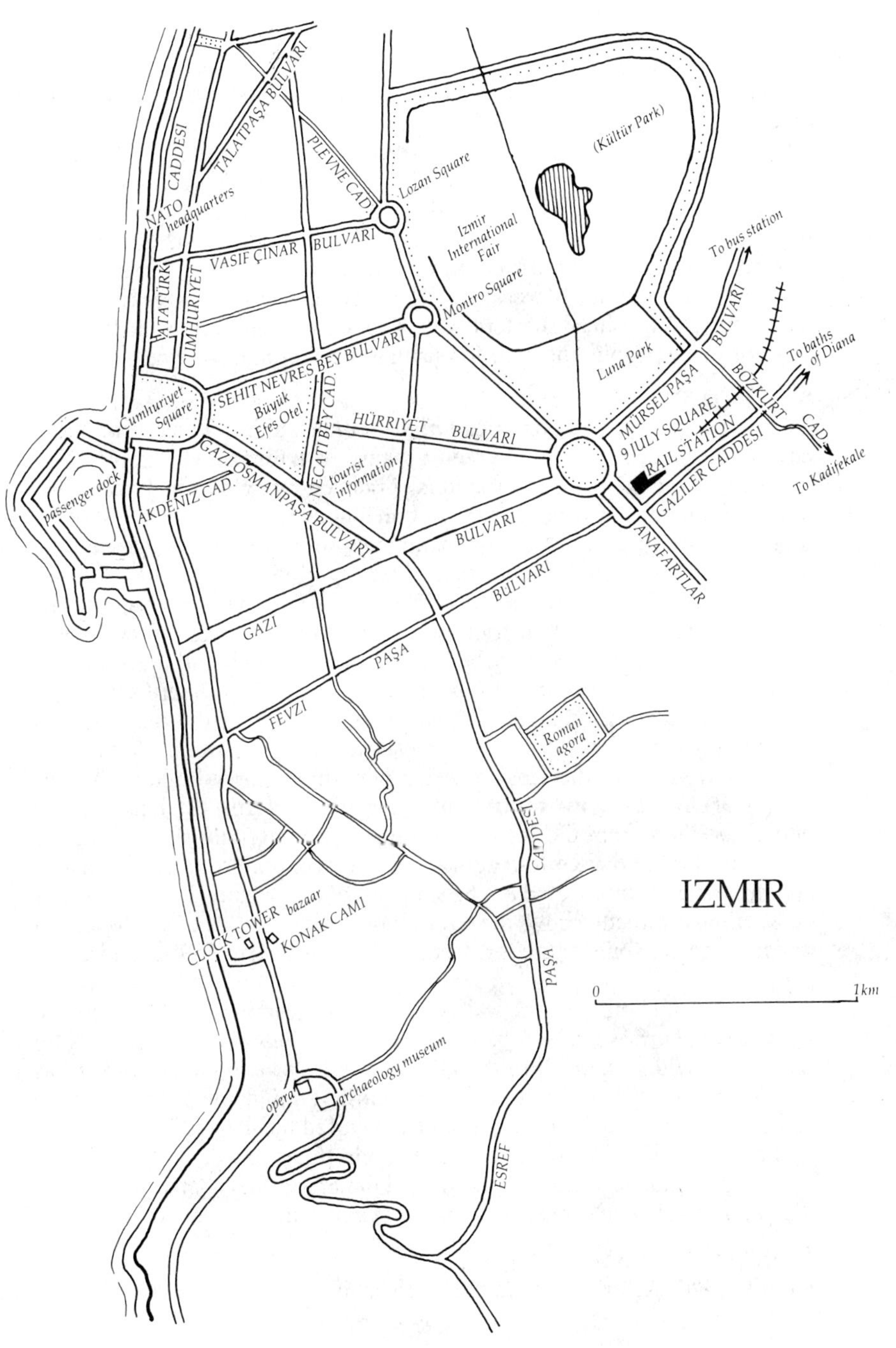
IZMIR
NATO CADDESI
TALATPAŞA BULVARI
PLEVNE CAD
Lozan Square
(Kültür Park)
headquarters
VASIF ÇINAR BULVARI
Izmir International Fair
To bus station
ATATÜRK
CUMHURIYET
Montro Square
BULVARI
SEHIT NEVRES BEY BULVARI
Luna Park
To baths of Diana
Cumhuriyet Square
Büyük Efes Otel
NECATI BEY CAD.
HÜRRIYET BULVARI
MÜRSEL PAŞA
BOZKURT
9 JULY SQUARE
CAD
RAIL STATION
GAZI OSMANPAŞA BULVARI
tourist information
GAZILER CADDESI
To Kadifekale
passenger dock
AKDENIZ CAD.
BULVARI
ANAFARTLAR
BULVARI
GAZI
PAŞA
FEVZI
Roman agora
CADDESI
CLOCK TOWER
bazaar
KONAK CAMI
PAŞA
0
1km
opera
archaeology museum
ESREF

majestic **Temple of Zeus** (second century AD), lying tantalisingly close to the highway (Rt 525). It's one of the few Corinthian temples along the coast; sixteen of its elegant columns and their architraves still stand in place.

Inland from here are four Carian cities with exasperatingly similar names. **Alinda,** once the capital of Queen Ada, sister of King Mausoleus and good pal of Alexander the Great, is on a height near the village Karpuzlu. Seldom visited and never excavated, it offers a romantic vision with its walls, theatre, and agora. **Alabanda,** near modern **Çine,** was also briefly capital of Caria, and still has its fine wall, bouleuterion, a theatre and a **temple of Apollo** mentioned by Vitruvius. The river Çine Çay with its gorge, is ruggedly picturesque, especially along the road between Çine and Yatağan Göktepe. In antiquity the river was called **Marsyas,** after the flute playing satyr who had the audacity to challenge Apollo and his lyre to a musical contest, with the Muses as judge. When the god was proclaimed victor, Apollo, never known for his sense of humour, flayed Marsyas alive and hung his skin on a tree at the source of the Çine Çay.

Lagina, on the east bank of the river, is the site of the **Hekateion,** an important Carian sanctuary, part of which survives. **Labranda,** the city of the double axe ('labrys' in ancient Crete) had another famous Carian sanctuary dedicated to Zeus. The remains here are interesting and include well preserved *androns* (palaces reserved for the royal family) notable for their windows. A Sacred Way linked the ten miles between Labranda and the city of Mylasa (modern **Milas**) in the fourth century BC, but nowadays, short of walking, access to the ruins is limited to those with four-wheel drive vehicles. In Milas is the large **Baltali Kapi,** the Roman gate 'of the axe' where the sacred way began. Milas is an interesting town with old Turkish architecture and three fourteenth-century mosques.

Back on the coast, **Iasos** has recently been excavated to reveal the best preserved Carian city; most memorable here is the **mausoleum,** which has been restored. For a while splendid mausoleums were the fad in Caria, inspired by the great model in Halicarnassus. Iasos is near pretty **Güllük,** an oasis on its own small gulf.

Bodrum

Whitewashed and flower-decked **Bodrum** is one of the most charming cities on the Aegean coast; but it's well known, and more people come every year. Located on the southern shore of the Bodrum peninsula, it lies in a sunny region of often spectacular scenery and sandy beaches; approaching it by land, it makes an unforgettable impression, even at night when its great landmark, the Castle of St Peter, is illuminated in a golden light.

Bodrum Castle and the Bay

HALICARNASSUS

Bodrum is on the site of ancient **Halicarnassus,** originally a Carian city and colonised by the Dorians around 1000 BC. It belonged to the Dorian 'hexapolis', which included the three cities on Rhodes as well as Kos and Cnidos, but when Halicarnassus began to dominate the league, the other cities expelled it. Later, it quickly came under the influence of the Ionians, and in 485 BC, Herodotus, the 'Father of History' was born here. The city's most glorious period, however, came under King Mausoleus of Caria, and was his capital during his reign from 377 to 353 BC. Under him, Caria became a powerful and independent state, and on his death, his wife and sister Artemisia built the famous Mausoleum for his tomb, one of the Seven Wonders of the World. When the city was later destroyed by Alexander the Great, with the assistance of Queen Ada of Alinda, the younger sister of Mausoleus and Artemisia, he spared the Mausoleum. The Knights of St John lost their castle in Smyrna to Tamerlane in 1402, and came here; finding the Mausoleum toppled, they used it as material to build their **Castle of St Peter.** Together with their fortifications on the islands of Kos and Rhodes, they dominated the southeastern Aegean, ruling the seas as privateers in their swift vessels.

One of the most interesting people to pass through St Peter's Castle was the Ottoman Great Pretender, Cem Sultan, younger brother of Beyazit II.

Cem thought the Knights would assist him in his frequent attempts to defeat and depose his brother, but the Knights, paid handsomely by Beyazit, had other ideas, and kept him as a hostage. They handed him over to Pope Alexander IV Borgia, who made a small fortune on the Sultan's ransom before poisoning Cem. The Knights themselves were forced to move on to Malta when Süleyman the Magnificent captured Rhodes in 1523.

THE CASTLE

The castle stands high on a small rocky peninsula just in front of the modern town. Because the Knights ruled the seas, they concentrated their defences on the landward side, and to enter the city you have to pass through seven gates, the first at the top of the ramp near the tourist office. This leads into the Northern Moat, site of the modern Bodrum Festival. Near the gate you see the first of some 250 coats-of-arms carved into the castle walls, as well as numerous reliefs and other architectural embellishments from the Mausoleum. A wooden bridge has replaced the drawbridge leading into the outer citadel. In the small Gothic **Chapel of the Knights,** a collection of Bronze Age antiquities from the area are displayed. This is the first of many well arranged rooms of antiquities in the castle, others are devoted to the Mycenaean Age and to a fascinating exhibit on **underwater archaeology** garnered from several wrecks of different epochs off the Anatolian coast, variously including a bronze statue of an African child, a bronze statuette of the goddess Isis, and a Byzantine steelyard. Most of these were found by the explorations of the University of Pennsylvania. Other museum rooms in the **Inner Bayle** house finds from the Hellenistic, Roman, and Medieval ages; the **Snake Tower** has a small theatre full of amphorae.

The Knights of St John, also called the Hospitallers, were often the second sons of noblemen, and coming from different countries, they divided themselves into different *langues* (tongues), each langue responsible for defending a certain area of the walls. In St Peter's Castle, there are four langue towers. The **German tower,** near the Snake tower, is currently being restored; the **Italian tower,** and the **French tower,** highest of all, in the centre of the citadel offer wonderful views of Bodrum and the two harbours of the peninsula; the **English tower,** on the south corner of the castle, has been done up in medieval style, with tapes of medieval music and young Turks dressed as knights. On the west wall, notice the relief of a lion and the arms of Edward Plantagenet; inside on the marble windowsills are names and dates carved during the many long hours of idleness.

THE MAUSOLEUM

The **Mausoleum of Halicarnassus** stood a bit outside the modern centre of Bodrum, to the west of the ancient harbour. Today, only the massive foundations are left but there are interesting models tentatively reconstructing the form of the Mausoleum. Most of its beautiful reliefs are in the British Museum in London. This was the biggest tomb ever built in the ancient Greek world; not only has the name come down to us, but, for hundreds of years, it was imitated (even in the Masonic Temple in Washington DC!). In Milas, the **Gümüşkesen** (second century AD) is believed to be an almost exact miniature of the great Mausoleum. The only ancient monument of Halicarnassus surviving is the **theatre,** with a seating capacity of 10 000, north of the Mausoleum on Göktepe.

Bodrum Peninsula

From Bodrum you can visit the ancient city of Cnidus (see below) on the other side of Gökova Bay. It is also an excellent base for visiting the beaches and fishing villages on the peninsula by minibus or caique, you can also charter a yacht for a leisurely cruise among the coves. **Gümbet** is the closest beach to Bodrum, some two miles to the west, with many hotels and restaurants. Caiques leave frequently from Bodrum for **Bardakçi** and Aktur, port of **Ortakeni,** noted for its architecture. At **Aspat** you can see the round **Çifit Castle,** once an outpost of the Knights, accessible by a narrow path. Below the castle, **Karaincir** has another, long sandy beach, protected from wind. **Turgut Reis,** at the west end of the peninsula, is named after the sixteenth-century Turkish admiral Dragut, who was born here and whose statue now stands by the waterfront. Dragut led the great siege of Malta in 1565 and died there, and Süleyman's fleet and army had to return empty handed, one of the first great setbacks for the Ottoman military. Two fine beaches lie on either side of Turgut Reis: **Akyar,** at a fishing hamlet and silvery **Gümüşlük,** the site of ancient Myndus, and one of the loveliest beaches around boasting some fine fish restaurants. **Yalikavak** is a scenic village, where many windmills still function, and **Bahçe** is a lovely place to camp. The northern shore of the peninsula is blanketed with pine forests that come down to the shore in many places; a popular spot here is the bay at **Türbükü** and **Gölköy**. Offshore from Bodrum **Karaada,** or Black Island, is known for its mineral waters that flow into a sea grotto, popular with bathers.

GETTING AROUND

For Euromos, take the bus from Söke to Bodrum and ask to get off at Selimiye, the nearest village. For the ancient cities further east, take the bus from Aydin to Çine and a taxi from there. Bodrum is easily reached from the coast from Izmir, Söke, or Marmaris (less easily) and even directly from Istanbul. There are frequent bus connections to Milas. The beaches and towns on the peninsula of Bodrum are very well served by dolmuş and mini-

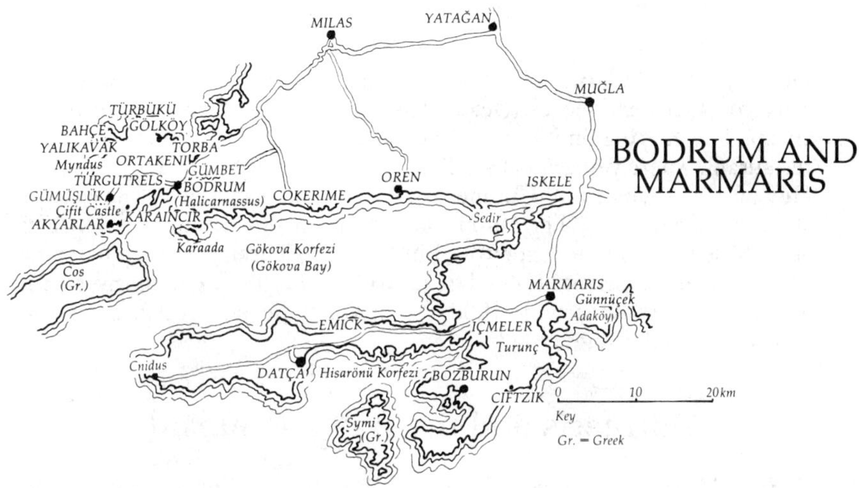

buses from the main bus station, as well as by boat taxis (dolmuş motorlari) that depart from Bodrum harbour. From spring to autumn there are boats to the island of Cos from Bodrum, and it's a port of call on the Turkish Maritime Lines cruise ship. There are also a number of companies offering excursions to the Datça peninsula and Cnidus.

TOURIST INFORMATION

12 Eylül Meydani, tel. (6141) 1091, Bodrum.

WHERE TO STAY

Bodrum has many hotels and pensions; prices are on the high side, but that doesn't keep them from filling up in the summer. If you're taking the kids, the **Gözen Oteli** at Cumhuriyet Cad. 18, tel. (6141) 1602 has a baby sitting service, is near the beach, and stays open all year, with a 30% discount in the off season. Singles with bath are 7500 TL, doubles 7000 TL. You can get a room with a view at the **Pansiyon Deniz** on Neyzen Tevfik Cad. where doubles are 3000 TL. **Belmi Pansiyon** nearby is the most pleasant of the inexpensive pensions, with beds for 900 TL; others are along Cumhuriyet Cad. On the peninsula Turget Reis has the most in the way of rooms and pensions; other pensions are at Gümüşlük and Torba, and in nearly every other village; rooms average 1200–2000 TL (double). There are also a wide choice in campsites—**Yuvam Kamping** is in Bodrum; others far nicer are near the beaches on the peninsula.

EATING OUT

Outside of Istanbul, Bodrum and its peninsula are the best places for rapturous gourmet experiences. Seafood is plentiful and fresh and relatively cheap. The **Körfez** on Neyzen Tevfik Cad. is the oldest and most famous restaurant, where you can eat a full fish dinner for 3000 TL. **Hey Yavrum Hey** on the beach just off Cumhuriyet Cad. is famous for its fish as well for about the same prices. The **Han** restaurant, in an 18th century caravanserai at 29 Kale Cad. is more expensive but has a live Turkish evening on many evenings. Less expensive is the **Turget Reis Lokanta** on Cumhuriyet Cad. where you can eat for around 1000 TL. In Milas, the **Sena** restaurant is also good, with similar rates.

Marmaris and the Datça Peninsula

By road **Marmaris** is reached from **Muğla,** the old capital of the region, with several fine old Ottoman mosques and homes. The scenery on the way is beautiful, reminiscent of California, and becomes spectacular as you descend to the lovely pine clad Bay of Marmaris. The city itself was devastated by an earthquake in 1958, and apart from the ruined fortress built by Süleyman during his siege of Rhodes, little of architectural interest remains. However, its lovely situation on the deeply indented coast, its access to the bay's beaches, and its fjord-like scenery has made it one of Turkey's major yacht ports. A number of companies offer charters along the peninsula and Lycian coasts.

East of Marmaris, over the wooden bridge, is **Günnücek Park** with a fine beach safe for children and a grove of rare frankincense trees. The west side of the bay has no fewer than fourteen campsites, all with beaches. Near the mouth of the bay are **Içmeler** with thermal springs, and **Turunç Bay,** with sandy beaches and chicken restaurants; across the bay are the **Phosphorescent Caves,** where the water glows when disturbed.

GÖKOVA BAY

On the other side of the peninsula in Gökova Bay lies the islet of **Sedir,** only a half mile long but very popular for its unusual snow-white sand with perfectly round grains, shipped to the islet from the Red Sea some 2000 years ago for Cleopatra. Then, a city called Cedrea stood on the islet; there are still the ruins of walls and a theatre. West along the peninsula, little **Datça** with its beaches has some pretensions to becoming a resort; the first half of the road there, climbing up to the top of the mountains, is quite dramatic.

Cnidus

Cnidus, at the very tip of the peninsula, was the headquarters of the Dorian Hexapolis. In ancient times it was famous for a statue of Aphrodite by the great Praxiteles, modelled on the renowned courtesan Phryne ('Toad' yet the first woman who won a court case by baring her bosom before the judges). The work was originally commissioned by the city of Kos, but the citizens there were too prudish to keep it, and Cnidus picked it up and made it one of the main tourist attractions of the coast. The base of the statue has recently been discovered in the circular foundations of a Corinthian temple in the city. The streets of Cnidus were laid out in a gridiron over a number of terraces; the walls and the theatre are the best preserved of the remains. The lovely statue of Demeter in the British Museum came from here, but no one has yet found the observatory of Eudoxus, a native of the city, student of Plato, and a pioneer in astronomy and geometry.

GETTING AROUND

Marmaris is another port served by the Turkish Maritime cruise boats, and it has one of the most reliable, year round ferry services to a Greek island, Rhodes; in the off season (even in early June) you can get a surprisingly low fare. Dalaman airport at Muğla is the closest airport, about an hour and a half from Marmaris (frequent buses) with regular domestic flights from Istanbul, Izmir, and Antalya, and an increasing number of international charters. There are frequent bus connections from Bodrum, and from Izmir and Fethiye; minibuses provide transport along the serpentine road to Datça and Cnidus. Boat dolmuş from Marmaris go to the many fine beaches and islets around the bay.

TOURIST INFORMATION

In Muğla, Özel Idare Işhani, tel. (6111) 1261. In Marmaris, Iskele Meydani 39, tel. (6121) 1035. In Datça, Belediye Binasi Iskele, tel. (6145) 163.

WHERE TO STAY

In Marmaris there are plenty of places to stay, from the **Atlantik Oteli** on the town beach (Atatürk Cad 34, tel. (6121) 1218), open year round, with singles for 6000 TL and doubles for 8000. Near the Atatürk statue at 32 Kordon Cad. there's the less expensive **Acar** with balconies offering a view of the harbour (tel. (6121) 11 17). There are also many small pensions and private houses with rooms, especially behind the Atlantik Oteli and on the far end of town near the bus station. In Datça there's a self contained holiday village, **Club Datça Tatil Köyü,** tel. (6145) 1170, open from May until October, with enough recreational facilities to keep the whole family busy; doubles are 12 000 TL. On the tip of town, there's the modern **Dorya Moteli,** tel. (6145) 35, where a double with bath is 12 000 TL. Datça also has a number of inexpensive pensions, and the **Bora** pension and restaurant in Cnidus, where you pay around 1000 TL for a bed.

Of the many campgrounds, the loveliest is **Çubucak Dinlenme Yeri Camping** on the south coast of the Datça peninsula, with restaurant.

EATING OUT

In Marmaris there is a solid block of restaurants along the yacht harbour, most of them expensive by Turkish standards though the food is delicious. For something less expensive, try the **Ayyildiz Lokantasi,** specialising in meat. In Datça, the **Sandal** restaurant is very good and worth it at 3000 TL for a meal. In Cnidus there are two small restaurants, and you can get food at any of the coves around Marmaris bay with a campground.

Part VIII

THE SOUTHERN COAST

A Lycian tomb in the sea at Kaş

The Lycian Coast: Marmaris to Antalya

In ancient times, when the indigenous Lycian people crowned this rugged stretch of coastline with a garland of lovely cities, the area was still something of a terra incognita for most Greeks and Romans. Even now the difficult mountainous terrain makes the interior hard to penetrate. Lately, however, the Turkish government has completed a coastal road, stretching around the Lycian bulge from Fethiye to Antalya. It was the last unfinished section of the coast highway, and its construction has opened to tourism a land that still retains its lazy charm, a transparent sea, every imaginable shade of blue and turquoise, spectacular scenery, and archaeological sites in varying stages of excavation, all settings that would delight any romantic.

The Lycians

The Lycians were a native Anatolian people Homer says that they fought with the Trojans under their leader Sarpedon, brother of King Minos of Crete, which led Herodotus to write that they were the descendants of an ancient Cretan colony. Most of the remains discovered along the coast,

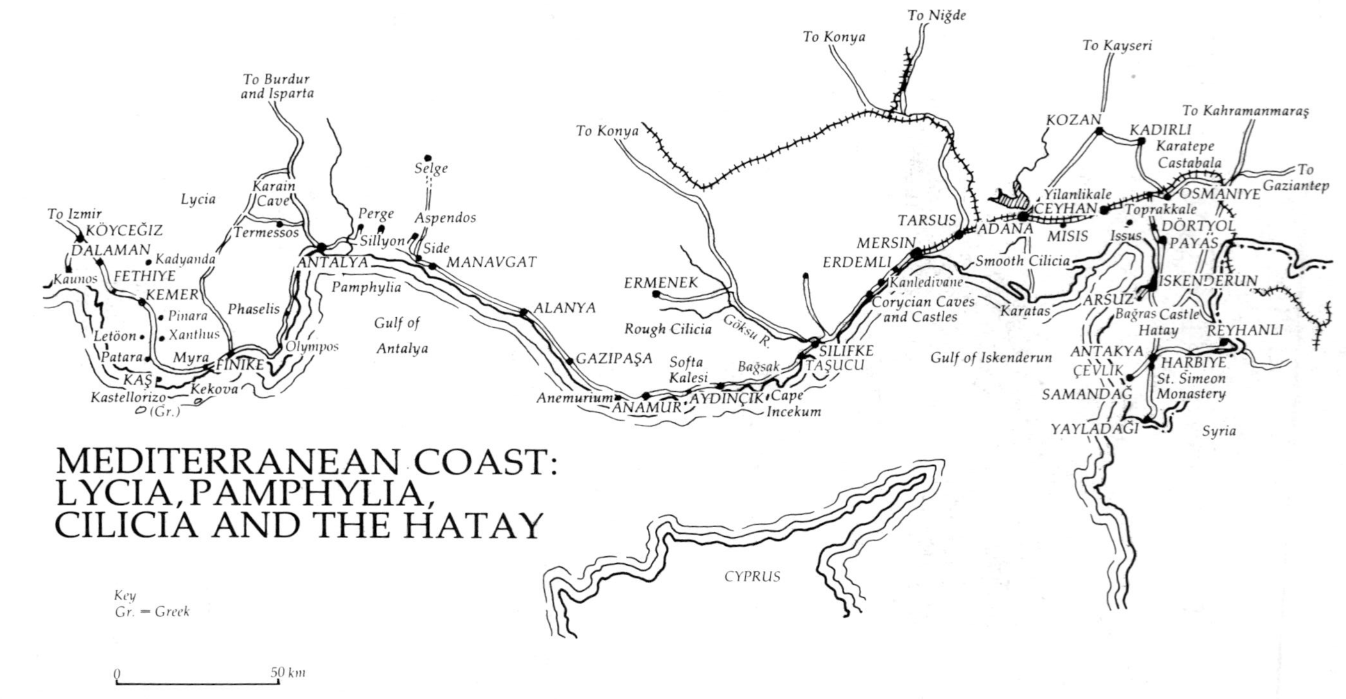
MEDITERRANEAN COAST:
LYCIA, PAMPHYLIA,
CILICIA AND THE HATAY
To Izmir
KÖYCEĞIZ
DALAMAN
Kaunos
FETHIYE
Kadyanda
Lycia
KEMER
Pinara
Xanthus
Letöon
Patara
KAŞ
Kastellorizo
(Gr.)
Myra
FINIKE
Kekova
Phaselis
Olympos
Termessos
Karain
Cave
To Burdur
and Isparta
ANTALYA
Perge
Sillyon
Selge
Aspendos
Side
MANAVGAT
Pamphylia
Gulf of
Antalya
ALANYA
GAZIPAŞA
Anemurium
ANAMUR
AYDINÇIK
Softa
Kalesi
Bağsak
Cape
Incekum
TAŞUCU
SILIFKE
Göksu R.
Rough Cilicia
ERMENEK
To Konya
To Konya
To Niğde
ERDEMLI
Kanlıdivane
Corycian Caves
and Castles
MERSIN
TARSUS
ADANA
Smooth Cilicia
Karataş
CEYHAN
Yılanlıkale
MISIS
KOZAN
To Kayseri
KADIRLI
Karatepe
Castabala
To Kahramanmaraş
OSMANIYE
To
Gaziantep
Toprakkale
Issus
DÖRTYOL
PAYAS
ISKENDERUN
ARSUZ
Bağras Castle
Hatay
REYHANLI
Gulf of Iskenderun
ANTAKYA
ÇEVLIK
HARBIYE
St. Simeon
Monastery
SAMANDAĞ
YAYLADAĞI
Syria
CYPRUS
Key
Gr. = Greek
0
50 km

however, date back only to the seventh century BC. Like Cilicia to the east, the rugged nature of the thickly forested terrain kept Lycia out of the pages of history, but by the time of Alexander—who captured the coast easily from its Persian satraps—it was more or less Hellenised, adopting many Greek letters into the alphabet, and Greek sculpture and architectural forms. The latter they adapted for their mortuary obsession, carving elaborate tombs with temple-like façades into the living rock, in some places so thick they resemble lost metropolises of the dead. Elsewhere, they made sarcophagi and tombs in the form of miniature houses of stone. These, often on high platforms, and the beautiful tombs carved into the steep cliffs overhead are the most distinctive features of the Lycian landscape.

Kaunos

Ancient **Kaunos,** westernmost on the coast, marks the border between the Aegean and Mediterranean seas, and between Caria and Lycia, and its remains show the styles of both cultures, as well as of later civilisations: there are Lycian and Carian tombs, a wall built by Mausoleus (king of Caria), medieval walls on the acropolis, a Roman fountain. Kaunos stands between Lake Köyceğiz and the sea, and can be approached by land or sea; the latter way goes via lovely Dalyan Bay and the canal that links the lake to the sea.

Fethiye

Fethiye, a modern town built over ancient **Telmessos** has Lycia's best harbour, protected by twelve islets. Telmessos means 'Land of Light' in Lycian, and is first mentioned in the fourth century BC. Most of it lies buried under modern Fethiye (itself rebuilt after an earthquake in 1957), with the exception of the **rock tombs** cut into the cliff near the bus station; these, especially the grand Ionic temple **Tomb of Amyntas** of the fourth century BC, are among the finest in Lycia. Here and there throughout the modern town you see large sarcophagi. The oldest and most interesting of these is the **Lycian Sarcophagus** next to the post office, carved from a single block of stone. The new **museum** is near the school, and has exhibits from Lycia, and an interesting sculpture garden.

Fethiye, though new, is not without a leisurely charm, and is the best base for visiting the Lycian sites in the vicinity. Public transport gives easy access to the several beaches in the area, most famously, **Ölü Deniz,** the 'dead sea', south, on a warm lagoon off the Gulf of Belcekiz, with a perfect two-mile beach; you have to pay to use the best part. This was once the haunt of pirates, and is very popular, but too large to get crowded. Other beaches are at **Katranci Bay** to the north, shaded by pine trees; nearest Fethiye is **Çaliş Beach,** opposite the islet **Şövalye,** which also has a beach. **Günlük beach,** just north of Fethiye, is in a grove of styrax, or liquid-amber trees. Above Fethiye, **Karmilassos** is a Greek ghost town, with forlorn houses and abandoned churches; as so often along the coast, when the Greeks left in the population exchange the Turks never liked to move in, preferring to let entire towns go to ruin.

AROUND FETHIYE

Inland from Fethiye you can explore, literally, three seldom-visited Lycian cities. **Kadyama,** northeast of Fethiye near modern **Yeşil Üzümlü,** has a well preserved theatre, a Doric temple, and baths, as well as other remains. **Tlos,** on the slopes of the White mountain, is 30 miles from Fethiye, near modern Kaleasar, on the other side of the River Xanthus, the modern **Koca-Çay.** Tlos was one of the most important members of the Lycian confederacy of the second century BC and remained inhabited through the Byzantine era; in the nineteenth century it served as the winter headquarters of the pirate Kanli Ali Ağa. As well as Lycian rock tombs, there are remains of Kanli Ali Ağa's fortress on the acropolis, Roman walls around the necropolis, a Roman stadium, baths, and necropolis, and a Byzantine church. On the other side of the modern village lies the theatre.

Pinara, another important member of the confederacy, is closer to Fethiye, on the west bank of the river Xanthus, east of **Kemer**; this is the **western** Kemer; there are two villages of this name, one at each end of Lycia. Pinara is one of the more romantic sites, on a height beneath the mountains, the ruins overgrown. Pinara is especially notable for its Lycian rock tombs; a Roman odeon and a Greek theatre are also easy to find. **Sidyma** lies nine miles off the coastal highway south of Pinara near Dodurga, and has more rock cut tombs.

Xanthus

Far more interesting, however, is **Xanthus,** the ancient capital and oldest city of Lycia dating back to the eighth century BC and famous in antiquity for its great resistance to Cyrus' general Harpagus who attacked in the mid-sixth century BC. Although they fought courageously, the Xanthians were outnumbered, and according to Herodotus, when they saw they were doomed to defeat, they retreated to their citadel, gathering together their womenfolk, children, and slaves, and locking them inside, set fire to the building and burned it to the ground, they then swore to fight to the death, and did. Indeed, when Xanthus was excavated, a heavy layer of ash was discovered over the ruins of that period.

Xanthus, rebuilt by the fifty families who had been away during the siege, prospered up until the Roman period, when it once again suffered a terrible devastation, this time at the hands of Brutus in 42 BC; rebuilt yet again with the aid of Mark Antony and Emperor Vespasian, the city survived until the twelfth century. Today it is one of the most revealing Lycian sites, most of it having been cleared, disclosing the layout of the city and its imposing funerary monuments. Unfortunately they were stripped of their reliefs in 1838 but these can now be seen in the Lycian Room of the British Museum in London, along with the entire Temple of the Nereids.

The funerary monuments are all near the Roman agora and theatre; the **Tomb of the Harpies,** high on its monolith is adorned with reliefs (plaster copies) of scenes from the Underworld. The winged female figures transporting souls, however, are not harpies but *kers*, who in true Greek religion, as opposed to the state mythology, performed that function. Next to the tomb is a Lycian tomb-sarcophagus (fourth century BC), high on its pillar. A similar tomb stands on the other side of the theatre. The **Inscribed Pillar** in the agora once supported the sarcophagus of a Lycian King; it is inscribed in Lycian on all four sides, and although this has yet to be deciphered, other evidence has led scholars to believe it was the tomb of King Kherei, who defeated the Athenians in a battle in the Peloponnesian War. Another well preserved, fourth century BC 'pillar tomb' is on the Roman acropolis, which served the Lycians as a cemetery (The Lycian acropolis was on top of the theatre, though the ruins there are all Byzantine.) An **arch** near the gateway in the south was donated to Xanthus by Vespasian.

Like the other ancient provinces of Asia Minor, Lycia had a federative sanctuary, a holy place shared by all the cities, the expression of their ethnic and religious unity. This was the **Letoon,** 4 kilometres south of the main road (the turnoff is just north of the one to Xanthus), was dedicated to Leto and her children, Apollo and Artemis. Although there was a small city here, the only remains are of the temples and a small but well preserved **theatre** on the hillside. Even though only foundations of three temples remain (the **Temple of Leto,** largest and easternmost of the three, the Temple of **Apollo and Artemis,** and a smaller unidentified one between them), the site is one of the most pleasant along the coast. The half-sunken ruins, including a huge and elaborate semi-circular **nymphaion** and a seventh century **monastery,** have become elegant pools for the lazy turtles and fat white ducks that abound near Leto's ancient spring, which still flows as freely as in ancient times. These peacefully share the spot with other exotic wildlife, including clouds of magenta dragonflies and frogs, straight from Aristophanes, croaking 'Brekekekex coax coax!' in the most correct classical Greek accents. On the floor of the twins' temple is a mosaic in the cella showing Artemis' bow and Apollo's lyre. Long inscriptions are everywhere; some have been removed to the nearby **museum.**

Apollo, surprisingly for a god of light and reason, proves a pretty shadowy character outside Greece proper. His mother Leto—etymologically and in religion the same as Leda, Latona, Lat, or however else she appears in mythology—seems to have been an old Middle Eastern version of the great goddess. Apollo, here, must appear in his role as god of the cult of Hyperboreans ('men from beyond the North Wind') centred at Delos, and extending, if the ancient historians are to be believed, from Britain to Palestine. At **Patara,** the next town along the coast, an oracle of Apollo existed that functioned only in the winter, the opposite of the oracle at Claros. In the summer, Dionysus presumably took over the temple while Apollo removed himself behind the north wind, to England, specifically to the temple founded in his honour (under a different name) at Stonehenge.

Patara

The next town along the coast, Patara's ruins lie 6 kilometres south of the main road along the shore. As you enter, you pass some fine **Lycian tombs** on the right-hand-side, and two apsed buildings, the **Roman baths** built by Vespasian, and a later **Christian basilica.** A three-gated monumental **arch,** stripped bare of its statues, adorned the town's main entrance. The **theatre** is in good shape, but partially covered by a tremendous sand dune, well over 100 feet high. Between sand, sea, and pines Patara is altogether one of the most attractive sites in Lycia.

Kalkan and Kaş

The modern village of **Kalkan,** and 26 kilometres beyond it, **Kaş,** both look like Greek island towns with everything, even the mosques, coated in whitewash. Kaş, a pretty town, has become a small quiet resort with a new yacht-harbour, offering perhaps the ultimate in sunny Mediterranean languor. There is a tall, lovely **tomb** in the centre of the town, with inscriptions in Lycian, and another on the hill just to the west on a narrow peninsula. The Greeks called Kaş Antiphellos, though the native Lycians called it Habesa. A **theatre** also survives west of the town with the ruins of a temple.

Coastline attractions

This part of the coast, heavily indented and full of isolated caves and islets, has some of Lycia's most spectacular scenery. Just a mile off shore from the town, the lonely little island of Kastellorizo marks the easternmost boundary of the Greek republic, inherited from the Italians after World War II with the rest of the Dodecanese. The few Greeks who live there come over to Kaş to do their shopping; a small company in the town runs unofficial day trips to the island—unofficial, as Kastellorizo is not a port of entry into Greece.

Among the attractions of this coastline, is a cave in which the rare Mediterranean seal lives; it is 5 kilometres west of the town under the low corniches of the coastal road. Then there is the **'Blue cave'** which was a pirates' lair in the Middle Ages. Just beyond it, where the Kaputaş stream cuts a big chasm through the rock wall, steps lead down to a secluded beach. East of Kaş, the main road leaves the rugged coast, and the only entry into the beautiful bay around **Kekova island** is the track south from the road near the ancient site of Kyanaei. All this country is dotted with Lycian tombs, hundreds of them, some rising picturesquely out of the waters of the coves. **Simena,** the coastal town at the end of the track, is below the ruins of a medieval castle. From here, you may walk to other ruins—the towns of **Aperlai** and **Apollonia.** In season, daily boats from Kaş leave for the Kekova Bay.

Demre

Going northwest, the next modern town, **Demre,** on a little plain full of small farms, is the descendant of ancient Myra, home of jolly St Nicholas, a fourth century prelate. He was actually born in Patara, but it was in Myra that he was bishop, beloved enough for his generosity and good deeds to get himself canonised. Before he became Father Christmas, he was known as patron of sailors; and the Greek Church still knows nothing of the Christmas duties he has in the west. Travel brochures have lately appeared with pictures of an American-style Santa Claus in front of the ancient ruins. Let us hope this doesn't get out of hand.

Follow the 'Baba Noel' signs in Demre to the **St Nicholas Church,** a fifth-century building with extensive eleventh-century additions, including a large barrel-vaulted nave and cloister. In the original structure there is some fine marble inlay work and much carved stone recycled from earlier buildings. Of the later frescoes, only one unidentified saint survives. This may well be the oldest surviving church building in Turkey.

Myra

About $1\frac{1}{2}$ km outside Demre, the ruins of **Myra** include an amazing collection of tombs cut out of the cliffs above the city, all in the form of temple façades. There are over a score of them, arranged on the cliff in an asymmetric jumble. Most are from the 4th century BC, and many contain funeral scenes in relief. Several of the façades have roofs carved to imitate wooden beams, suggesting that they are copied in form from wooden temples or other buildings that have not survived; the same is true of the Phrygian cliff-face façades west of Ankara.

Myra's other attraction is its **theatre,** a late Roman work with some uninspired sculpture. From its huge orchestra, we can guess it was used more often for games and animal shows than classical drama. In the vicinity are a number of Byzantine structures protruding from the surrounding farms and greenhouses, and, a few miles to the southwest a **Roman granary,** one of many in Lycia, decorated with a relief of Hadrian, who built it.

Around Finike

From **Finike,** a nondescript modern town 30 kilometres west of Demre, you have the choice of continuing along the coast, or striking inland through the mountains. Either way will take you to Antalya, though the recently built coastal route is considerably shorter. Travelling inland, you encounter first the ruins of **Limyra.** In the early fourth century BC, this was the most powerful city of Lycia under King Perikles, founder of the Lycian League of cities and a fighter for Lycian independence against Mausoleus of Caria. The site is worth a visit for the tombs—if you haven't seen enough yet—spread all over the outskirts of the ancient town. Notable among them is the **Heroon of King Perikles,** in the form of an Ionic temple, though some climbing will reveal several others that rank among the best Lycian tomb architecture.

North of Limyra the road passes Arkyanda, another ruined town, and then two lakes, **Avlan Gölü** and **Karagöl,** the 'Black lake'; its waters are held back by a dam of natural rock spilling dramatically through a chasm in the cliff.

Olympos and the Chimaera

Along the coast, the road skirts the grand massif of the Bey Dağlari, the 'Bey's mountains' around Cape Gelidonya, a familiar landmark to sailors ancient and modern. Heading northwards, **Olympos** is another ruined town in a pretty setting, though little remains of it. If you pass at night, you see a small flame rising from the mountains above the town. All the ancient geographers mention it, and it takes its name, the **Chimaera** from the myth of Bellerophon. The Lycian King, Iobates, sent Bellerophon to kill the fire-breathing monster, part lion, goat, and serpent. With the aid of the winged horse Pegasus, he succeeded, and returned, after other tasks set by Iobates, to Xanthus where he married the King's daughter and became heir to the Lycian throne. Carried away by his success, Bellerophon tried to ride Pegasus up to Mount Olympos; and for his presumption, earned a great thunderbolt from Zeus.

The real Chimaera isn't at all monstrous; in the daytime it isn't even visible. Whatever combination of gases causes it has never been satisfactorily explained, but if you care to make the half-hour climb up to the spot, you find it can easily be extinguished, only to relight itself after a few seconds. Apparently in ancient times it put on a better show. Nearby are the ruins of a temple, of Hephaestus of course, and the old writers describe it as only one of a number of fiery manifestations on the mountain's slopes.

Bellerophon didn't have to go far to reach the home of the gods. The Lycian Olympus, one of at least three mountains of that name and fame in Asia Minor alone, is now called **Tahtali Dağ,** the highest peak of the Bey's mountains.

Beneath Tahtali Dağ on the shore are the ruins of **Phaselis,** one of the foremost cities of Lycia. Founded by Rhodes in the seventh century, Phaselis often stood apart from its neighbours, even to the extent of supporting Mausoles against the Lycian League. The Phaselitians, like the people of Side, had a reputation as cutthroats and schemers; once, desperate for cash, they offered Phaselitian citizenship for sale to all comers. They met their match when a real cutthroat, the pirate Zenicertes, sacked the town and made it his headquarters, c. 90 BC. The ruins left today are all from the rebuilt city of Roman times. Its three harbours can easily be seen from the shore, also a **theatre, aqueduct,** and a number of **tombs.** Now, as in ancient times, Phaselis though lovely is famous for being infested with nasty hornets. These may or may not be in the mood to annoy you when you visit.

Beyond Phaselis, the highway passes more wonderful corniche scenery through mature Mediterranean pine forests. The broad curve of the Lycian shore ends as it began, with a village called **Kemer,** a growing resort town, its name fittingly meaning 'band' or 'arch'. From here, Antalya is just over the horizon.

GETTING AROUND

By air: Getting to Lycia is relatively easy, as there are airports at either end of the coast at Dalaman and Antalya (see the preceding and following sections).

By road: The only entrances apart from the coastal road are the two roads over the mountains from Isparta and Denizli; both are long, and the latter is unpaved for long stretches. Buses to and from Muğla and Antalya run very regularly along the coast, and if you're using them to hop from place to place, you shouldn't have much of a wait.

By sea: Since the late 1960s 'Blue Voyage', a yacht cruise along this beautiful and unspoiled coast up to Antalya has become very fashionable. Arrangements can be made through travel agents in Istanbul or in Fethiye, Kaş, or Bodrum, or through the agents of yacht-chartering firms in the US or UK. If you join with some friends, the price per person per day is very reasonable, usually less expensive than staying at a nice hotel.

Turkish Maritime Lines coastal steamers call at Fethiye, and occasionally at Kaş and Finike.

To the sites: Getting to most of the ancient sites is possible without a car, though not always easy. From Fethiye, you can take a minibus to Sidyma, Araxa, Tlos, Xanthus, the Letoon, and Patara; all will require some walking once you get there. For all those close to the coastal road, you can be fairly sure of finding some minibus, dolmuş, or even intercity bus to pick you up on your way back. For Kaunos, take the coastal bus to Köyceğiz and a taxi from there. Ölü Deniz is connected by frequent dolmuş-minibuses from Fethiye.

TOURIST INFORMATION

Fethiye: 1 Iskele Meydani (harbour square), tel. (6151) 1527.
Kaş: 6 Cumhuriyet Meydani, tel. (3226) 1238.
Kemer (near Antalya): Belediye Binasi (city hall), no tel.

WHERE TO STAY

There are pensions in Köyceğiz near Kaunos, and a wide range of accommodation in Fethiye, including the **Likya Oteli** (H4) at Karagözler, tel. (6151) 1169, modern and on the sea; a single here is 4200 TL, a double 5500 TL (open April–October). Cheap rooms can be found everywhere in town, and there are a number of campsites at Çaliş beach and Ölü Deniz (at the latter, the **Deniz Kamp** is open all year). There's also one motel at Ölü Deniz, the **Meri** (M1), also open year round, with singles for 6000 TL, and doubles for 7500, with private bath and 40% reduction in the off season.

Kalkan and Kaş at the moment have only small pensions, although there are big plans to change this soon in Kaş, where a multi-million dollar giant hotel complex is going up. In Kalkan, the most charming place to stay is the **Pasha's Inn** at 10 Sokak #8, tel. 77, where one of the six rooms and breakfast is 4500 TL single, 5750 a double. In Kaş, the **Motel Andifli,** tel. (3226) 42, is on the beach, and not a bad deal at 1000 TL for a single, 1500 a double, though water may be a problem. In Demre, there's the **Myra Pension** at Müze Cad. 4-B, open year round, with basic rooms at 1100 TL for a single, 1500 for a double.

EATING OUT

Some of the campsites at Ölü Deniz have restaurants, and there's the

Pirate's Cove where you can get excellent chicken curry for about 1000 TL. In Kalkan, the **Deniz** has delicious fish from around 6000 TL. In Kaş there are many good places to choose from: **Mercan** in the harbour is moderately priced. In Finike, the **Petak Restaurant** is good and inexpensive (1500 TL or so).

Antalya and the Pamphylian coast

In the twilight of the Aegean Bronze Age, a time when history passes into myth, the Greeks wrote of the 'mixed multitude of peoples' set in motion by the fall of Troy; many of these found their way to the land between the mountains of Lycia and Cilicia. Historians think it likely that settlement of this region actually preceded the breakdown of civilisation in the twelfth century BC. The Greeks later came to call this region **Pamphylia,** 'land of all tribes'. Its ancient borders are marked by the two largest modern towns in the area, Antalya and Alanya. Its cities, Perge, Side, and Aspendos all prospered on the fertile plain, becoming rich and thoroughly Hellenised by the time Alexander came. From their early history, more within the Hittite–Anatolian world than the Greek, they kept stories, some from Homer, of their foundation by the seers Mopsus and Amphilochus, who had been with the Achaeans at Troy.

Antalya

The coastal plain begins at **Antalya,** which with Alanya, is lovely, and skirted by long perfect beaches; both towns are becoming major tourist resorts, being described in phrases like 'the Turkish Riviera'. Here the Lycian mountains abruptly end to form a spectacular backdrop for the city. Prosperous for the first time in 700 years, Antalya is beginning to take on the air of a charmed Mediterranean resort city, sprouting palm trees and bright new buildings to go with the sunny, sleepy contentment; the local economy is booming and Antalya's population has recently reached 200,000.

HISTORY

Unlike so many of the coastal cities vacated by the Greeks, Antalya has been continuously occupied, and consequently very little is left to mark its history. King Attalus II of Pergamon, given this stretch of coast by the Romans for safe-keeping in 188 BC, founded the city when Side refused to acknowledge his authority. Called Attaleia, it soon surpassed Side and the other Pamphylian cities, gaining further impetus under the Romans when

Augustus settled a colony here in 6 BC. When Mediterranean civilisation collapsed, Attaleia showed more resourcefulness than other cities, setting up a fleet to defend itself against pirates, Arabs, and occasionally the Byzantine taxman, and consequently survived in a reduced state despite the contraction of seagoing trade.

Recovery came with the Selcuks in the early thirteenth century; although various Turkish tribes had already held stretches of coastline, the Selcuks were the first to develop the area, rebuilding Attaleia and Alanya, linking them to Konya with a string of caravanserais. The Sultans often spent their winters here. Had it not been for the disruptions caused by the Crusaders, and the stranglehold that Venice and Genoa kept on the eastern trade, the Selcuks might well have brought the old Eastern Mediterranean world back to life with a Turkish–Moslem slant.

THE OLD TOWN

Old Antalya's walls were removed long ago, but their course is followed by two modern boulevards, Atatürk Caddesi and Hastane Caddesi, separating the old and new towns. Where these streets meet, a surviving bastion of the Selcuk wall has been converted into an odd **clock tower.** To enter the old town in style, walk a few squares along Atatürk Caddesi to the restored **Hadrian's Gate.** Its three arches are decorative, but hardly a solid link in a fortification; in Hadrian's time, so secure was the pax Romana that it seemed cities would never again need real walls. In many places in Asia Minor there are purely ceremonial gates like these, or their ruins. This one was constructed in honour of Hadrian's visit in AD 130, and there may have been a statue of the emperor originally on top.

Towards the south end of the old town, among streets of pretty Ottoman houses, is the **Kesik Minare,** the 'broken minaret' struck by lightning long ago. The mosque it serves was originally a Byzantine church built in the fifth century, rebuilt and restored many times since. Continuing further, towards the sea, you come across a squat stone cylinder, the **Hidirlik Tower,** believed to be the tomb of a second century Roman consul; traces of a carved fascia, symbol of the consuls' authority, can still be made out. The people of Antalya take great pride in their **City Park,** on the sea cliffs at the end of Atatürk Caddesi, with its fountains, palm-lined promenades, and beds of roses and lilies. The walk built around the shore gives an exceptional view of the city and the mountains behind.

Surprisingly few Selcuk buildings remain in Antalya. The most important is the city's landmark, the **Yivli Minare,** the 'grooved minaret', typically Selcuk in its heaviness of form and unerring sense of proportion. Its lobed shaft and stalactite balcony are unique—one of the few of Turkey's fine minarets the visitor will remember. There are some surviving sections of the

walls nearby, along with more lovely Ottoman houses. It's impossible to date the houses; the same style, with low tiled roofs, stucco or half-timber walls, and second floor balconies, continued for three centuries; some of them actually were built in the 1920s. Fortunately, Antalya now has both the desire and resources to have many of them restored. An Ottoman mosque, the sixteenth century **Paşa Cami,** is nearby, just behind the clock tower.

Another job of restoration—on a grand scale—has been performed on old Antalya's **harbour.** Only a few years ago this entire area was falling into ruins; the city's ambitious plan for saving it, though not yet completed, has already won an international architectural award. Around the newly constructed basin for yachts and other pleasure craft new roads, fountains, hotels, parks, and terraced cafes have grown up; when it is finished, the centre of the city's activity will be back in this beautiful spot where it belongs.

At the top of the cliffs, on Hastane Caddesi, take a moment to admire the glory and grandeur of the most audacious indescribable, **Atatürk Monument** in all Turkey. May it stand forever.

MUSEUM

West of the old town, Konyaalti Caddesi heads towards the mountains, the long beach on one side, an equally long row of modern apartments on the other. About a mile out, it passes the new **Antalya Regional Museum.** Of all Turkey's museums, this is the most attractive in its arrangement of exhibits, and the simplest for the visitor, with clear, multilingual explanations; it contains one of the largest and best collections in the country. Its exhibits range from the stone age remains from nearby Karain Cave, the earliest habitation yet discovered in Turkey, to a beautiful sixth-century relief of the archangel Gabriel. Greek and Roman sculptures fill several large halls. One great sarcophagus, carved in the form of a temple, portrays the twelve labours of Hercules; another supposedly held the remains of St Nicholas of Myra (but don't tell your children you saw Santa Claus's grave); a group of huge Olympian gods, and some equally large emperors, Hadrian, Septimus Severus, and Trajan, a relief of the twelve Lycian gods and a famous icon of the Artemis of Perge. Best of all, perhaps, is a remarkable, almost impressionistic scene of the underworld from a grave stele, hung inconspicuously behind the Hercules sarcophagus. The Byzantines are well represented in all periods. The final rooms have a very good ethnographic collection, covering local life and crafts with a special section on the Yürük nomads of Anatolia.

BEACHES

Konyaalti Beach, extending for miles, is an extremely popular spot, barely visible from the street for all the restaurants, cafes, and cabins. Still, there's room for all; you just need to go a little further out to be alone. Many visitors prefer the fine sand at **Lara Beach,** about 11 kilometres southeast of town, and here also are the **Düden Waterfalls,** plunging dramatically into the sea.

Around Antalya

Taking the northern road, high up into the mountains from Antalya towards Burdur and Isparta, after 10 kilometres, at a crossroads, there is a choice of excursions. The right-hand route leads past a lovely forested picnic spot, the **Düzler Park,** towards **Karain Cave,** where human remains some 50 000 years old were found. Beside the cave which is a long climb up the mountain, there's a small museum, probably only of interest to the most fervent aficionados of the Paleolithic.

TERMESSOS

Up here in the mountains, we have left classical Pamphylia completely behind. Until Roman times, the influence of the Hellenised Greek cities never extended much beyond the coast; this mountainous region was known as Pisidia, the region of a fierce confederation of native Anatolian tribes who were better left alone. Their greatest city was **Termessos,** its ruins accessible on a new motor road 26 kilometres down the left-hand fork at the crossroads. The people of Termessos called themselves Solymians, giving the name to the formidable crag, Mt Solymos, under whose shelter they built their city. King Isbates, as mentioned in the *Iliad,* sent Bellerophon against the Solymians and he served them just as he had the Amazons, bombing them into submission with great boulders hurled down from Pegasus.

Other would-be conquerors did not fare as well. The Termessians liked to say they'd defeated Alexander, who abandoned a siege here on his way to Sagalassus in 334 BC. Throughout the Hellenistic era the coastal cities were constantly at odds with the Termessians, and the Romans discreetly signed a treaty declaring the city 'friend and ally of the Roman people'. Termessos remained autonomous throughout the Roman period, and showed it by not even bothering to put the emperor's picture on its coins.

The ruins are well preserved, but not excavated; the difficult mountainous site is an attraction in itself, altogether different from the coastal towns. Most of the ruins are from Roman times, and in no way unusual. There is a **theatre** in good condition, an **odeon** nearby, and a small indoor theatre that also served as a bouleuterion. Like Athens, Termessos has its **Stoa of Attalus,** in the agora just behind the odeon, built by the Pergamene king. The main thoroughfare, called King Street by the Termessians, touches the western edge of the agora on its way north, where it turned into a **colonnaded street** of shops, once lined with statues of prominent citizens; all these are gone, but the inscriptions tell us that many were champion wrestlers; this sport was a speciality of the city, and indeed all of Pisidia, as it is among the Turks today.

An outstanding feature of Termessos' remains, if you have the time to search them out among the bushes, is the large number of **tombs,** all around the slopes to the east, west, and south. Some are mere sarcophagi, others elaborately built in the form of temples (the best are to the south) and yet others, on the northwest slopes, are façades carved out of the rocks in the manner of the Lycians. Most have inscriptions, but not all are tributes to the dead; many warn of the fines grave robbers, or anyone attempting to re-use the tombs would incur, all mentioning specific amounts, payable to, for example, the Temple of Solyman Zeus. There are references also to the amounts payable to informers for catching the evil doers in the act.

GETTING AROUND

Outside of the coastal road, the only route into Antalya is the mountain road to the north from Burdur and Isparta, which also passes near Termessos. There is no rail service in the area, but buses to and from Antalya from all points are very frequent. The bus station is conveniently located in the centre, on Kazim Özalp Caddesi. Turkish Maritime Lines' summer cruises all call at Antalya, and the city's new airport receives daily flights from Ankara and Istanbul and charters from abroad, mostly from Germany.

Within the city, most sites are within easy walking distance of each other; for the museum and Konyaalti beach, it's easy to take a dolmuş down Konyaalti Caddesi (called Hastane Cad. in the centre) the main street.

TOURIST INFORMATION

33 Hastane Caddesi, tel (311) 11 747.

WHERE TO STAY

As Antalya booms, a crop of elaborate holiday hotels are springing up, starting with the **Talya Otel** (HL) on Fevzi Çakmak Cad., tel. (311) 156 0019, on the beach, with all the amenities. Singles here are 18 000 TL, doubles 26 000 TL. Most of the other beach hotels are around Lara Beach, to the southwest, such as the **Antalya Motel** (M2), on Lara Yolu 87, tel. (311) 14 609), with singles for 3400 TL, doubles for 5550 TL. Both these hotels definitely require reservations in season. For something cheap, try the **Öncel Pansiyon** at Karaalioğlu Sok. 6, tel. (311) 12 199, where doubles are 3000 TL. A little more expensive but sweet and small is the **Pansiyon Olimpiyat,** 17 Anafartalar Cad., tel. (311) 12 890, near the Yivli Minare. Prices are 3500 TL for a single, 5000 TL for a double.

EATING OUT

Konyaalti Caddesi is the place to look, with a number of fish restaurants behind the beach; none in particular stand out. Less expensive places can be found around the city's old marketplace, near the clock tower.

East from Antalya

The road east from Antalya does not follow the coast. It doesn't need to; the land is flat and there are farms, citrus groves, and banana plantations on either side as far as Side. Much of this land is haunted with ruins, and it is no surprise to see an ancient column sticking up in a field or along a side road, not always easy to distinguish from the aeration stacks of the irrigation system. Except for Antalya and Side, all the ancient cities of this region were built inland, their ports being nothing more than a landing stage at the highest navigable point of the closest river. Consequently, all the yellow signs marking the turnoffs to sites are on the north side of the road.

Perge

Perge, the first of them, is only two kilometres from the highway. Perge, claiming Mopsus and Calchas as founders, prospered throughout the Classical period and into Byzantine times. Although its ruins do not show a city of great size, its theatre could seat 15 000, as many as Side or Aspendos. Perge's most famous citizen, the mathematician Apollonius (third century BC), was a follower of Euclid who did important work with ellipses and conic sections, contributing much of the background of Ptolemy's epicyclic theory of the universe.

The modern road to Perge passes between the **stadium,** one of the best preserved in Turkey, and the **theatre** before it reaches the parking lot at the main gate. Although as yet unexcavated, the theatre shows promise of having been an even more impressive sight than those of Aspendos or Side. Its stage building is still present in part, along with some of its sculpted frieze; among the recognisable tableaux are scenes of Eros and Psyche, and Dionysus and Ariadne. In the stadium, the space facing the outside under the seats was rented out for shops, just as they are now in some modern Turkish stadia. Some of the runners' names and trades can still be read on the walls. Interestingly, the stadium seated fewer spectators than the theatre.

Perge's **main gate,** at the centre of the southern walls, is its outstanding feature—the Hellenistic inner gate, which the Pergeans made into a grand ceremonial entrance. The outer gate, added in the third century AD, is strictly utilitarian. Between the two, a large courtyard full of monuments and statues was flanked on one side by a colonnade and on the other, by the **propyla,** a formal entrance to the baths, and the fountain or **nymphaion** that looked like the façade of a theatre. Many of the statues found here are now in the Antalya museum.

To the two round towers of the gate still partly standing, the Pergeans of the second century AD added another courtyard in the shape of a horse-shoe, lined with statues of the city's founders. Then 'founder' did not necessarily mean one had 'founded', but could be anyone who financed any great public improvement. And so next to Mopsus and Calchas (the statues are gone but the inscriptions remain) there are such men as M. Plancius Varus and C. Plancius Varus, both identified here by their relationship to a woman—father and brother. This becomes less surprising when we get to know the lady. Plancia Magna, whose statue can also be seen in Antalya, was a member of a talented family that had migrated from Italy to Perge and become wealthy through land holdings. One of the men attained the office of Roman consul and Plancia, as well as being a great civic benefactress, was also chief priestess of Artemis, the major cult of the city, and, for a time, even held the highest civic office in Perge, that of demiurge. Great ladies in public life were not unknown in the ancient world, but for one so completely to dominate a town—inscriptions bearing her name are found everywhere—is exceptional.

Curiously enough, in Perge, the worship of Artemis, a Hellenised abstraction of the old Anatolian goddess Cybele, was far more important than that of any of the male gods. One of the archaeological puzzles here is where the Temple of Artemis, a building mentioned by many ancient writers, is located.

Compact and rectangular, Perge was cut into quadrants by two colonnaded streets and enclosed on three sides by walls, and on the north by a low hill that served as an **acropolis,** probably the original settlement of Perge. Little remains there now. The main streets had to be very wide as the depressions in the centre of them between the columns were water channels, not for sewage, but probably just a unique civic embellishment, the inspiration for the similar canal that runs down Atatürk Caddesi in Antalya today.

Inside the walls most of the remains are early Byzantine, a time when Perge was still prosperous: there is the small church next to the **agora,** adjoining the inner gateway on the eastern side, and further up the main street, on the left, the foundations of the **cathedral** remain; at the end, under the walls of the acropolis, was another nymphaion. Towards the west gate, the **palaestra** built during the reign of Claudius is one of the better preserved structures.

Sillyon

Like Perge, **Sillyon** was first built on a low, defensible hill; you must climb a bit to see what's left there. To reach it, take the signposted road to the north, some 15 kilometres past Perge on the coastal road. It was never a very important town, managing to avoid most of the quarrels of its contentious neighbours and figures only in history when Alexander passed through. The remains consist of foundations and streets and steps cut out of the rock of the hill. Some of the fortifications, including one complete square tower remain, and a few well preserved Byzantine buildings. A recent landslide swept away most of the theatre and all of the odeon.

Aspendos

The next ancient town, **Aspendos,** also lies north of the coast road on the banks of the Köprü Çay, the ancient River Eurymedon, then a much larger river than now. In 468 BC the final battles in the long wars between the Persians and Greeks were fought here and resulted in such crushing defeat for the Great King that Persia finally abandoned its attempt to subdue the Greek world. In a single day, the boldness of the Athenian admiral Cimon won two victories at once, on land and on sea. Both the Persian fleet and their army were concentrated at Aspendos for another assault on the Aegean. Cimon successfully drew the fleet from its harbour in the Eurymedon, and defeated it in a day-long battle, capturing many of the Persian ships; not content with this, he dressed some of his small force of marines in Persian uniforms and sent them up the Eurymedon, where they created a diversion so that Cimon and the rest of his men, secretly landed up the coast, were able to disperse or capture the entire, bewildered Persian army.

Aspendos and Side were usually considered the two leading cities of Pamphylia, which is perhaps why they never got on well with each other. After the Romans finally made them agree, Aspendos thrived until well into the Byzantine era; little is known of its eventual abandonment; the wars and disruptions caused by the seventh-century Arabs certainly had much to do with it. To get to the site, take a side road for four kilometres from the main road, passing a beautiful arched **Ottoman bridge** over the Eurymedon. The road may or may not be asphalted; work is in progress.

THE THEATRE OF ASPENDOS

Aspendos' theatre is the best preserved **Roman theatre** anywhere in the Mediterranean. This is no exaggeration; not only is the entire cavea intact, along with the arcade at the top, but the entire stage building has survived. Credit is given to the Selcuks for some preservation work, but no one yet knows what use they made of the building.

At the present entrance, a door in the centre of the stage building, is a small plaque with a message from Atatürk; his government made restoration of this theatre its first major archaeological project, and the inscription records Atatürk's wish that the Turks should not 'lock it up like a museum piece', but use it for performances of classical drama—and wrestling. This is not so strange; throughout this part of Asia Minor, wrestling matches were commonly staged in the theatre. Currently, plays are produced here during the September festival, but wrestling, as elsewhere outside Thrace, is becoming increasingly rare.

Whichever you would prefer to imagine on the cards, stepping inside the theatre magically transports you into the past, evoking the lost Graeco-Roman world in a way few ruins ever can. Not that it is a building of any great architectural distinction—no offence to Zeno, its architect (second century AD)—it is simply that it has survived. Even without its marble veneer or the statues that once graced the interior of the stage building, it is easy to imagine what a night at the theatre in old Aspendos might have been like.

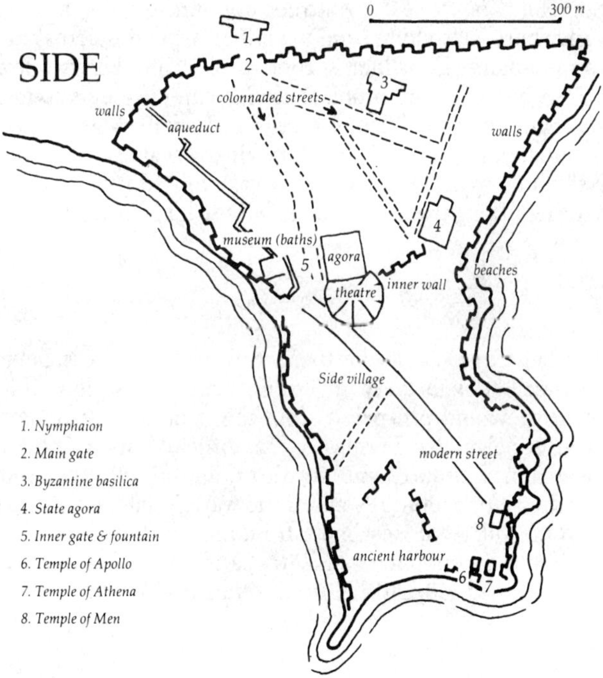
0
300 m
SIDE
walls
aqueduct
colonnaded streets
walls
museum (baths)
agora
inner wall
theatre
beaches
Side village
modern street
ancient harbour
1. Nymphaion
2. Main gate
3. Byzantine basilica
4. State agora
5. Inner gate & fountain
6. Temple of Apollo
7. Temple of Athena
8. Temple of Men

All the theatres of the Pamphylian cities had stage buildings; all were built by the Romans after this innovation had come into vogue. Earlier Greek and Hellenistic theatres had been open, as at Epidauros in Greece, sited with a striking natural backdrop for the action in the skene and orchestra. Under Roman influence, the plays moved up to a raised stage, or proscenium, and stage buildings were used both for manipulating the sets and props, and to shut out the outside world.

Of the sculptural scheme, all that survives is a frieze of Dionysus, but on the right, some plaster with a red and white zig-zag design can be made out. This has been identified as Byzantine work; there are similar designs in the castle towers of Alanya. Climbing to the arcades on top for the view, or to find a short cut into the city, is disappointing as the hill on which the theatre is hung is separated from Aspendos proper by a ravine. To see the rest of the town you must go around it; both sides lead to gates from which paths lead up to the city.

Aspendos has not been excavated, apart from the theatre, but there are remains of a few public buildings, a stoa, bouleuterion and basilica around the agora; all the more substantial ruins are Byzantine. The reason for making the climb is to see the **aqueduct,** one of the best preserved examples anywhere, stretching from the hill of Aspendos across the plain to the distant mountains. Four long sections still stand. The two towers may seem puzzling, but it was no problem for Roman engineers to make water flow uphill, using the principles of gravity and capillary action; the towers served to regulate the pressure and allow air to escape.

Back at the bottom of the hill you may wish to visit the two **baths,** to the left of the theatre along the access road, and the half-buried **stadium,** to its right.

Selge

Another Pisidian city that can be reached from the coast is **Selge,** which originally was called by the very un-Greek name of Estlegiys; as it became Hellenised, it grew and prospered from the manufacture of storax gum, used as incense. Selge, like Termessos in a difficult but beautiful mountain setting, has a ruined **theatre** and **stadium,** and a well preserved Roman **bridge** over the Eurymedon. It's out of the way, 34 kilometres north of the coast road to the village of Beşkonak; from there a track leads the last few kilometres up into the mountains. Nearby, a few miles north of Beşkonak, is the recently opened **Köprülü Kanyon National Park**.

Side

All these cities, interesting as they are, must be taken only as a prelude to **Side.** First among the Pamphylian cities of antiquity, or so it boasted, Side now must be considered the first among Pamphylia's ruins; it was the first to

The aqueduct by the Homer Road, Side

be substantially excavated so a visit here will prove much more rewarding to the non-specialist.

In the 1890s, when Crete was freed from Ottoman rule, a community of Moslem fishermen from there came to settle here. They built a village among Side's ruins and resisted all attempts by archaeologists and the government to relocate it. They're still trying, but in the meantime the villagers have made the most of their opportunity, turning their town into one of Turkey's most improbable tourist traps. Its main street, full of ice-cream parlours, bars, and trinket-stands, follows the route of old Side's colonnaded street, and the ancient residential quarters are filling up with hotels and pensions. It's pleasanter than it sounds. The beaches around Side's peninsula mainly attract Turkish and German families, the restaurants are good and the atmosphere relaxed. There is a noisy disco, but it's out in the ancient suburbs near the Byzantine basilica.

HISTORY

Cyme, the Ionian city near Smyrna, founded Side as a colony in the seventh century BC; it is thought that despite the Greek colonists, Side remained very much a city of native Anatolians, speaking their strange language which had been replaced everywhere else by Greek.

'Side' means pomegranate, and the fruit was often depicted on the city's coins, so many of which survive as to suggest great prosperity, lasting well into the sixth century AD. How they made their money is another question. Sideans, even more than the rest of the Pamphylians, had a well earned reputation for being scoundrels, both in business dealings and in relations with other towns. In the second century BC the city had an arrangement with the Cilician pirates and acted as their fence, circulating not only stolen goods, but also the pirate captives. Until Pompey put the pirates out of business, Side ran a slave market that, if ancient writers are to be believed, handled thousands of poor souls every day.

Despite this, the Sideans never fell foul of Rome. Most of the slaves ended up in Rome, and Sidean prosperity was not affected by the Roman takeover. By the fourth century AD, however, Side had so dwindled that it built a new wall near the theatre, reducing itself by half. After a revival in the fifth and sixth centuries, the depredations of the Arabs put an end to Side after a thousand years of urban life. Most of the inhabitants gradually resettled in Antalya.

REMAINS OF THE CITY

There is no difficulty in finding Side; even before the turnoff is reached the forest of signs for restaurants and pensions springs up, growing thicker as you approach the town. The modern road enters very near the ancient **main gate,** with a small semi-circular court just inside; not for decoration, as at Perge, but for defence. The ruins just outside the gate belong to the **nymphaion,** or fountain. It's a mystery why the fountain should be left outside; the long **aqueduct,** which passes through the walls three towers to the right of the gate, could have brought water anywhere it was wanted. Perhaps this was for vanity's sake, for dusty travellers to clean up before entering the city. Sections of the aqueduct in good repair can be seen for some distance north of the city, and its path inside the walls can be traced through the 'Quarter of the Great Gate', as the northernmost district by the baths and theatre is described in inscriptions.

Inside the gate, two **colonnaded streets** begin. That on the right, leading towards the theatre, was the main thoroughfare of Side, while the street on the left goes through the Quarter of the Great Guild, heading due south. Colonnaded streets like this were the status embellishment of Roman cities, shady arcades for business and shopping that gradually replaced the old Greek agoras as the places to see and be seen. The two in Side, totalling over a mile in length, testify to the great wealth of the city in Roman times; no other city in Asia Minor, not even Ephesus, had as many. Most of the surviving structures in the Quarter of the Great Guild date from the Byzantine afterglow, including a huge **basilica,** on the left side of the colonnaded street, a church, and an unidentified building off to the right.

Just before reaching the inner gate, the other street passes the Roman **baths** to the right and the large **agora** to the left. This was used in the second century as the slave market, and it isn't difficult to imagine the crowds of woebegone captives chained to the columns. On the centre of the agora, the circular foundation and ruins belonged, quite fittingly, to the Temple of Fortuna. Another open square, the **state agora,** stands a few hundred feet to the east, near the old sea wall. As its name implies, it was the governmental centre of Side. Most of this part of the city is partially buried under sand dunes that have accumulated over the centuries, and has not yet been excavated.

The baths, going back across the narrow neck of the peninsula, have been incorporated into the **Side Museum,** with an excellent collection solely on the strength of what the archaeologists found here: there are lots of Roman statues, including some excellent copies of earlier Greek works; reliefs of uniforms and weapons, found near one of the city gates, probably commemorate the spoils won in a victory over Pergamon, when King Attalus tried to conquer the Pamphylian coast; some wonderful sarcophagi show the sentimental side of the ancient world's attitude to death, portraying death's door, one with the deceased's faithful dog peering out; another, a child's, is carved with birds and butterflies.

The great arch of the **inner gate** still stands, simply because, at some later time, the citizens were compelled to wall it up, leaving a smaller entrance in the centre. It is thought that a statue of an emperor in his four-horsed chariot crowned the gate, hence the name of the neighbourhood, 'Quarter of the Quadriga'. In every Pamphylian city there is evidence of gradual impoverishment; marble façades on concrete, or sarcophagi re-used and statue bases with the old inscriptions blotted out and new ones added. Here, the grand **fountain** to the left of the gate was originally a monument in honour of the Emperor Vespasian, moved here from somewhere else in the city.

Here the modern village begins, built around the ruins of the old, down the colonnaded street to the end of the peninsula. The town is closed to traffic, but you may take your car if you're staying at one of the hotels or pensions. Side's well preserved **theatre,** adjoining the inner gate and facing the agora, dominates the centre of the city. On this flat peninsula, with no natural hillside out of which to carve one, the Sideans had to build a theatre themselves. The cavea, the largest in Pamphylia with room for some 25 000 spectators, is supported by an impressive system of vaults and arches.

A four-foot wall was built around the bottom row of seats to seal off the orchestra when combats and wild beast shows began to shove drama off the stage. The remains of two chapels, on either side of the stage building, and some inscriptions showing the seats, reserved for priests, reveal that somewhere in the early Byzantine era, it was used as an open-air church. Most of the sculptural friezes on the stage buildings remain in place, but the reliefs, probably scenes from the myths of Dionysus, are so completely effaced that early Christian vandalism is suspected.

Once in the modern town, you're on your own trying to find the other homes, baths, and temples of old Side. The newer buildings, in and around the ruins, exasperate the archaeologist, but make a picturesque setting. Ruins of some of the more important of the city's temples have been excavated at the very tip of the peninsula overlooking the **harbour,** now silted up. There are no natural harbours on the Pamphylian coast and Side, the foremost port city, was forced to make one out of almost nothing and dredge it continuously. 'A harbour of Side' became a figure of speech, like the labours of Sisyphus, for any unending task. Just where the water's edge once was, the platforms of the **Temple of Apollo** and the **Temple of Athena** are visible; the surrounding ruins belonged to a huge Byzantine **basilica** built over the temples, which were presumably demolished. Behind these, in what must have been a square at the end of the colonnaded street, are more ruins, of a Byzantine **fountain** and a temple (third century AD) devoted to Men, the Anatolian moon goddess.

ATTRACTIONS NEAR SIDE

While in Side, incidentally, avoid all proffered excursions to the **Manavgat Falls** in the mountains above Side, unless you need more souvenirs, or the prospect of a three-foot waterfall excites you. Leaving the town on the way to Alanya, you pass two caravanserais of the Selcuks; **Şarapsahan,** 15 kilometres west of Alanya on the coast, and **Alarahan,** on the side road 9 kilometres up in the mountains. Şarapsahan is fortified, testifying to the uncertainty of the sea lanes even in the best days of the Selcuks. Near Alarahan, the **Alara Castle** is a steep climb, but gives a spectacular view over the valley. Five kilometres before Alanya, the highway department has constructed one of its **roadside beaches;** this one is cleverly designed; a steep embankment had to be built for the road, a hundred feet above the sea, so they simply added steps and built dressing rooms into the side. The effect is one of perfect isolation.

GETTING AROUND

All the sites can be reached via the busy coastal road. If you don't have a car, buses and minibuses ply the Antalya–Side route with great frequency, so you'll never have long to wait. Side is the base for seeing the ancient sites; its taxi companies make a business of such excursions, and post their rates on blackboards in town. All the turn-offs from the main road are marked with yellow signs; prepare for some rough roads if you're heading for Selge or Sillyon.

TOURIST INFORMATION

In Manavgat (a modern town near Side) 273 Antalya Cad., tel. 1645.

WHERE TO STAY

Side is filled with innumerable small motels and pensions, both around the town and among the ruins. There's plenty of room, and the proprietors have adopted the habit—unusual for Turkey—of hanging out vacancy signs. Most are simple and all seem alike; if you want TV and air conditioning, try the **Defne Hotel** (H3), tel. 188–133, where singles are 11 000 TL, and doubles 14 000 TL.

EATING OUT

As a former fishing village, Side is full of fish restaurants, among which the **Aphrodite** at the end of the main street is worth special mention (6000 TL). In Antalya, Hastane Caddesi, the main street to Konyaalti Beach, is the place to look for dinner.

Fruit growing near the coast

Cilicia

This coastal province is ready-made for tourist brochures; the historical background is as good as even the wildest imaginings of a copywriter. Mark

Antony did present Cilicia to Cleopatra as a love gift, not for the sensuous coastal scenery or the forests and peaks of the beautiful Taurus mountains. Cleopatra, always a sharp girl chose in this case not to see the wood for the trees. Cilicia's timber happened to be Egypt's biggest import, and the Queen simply wanted to get it wholesale. Besides, these two lovers had a navy to build.

Half of Cilicia, like Lycia, is difficult country; the ancients commonly referred to the western portion as 'Rough Cilicia' and the eastern as 'Smooth Cilicia', the latter a plain created by deltas of several rivers around the present-day metropolis of Adana. Both sections have always lacked big towns and culture; rough Cilicia because there's nothing but mountains and trees, and Smooth Cilicia partly because of its location on a major medieval conqueror's highway through the Cilician Gates, and partly because of the mosquito. Malaria was a problem until recent times. Few of the armies that have passed through ever felt inclined to stop, and history has mainly avoided both the Cilicias. Rough Cilicia, impenetrable and indeed almost unknown to the Greeks and Romans, enjoyed its best hour just a century before Antony and Cleopatra had their fling, as the most notorious pirate's nest in the entire Mediterranean. Following the example of Tryphon the Voluptuary, a Governor of Kalonoros who turned to piracy after an unsuccessful revolt against the Seleucid King Antiochus, the Cilician pirates ruled the waves for a hundred years until the Romans decided to wipe them out; in 67 BC, they sent Pompey in with more ships and money than he asked for, and within six weeks the great Roman general had either killed, coerced, or bought off the lot of them.

Piracy made a comeback with the Arab invasions of the seventh century and Cilicia, never really prosperous at the best of times, degenerated into a beautiful wasteland. Ottoman rule did nothing to help, and until the Turkish republic, Cilicia remained the poorest, most backward and disease-ridden corner of Anatolia. In the last thirty years, the change has been dramatic. Modern Turkey's extensive water projects have turned the once useless coast into a garden of citrus and banana groves, with cotton the major crop on the plains.

Alanya

In **Alanya,** the 'pearl of the Turkish Mediterranean', not agriculture but tourism has accomplished the work of transformation. In ancient times writers included this city sometimes in Pamphylia, sometimes, in Cilicia. Its great rock of a peninsula that the Greeks called **Kalonoros** or the 'beautiful

The Kizil Kule at Alanya

mountain' makes a natural boundary stone between the two provinces.

Even in the worst times, Kalonoros continued to be inhabited. As an almost impregnable spot, it was a good place to hold. Alâeddin Keykubad discovered this to his dismay when he tried to take the citadel in 1220. Various stories still circulate as to how he finally got in; one has him marrying the commander's daughter and taking the whole family back to Konya, while another says that, in a final desperate move, he had his men tie torches to the horns of thousands of goats and drive them up the hill at night, tricking the defenders into thinking a great army was coming after them; one imagines they would have found the battle cry somewhat suspicious. The most plausible version has Alaeddin making a deal with the Armenian prince who held Kalonoros—offering him another piece of land instead, and saving them both the trouble of a siege.

Alâeddin renamed the city after himself, 'Ala' iyeh', and Atatürk, on a visit during his Westernising campaign, changed its name to the more euphonious 'Alanya'. Recently, with the most beautiful setting along the Mediterranean coast and miles of beaches, Alanya has become a major area for tourists from Turkey and abroad. The lower town around the harbour and the coastal highway past the beaches on either side (those west of the citadel are less popular and less crowded) are all full of tourist clutter in the manner of a Greek island. The Alanyali take refuge, as they have done from so many other invaders, up in the lovely old neighbourhoods above the citadel.

THE HARBOUR

In the harbour, beside the fish restaurants, cruises to everywhere and terraced tea gardens, you'll find the **Red Tower,** Alanya's landmark since Alâeddin built it in 1226. The government completely restored this octagonal 115-foot bastion in 1955, and now it houses a small ethnographic museum. The top floor, crenellated for cannons, offers a fine view of the city; note here how the floor is sloped with channels towards the middle—the centre of the building is one great cistern. This tower, a purely functional defensive work, that nonetheless ranks among the highlights of Selcuk architecture, was constructed to protect the **naval dockyards** built at the same time; they are joined to the tower by a short stretch of wall now surrounded by gardens.

From the start, the Selcuk aim in seizing coastal towns was to become a force at sea as well as on land, as they never had enough time to really get under sail, the birth of Turkish seapower was deferred until the Ottomans, some two centuries later. The enclosed dockyards, connected by archways, are a cool, quiet and interesting place to visit. Judging from the remains of an old beak-prowed fishing boat in one yard, it seems they have been in use until recent times. The other side of the yards is protected by another tower, **Tophane,** literally the 'ball house'—an arsenal.

ON KALONOROS

Besides the dockyards, the Red Tower also guarded the approaches to the citadel. From here the modern road climbs up through the **main gate** with its Selcuk inscription—in Persian, curiously—past old Ottoman-style houses and gardens. The grandest of these, conspicuous on the lower slopes, was restored by a former American ambassador to Turkey. Where the road passes through the second level of the fortification, traces of the original Hellenistic-era wall may be seen underlying Alaeddin's work; just to the right is a small Byzantine chapel, with the walls carefully built around it.

Further on, the road skirts a section of old Alanya within the walls that has survived as perhaps the most charming and serene place in Turkey, all overgrown, with plane trees and flowers among the stone walls and venerable cottages. This neighbourhood is now called the **Ehmediye.** At its centre, there is a **bedesten** and **caravanserai** built by the Selcuks with an unusual tomb, the 1230 **Aksebe Türbesi** and also the fine sixteenth-century **Sülemaniye Mosque.**

Tourism has touched the Ehmediye only slightly. Some of the more enterprising residents have set up a souvenir stand on the road offering two local specialities, lace, and gourds painted with the faces of—we can only guess—Cleopatra and Bugs Bunny. A few hundred yards further on and the road reaches the **Iç Kale,** the inner fortress. Once reached, a quick look down suffices to explain why the citadel was never taken by force.

Most of the buildings around the Iç Kale have gone to ruin; some are certainly part of the palace or governor's residence that existed here; another building with extremely thick walls can only have been a magazine. Best preserved, surprisingly, is a **Byzantine Church** that may be as early as sixth century. Inside, there are still remnants of the original frescoes on the walls. The four evangelists must have been the theme on the pendentives, for on one a lone, fading evangelist, his attributes gone, can still be seen poring over his book.

Much of the citadel walls have been restored in recent years. In one corner, called the **Adam Atacaği,** a platform has been erected for the view; here, according to a highly improbable local legend, condemned criminals were tossed off. The Adam Atacaği looks out over a narrow spit of land extending southwest from the rock of Alanya called **Cilvarda Burnu,** on which stand the ruins of a tower, a Byzantine monastery and chapel, and a building the Turks call the Darphane, or mint. There is no way of getting there on foot, but boats in the harbour take trips to the rock and to other spots around it: the huge **Pirate's Cave** and a **phosphorescent cave,** among others, and of course you'll be shown where Cleopatra took her dip in the ocean.

One final cave, the best of all, can be reached from near the beaches to the west of the rock. **Damlataş Cave** with its forests of stalagmites in delicate colours, was discovered only in 1948. Most visitors come just to look, but sufferers from bronchitis and other ailments find its mixture of radioactivity and high humidity to have curative properties. Not far from the cave, the **Alanya Museum** in a new building contains local archaeological finds.

GETTING AROUND

Although Alanya has no air or rail connection, regular buses travel to points along the coast and inland to Konya. Turkish Maritime Lines ships call often in the summer. As in Antalya, the coastal road is also the main thoroughfare of the town, and the dolmuşes can take you to any point along the beaches. There's a city bus service from the harbour up to the citadel, with stops all along the way.

TOURIST INFORMATION

56 Iskele Cad., tel. (3231) 1240.

WHERE TO STAY

Alanya has more hotels than any other place on the Mediterranean coast; a wide choice in town, on the beaches to the east and west, and at the Incekum beach 15 kilometres to the west. None are particularly noteworthy, except the **Alara Motel** (M1), (tel. local 46), at Yeşilköy, a fancy, riviera-style establishment on a beach along the Side road, with singles for 9000 TL, doubles 11000. If you're travelling on the cheap, there are plenty of pensions, some of which stay open all year, like the **Neslihan Pension** (P2) at 93 Atatürk Cad., tel. (3231) 1922. On Incekum beach, the most comfortable place is the **Aspendos Motel** (M1), tel. (0491) 92, open May–October and boasting a pool and tennis courts. Rates are 6300 TL for a single, 8250 for a double.

EATING OUT

Alanya has lots of restaurants; fish places like the **Havuzbaşi** and the **Meram** on the waterfront near the city park (5000–6000 TL). There is a wide variety of inexpensive places with Turkish specialities nearby.

Alanya to Silifke

Leaving Alanya for the east, the Cilician coast road follows the beaches for some distance before the steep slopes of the Taurus, plunging directly into the sea—as they do all the way to Silifke—compel it to climb into a scenic corniche, bordered by thick pine forests that in summer give an almost overwhelming fragrance. The Turkish forestry service takes good care of them, the most extensive forests in the country, and no knowledge of Turkish is needed to understand the signs, up every few hundred feet, warning about forest fires. Towns are few, but the entire coast is littered with ruins; Byzantine buildings and churches near the shore, and crumbling fortifications of different ages on the heights.

Castles along the shore

The best part of the drive begins at **Gazipaşa,** a fishermen's town with a beach near the ruins of an ancient town named Selinus. Some 20 kilometres further, at the boundary between Antalya and Içel (Mersin) provinces, another undeveloped beach runs along the edge of a narrow enclosed plain full of banana fields. The village of **Kaladiran** nearby, stands in the shadow of a ruined Hellenistic castle.

Anemurium, a town founded in the late Hellenistic era, occupied the southernmost point of Cilicia, at the cape now called Anamur Burnu. Its ruins seem shabby compared with the towns of Pamphylia—not a scrap of marble, only the dark, conglomerate archaeologists call 'pudding stone'; but they are substantial: a church and the arcades of an aqueduct on the hillside, with a castle on top. Near the beach, there are towers and ruined tombs. A few kilometres to the east, the **Castle of Anamur,** built in the twelfth century by the kings of Little Armenia, are directly on the shore, a peaceful, dreamy setting between two long beaches. The castle is almost completely intact, not through any virtue in its construction; the Ottomans kept it in good repair after the British occupied Cyprus, and used it as a fortress again in World War I. The small mosque inside is still in use.

The coast road continues east, climbing ever higher up and down the edge of the Taurus. On the very clearest days, they say that the mountains of Cyprus, 50 kilometres to the south, can be seen. **Softa Kalesi,** on a peak just after the holiday village of Bozyazi, was also built by the Armenians. 'Softa', in Turkish, means a student of theology, and the castle probably got its name from the chapel, still visible from the road below. On this stretch, there are several isolated beaches, but near Ovacik the road cuts inland for a while, up the forested Akdere (White Valley) and back.

When it returns to the sea, the road reaches its crescendo of scenery just before the plain of Silifke, at **Bağsak,** a pretty bay with beaches and the ruins of a medieval fort; this, and the crumbling chapel on the bay's islet, was built by the Knights of St John. While this order still occupied Rhodes and Bodrum, its fleet often gave it control of all the southern Turkish coast. **Taşucu,** an old village with a good harbour, has developed recently into a small, unhurried and unpretentious beach resort; from here you can take a trip on the regular ferry to Girne in Northern Cyprus.

Silifke

Like Alexander the Great who left 'Alexandrias' all over three continents lest we ever forget him, his generals and their successors who founded the Seleucid Kingdom of Persia and Syria bedevilled mapmakers with a score of 'Seleucias' all over the Middle East. Most have fallen to ruins long ago. One survived, and almost kept its name. Ancient **Selucia ad Calycadnos**, once a great, thriving city, has been whittled down by the years to plain **Silifke** on the Göksü, a piquant and humble Turkish town. There are no signs of Seleucia apart from a single standing column and traces of a theatre south of the Göksü, but the **Byzantine Castle** still peers down from the nearest crag, and on a slight rise near modern Silifke, in the east of the

Göksü plain near the coastal highway, stand the ruins of a Byzantine religious complex the Turks call **Meryemlik,** with the once great **church of Saint Thecla.**

This saint, according to the imagination of the hagiographers, was the first girl to throw over her fiancé for a life of chastity, and soon became the first female Christian martyr. Foundations of a colonnaded building that was once part of the monastery remain as well as the still-standing apse of the large basilica. Beneath it, recent excavations have uncovered a cavern, later carved into a chapel, where the early Christians hid. There are bits of mosaics and frescoes in the chapel, and the municipality has made it a small museum for architectural sculpture found throughout Silifke.

The Göksu, though a poor excuse for a river until the spring floods, once changed the course of European history. The Germans like to think of their old Barbarossa, Kaiser Frederick II of the Holy Roman Empire, as asleep under his mountain, like King Arthur. By 1190 Barbarossa had made the Empire a going concern, the most powerful state in Europe; he was on his way to the Holy Land to teach the Saracens a lesson when he met his match in the Göksu. According to the chroniclers, he unaccountably fell off his horse in the stream, and drowned before anyone could reach him, in six inches of water. The crusade was aborted, and German unification postponed 700 years. Upstream from Silifke, a small plaque marks the spot in the lovely **Göksu gorge** along the road to Konya.

Across Rough Cilicia, there have been few opportunities to strike inland to look at the Taurus Mountains; most of the roads are unpaved and the region remains as isolated and wild as in ancient times. The Byzantines called this land Isauria, and while its barbarous natives helped wreck the urban life of the coasts in the fifth and sixth centuries, in the process they themselves were becoming Christianised. By the eighth century they were producing Byzantine emperors, like Leo III, the famous Iconoclast.

Uzuncaburç

In ancient times, however, the furthest Greek civilisation ever penetrated the Taurus was the mountain city of Olbia, founded in the third century BC, known as Diocaesarea to the Romans and **Uzuncaburç** to the Turks. This is your chance for an excursion into the mountains. Not only are the ruins worth the 30 kilometre drive, but the road itself passes through a charming landscape of rolling, well-tended farm land, reminiscent of some corner of Italy. On the way, there are three **Roman tombs,** small temples in form, and almost entirely intact; two, at **Çifte Anit,** are visible from the road, and one of these is an unusual two-level temple with an arched vestibule and Corinthian columns.

Uzuncaburç means 'tall tower', referring to the two 70-foot Hellenistic towers, one in the city and another on a nearby hilltop, perhaps the best preserved examples in Turkey. It's believed there were others, forming a kind of communications system with the coast; messages were sent by flashing the sun off polished shields in a kind of Morse code. The city itself is a much more pleasant site than any on the coast in Pamphylia, a bucolic ruin shaded with walnut and fruit trees, among vineyards and goats.

You still enter the city through the **monumental gate,** with corbels and niches for long-vanished statues, leading to the usual **colonnaded street.** Just outside the gate is the theatre, unexcavated and overgrown. The pride of the ancient city, the **Temple of Zeus Olbios** is the oldest structure yet discovered using the Corinthian order (third century BC). The capitals are mainly on the ground, though several columns have been re-erected; the proto-Corinthian design shows traces of the Ionic scrolls from which it evolved. An apse still stands at the east end, reminding us that the temple was later pressed into service as a church. The sculptural friezes have been gathered in the garden, their cartoon lions, boars, bulls and leopards show a distinct decline from the best work of the Greeks, but have their charm, just as have the very similar carvings in many medieval cathedrals. From here, a crossroads of colonnaded streets will take you either to a rare, surviving arched **city gate,** or to the **Temple of Fortuna** (first century BC), which, as fortune would have it, has now become a social club for goats. Outside the city, you may also visit the large **necropolis** of tombs, some separate, some cut into the rock, and simple sarcophagi—many with the bones still inside.

Corycian Castles and Caves

Back along the coast, a small local tourist industry has grown up around the curiosities of **Korykos** (Corycia), an ancient settlement and religious sanctuary. First, at Narlikuyu, a small fishing harbour full of restaurants, Turkey's smallest national museum consists only of one small room with a fountain and a famous relief of the **Three Graces,** Aglaia, Thalia, and Euphrosyne, looking much as they do in Botticelli's painting. In the fourth century, there was a Roman spa around the spring here.

The Corycian caves, **Cennet** and **Cehennem,** can be most easily and truthfully explained as two great holes in the ground. They're interesting enough for the Turks, who coined these names 'heaven' and 'hell' for them, and they so fascinated the ancients that an important sanctuary of unfathomable antiquity was maintained in Cennet; it may have hosted mysteries such as those in Eleusis, or perhaps an oracle—Delphi also had a 'Corycian

Cave'. Cennet, an enormous chasm difficult of entry, can be explored with the aid of a guide; at the bottom, the remains of the old sanctuary have been incorporated into a fifth-century church. The little church was never an important site for the Christians; apparently they hoped to keep the old pagan demons deep inside by building it there, like the stopper in a bottle. The chasm, turning into a cave, continues on with an underground stream, no one knows how far; many believe the stream flows to the spring of the Three Graces.

Cehennem cannot be entered at all, except by a multitude of birds; their chirping echoes weirdly through the chasm. Like its counterpart, it is enormous and bottomless. A team of alpinists went down recently, and found only the bones of the few unfortunates who had fallen in. To the Greeks, this was the lair of Typhon, the monster of monsters spawned by Mother Earth in revenge for Zeus' defeat of the Titans. Typhon actually defeated Zeus and dragged him here, where he only escaped through the cunning of Hermes. Before succumbing to thunderbolts, however, Typhon managed to start a fine family; according to Hesiod, his offspring included the Hydra, the Chimaera, and Cerberus; his grandchildren, the Sphinx and the Nemean Lion.

Korykos was never a large town, though it's remembered as the place where Cicero spent two years of his exile from Rome as governor. **Ayas,** a few kilometres to the west, has a much more substantial appearance today, including the apses of two large basilicas visible from the road. In ancient times, Ayas was known as **Elaiussa-Sebeste,** but it was not to achieve prominence until the Rubenid kings of Little Armenia made it their capital in the eleventh century.

This odd state, formed by an opportunist group of refugee nobles after the Armenian homeland was overrun by the Selcuks, managed to survive for three centuries by a system of alliances, first with the Crusader states, and later, with the Ilhanli Mongols. Life as a Christian principality surrounded by Moslems became increasingly precarious in the fourteenth century, though ironically it was Peter I, the French-born king of Cyprus, who contributed the most to the end of Little Armenia. The last ruler of any independent Armenian state, King Leon VI, went into exile in Paris, where he is buried at St Denis.

Near Ayas, on the shore between two large, popular beaches, the Armenians concentrated their military forces at the **Castles of Korykos.** These two large fortifications, which also served as the port, were begun by the Byzantine admiral Eustachius; the Armenians enlarged and improved them, using lots of stone from nearby ancient cities including an entire Roman gate rebuilt into the new wall. The smaller castle, called locally the Kiz Kalesi or **Maiden's Castle,** stands romantically offshore on a small island; in the Middle Ages the Armenians joined it to the mainland with a causeway that formed their harbour, but today you either have to swim or hire a boat, if you want to see it. One of these castles has a role in an elegant fairytale recorded by Mandeville in his thirteenth-century book of travels. In the tale, the castle held a sparrowhawk upon a perch, and 'a fair lady of faerie that keepith it'; whoever went there and stayed seven days alone without sleep, the lady would appear to and grant a wish. A King of Armenia stood the trial, and when the lady appeared boldly stated he'd had enough of power and wealth, and demanded the lady herself. To such impudence she could only curse him and his nation to unending strife and impoverishment, and Little Armenia withered ever after. Other men fared better in the Castle of the Sparrowhawk, though Mandeville warns that if any should fail and fall asleep he will be forever lost. From here, the road passes more ruins, of the ancient towns **Kanlidivane** and **Soli,** as the coastal plain opens outwards into the flatlands of Smooth Cilicia.

The Plains

In the last forty years, much to the surprise of its inhabitants, this region has made the remarkable transformation from being one of Turkey's very poorest areas to one of its richest. With the natural fertility of the soil and some intelligent planning and a double dose of DDT, the people of **Çukurova,** as the Turks call this plain, began with cotton fields and turned them into an enormous textile industry. Adana and its port Mersin, the two largest cities of the Çukurova, have grown from almost nothing to sophisticated, up-to-date cities full of palm-lined boulevards and modern office blocks.

Nothing in **Mersin** is very old or of particular interest, but the city is well-built and attractive, with a lovely park running almost the entire length of its shore. Ironically, it is one of the oldest towns in the world; remains of a 6000 year-old culture, related to that of Çatal Höyük, have been dug from a mound called Yumuk Tepe, but from then to now, there have only been small settlements. **Tarsus** lies inland 27 kilometres to the east and St Paul would be surprised to see his native town, an almost abandoned ruin two centuries ago, grown into a manufacturing city of 100 000. All that survives of the ancient city is a stretch of wall and a simple, unembellished gate along the Mersin road. Antony met Cleopatra in Tarsus, so naturally the only ruin left has become **Cleopatra's Gate.** If you stay long, they'll show you the well from 'St Paul's house', too. Some more ruins can be seen at the old port of **Gözlükule,** dating from the Hittites up to Roman times.

Like Mersin, **Adana** has been here for a long time but only blossomed recently. As centre of the textile industry, the town has become Turkey's fourth largest. With so much expansion and prosperity, the old town, unfortunately, has become shabby and neglected, and even in the new districts in the north, apart from a few truly sumptuous boulevards, the city has had trouble managing its good fortune. Old Adana grew up around the **Taşköprü,** the long Roman bridge across the Ceyhan. Built under Hadrian and restored under Justinian and many other rulers since, the bridge has acquired an oddly lopsided appearance; all its arches are different sizes.

In the bazaar area, just around the corner from the nineteenth century **clock tower,** is the **Ulu Cami,** a very unusual sixteenth-century work with towers and recesses in stalactite patterns and a unique squat minaret that resembles a lighthouse. Just outside the north edge of the city, **Seyhan Dam** backs up a lake that has become a popular recreation area for local people.

With all the armies that have marched through this historical crossroads, down from Anatolia by way of the Cilician Gates, or along the coast, it's not surprising that so much has been built on this plain, or that so little has endured. Castles sprang up here like ice-cream stands around a carnival, over forty of them in Adana province alone, as well as remains of civilisations from the Hittites to modern times.

There is another Roman bridge at **Misis,** just east of Adana. This town's ancient name, Mopsuestia, recalls the Homeric seer Mopsus, who was associated with so many other Cilician towns. In Islamic folklore, this was the home of the great Doctor Luqman, a prototype of the physician–sorcerer of long ago. Just before the town of Ceyhan, the road from Adana passes under one of the mightiest of the medieval castles, **Yilanlikale.** The Armenians probably built it, and the emblem between two rampant lions over the gate is thought to be the arms of the Rubenid house. During the Crusades, the Knights of St John occupied and extended Yilanlikale. The popular name 'Castle of the Snake' may refer to the long silhouette of the walls as much as anything in its admittedly sinister aspect; the castle consists of three successive courts, each one higher and stronger than the last.

North of Ceyhan, the assiduous Armenians built two other formidable castles. **Tumla,** from the twelfth century, fell to the Mamelukes of Egypt, traditional enemies of the Armenians as they would later be of the Turks, in 1375. **Şiş,** overlooking the village of Kozan, was the last stronghold of the Armenians, and when a spy betrayed it to the Mamelukes in that same year, the story of Little Armenia came to its unhappy end.

Few spots in Turkey are planted as thickly with relics of the past as the environs of **Kadirli,** a little town on the Ceyhan River. The ruins of no fewer than eight castles can be seen in the vicinity, also neolithic village mounds, Hittite rock reliefs, an aqueduct that served the Roman town of Flaviopolis, and at least two ruined cities. Few of these are impressive and few of the roads paved; the best bet for a detour from Ceyhan into the area would be to avoid Kadirli, and head north to **Karatepe,** a Hittite city second only to Boğazköy in the wealth of reliefs and artifacts found there.

On the way, you'll pass the ruins of **Castabala,** also known as Hierapolis, a small Roman town where there are still some temple columns and buildings under a rambling Ottoman castle on a low crag.

Karatepe

From Castabala, the road is awful, but the countryside very lovely, with well tended farms and fragrant pine forests reaching their peak at **Lake Aslantaş,** as fair as any spot along the Turkish coasts. King Asitiwanda, who built Karatepe as his summer palace, could not have enjoyed the view as much; the lake is brand new, formed by the Aslantaş Dam downstream. Here, on the thirty or so reliefs arranged under two pavilions in the open-air museum, you should expect none of the weighty religious or statist themes of the art of Yazilikaya or Boğazköy. Perhaps by reflex, the Hittite artists added a few of their favourite fearsome lions and marble-eyed sphinxes, but most of the panels show domestic scenes—musicians with pan pipes and tambours, a mother giving suck, a merchant ship, even the king himself dining while a monkey under the table waits for handouts. Some reliefs are of gods, but they belong to an entirely different pantheon from those at Boğazköy; characters such as the chubby Phoenician god Bes, a bird-headed 'sun god', a centaur, and an unusual 'good shepherd' figure (like the early Christian representations of Jesus) show the influence of other cultures on the tolerant and syncretic Hittites. Excavations are still underway at Karatepe, and archaeologists have yet to get the actual palace and fortress in shape for visitors.

One last castle you meet, whether your route takes you to the Hatay, or to Southeastern Anatolia, is **Toprakkale,** its grim bulk guarding the crossroads now, as it did in the Middle Ages when Crusaders and Saracens, Armenians and Mamelukes contested for its ownership. As often as it was besieged and taken, it was repaired; the key to the plain of Cilicia, Toprakkale remained in good condition for centuries.

GETTING AROUND

Two roads cross the formidable Taurus Mountains, from Cappodocia to Tarsus (the E-5), and a more picturesque route, from Karaman to Silifke down the Göksu valley. Along the coast, the scenery is better than anywhere else, but if you're driving, note that services are sparse between Silifke and Alanya. The coastal highway is constantly being improved and widened, 10 kilometres at a time. There are no possible detours so watch out for delays.

Turkish Maritime Lines' summer cruises stop at Mersin, sometimes Iskenderun. There are daily flights to Adana from Istanbul and Ankara; for the western part of the region, you're better off going through Antalya. Adana is connected by rail with Istanbul and Ankara; the station is a kilometre north of the city centre of Ziya Paşa Caddesi. Buses go everywhere without difficulty. Within the cities there should be no need for transport; all are small and centralised.

TOURIST INFORMATION

In Anamur, 24 Atatürk Bulvari, tel. 1677. In Taşucu: 18A Atatürk Cad.—Gümrük Alani—near the harbour, tel. 234. In Silifke, 2/1 Atatürk Cad., tel. (7591) 151. In Mersin, Inönü Bul., at the harbour, tel. (741) 11 265. In Adana, 13 Atatürk Cad., tel. (711) 11 323.

WHERE TO STAY

Hotels in the smaller resorts of Cilicia are generally cheaper than Alanya, like the **Karan Motel** (M2), tel. 1522, in Anamur, with singles at 3050 TL and doubles for 4650 TL. Anamur also has pensions, as do Gazipaşa and Taşucu; the **Taştur** Motel (M1) in Taşucu has obligatory full-board, a good restaurant and a lovely setting, tel. (4590) 290, singles for 1200 TL half-board, doubles at 1700 TL. The beaches between Silifke and Mersin have only pensions, except the **Yaka Motel** (M4) near the Kizkalesi (4500 TL for a single, 6500 TL a double). Among the hotels of Adana, the **Erciyes Palas** (H4), 53 Özler Cad., tel. (711) 18 867 is a bargain, though some of the rooms don't have baths (4500 TL for a single, 6500 TL for a double).

EATING OUT

Restaurants along this coast means mostly fish; and on the whole, they're very good. In many places you'll find an unpretentious little place by the roadside with its fishing boat on the beach nearby. One of these is the **Melleç,** just west of Anamur, where you can just look in the cooler and pick out your fish (around 5000 TL for a meal). Besides the Melleç, there's the **Sato Restaurant** next to the castle in Anamur; in Aydincik, the **Arsinoe** on the yacht harbour is good. More fish in Taşucu and Narlikuyu harbours, the **Narli** and the **Alibaba** (both around 6000 TL). In Osmaniye there's the **Karadeniz Lokanta,** hard to find in a little arcade off the main street (2000 TL).

The Hatay

This little tongue of land projecting into Syria to spoil Turkey's rectangularity, marks the only changes in the nation's boundaries since the founding of the republic. Apart from the small chain of the Amanas Mountains running to the sea along the Gulf of Iskenderun, Hatay province is really the ancient city of Antioch, now Antakya, and its hinterlands on the lower valley of the Orontes.

During World War I, General Allenby's Egyptian Expeditionary Force captured the Hatay for Britain but a League of Nations mandate gave the French the territory; they spent considerable effort and money over the next sixteen years trying to win the goodwill of the inhabitants. When the date for the plebiscite ordered by the League finally arrived in 1939, the vote went overwhelmingly to join Turkey, and the French 'Hatay' became a historical curiosity remembered only by philatelists.

Whether you enter from the flat plain of Cilicia or the arid southeastern plateau, the contrast is striking. The fertile and well-tended countryside, its roads often lined with plane trees and oleanders, makes the Hatay one of the most civilised landscapes in Turkey. Along the coast, as soon as you have passed Toprakkale and have the Gulf of Iskenderun in sight, you will be on the plain where one of the most significant battles of ancient history was fought.

From Issus to Iskenderun

In 334 BC, Alexander the Great began his eastern campaign by invading Asia Minor; right across the peninsula, while reducing towns and dismantling satrapies, he had been seeking a final showdown with the Persian King Darius. That November, he caught him at **Issus,** near the Turkish town of Dörtyol. Most historians credit the Persians with some 400 000 men; nevertheless the fighting was brief and one-sided. Darius barely managed to escape with his life, and Alexander informed him, in the subsequent diplomatic correspondence, that any future messages to him should be addressed to 'King of All Asia'. Two years lapsed before Alexander finally entered Persepolis—there were other distractions, such as the conquest of Egypt—but the Battle of Issus had already made his title a reality.

Payas, the first town after Dörtyol, lies in the shadow of a large modern steel mill; in the sixteenth century, it was the major port of the region, and substantial buildings from that period remain, notably the **Selimiye complex,** built by Yavuz Selim in 1574, and a harbour castle thought to have been begun by the Venetians some centuries before. Payas' harbour silted up, and since then, **Iskenderun** has become the port of the Hatay and one of the largest in the Mediterranean; the ships waiting for dock-space often fill the horizon, as they do in Istanbul or Piraeus. As terminal of the busiest Middle East pipeline, the port handles all Iraq's oil exports. 'Iskender' is the Arab and Turkish form of 'Alexander', and the city can trace its origins to the Macedonian foundation; other than that, Iskenderun is wealthy and pleasant and remarkable only for being almost indistinguishable from Mersin.

From Iskenderun the coast road can penetrate only as far as the fishing village and beach resort of **Arsuz.** South of here ruins of a Crusader castle can be seen by boat, but a better and more accessible one lies near the route from Iskenderun over the mountains, at **Bağras,** built by the Templars in the twelfth century and captured soon after by Saladin himself. The castle is partially ruined, but the Gothic chapel and refectory remain.

Antakya (Antioch)

Throughout most of the Roman Empire, Antioch, now **Antakya,** was the third largest city of the Western world, surpassed only by Alexandria, and Rome itself. Seleucus Nicator, Alexander's general, who later created his own empire by defeating a sufficient number of his former comrades-in-arms, founded Antioch in 300 BC; as the Seleucid capital, it was the agent for introducing Hellenic culture into Syria, and as trade routes across the new Greek Middle East grew, so did Antioch, at a rate that astounded contemporary chroniclers. Just at this time, the Mediterranean world had become rich and cohesive enough to trade on a large scale with India and China; the Seleucids, in the middle, collected all the transport charges. Antioch, the metropolis of the Hellenised Syrians, renowned throughout the ancient world for their craft and subtlety in business dealings, became the first western terminal of the Great Silk Route.

Secure under the Pax Romana, after 64 BC Antioch's population at one time exceeded one half million. Roman client kings of the Middle East, like Herod of Judea and the Kallinikos dynasty of Commagene, brightened their images by endowing the city with great temples and public works. Learning and art were prized, even by the high standards of the time and place, and Antioch, before long, vied with Athens for intellectual leadership of the Empire. One of the first Christian communities was started here by St Peter himself; it grew so rapidly it became the greatest stronghold of the new faith, with enough of a hold on the population, even the upper classes, to resist most of the Emperor's intermittent persecutions; even though Diocletian burned down all the churches in 301.

For a time in the fourth century, Antioch competed with Constantinople for pre-eminence in the East, and as the city was a bastion of the Arian heresy, the two became doctrinal enemies as well. Constantinople's rise meant Antioch's decline; the capital could collect taxes and draw away all the trade, although it lacked the strength or will to defend its outpost in Syria. Before the seventh century, Antioch was sacked six times by the Persians and Arabs. After a revival as a part of the Crusader kingdoms, it was sacked once more by the Mamelukes of Egypt in 1268. That was the end; the modern city was a struggling village only a century ago.

As much of its growth took place under French rule, in the period 1920–1939, Antakya has very much the aspect of a French colonial city, with a slight excess of boulevards, traffic circles and palm trees. The traffic circle on the banks of the Asi, the ancient River Orontes, was obviously planned as a kind of civic centre; but here, the grandest French building is not a government headquarters or school, but an Art Deco film palace. Of the ancient city, all you see are marble blocks built into the walls and streets of the pretty old village, across the river from the new town. Kurtuluş Caddesi is its main street, generally following the route of the famous colonnaded avenue of antiquity; on it the **Habib Neccar Camii** is an exceptionally fine seventeenth-century mosque. On the mountains above the city, some parts of the ancient walls are well preserved, but they are difficult of access.

The main reason for visiting Antakya is the collection of Roman mosaics in the **Archaeology Museum,** perhaps the finest in existence, recovered from the city and its suburb of Daphne. These mosaics, in colour and detail, and in the expressiveness of the portraiture, must be counted among the greatest works of the Roman world. A face as perfectly captured as that of the unknown lady named 'Soteria' brings that world back to life, while mythological scenes like the room-sized 'Marriage of Tethys and Oceanus' attended by all the creatures of the sea, gently reproach us for not crediting the late Roman world with enough imagination.

AROUND ANTAKYA

The Hatay has been a civilised country since Neolithic times, and the plain around Antakya is littered with mounds and ruins. Just north of the city along the cliffs, is what the locals claim is the oldest Christian church in the world still in use. The name **St Peter's Church** was natural, for St Peter himself is said to have preached here. It is a cave, with a tunnel for escape during the persecutions, a cistern and, on the floor, the remains of mosaics. The carved façade, cut out from living rock, was added by the Crusaders. Antakya has a small Catholic community, and mass is said here, and in the nineteenth-century church on Kurtuluş Caddesi on alternate Sundays.

Along the cliffs to the left of the cave are a number of rock tombs, and a mysterious relief of a woman carved in the second century BC.

The most renowned pleasure dome of the ancient world was Daphne, at **Harbiye,** a beautiful spot overlooking the Orontes with small waterfalls cascading down a series of terraces, and groves of pine and plane trees. It isn't associated with the myth of Apollo and Daphne that all happened in Thessaly but the Hellenised gentry of the Seleucid Kingdom thought it would have made a fine setting for the myth. A famous temple of Apollo was erected here, and the well-to-do of Antioch surrounded it with their villas and gardens. Antony and Cleopatra courted here, and in the Roman era, the Antioch games held here surpassed the old games at Olympus in popularity and importance.

Roman emperors spent time in Antioch whenever their responsibilities permitted; Julian the Apostate, having grown up here, especially favoured it. When he returned in AD 363, on his way to campaign against the Persians, and saw the Christian population wrecking the beautiful temple of Apollo at Daphne to get stone for churches, he was furious. He had it rebuilt, but the Christians immediately burned it down. Daphne shared in Antioch's misfortunes; various earthquakes knocked down what the Christians hadn't and rearranged the topography, somewhat for the worse. Today the place is known by the incongruous name of **Harbiye** 'war college', but it is still a favourite resort of local people, with restaurants and picnic grounds among the waterfalls. It can be reached along the main road to the south six kilometres from Antakya.

There was a dark side to Antioch's early Christianity, leading to odd extremes. In Antioch, instead of a blossoming of innocence and faith what happened was an outbreak of neuroses no one could have foreseen. One outstanding manifestion was the fashion for pillar-sitting, begun by St Simeon Stylites in the fourth century, lasting for over a century. St Simeon spent some 25 years in the air, on a series of progressively taller columns, attracting great crowds of pilgrims and penitents and interfering in Imperial politics and public morals through his pronouncements from on high. Pillar-sitting became fashionable, and at one point, Church chronicles report no less than two hundred copy cats up in the air together.

The hill where all this took place, with the ruins of the fifth-century **St Simeon Monastery,** are off the road from Antakya to the west. A number of other old monasteries in various stages of disrepair, lie on the hills around Yayladaği near the Syrian border.

The road from Yayladaği to the coast leads to **Samandağ,** and from there north to **Çevlik,** near the ruins of Antioch's old port, **Seleucia ad Pieria.** Gradually abandoned as its harbour silted up, the town has little left to see except the **Tunnel of Vespasian,** a series of great halls with 50-foot ceilings carved out of the rocks near the sea, used as part of Seleucia's water supply system. Even though a smaller irrigation canal was recently built through it, you can walk through this cool and lovely spot, passing in and out of the mountain, listening to the frogs. Fine beaches line the shore all around with a beautiful backdrop of green mountains, some in Turkey, some in Syria.

GETTING AROUND

The Hatay is off the major routes, and getting there by bus (there are no rail or air connections) may be difficult. Nothing serious, only that you may wish to check with the bus lines in advance for times, and you may be stuck on a bumpy minibus, especially if you're coming from the east. St Peter's Church is within walking distance of the centre of Antakya, but for many of the other early Christian sites you'll need a car. Even with one, you may skip St Simeon's Monastery; it's 15 kilometres of really bad roads. Harbiye is easily reached by dolmuş.

TOURIST INFORMATION

In Iskenderun, Atatürk Bulvari, at the City Pier, tel. (881) 11 620. In Antakya, 41 Atatürk Cad., tel. (891) 12 636.

WHERE TO STAY

Antakya doesn't get many tourists, and the choice is limited to the **Atahan** (H2), tel. (891) 11 036 on Hürriyet Cad. (which has a good restaurant and rooms for 5000 TL single, 6500 double), and the **Divan** (H4), tel. (891) 11 518 on 62 Istiklal Cad.; if you choose to stay at Harbiye (Daphne), the **Deliban** (H2) is a bargain (tel. 54–55), with TV and refrigerators in each room for 5000 TL a single, 6400 a double. The beaches around Samandağ and Arsuz mainly have pensions, and the **Arsuz Hotel** (H4) on the beach (tel. 11–12) where a single will set you back 5100 TL, a double 6500 TL. The best hotel in Iskenderun is also good value: the **Hatayli Oteli** (H2), at 2 Osmangazi Cad., (tel. (881) 11 551) with a single for 7000 TL, and doubles at 10 100 TL.

EATING OUT

Antakya has good restaurants; besides the fine one in the Atahan Hotel, there's another on the same street, Hürriyet Caddesi, the **Zümrüt,** with an outdoor terrace (6000 TL). This street, in fact, at the centre of Antakya's old town, has almost all of the city's eateries, from tiny kebab houses to the two fine establishments mentioned above. In Iskenderun, the **Saray Lokantasi** (about 5000 TL) on Atatürk Bulvari, is a popular spot in the centre. Harbiye has a surprising number of places, but the most enjoyable are the informal outdoor restaurants in the park, only a shed or tent with picnic tables among the waterfalls and pines. At these you can get a good fish or kebab dinner at lower prices than elsewhere.

Part IX

THE BLACK SEA

Orchards on the North Coast

Turkey's longest coast has always been the marine back door, less favoured by nature and less prominent in history than the lands along the Aegean and Mediterranean. Jason and his Argonauts may have sailed it, but the Greek merchants and colonists behind the myth founded only a few towns, none of which ever attained much status in the ancient world. From Jason up to the present, in fact, the only intrusion the shores of the **Pontus Euxinus** ever made into history was the rise of the Pontic Kingdom in the wake of Alexander the Great's conquest in the fourth century BC. The Pontic Kings gave Rome fits for a century, but when they finally succumbed to the tenacity of the legions, it put an end to Pontus as a nation forever. Since then, with the exception of the short-lived but colourful Empire of Trebezond, these shores have managed well enough to stay out of trouble.

Recently, the Black Sea has been just as successful in avoiding tourism. Both the coast and the forest-clad mountains that rise behind it have their share of scenery, more in the western half than in the east. There are a few good beaches, but the climate lacks that Mediterranean perfection; the season is short, and rains are frequent, even in the summer. Even in the west, the best part of the coast begins only at Samsun; like the area around the Marmara, the coast, from Istanbul eastwards has become industrialised over the last forty years.

BLACK SEA COAST

All along the Black Sea, with the exception of a few local resorts, there is little accommodation and few restaurants. Though this is gradually changing, as yet the package tours and the magnates of the holiday industry are nowhere to be seen, and if you're not too demanding in your stretch of seaside, and wish to avoid knocking elbows with your countrymen, the Black Sea may be just the place.

From Şile to Giresun

Travelling east from Istanbul you come to **Şile,** a beach resort popular with the people of the city. Genoese merchants built the little **castle** here to protect their interests in the Black Sea back in the days when they were snatching the Byzantine Emperor's commerce out from under his nose. After Kandira, 82 kilometres to the east, the road leaves the coast, bypassing the promontory of Calpe and its islet just offshore, where a vision of Apollo appeared to the Argonauts; in classical times a Temple of Harmonia was built in commemoration, but not a trace of it remains.

The next good beach, at **Akçakoca,** with another ruined Genoese castle, was named after a general of Sultan Orhan's who captured it, the first Ottoman foothold on the coast. Akçakoca is often crowded with families from the big towns to the east: **Ereğli,** where the Middle East's largest steel mill adorns the coast, and **Zonguldak.** This latter city has been around since the Hittites, but only since the coal seams around it were first mined in the 1920s has it become important. Now, besides shipping out most of Turkey's coal through its large port, Zonguldak has become the centre of the country's major industrial region. Despite the smokestacks, it's not so bad that people stay away from the fine beaches along the coast towards **Amasra,** a town founded by colonists from Miletus, with yet another Genoese castle on its citadel.

Bolu and Lake Abant

Leave any part of this coast, and you eventually find yourself in the **Köroğlu Mountains,** a long chain that separates the plains around Ankara from the sea. Though not as steep as the mountains along the eastern Black Sea, these are heavily forested, not only with pines and poplars, but with groves of oak and other deciduous trees not often seen in Turkey. **Bolu,** south of Zonguldak, lies at the centre of the country's most popular mountain recreation area. Whenever you see 'bolu' in the name of a Turkish town, as in 'Inebolu', 'Safranbolu', you know it's at least as old as the

Romans; it's how the Turks came to pronounce 'polis', and this 'Bolu' was originally Claudiopolis. Nothing very old has survived, but there's a fine **Ulu Cami** built under Yildirim Beyazit. Bolu has a reputation for producing the best cooks in Turkey, but its citizens complain that they all go to Istanbul.

Beautiful **Lake Abant,** just to the southwest, is perhaps the best known mountain resort. Nearly a mile above sea level, the Turks keep it well stocked for trout fishermen. If one lake isn't enough, try the **Yedigöller National Park** where there are seven, among forests of oak, elm, and beech; here you may stalk the rare and elusive wild tulip. There's skiing at **Kartalkaya,** southwest of Bolu on the slopes of Köroğlu Dağ, the highest peak of the chain.

KÖROĞLU, THE ROBIN HOOD OF TURKEY

'Köroğlu' means 'son of the blind man', and behind the name stands a personality you should get to know if you plan to spend much time here. For these mountains are Turkey's Sherwood Forest, and Köroğlu, a real bandit who flourished at the end of the sixteenth century, is his country's Robin Hood. The historical evidence is limited to letters from the Governor of Ankara demanding Köroğlu's arrest; there are quite a few of them. The legends, still heard in rural corners here and in eastern Anatolia, are all we have beyond the letters, and they start Köroğlu out in life in much the same way as his English counterpart, sworn to outlawry to avenge a wrong done by the authorities.

His father, a groom for the lord of Bolu, had been charged with the duty of selecting a gift horse from among the herd of a neighbouring *bey*. He picked a lean, crippled colt, so enraging his master that he had the groom's eyes put out. Köroğlu promised revenge, and with the aid of the colt, now grown into a magic grey horse called Kirat, spent a long career doing just that. With him, at his mountain hideout somewhere near **Gerede,** lived 500 warriors, some heroes in their own right, like Demirioğlu, 'son of the blacksmith', the very picture of a Turkish Little John. **Nallihan,** the tiny village south of Bolu, is a centre of the Köroğlu legend, and here you may see one of Kirat's horseshoes still nailed to a stone wall. Strangely, these stories were always most popular out east, and another cycle of them has Köroğlu's band robbing fat merchants on the pass of Çamlibel, near Sivas.

PROVINCE OF BITHYNIA

In Roman times, these mountains formed part of the province of Bithynia; one thing they have in common with the old Bithynian villages around Bursa is the style of the houses. These square, half timber buildings, with their tile roofs and medieval overhanging second storeys, can best be seen in towns like **Safranbolu, Bartin** near the coast, and in the cosy little provincial capital of **Kastamonu.** The castle from which this town derives its name is, in one respect, unique in Turkey; it wasn't wrecked by Tamerlane—he built it. In modern times, the greatest thing to hit Kastamonu was Atatürk's speech here in 1925, proclaiming the Hat Reform, and the abolition of the fez. You can learn all about it (if you understand Turkish) in the pretty old building that houses the **Kastamonu Museum,** with a good collection of Roman era sculpture.

Sinop

Returning to the coast, you'll find more beaches in the pleasant stretch around the fishing towns of **Inebolu** and **Abana.** From there, it's a long and nondescript ride as far as **Sinop,** on the only remaining unpaved section of the coastal road. Long ago, the sailors of the Black Sea had a saying that the only reliable ports on the southern shore were 'June, July, and Sinope'. Originally a Milesian colony like Amasra, Sinope grew to become the preeminent town of Pontus during the Hellenistic era, and was a free trading city that maintained its liberty until the first King Pharnaces annexed it to the Pontic kingdom in 183 BC. As first city and occasional capital of this kingdom, Sinope was more than compensated by the many temples and monuments the kings bestowed upon it.

Sinope contributed two tough customers to the lore of classical antiquity. The lady after whom the town was named was an Amazon queen whose charms attracted the attentions of Zeus. When the god came courting, he promised Sinope any gift she desired; she chose everlasting virginity, and lived happily ever after. In 413 BC, Diogenes, the original Cynic, was born in this city. This is the fellow Alexander the Great found one day sitting in his usual tub; the prince, always kindly disposed to cranks and philosophers, asked if Diogenes desired anything of him, and received the famous reply 'Yes, stand out of my light'. Alexander is later said to have commented, 'If I were not Alexander, I would rather be Diogenes'.

As the Black Sea trade dwindled during Roman times, so did Sinop (this is the modern spelling), and today the only natural harbour on the coast finds itself eclipsed completely by artificial ones at Zonguldak, Samsun, and even Trabzon, originally a colony of Sinope. The town still makes its living from the sea. It may be a good spot for a fish dinner along the quays, but for all its past, little is left. The **castle,** built on the foundations of Mithradates' stronghold, is a Byzantine work, and the most notable building is from the thirteenth century, the **Alâeddin Camii,** one of the last mosques built by the dying Selcuk Empire. Outside of the town, there are good beaches at **Akliman,** an isolated spot on the bay, and at the fishing village of **Gerze.**

Samsun

Samsun, the largest city on the coast, is exactly the opposite of Sinope—all present and no past. The Milesians were here, too, and Samsun is just as old, but never had anything to show for itself until this century. Wherever you walk in the city's nondescript gridiron of steets, the sweet aroma of freshly cut tobacco fills the air, rising from the enormous old Tekel factory in the middle of the town which produces most of Turkey's cigarettes. Nobody smokes like a Turk, as you will have noticed, and Samsun is doing very well. The modern and well-planned centre of the city reflects this, with its shorefront boulevard, lined with palms and smooth, cleanly-designed new buildings. Samsun could well afford to put up the largest **Atatürk Monument** outside Ankara, but it also had good reason; in some ways, the Turkish War of Independence began here, with Atatürk's escape from Istanbul on the steamer *Bandirma.* Instead of inspecting the army, as he had fooled the Sultan's government into ordering him to do, he started making speeches to it and issuing manifestos to the patriots of Anatolia. Samsun welcomed him with bands and cheering crowds, and it has been a stoutly republican town ever since; ironically, it also has a reputation for being one of the most conservative Moslem cities in Turkey.

Samsun divides its busy port from the rest of the town with its **Fair,** a big park like the one in Izmir, that contains the stadium, train station, public auditorium, the Luna Park, acres of gardens, and the **Atatürk Museum** which resembles a lost pavilion from some forgotten exposition. The whole of old Samsun, full of market stalls and questionable restaurants is in the city's west end; here the memorable structures are not old mosques but the wonderfully overdone public buildings and banks, all in a bastard French, Second-Empire style.

Hazelnuts and cherries

Leaving Samsun, the first town you reach is Çarşamba, which means 'Wednesday' in Turkish (*Perşembe*, meaning Thursday, is 110 kilometres down the coast and looks just like it. *Pazar*, Sunday, is near the Russian border). From Çarsamba, the road takes a shortcut across the delta of the Yeşilirmak. This area, and really most of the Black Sea region, is extremely good farmland. From Sinop to Çarşamba, and inland along the Yeşilirmak valley, Turkish tobacco has been the major crop. Now, along the roadside up to Trabzon, there are mostly hazelnut plantations; the little *findik*, as the Turks call it, is a surprisingly important export crop. After Trabzon, tea plantations cover most of the land. Throughout, however, on the mountain slopes that never stray far from the sea, one more local speciality keeps the Black Sea farmers prosperous—the best cherries anywhere. They're indigenous here; the Romans first brought cherry trees from the Black Sea into Europe, and from there, they spread throughout the world.

Ünye and Ordu

If any town on the Black Sea shows promise of becoming a big seaside resort, it's **Ünye,** on a pretty half-moon bay with beaches, restaurants, and camping sites extending for several kilometres on either side of the town. Ünye itself, built around a beach and a shady promenade, retains traces of fortifications constructed when it was ancient Oenae. Caves along the shore near the town are one of the few Black Sea haunts of the *foca,* the Mediterranean seal. Between Ünye and **Ordu** the road, placid enough since Samsun, suddenly climbs into an exuberance of corniche turns, up and around the rugged peninsula the Greeks called the Promontory of Jason. Below the cliffs, lie secluded fishing villages and untouched beaches; the best of these faces an islet, within easy swimming distance of the shore, where a ruin has become a home for great flocks of sea gulls. Perhaps this is the 'Island of Ares', where the Argonauts were attacked by a flock of birds dropping feathered darts. A temple of Ares was said to have been founded on the island.

Not long before the Argo was launched, according to the generally accepted order of myths, Hercules had tramped these shores on his ninth labour securing the girdle of the Amazon Queen Hippolyte. The Amazon city Thermiscyra and its River Thermodon may have been at Terme, or near Ordu, if indeed it ever existed in the form mythographers have made for it. To the Greeks, this part of the Black Sea has always been associated with the Amazons, a confusion perhaps from Bronze Age Achaean merchants encountering matriarchal tribes during their exploratory voyages into Pontus.

Ordu, a real Greek foundation named Cotyora, keeps some reminders of the days of King Mithradates; the **Caleoğlu Castle** 5 kilometres inland, and some cliff tombs like those in Amasya. There's a large beach east of the town, but if you're looking for something a little different, try the crater lake up in the mountains at **Çambaşi,** some 70 kilometres south of Ordu, which is completely encircled by beaches.

Giresun and the route to Trabzon

The next town, **Giresun,** surrounds a small table-top peninsula with a Byzantine castle perched on top, a striking sight that is almost a mirror image of Alanya on the Mediterranean coast. As well as the castle, the town has an eighteenth-century Greek church and the tomb of Seyit Vakas, who won Giresun for the Ottomans in 1461. **Giresun Island,** just offshore, and another candidate for Jason's Island of Ares, is the largest of the Black Sea islands, and the only one inhabited. You sometimes hear it referred to as 'Amazon Island'; locally it's believed the ruins belong to Ares' temple and the palace of the Amazon queens who built it.

After Giresun, the wild mountain scenery once more commands your attention. All along the route, those Pontic mountains have lurked close to the shore; now their wooded slopes press in closer, in a shade of green you would never expect to see this close to the Mediterranean, more like England, than Turkey. From Samsun to Trabzon, there are no good roads inland, across the mountains; this is one of Turkey's greatest areas of wilderness, and the difficulty of the terrain ensures it will remain so.

Further along the coast, the castle you pass at **Akçakale,** built by the Emperors of Trebizond, serves as a reminder that you are near the borders of that lost realm. As you get closer to Trabzon, the villages begin to look suburban, first **Vakfikebir,** then **Akçaabat,** renowned for its folk dancers.

GETTING AROUND

A good, two lane highway runs along the entire coast, except for a short stretch west of Sinope, though this is a high priority with the highway department, and may be completed soon. Zonguldak, Samsun, and Trabzon (see next section) are the big centres for **bus traffic,** both within the region and to other points in Turkey. One large bus company, Ulusoy, carries much of the trade in this region; they usually give a good ride.

The only **railroads** that reach the Black Sea are the dead-end Ankara–Zonguldak and Sivas–Samsun lines, but there are two other alternatives for getting to the region—THY's **flights** to Samsun from Ankara, and the weekly Turkish Maritime lines (TC Denizyollari) **ferry boats** that take three days to poke along the coast from Istanbul to Trabzon, stopping at Sinop, Samsun, and Giresun.

TOURIST INFORMATION

Bolu: Stadyum Caddesi, tel. 3632
Sinop: Iskele Meydani, tel. 299
Samsun: Özel Idare Işhani, Irmak Caddesi, first floor—near the Atatürk monument, tel. 11228
Ordu: Belediye (town hall), Sahil Caddesi, tel. 14178
Giresun: Vilayet, tel. 3560

WHERE TO STAY

Most of the small coastal towns with beaches have only very limited accommodation, with inexpensive pansiyons the rule. Şile, with large hotels like the **Değirmen** (H3) on the beach, tel. 48–148, is an exception, popular among Stamboulu. Rates here are 4500 TL a single, 7600 a double. In the mountains near Bolu, the Turkish Automobile Club has built the large, Alpine-style **Koru Hotel** (H2), tel. 2528, with very comfortable rooms for 6400 TL, doubles for 10 500 TL. The Turban chain has a hotel on Lake Abant (H2), tel. 04, with a sauna and pool for 6000 TL, 8000 TL for a double, all rooms with bath.

EATING OUT

Bolu's cooks have a good reputation, which you may test at the **Idris Lokanta,** near the town hall (about 5000 TL for a meal with wine). Fish restaurants along the coast do exist, but are not numerous; in search of the renowned palamut, try at Sinope, Ünye, Şile, or near the Fair in the centre of Samsun.

The Monastery of Sumela, Trebizond

Trabzon

Trabzon, Trebizond, Trapezus: whatever transitions the name has undergone since the merchants of Sinope founded it in the eighth century BC, it has always had an exotic ring to Western ears. When the Greeks first came, they returned with shocking tales of a people called Mosynoecians, practitioners of open-air fornication, who lived in wooden castles (they may have been related to the Picts of Scotland). For centuries after the founding of the city, Trapezus was the easternmost limit of the Greek world.

In spite of the difficulty of crossing the steep coastal mountains, Trapezus somehow managed to become an important entrepôt for trade to the east. During the Byzantine period, after trade in the Mediterranean was disrupted by the Arab conquests, all the caravans, from Persia and beyond, with goods to sell to Constantinople or Europe found their way here. By now the name had become Trebizond, and the city had reached its balmiest days when the Crusaders sacked Constantinople in 1204. Alexis Comnenus, a member of the former dynastic family whose intrigues and corruptions had contributed much to the Byzantine decline, escaped from the fallen city; in his flight he raised an army of mercenaries in Asia from what he had of the family's wealth, occupied Trebizond and proclaimed it capital of a new empire, headed by himself under the title of Grand Comnenus.

THE COMNENES

Alexis had chosen well; not only was his new city impregnable, but it brought him a good income, and the Greek population was glad to have him. He, and his successors of the Comnenus house brought all the oriental luxury and ceremony of Constantinople with them; having once more the chance to indulge in their fantasies, the Comnenians spread Trebizond's fame throughout the world; in the European geographies and chronicles of the day, it conjured up the same half-legendary aura as did Baghdad or Samarkand. Its military fortunes rose and fell; at its greatest extent it occupied all the Black Sea coast, but near its end, only the city itself. The Comnenes kept their state afloat, less by military prowess than by craft, making good use of diplomacy, and ladling out tribute money to the Selcuks, Mongols, and Ottomans when that failed. Like the Hapsburgs, Comnenes were always careful to marry well; contemporary accounts suggest that the dynasty's greatest resource was cute princesses, much desired by the neighbouring potentates; this allowed the Grand Comneni to keep their web of alliances intact at all times.

By the middle of the fifteenth century, unfortunately, the only neighbour Trebizond had left was the voracious Ottoman Sultan, who already had enough wives. After Mehmet Fatih captured Constantinople, Trebizond, the last free Greek state, was obviously next on his list. Mehmet appeared in 1461, with the greatest army and fleet ever seen in the Black Sea, before or since. It made the desired impression on David Comnenus, the last emperor, who surrendered the city without a shot. The Turks treated Trabzon (as they came to call it) very well, but as Genoa, and later Venice, drew off all the Eastern trade for themselves the city inevitably declined. The

Russians did considerable damage when they captured the city in 1916, but Trabzon has been recovering gradually. Today, its port is busy, its suburbs expanding, and best of all, its football team is consistently one of the most successful in Turkey.

THE MODERN TOWN

Don't be discouraged by the entrance into the town. The neglect and squalor of the port area and coastal highway, with their vistas of rubbish and broken concrete, is unnerving enough to make visitors pass right by. You have to climb the hill to get into the city, going up Iskele Caddesi to the **Meydan,** the main square of the modern city; once up there, you'll be relieved to see that Trabzon is quite an agreeable town after all. The square, with its shady park, city hall, and fire station, with shiny red engines out on display for all to admire, is not only the centre of the business district; almost all the hotels and restaurants congregate here as well. Next to the fire station, the sixteenth-century **Iskender Paşa Camii** commemorates a popular Ottoman governor; its shallow dome, curved like an upside-down soup plate, shows Byzantine influence.

ALONG MARAŞ CADDESI

Either of the two big streets leading west from the square, Maraş Caddesi or Hükümet Caddesi, will take you to the old Greek city, but Maraş Caddesi is by far the most interesting; it skirts Trabzon's **bazaar,** a large and colourful district of narrow streets where many of the crafts that once brought Trabzon fame—all manner of work in copper, silver, and gold—are still going strong. As is common in Moslem cities, no need is seen to separate religion and commerce. The attractive 1839 **Çarşi Cami,** right at the heart of the market district, is directly connected to the sixteenth-century **bedesten.** All around, the maze of blind alleys and old *hans,* with a talent for somehow looking even older than they really are, give the place an air of mystery and impenetrability, rare even for a Turkish market.

Further along Maraş Caddesi, peering out from a tiny square, stands the oldest Byzantine church left in Trabzon, **Ag. Anna,** built in the seventh century and restored in the ninth. Plain as it is, there is something endearing about this forlorn, padlocked little church. The basilica form is unusual in Byzantine buildings—except in Trabzon, a town strictly orthodox in doctrine (St Athenasius himself is said to be buried in Trabzon), but heretical in architecture. The basilica of Ag. Anna's set the pattern early, and even when later churches began to sprout domes, Trabzon's churches eschewed the centralised pattern of their counterparts in Constantinople and elsewhere. The plan of Ag. Anna has three parallel naves, the one in the centre raised to form a clerestory with a few small windows.

OLD TOWN AND WALLS

To get into the old town, find your way back to Hükümet Caddesi. You soon come to the high **Tabakhane Bridge,** and beyond it, a panorama of the walls of Trebizond, rising sheer and hard above the narrow valley. From the bridge it's easy to see how the city got its name. On the opposite side there's a valley and a bridge just like this one, and between them, the old town, which the Turks call the **Kale,** stands up high very like a table—*trapeza* in Greek. Also, you can see how the city got its reputation for impregnability; above the two ravines, now picturesquely filled with orchards and market gardens, the cliffs, and the walls above them, rise as high as 150 feet. No army ever actually took Trabzon by force of arms; when the Selcuks, under Alâeddin Keykubad tried to, all their assaults failed and their army was washed away in a sudden flood through the ravines.

The long, straight Iç Kale Caddesi splits the old town from north to south; old Trabzon's busy centre lay at the spot where the Iç Kale meets the roads from the two bridges; today this spot is occupied by a little square full of chairs and sleepy Turks, between the Vilayet and the **Ortahisar Cami;** this is no less plain and severe as a mosque, than it was as the Panayia Chrysokephalos, the 'Church of the Golden-headed Virgin', built by the Comneni in the thirteenth century. Behind it, along the western edge of the walls, once stood the **Palace of the Comneni,** of which nothing now remains except a few arches and sections of wall between the more recent houses of the district. Nothing much is left either at the southern end of the Iç Kale, where the offices of the Trebizond state and army had their quarters, at the highest and least vulnerable end of the 'table.'

BYZANTINE MONUMENTS

If you follow Iç Kale Caddesi beyond the walls to the south, you will enjoy the best view of the city and its extensions up the surrounding hillsides. From out here, you can pick out three other Byzantine monuments in the steep neighbourhoods south of the Meydan; they are then easier to find if you wish to visit them. Following Boztepe Caddesi south from the Meydan takes you to two of them. One of them is the **Ag. Eugenios,** one of the first works of the Comneni after their arrival, built on the site of an older church and dedicated to Trebizond's patron saint. Mehmet Fatih converted it into a mosque on the first Friday after his conquest of the city, and it has been called **Yeni Cuma Cami** (New Friday Mosque) ever since. On the other side of the hill called Boztepe stands the **Teokephastos Convent** of the same period. One of the last churches to be built, the fourteenth-century Ag. Philipi, is now the **Kudrettin Mosque.**

Leaving the Kale over the western **Zagros Bridge,** you soon find yourself in another pleasant square, with mighty plane trees surrounding Trabzon's finest Islamic work, the **Hatuniye Cami,** built by Sultan Selim I in honour of his mother; her tomb stands just outside the entrance. A surviving stretch of the city's **outer walls** can be seen nearby, running parallel to the street that leads to the seashore.

AYA SOFIA

If Trabzon's most famous building must be mentioned last, it is only because it's the furthest from the centre, a good mile walk or dolmuş ride from the Kale. Set on a little hill planted with roses above the awful, but fortunately invisible coastal highway, stands the **Aya Sofia Church.** Even though Trabzon, before 1920, had one of the largest Greek populations in Asia Minor, this church had been neglected for centuries, and was on the verge of collapse when a team of archaeologists went to work on it in the 1950s. Many parts, including the cylindrical dome, have been almost completely reconstructed, but, more importantly, the original frescoes have been recovered from beneath the plaster and restored. Today, the frescoes are Trabzon's greatest tourist attraction, the finest late Byzantine art east of Istanbul.

The Aya Sofia is a building of much architectural interest, but not in the way you might expect. Most of the elements of a Byzantine church can still be recognised: the dome, the small apses and the vestiges of a central cross plan, but it seems that after so many centuries—over a millennium of Greek Christian architecture—inspiration had finally given out. Emperor Manuel Comnenus had the church built in 1245, one of the last great buildings the Greeks made when time was running out for them in Anatolia. Between the Romanesque arches, the Western-style naves with their barrel-vaulted ceilings, and the sculptural frieze on the south porch, there are almost as many West European and Armenian elements in the design as Byzantine. What the builders lacked, the artists more than made up for; Aya Sofia's thirteenth-century frescoes, with their perfection of line and colour, have a special place in the story of the last Byzantine renaissance, the efflorescence of painting in the Greek twilight, whose influence helped make possible Western Europe's own Renaissance.

Almost one half of all the original paintings survived sufficiently to be restored. The best, perhaps, are in the narthex, scenes of miracles from the life of Jesus. There are many other familiar themes: the Annunciation, and the Four Evangelists with their attributes. The Virgin Mary in the Ascension takes her place in the central apse, while a huge, half-effaced figure of the Christ Pantocrator looms over all, from the dome. Most unfortunately, another scene in the porch depicting the Last Judgement in the manner of Bosch or Brueghel, is almost completely lost; among the remnants a lone wolf devouring souls can be made out.

The Zigana Pass

Even if you intend to push on to the end of the coast, the temptation here will be strong to turn inland; the Trabzon–Erzurum road, the last stretch of the Silk Route in the days of the Comneni, is today the only decent road over the steep eastern Black Sea Mountains between Samsun and Artvin. Even so, crossing over on the bus is an adventure, and driving, it could be an epiphany of terror. Zigana Pass, climbing up to the 6300 feet, the narrow road ascends more sharply, contorts along more hairpin turns, and looks down over more bottomless cliffs than any mountain road you've ever seen. For your trouble, the views will be reward enough; all around, the slopes and crags are covered with forests and banks of wild flowers, at least until the treeline is crossed, which is shortly before the eternal snows of the pass. (The rest of this route is described under **Erzurum,** p. 327.)

SUMELA MONASTERY

On the way, a detour at the pretty village of **Maçka,** with its hog-backed Ottoman bridge, will take you up another narrow valley to an unforgettable sight, the **Sumela Monastery,** its white walls standing out sharply from the grey, one thousand-foot cliff in which they are embedded. Monks had lived in the caves of this cliff since the fourth century, when an icon of the Virgin Mary painted by St Luke was brought here. Later Byzantine Emperors extended the complex, but exactly which of the Comneni was responsible for its final form, the pale, magnificent seven-storey complex crumbling away on the cliffs today, is not known. Sumela ranked as a monastic establishment second only to Mt Athos, but with the expulsion of the Greeks in the 1923 exchange of populations, it was abandoned; after decades of vandalism, very little is left inside. If you climb the long stone steps cut out of the rock, you will be disappointed, but you'll probably have the whole huge building to yourself. Several other convents and monasteries can be found in the surrounding area, but they have fared little better.

East of Trabzon

East of Trabzon, the Empire of Tea truly begins. By now, even if you've spent only a little time in Turkey, you'll have had countless glasses of tea thrust in front of you; it all comes from these green mountain slopes. Demand is high, and this far corner of the nation has become quite prosperous in a modest way. Many of the people here are Laz, a folk of obscure Caucasian origins who have been here a long time without causing anyone any trouble; you see the old men in the cafes and buses, with their berets, big mustaches, and long watch chains, eternally jolly and easy going; the

Turks secretly envy them. Many others are Georgians; Soviet Georgia is just across the border.

Rize, the capital of the tea region, barely squeezes in between the mountains and the sea. Here, behind the tea slopes, mountains rise as high as 12 500 feet. Behind them is the valley of Çoruh, in which, in **Artvin** and surrounding villages such as Ardanuç and Şavşat, simple Georgian churches and monasteries still stand; this valley remains one of the most contented, though least visited, sections of Turkey. Times were not always so good, as the many castles around the valley testify. Artvin and **Ardahan** have two of the largest, built by Selim the Grim in the sixteenth century when the Ottomans were consolidating their power in the northeast.

GETTING AROUND

Trabzon can be reached by bus or by Turkish Maritime Lines ferries from Istanbul. The coastal road is good the entire length of the section, but any of the roads over the mountains to the south can be a real problem in the winter—especially the Zigana Pass south of Trabzon, where silk and spice caravans disappeared with regularity in the old days.

Trabzon is the only city on the coast too large to see everything on foot. The dolmuş lines along Maraş Caddesi, connecting the town square with Aya Sofia, can take you to most of the sights, but to reach the old churches and monasteries of the periphery, it's either a long hike or a taxi ride. The main **bus stops** and **taxi stand** are in the square, where gleaming '60 Chevies await your call—just remember they're more expensive than smaller taxis, since they use more petrol. You'll need a taxi to see the Sumela Monastery—buses only go as far as Maçka.

TOURIST INFORMATION

Trabzon's trilingual and very helpful **Information Bureau** is on the square, next to the Özgür Hotel (tel. (031) 12722 or 13827).

WHERE TO STAY

In Trabzon most hotels are around the square. The **Özgür Hotel** is perhaps the fanciest (though not by much!); it's at Atatürk Alani 29, tel. (031) 113 19–127 78 and costs 4050 TL a single, 5400 TL a double. Of the really inexpensive, the **Anil Hotel** is best—avoid the **Kalfa,** on the square where some taxi drivers would like to take you, but most of the other establishments—all quite inexpensive—should prove adequate. In Hope, Artvin, and the other villages in the far northeastern corner, accommodation is sparse and simple. There's one hotel in Hopa, the **Papilla** on Ortahopa Cad., tel. 1440, with rooms between 3600 and 5400 TL.

EATING OUT

The Özgür restaurant attracts most tour groups, but there are other good, cheap restaurants in Trabzon; quite a few may be found in the square near the firehouse, setting their tables out on the sidewalk in friendly competition. Outside the centre, **Piknik Restaurant** on the hill of Boztepe with a view of the city (about 6000 TL) and the **Kavalik Restaurant** on the coastal road west of town are among the best.

Part X

NORTH-WESTERN ANATOLIA

The Green Mosque at Bursa

Bursa

Fortune has always been unusually fickle, especially in the cities of Asia Minor. The soil here is fertile but thin; it is hard for a city to take root. Think how Antioch or Miletus have fared, or see how many towns have completely succumbed to trade dislocations, the silting-up of harbours, and the Alexanders and Tamerlanes. Bursa, however, has been highly favoured; it is a capital of grace, a tribute to what any city can do if left in peace long enough.

King Prusias I of Bithynia founded Bursa—then **Prusa**—in the second century BC. The Ottomans made it their temporary capital in 1326, while waiting for Constantinople to fall to them. In a sense, Bursa is Istanbul's little sister, and even if you're fond of Istanbul, coming here will be a breath of fresh air, figuratively and literally; up on the slopes of the 8300 foot Uludağ, the snow on its peaks lingering well into the summer, the Mediterranean seems far away.

Added to this Moslem Alpine setting are famous thermal baths, a funicular railway, and plenty of trees. Its citizens call it *Yeşil* Bursa, 'Green Bursa', a title of honour they strive to maintain by meticulously caring for their

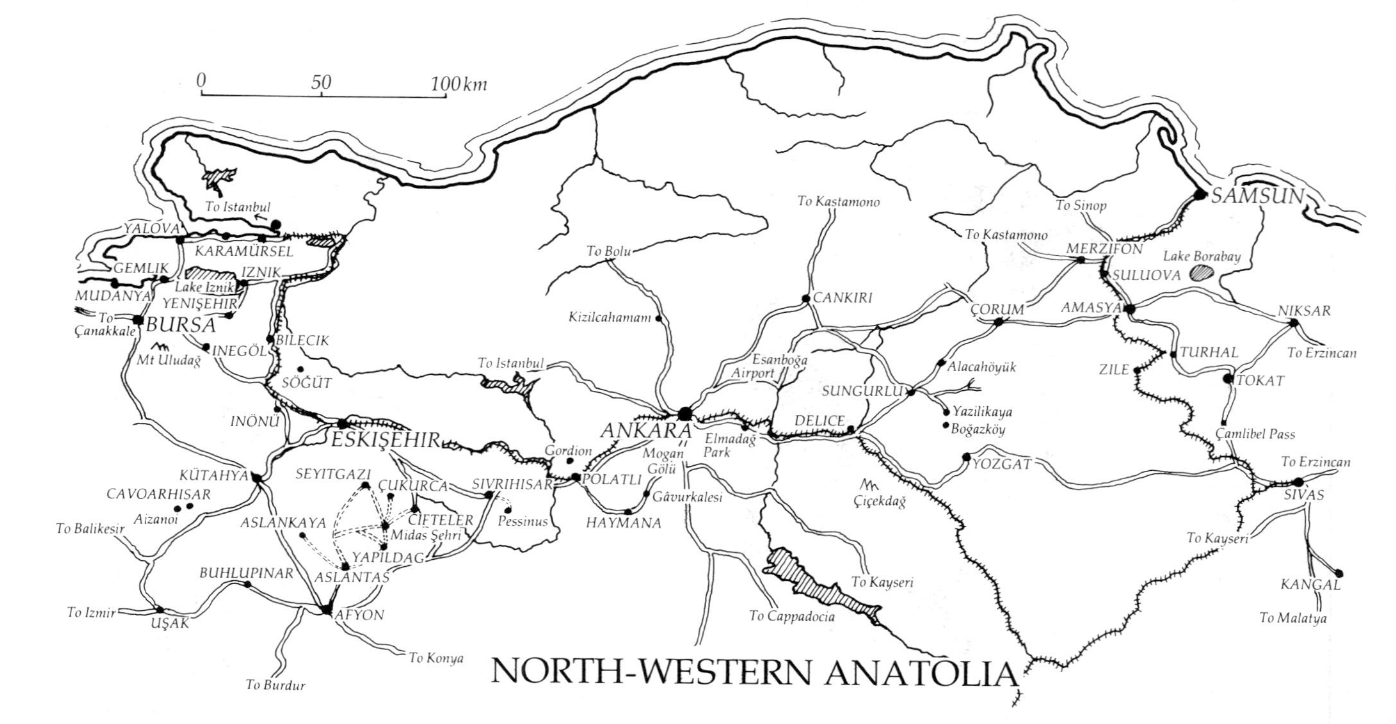
0
50
100 km
To Istanbul
YALOVA
KARAMÜRSEL
GEMLIK
IZNIK
Lake Iznik
MUDANYA
YENIŞEHIR
To Çanakkale
BURSA
Mt Uludağ
INEGÖL
BILECIK
SÖĞÜT
INÖNÜ
ESKIŞEHIR
KÜTAHYA
CAVOARHISAR
Aizanoi
To Balikesir
SEYITGAZI
ÇUKURCA
CIFTELER
Midas Şehri
ASLANKAYA
YAPILDAG
ASLANTAS
BUHLUPINAR
To Izmir
UŞAK
AFYON
To Konya
To Burdur
To Istanbul
Gordion
SIVRIHISAR
Pessinus
POLATLI
HAYMANA
Gâvurkalesi
Mogan Gölü
ANKARA
To Bolu
Kizilcahamam
Elmadağ Park
Esanboğa Airport
To Kastamono
CANKIRI
DELICE
SUNGURLU
To Cappadocia
To Kayseri
Çiçekdağ
Alacahöyük
Yazilikaya
Boğazköy
ÇORUM
YOZGAT
To Kastamono
To Sinop
MERZIFON
SULUOVA
AMASYA
SAMSUN
Lake Borabay
ZILE
TURHAL
TOKAT
NIKSAR
To Erzincan
Çamlibel Pass
To Erzincan
SIVAS
To Kayseri
KANGAL
To Malatya
NORTH-WESTERN ANATOLIA

beautiful parks and gardens, as well as the venerable plane trees that adorn their streets. You can't help but notice Bursa's resolute civic pride; cleanliness and order extend to an almost Victorian fussiness. Prosperity helps, of course. On the main road into the town you pass Turkey's largest car factory and along with Turkish Fiats and Renaults, Bursa ships out tons of soda-pop, bathtubs, clothing, knives, cannons for the army and hosts of other products.

Although today Turkey's sixth largest city, in ancient times Bursa was never more than a minor provincial centre. What little is known of it comes from the letters of Pliny the Younger, the governor under the Emperor Trajan. To the Byzantines, the town was a fashionable resort for its baths; but the Ottomans put Bursa on the map. Sultan Orhan captured it in 1326 and made it his capital, a position it held on and off until 1453. Here the Ottomans began to sponsor great religious architecture. Drawing on the traditions of the Selcuks and Byzantines to develop a style that would be a fit heir to the past, and complement the ambitions of the Sultans, their architects crowned Bursa with mosques, schools, and mausoleums solidly and honestly medieval, possessed of an austere but very present spirituality that earns them a place beside the more elaborate creations of Istanbul.

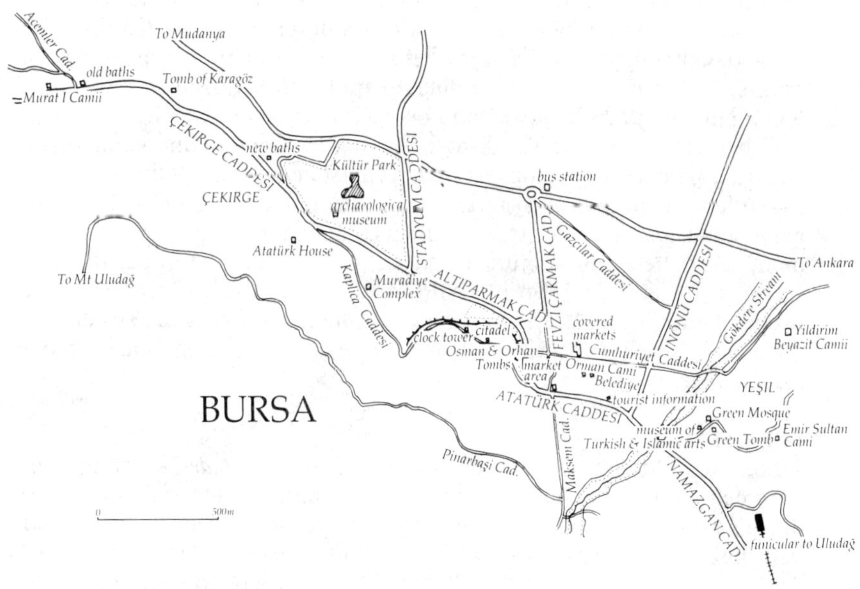

SEEING BURSA: THE MARKET AREA

A good place to begin a tour of Bursa is at the first Ottoman mosque, the **Orhan Camii**, built by that Sultan in 1335, and restored after a Karaman invasion damaged it in 1413. This small but lovely mosque is the pattern for later works in Bursa; its best features its simple but graceful porch and fountain. Inside, the central dome is supported, not by pendentives, but by semi-domes in the corners. In some ways, this is the structural system of older buildings like the **Aya Sofia** turned inside out; it would not work with a larger dome. The outlandish geometry that decorates the semi-domes is just that, decoration, not part of the structure. Such polygens run amok are a recurring conceit in Bursa's mosques.

Just across the street, Bursa's *Belediye* (City Hall), is not in tourist brochures, but it's probably the largest piece of folk-art in Turkey, and the prettiest City Hall. Its construction of half-timber, with horizontal, vertical and diagonal beams in a seemingly haphazard manner, with bricks in between, is common in the older village homes. Here, with its painted designs of flowers and trees, and illuminated with strings of coloured lights, it's one of the unexpected delights of Bursa.

Bursa's **market district** encompasses everything north of Atatürk Caddesi. The network of covered bazaars and *hans* is not as large as Istanbul's, with less jewellery, and more bath towels and tea sets. Just the same, it's tidier and has better bargains. The arcades destroyed in a 1955 fire have been rebuilt much as they were before. Near **Kapali Çarşi**, the main arcade, is a lovely complex containing the **Ipek (silk) Han** and the adjoining **Koza Han** with a little *mescid* built over a fountain at the centre.

Other *hans* in the market district, on Atatürk Caddesi and Cumhuriyet Caddesi, are currently being restored. As in Istanbul, many of the surrounding streets are given over to a particular trade; in Demirciler Caddesi, as its name implies, is a whole street of smiths, hammering away in ferrous harmony. Also here, on Atatürk Caddesi, is the Grand Mosque, the **Ulu Cami**, completed in 1396 by Yildirim Beyazit and twice restored. Here twenty domes, two graceful minarets, and the more than usual austerity of the outside give way to a virtuoso display of Arabic calligraphy and a famous carved *mihrab* within.

THE CITADEL

To the west, Atatürk Caddesi curves around the old *citadel*, which is in an extremely strong position. Undoubtedly it had much to do with maintaining Bursa's peace and quiet over the centuries. Not much remains of the old walls built by the Ottomans, but on the slopes down to Atatürk Caddesi, modern Bursa has turned the old fortress into a modern-day version of Nebuchadnezzar's hanging gardens; the slopes, with stairways and terraces full of trees and flowers give ever-changing views over the old city. There are also many cafes, in which the people of Bursa practically live; wherever there's a beautiful view, common enough in this city, you'll find a pleasant spot to sit and reflect.

On the citadel you'll find the oldest houses in the city. Many are in disrepair, but more than elsewhere, Bursa has made an effort at historic preservation, noticeable in such streets as **Kale Caddesi**, lined with homes of the seventeenth to nineteenth centuries. Near the **clock tower**, a landmark visible from most of Bursa, are the tombs of the first two great Ottoman leaders, the **Osmangazi Türbe** and **Orhangazi Türbe**, both restored after heavy damage in the earthquake of 1855. Orhan's sarcophagus lies beside that of his wife, Nilüfer Hatun, a Byzantine princess married off for reasons of political expediency, who became the first of the great ladies of the Ottoman Empire; the building she founded for travelling dervishes in Iznik now contains that city's municipal museum.

Two routes lead down from the citadel, one through the meandering streets westwards to Kaplica Caddesi, leading eventually down to the Kültür Park and suburb of Çekirge (discussed below), or the other going back through the hanging gardens. From here, **Atatürk Caddesi**, the modern business street, continues eastwards around the market district. Just beyond Atatürk's statue, the street goes over a small bridge that crosses the narrow chasm of the **Gökdere stream**. Small cafes overlook the stream, with lawns and flowerbeds arranged in patterns and scrolls, but you can't get to it from the cliffs. Just beyond in a little square overshadowed by an enormous plane tree, a road branches off to the left for the **Yeşil** ('the Green'), loveliest of Bursa's neighbourhoods. This road, the Yeşil Caddesi, goes to the Green Mosque and the Green Mausoleum. Even the street signs here are green.

YEŞIL CAMI

It has to be said that the **Yeşil Cami (the Green Mosque),** is the finest mosque in Turkey, a marvel not only in the perfection of its form and decoration, but for the way these two elements, the simple structure and the lavish stonecarving and coloured tiles, are combined into a harmonious work of art.

We read in the history books of the early Ottoman Turks as grim and resolute Gazi warriors, still attached in many ways to the kind of life their nomadic forefathers led out on the Asian steppe just a few generations before. Their detractors, historians like Gibbon and the Byzantine apologist Steven Runciman, paint them as semi-barbarians who could build an empire but didn't know what to do with one. Such a building as this makes us pause to reconsider. Mehmet I had the Yeşil Cami built in the second decade of the fifteenth century, at a time when all the Ottomans' resources must have been needed for the reconstruction of the state, so soon after Sultan Beyazit's disaster at the hands of Tamerlane. Nevertheless, the necessary money and attention were found to construct this masterpiece.

Mehmet's architect, Haci Ivaz Paşa, attempted no radical departures here; the Ottomans had been building in this style for a half century already, in Bursa and elsewhere. Rather, this mosque represents the culmination, the perfection of that style. If the Ottomans had met an early end like the Selcuks, if they had never captured Constantinople and acquired the resources to build so many copies of the Aya Sofia, the Yeşil Cami would have its page in the art histories as the greatest work of the deceased nation; we would mourn the Ottomans as we do the Selcuks, thinking, 'If only they had been around to build more'. Decadence is a subtle disease; nations do not always reach their political artistic peaks at the same moment. If you wish to see how the Turk could build before Roman success and Greek luxury made him drowsy, come to the Yeşil.

Most visitors come down Green Avenue to the place where the Green Mosque and the Green Mausoleum face each other across the street and immediately head for the latter, their eyes caught by the masses of green tile. Tile, from Iznik, in the very same beautiful sea-green is used around the windows of the mosque, though sparingly, to call attention to the excellent carved stonework. No windows like these exist in Istanbul and certainly nothing like their flowery decoration, an inheritance from the Selcuks, as is the fine gateway with its concave 'stalactite' recess. Similar entrance gates are the principal adornment of most of the older Turkish mosques in the interior.

Inside, any impression that Mehmet was being cheap with the Iznik tiles is immediately dispelled. The mihrab, the ceilings, the upstairs galleries, and all the walls up to six feet are covered with them, in blue and green, many with floral designs. The plan is a simple one: a central hall under two shallow domes, one slightly higher than the other, a common form for the smaller early Ottoman mosques, as in the Orhan Camii. The Islamic fascination with geometry is here on display, from the unusual three-dimensional shapes that support the domes to the intricate patterns, carved into the walnut doors, shutters, and mimber, and the geometric medallions intertwined with Koranic calligraphy along the walls.

Some features are unusual. The ribbed interior of the domes shows a Greek influence, recalling the Istanbul Byzantine churches like the Kariye. In the dome near the entrance an oculus sends down a sunbeam at high noon over an exceptionally beautiful fountain, carved from a single piece of marble. The galleries around it, with some of the best Iznik tiles, were meant as private boxes for the Sultan and his harem. Two *eyvans*, or chambers, flank the central hall, once used for the reception and repose of travelling dervishes.

In the Green Mosque, the skill of the architects and the exuberance of the artisans who embellished it, and also what we can imagine to be the munificence and careful eye of their patrons, all conspire to impress upon one a single idea: that this is ripeness, the best work of a mature culture, a culture that in 1413 had lost little of its heritages of ancient Greek and Roman, Arab and Persian. More than that, it is a great work of Islam, a tribute to the sustaining faith that made such continuity possible. However much knowledge of Islam the western visitor brings here with him, he will know more when he leaves.

The Green Mausoleum

Mehmet the First, who put up the work, did not command the respect of the other early Ottoman sultans, pre-occupied as he was through most of his reign with defeating the intrigues of his brothers and cousins, and with reunifying and rebuilding his shattered state. His conquests were few, but his achievements, in the worst of times, have earned him more than he usually gets. His grandfather, the first Murat, had been illiterate, but Mehmet can be accounted the first cultured man among the Sultans. He had expressed a wish to be buried here, beside his great mosque, and during the reign of his son Murat II, the **Green Mausoleum** was built for his remains.

If the mosque had been for Allah, this was for the family. The architect was the same, Haci Ivaz Paşa, but if he and Murat were not able to confer the same perfection of spirituality upon this tomb, at least in the best family manner they spared no expense, pouring in the rich Iznik tiles in such profusion as is not found anywhere outside of the Blue Mosque in Istanbul. Almost as many are to be found inside, sheathing Mehmet's immense sarcophagus, painted with sayings of the Prophet in a bold flowing calligraphy.

The Green Medrese

A third and equally worthy member of this complex stands just a block away on Yeşil Caddesi; the old theological school called the **Green Medrese** has lately been restored and converted to house Bursa's **Museum of Turkish and Islamic Arts.** The large ethnographic collection occupies the students' cells and the central courtyard; outside there's a pretty garden with a view over the Gökdere stream and the rest of Bursa. Inside are fine silver, carpets, and swords, Selcuk architectural decoration, books and almanacs, and some very unusual nineteenth-century pottery from Çanakkale, a centre of the ceramic craft after it had died out in Iznik. Overhead in some of the domed ceilings around the cloister is more first class tile work.

One speciality of the museum is figures from the old Turkish shadow play, *Karagöz*. Bursa likes to claim Karagöz and Hacivat, the traditional Punch and Judy of this ancient entertainment, as its citizens; their 'tomb' is in the suburb of Çekirge. On one puppet you can see the mechanism whereby Karagöz's hat pops up whenever he is surprised, revealing his bald head.

THE MOSQUE OF YILDIRIM BEYAZIT

Continuing beyond the Yeşil into the eastern edges of Bursa, there are two mosques of the same era, both set up on hills among the rambling cottages and stone walls of this delightful area. The **Emir Sultan Camii** (1431) stands on the street of the same name, off Yeşil Caddesi; it was built by one of the daughters of Yildirim Beyazit in honor of her deceased husband. From here, Davutkadi Caddesi heads northward some ten blocks to that Sultan's own complex of religious buildings, the **Yildirim Beyazit Camii** (1395). In both of these, it's interesting to make architectural comparisons with the Green Mosque, but we can only guess at their original decorative scheme. Like the tombs of Osman and Orhan, and indeed almost everything else in Bursa, these mosques were hit hard by the 1855 earthquake; apparently the city only had resources enough to do a complete job of restoration on the Green complex, and as a result, Beyazit's and Emir Sultan's foundations were left with plain interiors that go well with the structure's formal simplicity, but are no substitute for the original.

Beyazit's mosque may have been an especially good one. Its *eyvans* and uneven twin domes recall the Yeşil Cami, and its arched portico and single slender minaret are fine elements. Before the earthquake, this mosque was the centre of a well-endowed *külliye*, a complex that included a hospital, schools, and dervish communities. Of the original eight buildings only the mosque, medrese, and Beyazit's tomb are left. This tomb, small and severe, is probably the most fitting memorial to the most ambitious and least cautious of the Ottoman Sultans. Undoubtedly, it would have been grander had not Beyazit's fourteen-year reign ended so ignominiously at the Battle of Ankara; here, the mercurial warrior, who expected to become the lord of Europe and Asia, instead ended up as lunch on Tamerlane's table. The Turks accepted it, as the Greeks would have, as divine punishment for hubris, and how else could the Mongols have been explained, but as a scourge of God? Later Sultans, for a while at least, took the lesson to heart.

THE MURADIYE

Returning to the citadel, and beyond it to the west end of Bursa, you may visit the works of a more fortunate monarch, Mehmet II, the Conqueror, at the **Muradiye Complex**, along Kaplica Caddesi just off the main street which, at this point, has changed its name to Çekirge Caddesi. Among the eleven buildings are a mosque, tombs, and schools, all plain, made in sandstone and narrow brick. There is none of the marble and fine sculptural detail of the earlier mosques here; this no doubt reflects the attitude of Mehmet, always with his eye on Constantinople. If he did not choose to embellish his *külliye*, at least he had himself buried here—next to his father, Murat II—who is interred in a simple *türbe* supported by ancient Corinthian columns with a wide oculus in the dome; Murat had requested that his tomb be open to the sky. The most elaborate tomb here, ironically, belongs to the celebrated upstart **Cem Sultan**, Mehmet's younger son, who rebelled and intrigued for years against Beyazit II, his brother. Cem's career as Ottoman pretender would have been an ideal subject for a novel by Sir Walter Scott, but one with a sad end for his partisans. Bayezid finally managed to pack him off to exile in Italy, where he died at the age of 34. As if in compensation, the Sultan brought him to this beautiful mausoleum, with its tiles and painted details in fairyland colours.

ÇEKIRGE

Çekirge means 'locust' in Turkish, and there are certainly enough of them in the woods that cover this slope of Uludağ. In the days of the Sultans, Çekirge, with its famous therapeutic baths and lovely views, was the favoured residence of the Imperial families. Today it's Bursa's wealthy suburb, with two miles of hotels and smart new apartments spreading westward from the city.

The people of Bursa like to come here to play at the **Kültür Park**. Turks in the big cities use their parks the way we would have a century ago, and it's charming to see the families in their Sunday best, dragging their children along and they, in turn, their balloons, all coming to see and be seen, to eat ice cream and inspect the flower beds. Here there is a blue lagoon with a fountain where young couples paddle canoes, an amusement park that must have half the neon in Turkey—its two giant Ferris wheels are among Bursa's landmarks—a football stadium, and acres of garden paths. Bursa's **Archaeological Museum**, in the centre of the park has a smattering of mainly Roman artefacts, and a large coin collection.

In the same Victorian atmosphere are the fine homes built a century ago in the streets across Çekirge Caddesi. Most are in the typical old Bursa style, in pastel plaster with enclosed wooden balconies, but a few, like the summer houses along the Bosphorus, could easily pass for American, Queen Anne homes of the 1880s, with more than a touch of Hansel and Gretel thrown in. The city put President Atatürk up in the best of them whenever he came to town, and this one has been preserved as the **Atatürk Museum**.

If Çekirge has been the fashionable end of the town ever since Roman times, the springs and thermal baths are the reason, widely prescribed for all manner of ailments and for one's general well-being besides. Most of Bursa's tourist trade comes for the waters, and several hotels in the district have their own springs. Two Ottoman foundations, called locally the **Old Baths** and the **New Baths**, the latter in a nice garden next to the Kultur Park, are open to the public and are quite popular.

Further west in Çekirge Caddesi, you pass a little monument called the **Tomb of Karagöz and Hacivat**. One story from old Bursa relates that these incorrigible clowns (the shadow-play figures) were workmen in the service of the Sultan; not merely did they never do their own jobs, but with continual arguing and joking, they so distracted the other workers that the Sultan was eventually obliged to put them to death.

Nearby, at the very end of the city, stands the oldest of the imperial mosques, the 1367 **Murat Camii**. At that time, Turkish architects had not yet found their classic style; this building, good as it is, can be considered an experiment on the way. Roughly square, the mosque occupies only the first floor, with one squat minaret in a corner. The second floor, behind a graceful loggia, was a theological school. The tomb of Murat I in the grounds has been restored too often to be of much interest, though Murat himself was a great soldier and statesman who contributed much to the growth of the Ottoman state with his Balkan conquests and rationalisation of the government. A Serbian prisoner stabbed Murat in the back in the Battle of Kossovo, his greatest triumph, and his son Beyazit brought him here to this *türbe*.

ULUDAĞ

If not for the waters, or the charms of the city itself, visitors come to Bursa to see **Uludağ** (8300 feet), literally 'great mountain,' the tallest peak in northwestern Turkey. From Bursa, the mountain may not at first seem impressive, only a steep emerald ridge enfolding the city and stretching to no great height. Take either of the roads around it, though, towards **Eskişehir** or **Kütahya**, and you'll see the true Uludağ, standing high above the surrounding plain in the same manner as the much taller mountains of Eastern Anatolia. The peak visible from Bursa is only the first of a series, stretching peak after peak into the southeast, with forests, meadows and mountain streams in between. The highest will be covered with snow well into the summer. Uludağ is a national park, with Alpine scenery, ski resorts with properly-Alpine lodges, and several hotels. You can get up there, either by the road off Çekirge Caddesi that runs for 32 kilometres almost to the highest summit, or by the long **funicular railway** with continuous service from the eastern edge of Bursa.

The ancients called Uludağ Mt Olympus, the Mysian Olympus, one of eight or so peaks around the Mediterranean with that name. The religious syncretism of the sophisticated Hellenistic world led men of letters to look for similarities in all the local cults and myths that soldiers and travellers brought back to them from the ends of their rapidly expanding world. Any mountain credited with being the home of the gods by the natives, as Uludağ was, became an 'Olympus', less a name than a category.

East of Bursa

Mysia was the province stretching from Bursa towards the east, and included much of the southern shore of the **Marmara** and the city of **Balikesir,** the ancient Paleokastro. Ancient geography, as is usual in Asia Minor, was never too clear about boundaries; for a while the Romans were wont to call the area around Bursa '**Phrygia Minor**', and the city itself, along with the territory to the cast, '**Bithynia**'. Today these lands along the valley of the Sakarya River, the ancient Sangarius, are in one of the more fortunate corners of Turkey, even if they no longer have a sense of being a distinct region. The countryside is green and good, and cultivated with loving care, and the villages, with their characteristic brick and timber dwellings drift through the decades in a permanent state of genteel dilapidation. **Bilecik** would have been the most interesting of them, had it not been destroyed in the War of Independence. Of its early Ottoman monuments only the Karasu Bridge, reputed to be the work of Mimar Sinan, remains.

Inegöl, to the west, is an agricultural town famous throughout Turkey for meatballs, *Inegöl köfte*, while in Söğüt, you may visit the **tomb of Ertuğrul**, founder of the Ottoman dynasty. In a way this Sakarya valley is the original Ottoman homeland, a secure and uncontested spot in the thirteenth century, a perfect place for an ambitious band of roving warriors to patiently await its opportunities. The Byzantines were too feeble to trouble them, and no serious enemies appeared from the east, either; despite all the talent of the early Ottomans, one can perhaps attribute much of their early success to just a very lucky choice of locations. And maybe the spot is always lucky for the Turks; just a few kilometres south of Söğüt, the climactic battle of their War of Independence was fought at **Inönü** in 1921. A few years later, when Atatürk decided that all Turks should have Western-style surnames, he himself conferred one upon his right-hand man, the general who had won the battle and halted the Greek offensive. Ismet Paşa now became Ismet Inönü, later to be the second President of the Turkish Republic.

Iznik (Nicaea)

Between the Sakarya and Gemlik Bay, an inlet of the Marmara, a circle of wooded hills isolates a large lake, **Iznik Gölü,** named after the ancient city

The Minaret of the Green Mosque, Iznik

on its eastern shore. **Iznik,** the ancient Nicaea, was founded in the fourth century BC, and for a while was the capital of the Kingdom of Bithynia before the Romans swallowed it up, but it wasn't until the Christian era that the city achieved its fame, or perhaps its notoriety, as seat of the two great church councils. First, in the fourth century and again in the eighth, the querulous bishops and bureaucrats of early Christianity met here to argue, anathematise their enemies, or smash them with bats and run up uncollectable bills at the local hostelries.

The Church Councils

Constantine himself first summoned them in 325 to decide the insoluble conflict between the **Arian** and **Athanasian** sects. His favourite, St Athanasius, came all the way from Alexandria to lead his partisans in the attack, demanding that every Christian admit both the divine and mortal natures of Christ. Arius, who has been called a 'unitarian', wished strongly to avoid having the godhead cluttered with extra, inessential 'essences', and got himself murdered here for his trouble, though his party won a short-lived victory. Nicaea, a beautiful resort city in a strategic location, central for the eastern half of the Empire, had already been a residence of Emperor Diocletian, and would be for several later emperors; the Church Fathers found it a wonderfully agreeable locale for conventions and they came often, most importantly for the great council of 786, when the bishops codified rituals and beliefs into the form still observed by the Greek Church today.

Empress Irene, who almost married Charlemagne but could not bear to part with the intrigues and luxury of Constantinople, may have been an outrageous tart, but she is remembered fondly by the Orthodox for calling this council to put an end finally to the Iconoclastic struggles that had so bitterly divided the Empire. Convening at Nicaea's Church of Aya Sofia, the bishops from as far away as Italy decided once and for all that holy images 'stimulate spectators to think of the originals', and therefore deserved at least a kind of adoration.

Nicaea's finest hour, though, came in the dark days following the Sack of Constantinople in 1204. The die-hard, Theodore Lascaris, brought the remnants of Greek resistance here and became Emperor-in-exile; he and his successor, **John III Vatatzes,** reconstituted the empire, carefully rebuilding its finances and its army for the day when Constantinople would once more be theirs.

The Selcuk Turks held the city and made it their capital for a brief period in the eleventh century, and it fell again, finally, to the Ottoman leader Orhan in 1331. As a Turkish city, Nicaea, now Iznik, gained fame throughout the Islamic world for its hand-painted ceramic tiles, made with a quality of colour and design that cannot be imitated today. Expensive though they must have been, all the early Ottoman Sultans demanded them in enormous quantity for their mosques, and today they can be seen on buildings across Turkey wherever earthquakes and decay have spared them. As the finances of the Empire declined, the market for these tiles disappeared, and the city with it; by the nineteenth century only a dismal village was left inside the old Byzantine walls; even that remainder suffered grievous damage in the fighting of 1922.

IZNIK TODAY

Today, some leftover grace from its days of greatness keeps Iznik free of the usual sadness that accompanies ruins. The town is simply too full of roses and children and green gardens to be melancholy. Indeed, the modest agricultural centre that Iznik has become cannot nearly fill the square mile or so within its Byzantine walls, and its people wisely use the remaining space for vegetable plots and olive groves. Not much happens there now, and whatever talent is left from the long-gone ceramic industries is devoted to making cinder blocks and roof tiles.

Even though the foundation of the city pre-dates the Romans, Iznik has the plan of a typical Roman provincial town: two broad main streets meeting at right angles in the centre, connecting the four main gates. Nearly all of Iznik's **walls** can still be seen, in various stages of decay, and along the garden paths and sheep trails you find the occasional arch or Greek inscription, towers, sally-ports and storage rooms. Two of the **gates,** the northern, or **Istanbul Gate** and the western or **Lefke Gate,** survive, with Roman triumphal arches between their inner and outer parts, inscriptions in Greek and Latin commemorating the visit of the Emperor Hadrian, and remains of marble reliefs. The Lefke Gate is the better preserved, and near it are parts of a much-weathered decorative frieze, also carved inconspicuously on the inside of the gate, something that is obviously and inexplicably a layout for the game 9-men-Morris. There is a similar one in the Basilica of St John in Selçuk, and if they're mason's marks, they're quite unusual. Outside the gate, the **Byzantine aqueduct** has suffered little from time, although it's no longer in use.

Inside the city, little remains of ancient Iznik. Near the ruined Yenişehir gate at the south entrance, the half excavated ruins of the **Roman Theatre** are visible behind a fence, and exactly in the centre of the town stands the derelict **Church of Aya Sofia**, an eleventh-century structure that replaced an earlier church from the era of Justinian, which hosted the ecumenical councils of the fourth and eighth centuries. Some fragments of mosaics and frescoes can still be seen. The conquering Ottomans added a minaret, and its stump is currently the home of one of Iznik's numerous storks.

Storks, surprisingly, spend their summers in Turkey. These have little to do with their North-European cousins, and they are said to spend their winters in far-off Morocco. Minaret stumps make perfect bases for their nests, combining good drainage, peace and quiet, and inaccessibility to weasels. Another nest may be seen on a ruined minaret near the Istanbul Gate, next to the Nilüfer Hatun Imareti, a fourteenth-century hospice for travelling dervishes that now serves as the **Iznik Museum.** Here a selection of artefacts from recent Turkish crafts going back to Paleolithic tools proves the long continuity of this site; more interesting are the grave steles and architectural fragments arranged in the garden outside. Ranging from the early Hellenistic to the late Byzantine, the steles provide a kind of glossary of symbols, a complete guide to the inexhaustible iconography of death that so long occupied the Greek world's fancy.

Not surprisingly, the most important part of the museum's collection is devoted to ceramics, some as old as 2500 BC, as well as the best Islamic work. A city map on the wall of the museum helps in finding your way through the village to the ancient sites and around the walls. Across the street from the museum, the **Yeşil Cami,** built in the 1380s, will catch your eye with what may be the prettiest minaret in all Anatolia. The blue and green tiles that cover it are not Iznik work, however; during restorations in the last century it was necessary to replace them all.

There are no good **beaches** on Iznik's lake shore, but people still come here, particularly from Bursa, to walk along the promenade outside the town's ruined **Lake Gate,** and to eat fresh fish in the restaurants on the water's edge. If you come here on just the right day in the spring, you can ski down Uludağ in the morning and swim in Lake Iznik or the Marmara in the afternoon.

GETTING AROUND

Bursa is often described as a day trip from Istanbul. This is possible but not much fun—four or five hours one way by road, and longer if you take the ferries from Istanbul to Yalova or Mudanya and wait for bus connections. Bursa deserves more than one day anyhow. Regular buses make the one-hour trip to Iznik, taking the scenic route along the southern shore of the lake.

Atatürk Caddesi, even though it changes its name three times (see map), is the main axis of Bursa, and the route of most buses and dolmuş. Taxis cruise, but are not as common as in Istanbul or Ankara.

TOURIST INFORMATION

The Tourist Ministry's Information Office is at 82 Atatürk Caddesi (tel. 12359) but if you visit the city's own office on the same street, just around the corner from City Hall, you'll have the pleasure of meeting Mrs Leyla Ilova, who has been entertaining visitors to Bursa for twenty years. Her office is next to what may be the world's only city-owned flower shop.

WHERE TO STAY

Most of the city's finest establishments are in the quiet Çekirge suburb, a mile west of the centre. Many of the hotels here boast thermal baths; oldest and most renowned of these is the Çelik Palas (H2) at Çekirge Cad. 79, tel. (241)196 00–6. Its name, 'Steel Palace' comes from the great steel dome that covers the baths. It also has tennis courts and nearly every other amenity for 14 000 TL for a single, 21 000 TL a double. In the same category, the **Dilman Oteli** on Hamamlar Cad., tel. (241)217 01–173 28, also has thermal baths but fewer luxuries for 11 000 TL for a single, 14 500 TL a double, reduced rates for children. The least expensive hotel with a thermal bath is the **Adapalas** (H3) 1 Murat Cad. 21, tel. (214). 192 00–1 where you can stay for as little as 2800 TL a single or 3600 TL a double, extra for private bathroom.

The **Akdoğan,** also on Murat Cad. 5, tel. (241) 247 55 57, is rated H1, but offers good value at 7000 TL for a single, 10 000 for a double; it has a Turkish hamam, TV, refrigerators, a swimming pool, and reduced rates for kids as well. In the city centre, the **Artiç Oteli** (H4) on Fevzi Çakmak Cad. 123, tel. (241) 195 00 is quiet, pleasant and inexpensive: 4000 TL for a single, 6000 TL for a double.

There is as much accommodation on Uludağ as in town, mostly in chalet-style ski lodges like the **Alkoçlar** (H4) in the national park, tel.

(2418) 1130–5, open December–April. For year round recreation on Uludağ, stay at the **Panorama Oberj,** tel. (2418) 1237, with a swimming pool, tennis court as well as winter sports; in the summer you can get a discount on the rates of 7000 TL a single, 9800 TL a double. Note that full pension is usually mandatory on Uludağ.

In Iznik, the **Iznik Motel** (M2) right on the lake shore, in an area within the walls now covered with gardens and olive groves, is the town's most prominent accommodation, tel. (2527)1041; rooms are clean but modest at 2000 TL a single, 3000 a double.

EATING OUT

In Bursa, among the large number of good restaurants, there's the **Özkent Lokanta** in an outdoor setting in the Kültür Park (7000–9000 TL) and an inexpensive local favourite, the **Nazar Restaurant**, (1000 TL) in the Iç Koza Han in the bazaar area. In Iznik, fish are easier to come by in a number of restaurants along the lakeside promenade; **Dallas Restaurant,** a good one, may be the only restaurant in Turkey with a German translation-by-telephone service. A fish dinner here runs at around 4000 TL.

Ancient Phrygia: Kütahya to Ankara

The countryside between **Kütahya** and **Ankara,** long ago the homeland of the Phrygians, is one of the drier corners of Anatolia. Its river valleys, like that of the Sakarya, are fertile and pretty, but between them stretch miles of bare hills, broken by occasional mountains.

Eskişehir

To make up for what nature has denied this land, the Turkish Government has spent a considerable part of its development effort here. As a result, **Eskişehir,** the provincial capital, has grown up to become one of Turkey's largest cities. It's a joke among people here that Yenişehir ('new town'), to the northwest is a crumbling old village, while Eskişehir ('old town') has become a thoroughly modern city, grown wealthy enough from its manufacture of locomotives and Meerschaum pipes to water its streets twice a day to keep down the dust—and they need it. This is one of a very few places on earth where Meerschaum is found, and when you see any of it in tourist shops elsewhere in Turkey, the chances are it was mined and crafted here; finely carved pipes and walking sticks can be bought very cheaply in a number of shops around town.

In ancient times, this was the Greek-Phrygian city of Dorylaeum, whose scant remains can be seen around the Selcuk castle northwest of the town. Grave steles and columns of Dorylaeum, some quite interesting examples in fact, are on display at Eskişehir's **Archaeological Museum**. On the eastern edge of the city there is the sixteenth-century **Kurşunlu Mosque,** a complex attributed to Mimar Sinan. Eskişehir is a pleasant and animated city; the Porsuk Su (Beaver Creek) and its tributaries and canals run all through it, crossed by hundreds of little bridges, but it hasn't much to show the visitor. Those who pass through are usually on their way to the Phrygian sites to the south, or to the famous **Temple of Zeus at Aizanoi,** some 130 kilometres to the southwest at the village of Çavdarhisar.

Aizanoi and the Temple of Zeus

Despite its location, Aizanoi draws its share of tourists, who come to see the best preserved ancient temple anywhere in Turkey; it is also one of the largest, almost a hundred feet in width across the bottom of its podium, and one of the last to be built in the second century during the reign of Hadrian. Despite the fashion of the day for the Corinthian order, the Temple of Zeus is Ionian, showing the Roman preference for tall elevations and narrow columns.

Most of these columns and half the walls of the cella still stand. Parts of the frieze connecting the tops of the columns are present as well, though the pediment and roof are long gone. This pediment had been decorated at its peaks and corners with huge *acroteria*, carved stone acanthus leaves, and bits of these lie on the ground. Hadrian's reign was one of the better times for Asia Minor and the rest of the Empire, when both prosperity and building talent were still undiminished. The style of the Temple may have been thought old-fashioned when it was built, and less charitable critics today may find it lacking in inspiration; with something of the air of a 1920s bank building, and erected by men to whom art no longer came easily, but who did their best to strive for a quiet tastefulness. The temple's form, which you can call *pseudodipteral* (having open corridors behind the columns instead of a second row of columns) is a copy of the Temple of Zeus Sosipolis at Magnesia (Manisa), a work much admired in that era.

One Roman innovation, made possible by the temple's great height, is the cellar, with its barrel-vaulted roof. Zeus had to share his temple with the goddess Cybele, which is not unusual in a town so near Phrygia, though in Phrygia proper Cybele's orgiastic rites were conducted in the open air; it's difficult to say what went on in her subterranean sanctuary here. Relegation to the cellar implies no disrespect for Cybele, but it does wonderfully symbolise the state of mind of the ancient world. Zeus, representing reason, order, and light, rules the upper world, while, just below the surface, lay mystery and the unconscious bound up in the formidable personality of the great goddess. One of the huge acroteria on the east front was a bust of Zeus, while that on the west depicted Cybele. Here the two co-existed in a hard-earned balance that was not lost until the coming of Christianity.

Little remains of the rest of Aizanoi; if you have time you can trace the outlines of the stadium, having an unusual arrangement in which the town's theatre closes its open end. The Temple of Zeus faced an agora fronting on the now intermittent stream the Greeks called **Rhyndakos,** where there are still remnants of bridges and quays.

Kütahya and Afyon

Kütahya, under its Ottoman castle, is the city closest to Aizanoi. When the art of ceramics declined in Iznik, Kütahya seized the opportunity, and still keeps up the craft, making fine china and porcelain as well as architectural tiles, used in the restorations of all the old Ottoman mosques. Kütahya has a few Ottoman mosques of its own, notably the fifteenth-century **Ulu Cami.**

From Kütahya, the first slopes of a broad mountain called **Türkmen Dağ** rise up over the horizon, stretching off to the east. On its opposite slope, in difficult hill country, is the source of the Sakarya River. There you will also find **Midas City** and nearly a dozen temple façades and tombs in the heartland of ancient Phrygia. There is no way over the mountain, unfortunately, and adventurous souls desiring to explore Phrygia must start from Eskişehir or **Afyon** to the north. Paved roads from either city will carry you thirty or forty kilometres into the area, but then, if you're not driving, you are at the mercy of whatever taxi drivers you can find in the villages of Seyitgazi or Ihsaniye. Afyon (it means 'opium'), a provincial capital set in an area famous for its hot springs, is guarded by a lofty **fortress,** present perhaps since Hittite times and rebuilt many times since. Some not-so-hot springs near the Gazligöl ('Lake Gas'!) supply the mineral soda water you find in little green bottles all over Turkey.

The Phrygian heartland

Anyone seriously interested in the fascinating world of pre-Hellenic Anatolia, with its native cultures such as the Phrygians, squeezed in between Persians and Greeks and influenced by both, should not be discouraged from pushing into this little-visited region. The Phrygian monuments in their lonely settings are well preserved and quite impressive, and you'll have a chance for some real exploration. No archaeological area in western Anatolia is less documented, many of the sites still being known only to the locals.

SEYITGAZI

If you go through **Seyitgazi,** probably the better choice, stop for the **Mosque and Tomb of Seyyit Battal Gazi,** the semi-legendary Arab warrior who died in battle here in 740, when the town was much more important than it is now. The tomb at the centre of this large complex was constructed in around 1200 by the mother of the Selcuk Sultan Alâeddin Keykubad; Seyyit Gazi lies inside a sarcophagus a full twenty feet long, next to his Greek wife Eleonora. The mosque and medrese were added in the sixteenth century by Selim I.

MIDAS CITY

If there's only time for one site, head for **Midas Sehri,** the so-called 'Midas City', 25 kilometres southeast of Seyitgazi. Here, bordering the modern village of Yazilikaya, the acropolis of a sixth-century Phrygian city, whose true name we do not know, rises up from the surrounding plains with little on the top, but a wealth of detail carved into its steep sides.

It was named Midas City by Captain Leake, a British traveller who discovered it in the early 1800s. At the end of the acropolis facing Yazilikaya (not to be confused with the Yazilikaya at Boğazköy) stands the largest and most striking monument, a temple façade some 70 feet high; at its top, Leake thought he could discern the letters 'MIDAI' in a long Phrygian inscription, and reported back to the world that he had found the grave of King Midas. In truth, the Phrygian language remains something of a mystery. Most of the letters were adapted from the Greek, though, and more likely than not, some 'Midas' had something to do with it; this is no tomb, however; the experts think of it as a kind of stage background for the outdoor rites of Cybele. Her cult statue would be placed in the niche at the bottom of the monument during the festivities.

Around the niche, the precise, symmetrical maze-like pattern that covers most of the monument's face shows the odd degree of abstraction the Phrygians had reached in their religious art. The pediment suggests roof beams resting on a central ridge-pole, and it may be that the cliff façades are representations of wooden temples that no longer exist. A second, somewhat smaller façade was carved into the north face of the hill, roughly the same in form, with a frieze along the top decorated with Greek-style acanthus-leaf designs. All around the other hillsides, both above and below the bits of the original defence wall, a day's exploration will reveal any number of other niches and altars, inscriptions, underground chambers, and other features whose uses can only be guessed at.

Sites near Midas City

A third temple façade, smaller and somewhat eroded, can be seen near Yazilikaya at **Arezastis.** You can compare all three with the entire temples in the same area, one cut out of the **Gerdek Rock** near the village of Çukurca, and another at **Hisar Kale,** 9 kilometres to the southwest at Yapildak village. Another site near Çukurca, perhaps the most unusual of all, is the **Doğanli Kale,** an outlandishly eroded crag of limestone, honeycombed with chambers and niches, with hollows that seem to have, at one time, held wooden beams and stairways. Again, whatever was the purpose of this lost little piece of Cappadocia is left to the imagination. Some of the work is said to date from Byzantine times, and like the similar oddities in Cappadocia may have been used as a monastery.

The road going west from Yazilikaya passes a **Phrygian tumulus** on its way to the village of **Kümbetköy,** which takes its name from a Roman-era tomb guarded by two lions in low relief, a recurring symbol in Phrygian art just as it was for the Hittites. South of here, on the way to Afyon, other Phrygian lions have given the villages of **Aslantaş** and **Aslankaya** their names. The temple façade at Aslankaya is a remarkable sight, carved out of a thin, twisted pinnacle of rock; two lions keep watch from its pediment while two other huge figures as high as the façade itself, though badly eroded, flank the monument. Both this and the smaller façade at Aslantaş are done in the same angular patterns as at Midas City.

PESSINUS

Pessinus, 16 kilometres south of where the Eskişehir–Ankara highway passes Sivrihisar, was the religious and geographic centre of Phrygia. Almost nothing can be seen on the site, but archaeologists have found a first century AD temple at the top of a broad ceremonial stair. A college of priests ruled the city; an inscription records that half were Phrygian and half Galatian. Even during the two centuries when Pessinus was under the sovereignty of the kings of Pergamon, these priests, or *galli*, ruled the city and its hinterlands as a theocratic state, and their influence spread far beyond Phrygia's borders.

The Romans put a stop to this in their usual ingenious fashion. In 204 BC, they instructed their Pergamene allies to send them the cult figure, a *baetyl* from Pessinus. King Attalos was glad to comply; the respected Sibylline Oracle had commanded it, and the *baetyl* (probably a meteorite, like the Kaaba in Mecca), was conveyed to Rome with all proper observances and placed in a temple specially built for it. The Romans expanded their power as much through this talent for taking over other people's religions, as by triumph of arms; one wonders what happened to all the statues, relics and cult objects they collected.

In Phrygia, the worship of Cybele had much to do with bees; Greek mythographers always associated her with Aphrodite Ericyna and her golden honeycomb, worshipped at Mt Eryx in Sicily. Today the site of Pessinus is known to the Turks as Ballihisar—the Honey Castle.

GORDION

Gordion, like Pessinus, is a site only an archaeologist could love; the early Phrygian capital contains no well preserved buildings or fine reliefs; only parts of it have really been excavated, though enough for specialists to have drawn up a ground plan of the major palace buildings.

Much more interesting is the **Great Tumulus** on the edge of the city, which, as you might guess, everyone calls **Midas' Tomb.** Gordion is reached from the same Eskişehir–Ankara road, 20 kilometres northeast of the town of **Polatli,** with yellow signs marking the route from there. Approaching the site, you see mounds of all sizes, gradually increasing in number. The largest, most likely, were for the kings, though even mere nobles apparently had the resources to build them. Few of the smaller tumuli have been excavated; the burials in them were cleverly placed off-centre to discourage grave robbers and archaeologists. One they did find yielded the remains of a five-year-old boy, with some charming toys that are now in the Ankara Museum.

The Great Tumulus

The Great Tumulus, now worn down to about 160 ft in height, must originally have been close to 250 feet. In Turkey only the mound called Alyatta's Tomb near Sardis is bigger, and it's difficult to think of another taller anywhere else in the world. Whether or not the king inside was a 'Midas' or a 'Gordius' is unknown—they alternated these names the way Danish kings do with 'Christian' and 'Frederick'—but he was a small man, no more than five feet two, and close to sixty years of age. The tomb at the centre of the mound has been thoroughly excavated, and you can reach it through the long, lighted tunnel, recently constructed. To build this mound, the Phrygians started with a double-walled wooden house set into the ground, covered it with stones and clay, and then piled up the earth above it. The wood—great logs of cedar that must have come from Lebanon, still sound after 2600 years under the earth—is mortised at the corners like a frontier cabin. Inside, no gold, but dozens of pots were found, some exceedingly well-crafted furniture, now in Ankara and, inexplicably, 145 brass *fibulae*—the archaeologists' word for 'safety-pins'.

The current excavations of the city are surrounded by a fence. Having been nearly completely covered with centuries of silt from the Sakarya's floods, you can now look down into the diggings and make out, at the south-eastern end, the **monumental gateway,** and behind it the palace buildings and a long row, somewhat like a modern residential terrace, that belonged to the palace household. The palaces themselves consisted of a row of megaron-style structures, with a central hearth surrounded by rooms and one large hall in front serving as the entrance; it is quite likely these had façades in wood similar to the temple façades mentioned above.

Story of Gordius and Midas

Arrian's life of Alexander mentions that the Gordian knot was kept in the Gordion acropolis. Since nothing like an acropolis exists here, the temple complex is probably what he had in mind. According to the myth as related by Arrian, Gordius was originally a poor farmer. One day an eagle perched on his wagon tongue, and Gordius, taking it as an omen, decided to visit an oracle at Phrygian Telmessus to ask its meaning. On the way, the eagle still riding along with him, he met a local priestess who instructed him in the proper sacrifices for the oracle; he married her, and she bore him a son named Midas. In the meantime, the Phrygian king had died, and the country was drifting into factional strife. The same oracle announced that a man in a ox-cart would come to bring peace to the land, and as that happened to be the unsuspecting Gordius, when he rode into the city one day, he found himself proclaimed king.

He founded the city of Gordion, the story continues, and laid up his wagon there. Over the years, a prophecy gained currency that whoever could solve the cornel-bark knot that bound the yoke to the wagon tongue would become 'master of Asia'. Much speculation has gone into the nature of this knot, although its presence here is historical fact. When Alexander passed this way—Gordion lay directly on the great trade and conquest route between Greece and Persia—he felt obliged to fulfil the prophecy, since becoming master of Asia was exactly what he had in mind. Most commentators claim he cut the knot with his sword, which provides the most poetic solution. Robert Graves believes the knot was an alphabetic cipher, expressing the secret name of a god (Incas and ancient Britons had such devices, so why not the Phrygians?); he sees Alexander's sword stroke as a historical turning point, at which the power of blind ambition and main force broke the last barrier to the destruction of the ancient authority of religion.

Of Midas, we learn that he planted famous rose gardens and was a great musician, taught by Orpheus himself. As well as the tale of the golden touch, Midas is said to have had a pair of ass's ears planted on him by Apollo; Midas unwisely voted against the god in the musical contest with Midas' countryman, Marsyas. His barber was supposed to keep the secret, (which Midas hid from others with a conical Phrygian cap, such as was the fashion during the French Revolution) but couldn't manage to; he dug a hole in the ground near a river and whispered, 'Midas has ass's ears!' into it;

most unfortunately for him, the reeds on the spot spread the message to everyone within earshot, 'Midas has ass's ears!'

Midas's name, like Gordius's, probably has a basis in history. He, or one of the kings with that name, appears in Assyrian records as 'Mita of Mushki'. This Mushki, perhaps, was the Phrygians' own name for their nation. 'Phrygian' is a Greek word meaning 'free men.' As a pastoral people without a strong state, they probably were just that.

Despite the wealth that lay behind the legend of Midas' golden touch, his capital was not to endure. The Great Tumulus was built around 720 BC, and the Cimmerians came to sack Gordion only twenty years or so later. Though it revived in the sixth century, by Roman times, writers were already sadly remarking that the once great city was dwindling into a mere village.

Finds from Gordion

Whatever finds from Gordion the government hasn't carried off to Ankara are on display in the small **museum**. Small bits of red, white, and black architectural ceramics give some idea of how the palaces originally looked; the rockpile that is Gordion today belies the Phrygian talent and liking for extensive decoration. Other artefacts include a wildly undisciplined geometric-pattern mosaic (from one of the megaron houses) that looks more Post-Impressionist than ancient Phrygian, and one perfectly serviceable pair of dice.

On your way back to Polatli, take time to notice the **Atatürk Monument** on the crest of the most prominent hill north of town. This could well be the only really successful modern memorial anywhere in Turkey; at least it's an interesting attempt at recapturing the ancient Anatolians' talent for monumental sculpture. Consisting of two long rows of marble columns of increasing height, tracing a gracefully curved silhouette over the hilltop, it's as abstract, and as memorable, as any work of the Phrygians.

GETTING AROUND

To see Aizanoi, you have to stay in Kütahya; any bus from there to Uşak or Izmir will stop at Çavdarhisar, the nearest village. To see the Phrygian sites between Eskişehir and Afyon without a car is chancy, but you'll probably find someone with a cab in Seyitgazi to take you around. Taxis from Eskişehir will do it, but at a very high price. If you have a car, your only problem will be finding the sites—some are really off the beaten path. Taxis in Polatli, a village along the Bursa–Ankara highway, are used to make the trip to Gordion, and do it cheaply.

TOURIST INFORMATION

In Kütahya, Yeni Hükümet Konaği (government house), tel. (2311)

2618. In Eskişehir, Vilayet, 2 Eylül Caddesi, tel. (221) 17 293.

WHERE TO STAY
Both Kütahya and Eskişehir are towns where you have trouble spending money on hotel rooms. Two hotels in Eskişehir have thermal baths, both rated H3 and next to each other on Hamamyolu Cad.: the **Has Otel Termal** at no. 7, tel. (221) 7819 and the **Sultan Termal Otel** at no. 1, tel. (221) 18 371. After visiting the Phrygian sites you may well appreciate the warm baths. Rates average 7000 TL for a single, 9000 TL for a double.

In **Kütahya,** the best by a nose is the **Gönen Oteli** (H4) on Menderes Cad., tel. (2311)1751–2144, with singles at 4000 TL, doubles 6000 TL.

EATING OUT
Restaurants are small and inexpensive and all about the same; this is not a well travelled region.

Ankara

Most people have the impression that Ankara, the capital of the **Turkish Republic** since 1923, is absolutely new, a modern toadstool of a city conjured up out of bleakest Anatolia by Atatürk as a symbol of his country's pride and aspirations. Modern it is of course, and toadstool beyond question, but underneath all the clutter of ministries, highways, and apartment blocks there is a genuine old city too, as old as the Hittites, and layered with memories of all the nations that have come and gone since then. Atatürk chose his capital more cleverly than at first appears. Above all, Ankara is an entirely Turkish city, and has been for eight centuries, even though the traces of the Phrygians, Greeks, and Romans that preceded the Turks are still out in the open for all to see.

HISTORY
A relief map shows why the spot has always attracted so much attention. Just to the east, a gap between the Köroğlu Mountains and the bare plateau south of them forms a natural corridor called the **Halys Gates.** The Persian Royal Road and the Via Regalis of the Romans passed through here, as did conquerors from Alexander to Tamerlane. The Hittites were the first to build on Ankara's lofty citadel, and the Phrygians after them made it one of their most important cities. Dozens of Phrygian tumuli once covered the plain, but almost all have vanished. The Galatians succeeded them—there are still plenty of red hair and freckles in this part of Turkey—and Augustus annexed their lands for Rome in 25 BC. By then, the city had assumed a variant of its modern name, **Ancyra.** Europe knew it for a long period as **Angora** and gave its name to the soft wool produced by the region's goats.

To Esenboğa Airport
Bentderesi Cad.
Roman baths
Temple of Augustus
Julian's Column
National Assembly Museum
Hisarparki Cad.
ULUS SQUARE
CITADEL
Sehit Kalmaz Cad.
Yenice S.
Çikrikçilar Cad.
museum of Anatolian cultures
Aslanhane Cami
Ahi Elvan Camii
Anafartalar Cad.
Saraçlar Sok.
Ulucanlar Cad.
SAMANPAZARI
Denizciler Cad.
Tavus S.
hippodrome
To Atatürk Orman Çiftliği
bus station
KÂZIM KARABEKIR CAD.
Istiklâl Cad.
Cumhuriyet Bulvari
GENÇLIK PARK
Luna Park
opera
HIPODROM CAD.
rail station
ethnographic museum
TALÂTPAŞA BULVARI
Hacettepe University
GAZI MUSTAFA KEMAL BUL.
ATATÜRK BULVARI
Kizilay Sokak
Hasircilar Sok.
Gevher Nesibe Yolu
university hospitals
Hacettepe Park
CEMAL GÜRSEL CAD.
Strasbourg Cad.
MALTEPE
Atatürk Mausoleum (Anit Kabir)
Tuna Cad.
ZIYA GÖKALP CAD.
GENÇLIK CAD.
MITHATPAŞA CAD.
NECATIBEY CAD.
tourist information
KIZILAY
Güven Aniti
FEVZI ÇAKMAK CAD.
ANKARA
To Eskişehir
government ministries
0
500 m
GÜLHANE CAD.
To Kavaklidere and Kuğulu Park
Grand National Assembly

Although continuously occupied through all the centuries since, Ankara was never a great city, but as Atatürk realised, it is a natural capital of Anatolia. Its fortunes have always risen and fallen with those of its surrounding country; with the neglect and peril that was life here until the Republic, it was never able to achieve much. Also, it's a good distance from Istanbul and the intrigue synonymous with the old capital, which enabled Atatürk to make a clean break with the past.

ANKARA TODAY

Two million people live in Ankara now. Those who have jobs work for the government or businesses attracted by proximity to the government; those who haven't get by as best they can while looking. Much of the city's phenomenal growth, like Istanbul's, has been the unplanned and unwanted migration of hundreds of thousands of villagers from every corner of Turkey. For all Turks, Ankara is just the symbol Atatürk wanted it to be, the nation's pre-eminent city of opportunity, and this is one of the side effects.

In no way can Ankara be called a pleasant city. Some quarters are almost that, but Ankara is big enough and diverse enough to accommodate a whole range of adjectives. 'Ill-planned' comes to mind first. Turkey's first town planners were more civil engineers than artists. Ankara has more gratuitous highway interchanges than all the rest of the country put together, some in the centre of the town where all can enjoy them. The exact centre, between Gençlik Park and the business district, is occupied by a sprawling railway yard. The highways and the railways combine to give the city the worst air pollution in Turkey. Don't imagine for a minute that any native of Ankara minds discussing these problems. Quite the contrary; like many busy and thriving big cities, Ankara seems almost to get a perverse joy from them. The city has skyscrapers, fine parks and residential districts, trendy stores, a good university, and nothing to envy in any other Turkish town, save Istanbul. And if they must sacrifice other amenities to gain these, what of it? Ankara is on top, and it knows it.

One thing the planners didn't do was to try to integrate the new Ankara with the old. As a result, the two exist uneasily side by side, with that freightyard for a border. As the newer, southern districts grow and prosper, the old town suffers. Some parts still retain the village atmosphere of old Ankara; some have deteriorated to nothing more than poor shops and junkyards, while still others have had new streets of modern buildings smashed carelessly through them. The planners seem to hope that one day the old town will just disappear.

MUSEUM OF THE NATIONAL ASSEMBLY

You must come here, though, to the **Ulus Meydani** (National Square), to see where modern Ankara and modern Turkey began. Most visitors don't stop at the little grey building just off the square, but you wouldn't go to Philadelphia without seeing Independence Hall and you should take a few minutes here to visit the **Museum of the National Assembly**. After the Erzerum and Sivas Congresses decided in 1919 to coordinate and extend the efforts of the local defence committees across Anatolia, elections were held wherever possible for the new Grand National Assembly; it met here for the first time on April 23, 1920. **Atatürk,** elected chairman on the first day, was at the time under death sentence from the Istanbul government. Greek troops were occupying the Aegean coast, and French, Italian, British, and Russian forces were also present on Turkish soil, and advancing.

Here in this hall, with its little school desks jammed together and the chairman within spitting distance of nearly every deputy, the Turks did the last thing anyone ever expected; they roused themselves as a nation, for the first time, and prevailed against a host of enemies. Not having attended a Turkish grammar school, you will not know all the serious-looking men in the photos that cover the walls, or be familiar with the significance of the letters and declarations on display in the glass case, but you will come away with the impression that some great work was done here, and your respect for the Turks and their revolution will be increased.

REMAINS OF OLD ANKARA

From here, you can walk six blocks north and 1600 years back to the Hükümet Meydani, and the tall, worn **Column of Julian.** The **Galatians** of Ancyra, who made up most of the population in the third century, had a reputation among their neighbours for piety to their cults of Cybele and the moon goddess Men; it's not all that surprising if they erected this monument in honour of the Apostate Emperor. Julian was a good general, and one of the last Roman emperors to make a serious effort to hold the eastern borders. He passed through Ancyra in AD 262 on his way to campaign against the resurgent Persians, and after a series of frustratingly undecisive encounters, he fell ill and died the next year, derided by the Christians but mourned by the poets, the soldiers, and all who wished the Roman cause well.

The Temple of Augustus

History has had its little joke with the Galatians. Their temple of Cybele, converted after the conquest to the worship of Augustus and of Rome, was to end its career as a Christian church; if they had not maintained it for so many centuries, the **Temple of Augustus** would not have survived at all. As it is, the pediment and all the columns have fallen, but enough remains to see that this, like the temple of Aizanoi, was, in its plan, a copy of the Zeus Sosipolis temple in Magnesia. The walls of the cella, the inner sanctuary, are inscribed with a long text in Latin and Greek, the 'Deeds of the Deified Augustus,' the longest Latin inscription found anywhere. Little of it is still legible, effaced less by time than modern Ankara's exhaust fumes; fortunately a scholarly sixteenth-century Spanish ambassador took the trouble to write down the full text.

Who knows what moved the Ancyrans to convert their temple to Emperor-worship; it may have been political expediency, or perhaps genuine gratitude for the *pax Romana*. Coercion from Rome is less likely. Unlike some of the later decadent emperors, Augustus himself was a good Roman and mildly disgusted by the idea of being worshipped. He permitted such worship only after his death, when his advisers convinced him that the people of Syria and Asia Minor, grown accustomed to divine rulers from Persian days, would expect it. Even then, he decreed that a divine personification of Rome should take precedence in the temples. What meant more to him was effective and just government, and he took pains to ensure that his biography and political testament, including a report on the state of the Empire he was leaving to his successors, would be carved into the walls of all his temple. Oddly, this is the only complete text anywhere, and the other fragments that have come to light are also in Anatolia.

Adjacent to the temple, the fifteenth-century **Haci Bayram Mosque** is one of the few in Turkey that is full of worshippers at Friday services. Haci Bayram was a dervish whose virtues and deeds gained for him almost the character of a saint. His memory is especially revered here in his home town, and his tomb is an object of pilgrimage.

Roman Baths

Ankara's other Roman-era attraction, the third century **Roman Baths,** stands just a little to the west on Çankiri Caddesi, the northern extension of the city's major thoroughfare, Atatürk Bulvari. Of these baths, erected by Emperor Caracalla, enough is left to work out the frigidarium and caldarium (cold and hot rooms) and other features of this direct ancestor of the Turkish hamam, and the adjacent cloistered quadrangle that served as the palaestra, or exercise yard. These aren't as big as Caracalla's famous baths in Rome, but in a provincial city like Ancyra, they are a remarkable monument to the perverted soul who spent whatever time he had left from murdering his countrymen on improving the hygiene of the survivors. Noteworthy here is a good example of that useful Roman invention, central heating. In many of the rooms are false floors raised up on blocks; hot air circulated through these spaces from the furnace.

THE HISAR

Everything else built by the Greeks, Romans, or Byzantines in Ankara still exists but the last Byzantines, and the Turks who followed them, carried it all up the hill to the *Hisar*, the citadel. And a most remarkable citadel it is; it's common in sites in Turkey for ancient stones to be re-used in fortress walls, but only here do you find a castle built of little else. Some parts of the walls are all marble and good sandstone, carved with pieces of a hundred different inscriptions and architectural trimmings. Whole courses consist of drums of ancient columns, lined up on their sides like rows of portholes on a ship. One could think of the Hisar as a huge jigsaw puzzle; if there were time and archaeologists enough, the whole of old Ancyra could be re-assembled from the pieces.

It's a stiff climb up, as many would-be invaders have found; today the formal entrance runs from Hisarparki Caddesi through a road lined with gardens to the top. Upon arrival, you find a tranquil old Turkish town unchanged and utterly remote from the city of skyscrapers down below. Cars can hardly get through the narrow bumpy streets, and so the neighbourhood inside the walls, though poor, is cleaner and quieter. The views from the walls are superb; to the south and west the modern city stretches to the horizon.

To the north-east, in the direction of the airport, are the plains on which Tamerlane's hordes overcame Sultan Yildirim Beyazit in the **Battle of Ankara** in 1402. The Turks attribute this disaster, the first serious defeat of the Ottomans, to a point of honour. Beyazit, abandoning the first siege of Constantinople and rushing his army east to meet the advancing Tamerlane, caught him completely by surprise. To take such advantage of a noble foe seemed shameful to the young Sultan, however, and he gave his enemy a day to collect itself and meet him in proper battle array. Beyazit's exhausted troops proved no match for the nomad horsemen and Tamerlane's elephants, and in the rout that followed the Sultan himself became another inmate of Tamerlane's sad menagerie of captured potentates. After this blow, it was a decade before the Ottomans recovered their strength.

GECEKONDU

If you look from the east wall, you will see how Ankara's other half lives. If you imagined the shanty town districts, the *gecekondu*, as dreary expanses of grim hovels, you haven't given Turkey's urban migrants, raised in their village traditions of self-sufficiency, anything like the credit they deserve. Gecekondu, in time, have a way of metamorphising into decent little cottages, and the areas they create, though completely unplanned, become real neighbourhoods. The view from the walls is startling; the gecekondu begin at the slopes of the citadel, fill the valleys around it and climb the next hills, descending, climbing again and again, as far as the eye can see. It is a panorama of hundreds of thousands of homes, unbroken by a single landmark. Some areas have utilities and schools, others are still waiting; the worst look full of despair, while the best seem almost garden suburbs. In all of them, what keeps people going in the struggle, making the long trips each day to the city centre on foot or in the tired minibuses that swarm around the Ulus district, which sustains them as they strive to find a job or keep one, is the quietly confident hope that they, or their children, will one day do better.

MUSEUM OF ANATOLIAN CULTURES

You have to climb halfway up the citadel hill at least to find the **Museum of Anatolian Cultures**. Many visitors to Ankara come only to see this surprisingly small museum, a beautifully restored Bedesten of the fifteenth century that was once the heart of the city's bazaar. Though small, there are few museums anywhere in the world that can offer so many treasures from the distant past.

That is how the Turks wanted it, if you are obsessed with efficiency, consider that by spending a single day here you can spare yourself the trouble of visiting several dozen of Turkey's best known ancient sites. Like Paris, Ankara is a cultural imperialist, and all the best Hittite reliefs, Phrygian pottery and Urartian metalwork have been brought here. It was Atatürk who first had the idea for such a collection. It was originally known as the Hittite Museum in an attempt to call the world's attention to the newly discovered works of the first great Anatolian nation, and at the same time, to be an inspiration to the new nation he was trying to build. As other sites came to light in the explosion of archaeological activity here, explorations that have reshaped our knowledge of the ancient Middle East, other fine artefacts have been brought here. The whole gives a solid education in this field from Paleolithic times up to the Greek colonisation. Unlike so many other museums, this one does not overwhelm with endless cases of broken pots, every piece is significant, and most are works of art in their own right.

From the Neolithic Period, the prize exhibits come from Çatal Höyük, the 8000-year-old town whose recent excavation has changed all our ideas of ancient history. One entire temple from the site has been reconstructed, with its bulls' head idols and sophisticated frescoes, and a host of figurines of the chubby mother goddess in both her forms, as fertility symbol and as mistress of wild animals. The Hittites, not surprisingly, occupy a lion's share of the exhibit space with plenty of their curly-maned lions in attendance, too. The large number of well-preserved reliefs in the museum's great hall come both from sites of the Hittite Empire, such as Boğazköy and Karatepe, and from the weaker kingdoms that followed its collapse. The Hittites used sculpture not only for serious religious and state subjects, but also to depict scenes both from everyday life and from pure fancy; as a result, the variety of their artistic themes ranges from gods and kings astride their sacred mountains to sphinxes, hunting scenes and domestic tableaux, children and musicians and a master, not a mistress, of animals leading them in procession like a Pied Piper.

With all the attention given to the Hittites, it may be easy to overlook the works of the Hatti and other early Bronze Age peoples who preceded them. The collection here remedies that. Some of their cast bronze works here must surely rank among the greatest ancient art; their style bears a striking resemblance to the celebrated bronzes of the *nuraghe* culture of Sardinia, whose ancestors may have been migrants from Anatolia. Most of these bronzes, found at Alacahöyük and other sites, seem to have been mounted on the tops of standards or sceptres. Some are stylised bulls and stags, but the most memorable are the circular or elliptical shapes, covered with various geometric lattice designs, many with stags, bulls, of asses in the act of passing through the circle.

The scholars call them cosmological symbols, which they undoubtedly are, and throw up their hands in despair of ever understanding them completely. These compelling symbols fascinate the modern Turks. The symbol of the government Tourist Ministry uses one, and on Ankara's Atatürk Bulvari a gigantic copy of one has been erected right in the middle of the city.

Two later nations with a marvellous artistic talent, the Phrygians and Urartians, round out the museum's collection with rooms of their own. The Urartian finds come from a wide area; their empire, at its height, reached from Sivas to western Iran, from Trabzon to Aleppo. Like the Phrygians, they loved detail and geometric patterns; these can be seen adorning a bronze warrior's shield, several delicately-inscribed bronze belts worn by Urartian kings and priests, and in a beautiful soapstone carving of the winged god Haldi, standing on the back of a lion under the towers and gables of a many-storeyed fortified palace. The metalwork commonly depicts gods or priests in processions, griffons or fantastical birds. The priests, if they are indeed priests, carry standards with a strange device, a square crossed by two diagonals, rare in Anatolia but a familiar symbol of the calendar in ancient Crete.

SAMANPAZARI

Southeast of the citadel, the quarter called the **Samanpazari** ('haymarket') contains, as well as the ramshackle bazaar, three of the oldest and most interesting mosques: the thirteenth-century **Aslanhane Cami** built by the Selcuks during the brief period they held Ankara, the **Yeni Cami,** and the **Ahi Elvan Camii,** built by the Ahi Brotherhood in the early 1400s.

NEW ANKARA

A broad new highway, Talatpaşa Bulvari, cuts off the old town abruptly, and all the land on the other side has been cleared for the huge campus of modern Turkey's educational showpiece, **Hacettepe University**. Where Talatpaşa crosses Atatürk Bulvari stands the **Ethnographic Museum,** the first important building created by the Turkish Republic, started by Atatürk in 1925 to further study and appreciation of native Turkish folklore and crafts. Atatürk himself lay in state here, from 1938 to 1955, when his mausoleum was finished. Today the museum is the largest of its kind in the country, with rooms devoted to costumes and embroidery, metalcrafts, weapons, calligraphy, and objects collected from the dervish *tekkes* after their dissolution. There is a seventeenth-century room from an Ankara home, furnished to recreate a picture of life from that era, and best of all, some excellent woodcarving from the Selcuk period, doors and mihrabs from mosques, even the throne of the Selcuk Sultans.

As well as museums, Atatürk thought his city should have formal European-style parks. The first of these lies catercorner to the Ethnographic Museum and behind the city **Opera. Gençlik Park** ('youth park') may not be quite as pretty as Kültür Park in Bursa, but its layout is much the same, with lagoons and island cafes, an open air theatre, and a **Luna Park**; this last isn't a name, but a word that has passed into the Turkish language. Wherever the first one may have been, every amusement park in Turkey now is a Luna Park.

The Modern Districts

Like most Turkish cities, Ankara is long and thin, growing up along the main streets and the bus and dolmuş lines that traverse it. Consequently it's almost a mile from here to the centre of the modern city, the intersection called **Kizilay** ('crescent') where a curving avenue crosses Atatürk Bulvari. The twenty-storey international-style skyscraper here was Turkey's first, a big deal twenty years ago, though no one gives it a second look today because there so many others. Across the street, the small park around the **Güven Aniti** ('Confidence Monument') is a small oasis in the middle of the crowds and ferocious traffic of this district, which has most of Ankara's shops, offices, and hotels. The monument itself, with its glowering Atatürk and Turks gazing hopefully into the future, will make a fine exhibit in someone's archaeology museum in a millennium or two.

Another half-mile south takes you to the corner of Gülhane Caddesi and the centre of Ankara's government district. Turkey is a very centralised nation, and here the office blocks go on and on, stretching towards infinity. In the middle, in a very tired style of government architecture, stands the **Grand National Assembly,** the parliament building. Still further south,

Atatürk Caddesi becomes Embassy Row, leading to the fashionable suburbs of Kavaklidere and Çankaya. Here is another of Atatürk's parks, called **Kuğulu Park** ('swan park') and there certainly are plenty of swans. It's a pleasant spot in which to watch the younger members of the Turkish élite disporting themselves, as far from the neighbourhood of the Hisar as London is from Ouagadougou.

TOMB OF ATATÜRK

Not far from the Kizilay, on a hilltop above the suburb of Maltepe, the **Tomb of Atatürk** rises like an ancient temple on an acropolis over Ankara. The **Anit Kabir** ('monumental tomb') means a lot to the Turks; it's the building they show every night as sign-off on Turkish television when they play the national anthem. At night the entire monument is illuminated to become the city's most conspicuous landmark. It took nearly ten years to build, and in it the Turks made a serious attempt to recapture some of the massive monumentality of the ancient civilisations, while establishing a new style of their own. They didn't quite bring it off although the effect is certainly impressive.

To get there, you first go down a long promenade lined with Hittite-style lions, leading up to a square of low stone buildings that contain a **Museum** of Atatürk and his works. The entire complex is packed with soldiers, an honour guard from each of the services, all enormously tall and decked out in American-style military pomp. The monument, a plain box with a decorated cornice and surrounding colonnade of square pillars, is reached by a long flight of steps. On the walls are lengthy quotes from Atatürk and Ismet Inönü, who is also buried here. Inside, the great building is empty save for Atatürk's huge sarcophagus, with glass walls affording views over the city he built.

AROUND ANKARA

Around Ankara a large number of recreation areas have sprung up to meet the needs of the capital. Perhaps the favourite picnic-spot is the **Atatürk Orman Çiftliği,** one mile west of the town. Late in his career, the Turkish leader decided to enjoy the delights of the gentlemen farmer, and started this as a model farm to introduce new agricultural methods into Turkey. Other pleasant resorts are around **Mogan Gölü** to the south, **Kizilcahamam** 80 kilometres to the north up in the mountains, and the skiing centre of **Elmadağ,** just southeast of the city. At **Gâvurkalesi** ('infidel's castle') 60 kilometres to the southwest, you can visit a religious site of the Hittites, consisting of an underground tomb and a relief depicting the weather god Teshub, his wife Hepatu, and their son Sharruma, the divine family of the Hittite pantheon.

GETTING AROUND

Ankara is one of the cities where taxis not only have meters but usually use them. You'll probably need one if you arrive by bus or train. Both stations are on Hippodrom Caddesi, a mile and a half from Kizilay, the centre of the city. From Esenboğa Airport, northeast of the city, you have a choice of a cab—about 2000 TL—or the usual THY bus to their office a few blocks from Kizilay.

Ankara isn't encouraging for those who like to explore cities on foot. As well as the dirty air, it is the typical Turkish strip-city blown all out of proportion; almost any destination will be on or near the three-mile length of Atatürk Bulvari. Buses (buy tickets in the booths at the major stops, as in Istanbul) and dolmuş are crowded but frequent, just look at the destination signs to see if they're going in the direction you want. If you're not ready to climb up to the Hisar, there are minibuses in the broad open space that serves as a terminal just east of Ulus Meydani.

The Anit Kabir, upon its hill, and the Atatürk Orman Çifliği are best reached by taxi, but all the recreation areas in the vicinity of the city can be reached easily by bus.

TOURIST INFORMATION

Right in the Ministry of Tourism building, 33 Gazi Mustafa Kemal Bulvari (tel. (41) 173012) just west of Kizilay. The Turkish Automobile Club office is at 4 Adakale Sokak, tel. (41) 186578.

WHERE TO STAY

Ankara's fanciest hotels are mostly around busy Atatürk Bulvari, between Kizilay and Kavaklidere: **Büyuk Ankara** (L) 183 Atatürk Bulvari, tel. (41) 34 49 20, is the most luxurious, with singles for 44 800 TL, and doubles for 56 000 TL. In an older building, but good value is the **Bulvar Palas** (H2) at no 141, tel. (41) 34 21 80 89, where you can get a TV and refrigerator in room as well as a private bath for 10500 TL a single, 14000 a double; or a mere 4500 TL a single, 6000 TL a double without bath. For a quieter setting, try the **Dedeman Oteli** (H1) near the embassies on Büklüm Sok. 1, tel. (41) 34 49 80 5, Ankara's largest hotel with 252 rooms; rates are 14400 TL for a single, 18000 for a double, with special reductions for the kids.

Many of the city's more modest establishments are in Ulus, in and around Denizciler Caddesi. None in particular stand out, but they are convenient to the museum and other sights of the old town. Around Kizilay, the quarters around Necatibey Caddesi and Bayindir Caddesi offer more of the same. There are several campgrounds and motels on the Istanbul road just outside of Ankara.

EATING OUT

Ankara is one of the three cities in Turkey (the others are Istanbul and Izmir) where you can take a day off from Turkish cuisine if you so desire. The **Italyan Restoran,** 200 Hoşdere Caddesi in Kavaklidere, (4000–6000 TL for the works), and **China Town,** 19 Köroğlu Caddesi in Gaziosmanpaşa (dinners for about 6000 TL) are two of the places that have grown up in the cosmopolitan suburbs in recent years. On the same street, the **Yakamoz Restaurant,** is well known for its fresh fish, a scarce commodity in Ankara, but expect to pay at least 5000 TL for a meal.

Behind the northeast quadrant of the Kizilay intersection, some streets have been closed off to traffic; these are a good bet for inexpensive kebab houses; Ulus is also full of these. As usual, the ones that look the best really are. The only chain of kebab restaurants in Turkey is in Ankara; avoid it.

To Boğazköy

Towards the east, just beyond Ankara lies the **Kizilirmak,** the Crescent River, curving in a broad loop from its mouth near Samsun around past Ankara and through Cappadocia, back to its sources in the east near Sivas. To the Greeks this was the Halys, a name famous from the campaigns of Alexander and Xenophon, but before that, its arc enclosed the home counties of the Hittite Empire, a fertile and defensible country with the Hittite capital of Hattusa, near modern Boğazköy, at its centre.

Today **Çorum** is the major town in this region. It has little to offer the visitor, an ornate clock tower in the square and a small Selcuk castle hidden away behind the school playground, but if you're bound for Boğazköy or Amasya, you'll probably pass through it. Have a look around; Çorum is a modern town, clean, well laid-out, and prosperous, with an air of happy contentment about its people. Ankara may have the skyscrapers, but it's in places like Çorum where you can see Turkey's future.

Boğazköy

Boğazköy itself is a small pretty village of prosperous farmers. All around it, in an area of roughly two square miles, lie the scattered remains of the capital of the Hittites, **Hattusa.** Most travellers' first great surprise on coming here is learning that all the excavated buildings, temples, and fortifications they visit among the farms and fields of Boğazköy were in fact parts of one city, a metropolis whose four miles of walls contained nearly two hundred towers. Tours of the site are organised through travel agents in Ankara, and occasionally in Çorum, but if you prefer travelling on your own, the best base for the expedition is **Sungurlu,** the closest town, located on the Ankara–Samsun road.

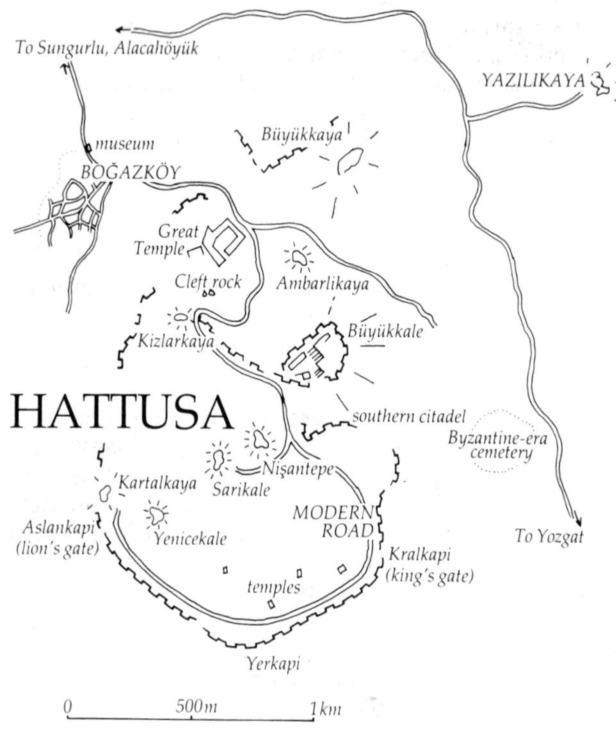

HISTORY IN THE HITTITE CAPITAL

The earliest traces of habitation at Hattusa go back as far as 3000 BC. By about 2000, there was a settlement around the citadel (Büyükkale). This would be a town of the people of Hatti, from whom Hattusa took its name, but it's uncertain whether it was their capital. From the many natural advantages of the site, we can guess that it might have been; besides the fertility and beauty of the area, its strategic location for trade, and its suitability for defence, there are natural springs everywhere. These ensured a source of water within the walls, and may, conceivably, have had some importance to the religion of the place.

The first written record mentioning Hattusa is unsettling. Anitta, king of Kushar, a city of unknown location, is the subject of the oldest tablet in the Hittite State Archive. The inscription recalls his total destruction of the city, and the curse he put upon it, which was that it never again be inhabited.

This was in about 1720 BC. We also learn from the archive, however, that by the late seventeenth century another king of Kushar moved his capital to Hattusa, and styled himself 'the man from Hattusa' or Hattusilis. A capital it remained throughout the Hittite old kingdom and empire (c. 1600–1200 BC), with one brief interruption when King Mutawalli moved his court to the southeastern city of Dattassa for what must have been reasons of temporary political distress. Shortly after it was restored, the great palace on Büyükkale burned down, perhaps as a result of civil strife, but both the city and its fortifications reached their highest stage of development under King Tudhaliya (c. 1250 BC) shortly before the catastrophe that ended the Hittite kingdom forever.

Symptoms of the coming end do not turn up clearly from the archaeological record. Reports of wars with the frontier tribes are common enough, and according to Dr Kurt Bittel, the archaeologist who devoted much of his life to the excavations at Hattusa, there was a noticeable decline in building standards in the city's last period. In any case, unknown invaders annihilated both the city and empire in around 1200 BC.

Afterwards, the city seems to have remained abandoned until the ninth century BC, when a Phrygian or Phrygian-influenced community grew up from the ruins of the Hittite palace, a well-built, important town that unfortunately isn't mentioned in a single ancient record. Most of its works have been cleared away by archaeologists to expose the Hittite levels underneath. The famous smiling Cybele in Ankara's archaeological museum was found in the Phrygian town.

YAZILIKAYA

Most visitors try to plan their trip to be in Hattusa at about noon when the reliefs carved into the rocks at **Yazilikaya** are best seen, and most begin their visit here, the national shrine of the deified Hittite kings. Yazilikaya is on the heights a mile and a half northeast of Hattusa.

The early Hittites seem to have conducted their rituals out of doors, not surprisingly for a people whose chief-deities were gods of sun and storms. The two chambers in the natural rock formation at Yazilikaya were thus open to the sky, even after the monumental gateway and complex of buildings (of which only the foundations remain) were constructed at the entrance to the chambers.

Bittel believes the **small gallery** to the right served for the funeral rites of departed kings. Certainly the reliefs carved in this shadowy, narrow chamber support this. Lion-headed figures, gesturing menacingly, guard the entrance, and once inside you are confronted with the bizarre and mysterious 'sword god', about whom archaeologists do not choose to speculate. This figure has the head of a god over a body which is a composite made up of four lions symmetrically arranged, and which terminates in a tapering sword blade, with its point downwards.

Another relief in this chamber shows **King Tudhaliya**—one of the four Hittite kings of that name—in the protective embrace of the god Sharruma, both of whom are in the conventional Hittite pose: standing in profile, with the left hand pulled back and the right extended. This is a particularly fine and well-preserved work, as is the famous frieze of the **'twelve gods'** on the opposite wall. These fellows, in a row as if a Bronze Age chorus line, carry curved swords or sickles and wear the conical hats allowed to Hittite deities.

Conventions of Hittite Art

This is a good place to explain some of the conventions of Hittite art and writing, as deduced by clever and erudite scholars like Dr Bittel from an absolute minimum of evidence. You recognise a Hittite king, such as Tudhaliya, by his rounded skull cap and earring, and by his *Kalmush,* the curving Hittite sceptre that resembles a monkey's tail. Note the Turkish slippers with the upturned toes, sported by both kings and gods. Among the ideograms that accompany the king will be a winged sun-disc, almost the same as that found in the art of the Assyrians and other ancient peoples. Beneath it, there is often a pair of what look like columns topped with Ionic capitals; these are taken to mean 'great king'. The other ideograms declare the king's name.

Gods are recognised by the pointed caps, and their standing in the divine hierarchy is indicated by the number of horns on the caps. Goddesses wear long pleated skirts and tall hats like those called *polos* by the Greeks, seemingly simulating the walls and towers of a city. Both are often portrayed with animal attributes, some stand on the backs of leopards or an eagles' wings, while the greatest gods often bestride sacred mountains. The ideogram for 'god' is an ellipse, divided vertically in half.

In the small gallery, there are also niches cut into the walls that may have held burial urns of the kings. At the corner near the entrance is a statue base that once supported a figure of the god Sharruma, and it's worth noting that the eyes of all the figures in the reliefs turn towards this spot.

To the left of the small gallery, a cleft in the rocks covers what seems to have been a well or spring; oddly, archaeologists make no mention of it. The large irregularly-shaped gallery, to the left of this, contains reliefs of 63 Hittite gods and goddesses; 42 gods marching from the left to meet 21 goddesses coming from the right. It is believed this chamber was important in the New Year celebrations that took place in the spring.

It's difficult to ascribe names or functions to most of these images. From left to right, the first twelve are the same chorus line of gods as are represented in the small chamber, in the same pose. The other goods on this panel are unknown. In the next section, the badly worn part that seems to be a kind of house is really, on closer inspection, two bull-headed gods supporting the sky. The four figures on the far right represent Shaushga, the local name of **Ishtar,** her two handmaidens and the familiar Mesopotamian water-god **Ea.**

The Hittite Pantheon

The next, and largest, section portrays the chief deities of the Hittite pantheon. The first two are unnamed gods of agriculture and weather; the next, the one with the most horns, is the Weather God of Heaven, **Teshub,** facing his consort **Hepatu** depicted astride a leopard. Her son **Sharruma,** also on a leopard, is directly behind. None of the goddesses that follow have been clearly identified.

Most of the names of these deities are from the Hurrians, the people to the south-east, who strongly influenced Hittite art and culture. It is interesting to speculate on the cultural sources of this complicated pantheon. If the Hittite religion followed the usual pattern of that era it may have worked like this: the northern invaders, the Hittites from the Balkans, brought down a Zeus-like storm god and grafted him and his companions onto a matriarchial system of the indigenous Hatti folk, represented by Hepatu. Her son Sharruma is a typical Tammuz-Adonis-Osiris figure of death and rebirth; his importance as mentor and examplar of the sacred kings betrays a strong conservative instinct in the religion. In the frieze in the large gallery, he stands among the goddesses, as one of the original deities of the country, while the imported goddess Shaushga-Ishtar keeps company with the males.

One mortal has elbowed his way into this divine congregation, and it is King Tudhaliya IV, carved into the opposite wall, larger than any of the gods, with his sacred mountains and his symbols exactly as in the portrait in the small gallery. It's ironic that the last known Hittite king should be the only one to receive this treatment, apotheosis, just before Götterdämmerung. As in so many other cases, for example with the Romans, the kingdom of Commagene, the Incas or Aztecs or old King Ozymandias, an excess of king-worship seems to be the sign of an overripe nation that has lost its mental balance. When Tudhaliya had himself immortalised on this rock, his civilisation had not fifty more years to live; perhaps his apotheosis speaks as clearly of the coming end as anything in the State Archive.

HATTUSA: THE GREAT TEMPLE

Coming to Hattusa itself, most visitors begin with the ruins of the **Great Temple,** at the modern entrance to the complex. Even though this temple, with the narrow storerooms surrounding it, was built in the last century of the Hittite Empire, about 1250 BC, its site is one of the oldest parts of the city, on the slopes just below the Büyükkale fortress. Nearby, excavations have revealed older buildings that belonged to an Assyrian trading colony, or *karum*, that flourished within the city during the Hittite old kingdom.

Here, as everywhere else in Hattusa that has been excavated, are neatly-squared stone foundations all rising to a single level, with nothing above. The Hittites used sun-baked brick, covered with plaster and probably painted, in their building; consequently, the actual walls disintegrated long ago.

Near the entrance of the temple complex are the remains of an enormous **ceremonial basin,** carved with lions. Though broken now, it was originally almost 15 feet long, carved from a single piece of limestone. The entrance itself, the once-imposing gateway, through which the Hittite king entered with his retinue on formal occasions, leads to a paved street where there is another basin. Here the street curves, and completely surrounds the actual temple which is recognisable by the larger and more carefully cut stones used for its foundation. In the temple, it's easy to distinguish the central courtyard and the most important chambers, which are to the northeast: two large rooms of equal size that contained statues of the weather god and sun goddess, illuminated by windows to the outside. It is likely that the temple, as well as the surrounding storerooms, were two, and, in some places, three storeys high, but there is no evidence as to how the outside of the temple and its roofline looked.

The temple storerooms must have contained the treasury, though nothing of this survived the sack of the city. Many of the cuneiform tablets that have contributed so much to our knowledge of the Hittites were found here, including one that contains a list of 208 members of the temple household, including,

> ... 18 priests, 29 women musicians, 19 scribes for clay tablets,
> 33 scribes for wood tablets, 35 soothsayers, 10 Hurrian singers...

The remainder is lost. Also in these storerooms are the huge jars for wine or oil, some of which bear inscriptions.

The rooms in this part of the temple were long and narrow, and opened out only onto each other at the points where there are the huge, U-shaped marble thresholds, with doorposts sunk into them. Archaeologists never mention the great green stone, found in a room at the southern end of the street leading from the gateway. It is carved into an irregular shape and polished as smooth as glass; its purpose is unknown.

To the southwest, across an ancient street, which incidentally carries the storm drains underneath it as do other streets in Hattusa, is another complex of rooms built around a courtyard; it is believed that this too was part of the temple complex. At its southern edge, a **subterranean fountain** was discovered in a small room with a corbelled roof.

THE FORTIFICATIONS

Looking out from here, two large rock formations rise up from the nearby heights to the south. The cleft parting them is partially man-made; apparently there was a well or spring inside. This area which stretches from the limits of modern Boğazköy in an arc across to Büyükkale in the southwest, marked the southern edge of the old city wall; its foundations, as well as some of the postern gates in it, are still present.

As you follow the modern road up to Büyükkale, you pass **Ambarlikaya** and **Büyükkaya,** other natural rock-heights to the left that the Hittites were forced to include in their defensive works. The walls that ran along between these were among the most impressive achievements of the Hittite architects, with gigantic earthen dikes supporting walls that in some places climbed slopes at an angle of 45°. Castles once perched on top of both these rocks.

BÜYÜKKALE

Büyükkale, the citadel and original centre of Hattusa served in late Hittite times as the capital of the state and the residence of the kings. The stairs you climb up are near the site of the original main gate, and lead to the lowest of three ascending courtyards, this one the so-called **state agora.** The complex to the west, consisting of four long rooms, was the **State Archive,** perhaps the oldest library building in the world. Among the thousands of records found here was the famous **Treaty of Kadesh,** signed with the Egyptians in 1259 BC. We owe its preservation, ironically, to Hattusa's anonymous invaders. When they put Büyükkale to the torch, the clay tablets were fired as if in a kiln; otherwise they would have disintegrated long ago.

It is believed that the middle courtyard was a kind of 'buffer zone' separating the bureaucracy from the royal residences in the upper courtyard, of which little remains but two large cisterns. On the southern edge of the citadel is a line of temples and state buildings; here some of the original brick still survives.

THE SOUTHERN WALLS

Sometimes after a period of crisis, cities realise that their fortifications, however impressive, are not good enough; they then exert themselves to extend them farther than earlier generations had ever dreamed of doing. Thus, Athens built the long walls to Piraeus, and Syracuse, after the Peloponnesian War, constructed the incredible series of fortifications up to Euryalos. Some episode in Hittite history caused its kings to realise that their city's Achilles heel lay to the south, where the land slopes gradually upwards to a ridge higher than Büyükkale itself. The rulers of fourteenth-century Hattusa solved the problem by building a broad arc of walls almost three miles long across their southern suburbs, thus completing one of the most magnificent urban **fortifications** anywhere in the ancient world.

On its way to these walls, the modern road passes several natural heights, fortified by the Hittites, that deserve a visit. To the left of the road, the **Southern Citadel** was probably of great importance to the city, but little has yet been excavated. To the right, is **Nişantepe,** the site of another castle notable for the large, but unfortunately indecipherable inscription on the eastern face of the rock, referring to King Suppiluliumas. The name of the castle means 'Mark Hill' or 'Target Hill', and from here most of the other monuments of Hattusa can be seen, as well as the infinite hills and mountains on all sides. The name is provocative, for standing here you have the sense that the city and its environs are somehow arranged, that this is one of the centres of a vast geomantic construction. If so, the key to it was buried with the Hittites.

Nearby, across a narrow saddle of land, is another large rock and **Sarikale,** the 'yellow castle', with rooms, courtyards and cisterns like a smaller Büyükkale. **Yenicekale,** a similar construction, crowns the mount furthest south. Foundations of four important **temples** have been discovered near the southeast corner of the walls, but the excavations are still underway.

Yerkapi

The **southern walls** themselves are a symmetrical configuration with the great gateway **Yerkapi** at its centre. Even in its ruined state, Yerkapi is perhaps the most memorable sight in Hattusa. Only the foundations of the double wall and towers remain, but these were built on a man-made ridge some thirty feet high, and here the slopes are paved to further disconcert attackers. Two long stairways, one on either side, lead down from the outer wall. The gate was decorated, or guarded, by finely carved sphinxes, one now in the museum of Istanbul, and the other in Berlin. There is a surprise directly underneath it, a strange, sloping 200-foot tunnel through the mound, built of rough cyclopean masonry corbelled inwards, altogether unlike anything else in Hattusa. Archaeologists call it a sally port, a gate from which the defenders could sneak out and harry their attackers from behind, but this is a poor explanation; the tunnel is too noticeable and too carefully built and sited (lying directly north–south, on the central axis of the city). It is more likely it held some religious or ceremonial significance.

Kralkapi and Aslankapi

A third of a mile away, two other important gates, **Kralkapi** and **Aslankapi,** can be seen on either side of Yerkapi. These are well known for the reliefs that give them their names which mean King's Gate and Lion's Gate, though they, like most of Hattusa's sculptures, have been removed to the Ankara museum and replaced with concrete casts. The king carved on Kralkapi is probably really a god protecting the gate. Whichever he is, it is one of the Hittites' best works. The god looks remarkably placid and confident, and the axe he carries looks very serious. So do the lions of Aslankapi, though they're not nearly as well preserved. The unusual and impressive architectural feature of these gates is their well executed parabolic arches, a form unique to the Hittites. We can give them credit for having mastered some quite complex mathematics; it is difficult to imagine anyone building a parabola freehand.

Many of the finds of Hattusa that are not in the Ankara museum are in the small **Boğazköy Museum** (you get in for the same ticket as Hattusa). These include some intricately carved seal rings, *pithoi*, and other ceramics, some Byzantine stelae, and an unimaginative reconstruction of the Büyük Mabet (Great Temple) of Hattusa.

Alacahöyük

A possible afternoon detour from Hattusa is to **Alacahöyük**, on a side road going back towards Sungurlu. Long before the Hittites ever entered Anatolia, as far back as 4000 BC, there was a settlement here of the indigenous Hatti people. In their best days, about 2500–2000 BC, the Hatti had one of the most advanced cultures anywhere outside Mesopotamia. Later occupations have covered up the Hatti at sites like Alacahöyük, and it's hard to tell what kind of talent they had town-building; apart from the later Hittite reliefs, there's really little left to see. Their wonderful metal cosmological discs and figurines have already been mentioned. Most of these are in Ankara, though copies may be seen in the small **museum** here.

The Hittite reliefs, contemporary with those at Hattusa (and like them, concrete casts of the originals), are a puzzle. Two musicians play outlandish instruments, while two other men climb a ladder to nowhere. One figure archaeologists have named the 'sword swallower'. There is a procession of animals, a seated female goddess, and a king and queen standing before an odd T-shaped object and what appears to be an altar with a bull on it.

GETTING AROUND

Some books recommend Ankara as a base for visiting the Hittite sites at Boğazköy. This may be the only acceptable way for travelling pashas, but it's 180 kilometres away and not at all necessary. Modest hotels exist at Corum, or best of all in Sungurlu, the closest town to the ruins. Sungurlu can be reached by any Ankara–Samsun bus or Ankara–Amasya bus. From there, about 6500 TL is the going rate for a complete trip (extra if you want to take in Alacahöyük too) taking half a day or more. You can avoid this by taking the Sungurlu–Boğazköy village bus and walking to the sites, but be warned it's a good eight-mile walk if you want to see everything.

TOURIST INFORMATION
Atatürk Caddesi, Sungurlu, tel. 752. In Corum, Şehir Işhani, tel. 4704.

WHERE TO STAY
The **Hitit Moteli** (King Suppiluliumas slept here often) just outside Sungurlu, is the best base for seeing Boğazköy; besides beautiful landscaping, with flowers and occasional nightingales, it has a good restaurant, and is located on the Ankara highway; most buses stop here; tel. 42 409, with singles with baths for 2000 TL, 2850 for a double. There's a new **Turban hotel** in Çorum in the Cepri district, tel. 5311–13, with singles for 4000 TL, doubles for 5000 TL. The old standard in Çorum is the **Kolağasi** (H4), 97 Inönü Caddesi, in the centre, tel. 1971, with singles for 3300 TL, doubles for 4000 TL. A guesthouse of sorts has recently opened in Boğazköy village.

EATING OUT
There are simple lokantas in Çorum and Sungurlu, as well as at Boğazköy itself. The restaurant at the Hitit motel is quite good and inexpensive, at around 2000 TL for a meal.

Sivas to Amasya

Leaving Alacahöyük, the road going east from Ankara, after the turnoff for Sungurlu and Corum, follows the green and pretty valley of the river Delice before reaching **Yozgat,** an agricultural centre, distinguished only by its Ottoman clock tower. After Yozgat, the road passes through one of Anatolia's emptier quarters for a hundred miles before rejoining the valley of the Kizilirmak at **Sivas,** a peaceful city of 150 000 people, founded during Roman times as Sebasteia.

Sivas

Sivas first gained importance during the Middle Ages, as erstwhile capital of the Selcuks and other Turkish emirs. This was Sivas's golden age, lasting until Tamerlane sacked it in 1395. Today, Sivas is most proud of its role at the beginning of the War of Independence; during the summer of 1919, when much of the country was under foreign occupation, the then-General Mustafa Kemal (Atatürk) called together the first national congress in this safe, remote city. On September the fourth, the decision was made to ignore the Istanbul government and work for the liberation of Turkey. Today, the place where the congress met, the old boys' high school on Konak Meydani in the centre of Sivas, is the **September Fourth Museum** with the congress hall and Atatürk's apartments kept just as they were during that eventful hour.

Selcuk Monuments

To the south, the square extends into a park that contains four of medieval Sivas's finest monuments, the **Kale Cami** of 1580, the **Şifa'iye Medrese,** and the **Çifte Minare** (twin minarets), these two facing each other across an ancient street, and the **Buruciye Medrese.** All of these last three structures were begun in 1271. Although by then the Selcuks had moved their capital to Konya, they still took great interest in the eastern marches. This complex, despite its ruined state, is as fine as anything they built in the west. All three have beautifully carved gateways, the Şifa'iye adorned with stern Selcuk lions, the Çifte Minare with acanthus-leaf capitals, probably borrowed from an earlier Byzantine structure. The two minarets, made from brick and blue Iznik tiles, and the exterior walls, are all that remain of the mosque. Already they list as much as the Tower of Pisa, so see them while you still can.

The park containing these structures was the heart of Selcuk Sivas. Above it rises the old **Kale** (citadel) on the hill, and although occupied since the Hittites, nothing remains today, and the old fort has been converted to a park. The neighbourhoods around it, to the south and west, are the oldest in Sivas, with quiet and pretty streets where the appearance of a foreigner is a rare event. Here stands the twelfth century **Ulu Cami,** and yet another Selcuk theological school, the **Gök Medrese,** also built in that great year of 1271. Although derelict, this is one of the most famous works of Selcuk architecture, for its splendid gateway, with its fanciful sculptured patterns that include a melange of styles from every corner of Anatolia, with some old Byzantine carved thistles and angels thrown in.

Outside Sivas, two long and graceful **Ottoman bridges** span the Kizilirmak, lying parallel to the modern roads to Ankara and Amasya.

Divriği

To see the greatest of all medieval Turkish mosques in this corner of Anatolia, you must make the long and difficult trip to **Divriği,** 150 kilometres southeast of Sivas. It is easier to reach by train than by the long and roundabout routes on unpaved roads. In the thirteenth century, Divriği was the capital of the short-lived Mengüçeh Turkish emirate. The **Ulu Cami,** near the town citadel, is, in form, similar to the Selcuk mosques of Sivas or Erzurum, with its short minaret, low sloping roof, and conical *türbes* protruding from the top. Its carved portals are judged among the best work of the age. Divriği was flourishing then as a stop along an important trade route, from Sivas down to the Euphrates valley; the sources of that legendary river are in the surrounding mountains and, consequently, a number of **caravanserais**, in various states of preservation, dot the Sivas road, most notably at **Kangal,** a village midway between the two towns.

Besides the road to Divriği there are three other routes from Sivas: the main highway east to Erzurum, the bad road over the Tahtali Mountains to Malatya, or a slight backtrack along the valley of the Yeşilirmak ('Green River') to the northwest. Of the three, this last is by far the most scenic, crossing the Yildiz ('star') Mountains at the pass of **Çamlibel** and then continuing through forest and mountains that become increasingly more rugged and green the closer you come to the Black Sea.

Tokat

The farmers of the Yeşilirmak grow tobacco, among other things, and one of the Turkish monopoly's most popular brands of smokes is named after **Tokat,** a lovely town on the river that has been occupied for thousands of years. Recorded history first mentions Tokat under the name of 'Comana Pontica,' the religious centre of Mithradates' Pontic Kingdom. Orestes, son of Agamemnon, is said to have visited here on his wanderings, introducing the rites of Artemis and leaving a famous image of the goddess that the Persian King Xerxes later stole.

Up on the slender peak that guards the town, the picture-book **castle** was built by the Byzantines and restored by the Turks. The Byzantines here only interested themselves in holding this strategic position; under them the city dwindled, reviving under the Selcuks and other Turkish emirates who contested for the town in the Middle Ages. Among Tokat's Selcuk legacy is the **Gök Medrese** of 1270, a medical college that is now the **Tokat Museum,** with the usual grave steles and Turk's attic of folk arts and crafts. One tomb in the medrese belongs to Mu'in al-Din, the Selcuk vezir who built the complex Ottoman contributions to Tokat include: the sixteenth-century **Ali Paşa Camii,** centre of a group that includes a tomb and baths; the **Hatuniye Cami,** built by Bayezid II; a fine stone bridge at the northern end of the town; and the **clock tower,** across from the Ali Paşa Camii in the town square. If all these clock towers, like the ones in Çorum and Yozgat, look alike, they should; all were built during the nineteenth-century reign of Abdul Hamid. He may have earned his reputation as a black-hearted reactionary in a thousand ways, but he did want the Turks to know what time it was.

Amasya

The great citadel of Tokat closes off one end of the valley of the Yeşilirmak, and its counterpart at **Amasya** seals the other. In between, the Yeşilirmak lives up to its name, for although the river itself is muddy brown with the soil of Anatolia, the land it waters between those two high citadels is one of the greenest and most fertile corners of the nation.

Amasya itself is small, but offers some of Turkey's best travel poster shots. Squeezed into a steep valley, under cliffs carved with rock tombs of the ancient Pontic kings, and with its old Ottoman houses overhanging the winding Yeşilirmak, Amasya qualifies as one of the loveliest cities in Anatolia. Its strategic position has also gained it the attention of kings and sultans throughout the centuries, and they have endowed it with many fine buildings.

The Kingdom of Pontus

In antiquity, the Yeşilirmak was called the Iris, the messenger of the dawn, and with good reason, for to the Greeks, this was one of the borders of the known world, beyond which lay only Amazons, Scythians, and other barbarians that gave the Greeks bad dreams. As a sometime capital of the various kings named Mithradates and their obstreperous Pontic kingdom, 'Amaseia' gave the Romans a big headache. Rome captured the city in 70 BC, but with the revolt of Phanarces, she was forced to send Julius Caesar to finish the job. After the battle at nearby Zile in 47 BC, and the destruction of the Pontic army, Caesar came up with the tag 'Veni, vidi, vici', a political slogan that was to carry him a long way.

Along the river

The centre of Amasya is a broad square on the river's edge, with one of the better equestrian Atatürks, a statue portraying the conqueror in his beaver hat surrounded by resolute soldiers and anxious women, gazing fiercely at the police station across the river. From here, a pretty shaded promenade follows the river and the main street, Ekin Pazari Caddesi, runs parallel towards the south. Between them, the shopping district surrounds a sixteenth-century **bedesten,** still in use. A few blocks further, past the twin domes of the **Sultan Beyazit II Mosque** complex, the city's most impressive, you come to the **Amasya Museum.**

This museum contains, in its large new building, a fair collection of artefacts from the various chapters of the past. There is a good-as-new Roman bathtub and two curious cylindrical sarcophagi, as well as local arts and crafts. Some of the most beautiful objects made in the Islamic world were astronomical instruments, and there are fine examples here. The undeniable attraction of the museum, however, is in the **Mongol mummies** in the adjacent Selcuk **Türbe of Sultan Mesut.** Mesut sleeps peacefully in the crypt, but the Mongols, Cumodar and Oshuga Nuyin, two governors of the fourteenth century who served under the renegade Khan Hülâgü and his successors, are displayed in glass cases, along with the members of an important Selcuk family and its children. The museum's sculpture garden surrounds the türbe, and the columns with Latin inscriptions there served as milestones and were found along the Roman road that traversed the valley of the Yeşilirmak.

Just around the corner from the museum is another *türbe*, that of **Halifat Gazi,** the best of the many tombs in this city. The asymmetrical decoration, with delicate geometric patterns inside small circles randomly arranged over the tomb, is a peculiarity of local architecture.

OTHER SIGHTS

Two other mosques can be seen in the district above Ekin Pazari Caddesi. Across from the old bedesten stands a ruined *han*, and on the hill behind it, the fourteenth-century Mosque of **Burmali Minare,** taking its name from the spirals of its 'twisted' minaret. A few blocks further uphill, the **Fethiye Camii** was originally a Byzantine church of the seventh century.

Beyond the square, the Yeşilirmak twists northwards. Following it along the main road, you'll find more of Amasya's medieval landmarks. First, the **Timarhane** of 1309, an insane asylum, founded during the period of Mongol rule. Despite its function, the Timarhane has been blessed with a gate as fine as that of any mosque. It remains unfinished, reflecting the uncertainty of the times after the collapse of the Selcuk state. A block further on lies the **Mehmet Paşa Camii** (late fifteenth-century) and beyond that, the early fifteenth-century **Beyazit Camii.** Through much of early Ottoman history, the sons of Sultans were shuffled off to Amasya as governors to keep them out of trouble until their turn on the throne. These two mosques, as well as many others in the town, are a result of the royal attention, as is the **Büyük Ağa Medrese,** just across the bridge from the Beyazit Camii. This beautiful octagonal complex, with its interior arcade and courtyard, was founded by Beyazit's Chief White Eunuch.

Maiden's Palace and Citadel

On this shore of the river, where the old wooden houses crowd against the banks, the huge rock crowned by the citadel rises straight up above them, with royal tombs burrowed out of its cliffs. According to the geographer Strabo, a native of Amasya who knew the city under both Roman and Pontic rule, the ledge above this narrow bank was the site of the Pontic royal palace, known locally as the **Maiden's Palace,** with walls that extended down to the river. Parts of these are still visible, built into the walls of the old houses of the quarter, though they're only visible once you climb the stairs of the palace proper. Here the walls have been restored in recent years, and amid the gardens, you can see remains of the painted arches and domes that were part of the baths built by Mithradates.

From the rock gardens, cut stairs lead up to the **tombs** of the Pontic kings. Marvellous as these seem from down below (the city illuminates them at night), little of colour or interest has survived the centuries, and it's impossible to tell which kings were buried there. Sockets cut into the stone indicate there must have been imposing stone façades and balustrades, but nothing of these or any other artwork or grave goods exist today.

Still, the effect is royal and grand enough. Visitors are usually surprised that the tombs are not merely façades themselves but entire buildings chiselled out of the dark basalt cliffs; you can walk completely around two of them, into the mountain and out again. Altogether there are four tombs here, but the surrounding region has ten more, all overlooking the Yeşilirmak, and they comprise the national pantheon of this forgotten kingdom.

In ancient times, Amasya's **citadel,** high above the tombs, was reputed to be impregnable, and from below it does in fact seem utterly inaccessible. However, there's a way around the back (yellow signs indicate the way from the vicinity of the Büyük Ağa Medrese) and the summit can be reached by car.

Here, in a kind of museum of masonry, the building styles of the ages betray the various reworkings of the fortress, and its continuous importance over two thousand years; first, there is ancient rough stone, then good square ashlar from the Hellenistic era, then Roman brick, and finally the characteristic Ottoman sandstone that comprises the greater part of the ruins. Flowers and some of the prettiest butterflies in Anatolia currently occupy the site, and, if the terrain is difficult, the panorama over Amasya's valley and surrounding mountains makes it all worthwhile.

At the entrance a marble lintel with a Greek inscription has been built into walls of a later era. In the derelict lower citadel, a cistern remains that provided the fortress with its water. The upper citadel is better preserved, and here you can find the famous secret passage: look for a large surviving stretch of wall, high but not broad, with an opening in it that looks, from a distance, like a keyhole. Near its base is a spot where the wall has crumbled away to form a set of steps on its jagged edge. Climb up, and you'll see a brick, arched tunnel with slippery descending steps. Supposedly it leads down to the tombs, but no one in Amasya, it seems, has ever tried it. Bring a flashlight and half a mile of rope.

Around Amasya

Today, as in the days of Mithradates, the area around Amasya is one of the most productive and densely populated farming regions of Turkey. The valleys of the Yeşilirmak and its tributaries, between the peaks and crags, are dotted with towns, each with its castle hovering over it, and some well-built foundations of the medieval Turks at its heart. **Zile,** where Caesar conquered, is one of these, also **Merzifon,** the ancient 'Phazemon'. **Niksar,** further east in the valley of the Kelkut Çayi, has kept its name since Roman times, or almost. The Romans called it Neocaesarea, but time has eroded the name just as it has the old fortress, one of Mithradates' strongholds. Niksar received some fine buildings from the Selcuks, notably the twelfth-century **Yağibaşan Medrese.**

It's out of the way, some 60 kilometres along mountainous roads from Amasya, but a trip to **Borabay Gölü,** a volcanic crater lake surrounded by forests, will reward you with some of the best scenery these mountains have to offer.

GETTING AROUND

You can't get to the Amasya region by train from Ankara, but there's the slow, infrequent Samsun–Amasya–Sivas line with good scenery through the mountains. There are no difficulties with bus connections anywhere, but trips through the mountains will take longer than you'd expect—though the network of paved roads is better than in most parts of Turkey. Both in Tokat and Amasya you can get a taxi to take you up to the high castles for about 2000 TL.

TOURIST INFORMATION

In Sivas, Vilayet, on the main square, tel. 128 50. Amasya and Tokat are among the few provincial capitals without tourist information offices, but we wouldn't be surprised if that changes soon. It's hard to find anyone who speaks English in this part of country, but everyone tries their best to be helpful.

WHERE TO STAY

Everywhere in this region, accommodation will be clean but modest; it's a pleasant part of Turkey, but hardly overwhelmed with tourists. In Amasya, the **Apaydin Hotel** (unlisted) on Ekin Pazari Cad. is typical of what you'll find, at 1400 TL for a single, 2000 TL a double. Other places may be as high as 3500 TL if tourist rated. Amasya has a **Turban Hotel** (H3) in Helkis, tel. 3134, 3750 TL a single, 4700 TL a double. Sivas has plenty of indistinguishable hotels, Tokat a few, and Yozgat just one. Rooms even plainer and cheaper may be found in Divriği, Niksar, Suluova, and Merzifon.

EATING OUT

Nothing either special or unpleasant is likely to come your way. The **Çiçek Lokanta** in Amasya is good and moderately priced at 4000–5000 TL; the same prices prevail at the **2 Eylül Restaurant** in Sivas.

Part XI

SOUTH-WESTERN ANATOLIA

The entrance to the Covered Hall of the Sultan Han near Aksaray

Konya

Some cities, such as Istanbul, are forced by their location to play a large role in the world's affairs; others may survive for millennia without contributing anything. Most fortunate of all, though, are the towns that at one time in their lives have a little empire of their own, and then move off history's stage into a long golden twilight. Bursa is one such Turkish city, Konya is the other.

These two have other things in common; they are the cleanest and best-kept cities in Turkey, and both have managed the difficult process of becoming modern and prosperous on their own terms. Turkey often advertises itself as the 'Land of Civilisations', and with the many peoples and cultural influences that have drifted through over the centuries, it is hard to isolate anything as specifically 'Turkish', until you come to Bursa or Konya, the most Turkish of the nation's cities. Konya has a reputation for being the most conservative and devout corner of Turkey; in truth, there are plenty of other candidates for that honour. This is nothing to be alarmed about; Konya is a city where culture and tolerance have always been accounted virtues. If it has a living faith to sustain it, so much the better.

HISTORY

The first we hear of Konya is as a Phrygian town called Kawania; later, under the Greeks and Romans it became Iconium, capital of the province of Lycaonia. The Selcuks, with whom medieval Konya is usually associated, were not the first Turks in the neighbourhood; other warrior bands were around as early as the ninth century, and the Arabs of the Abbasid Caliphate had arrived before them, twice capturing the city from the Byzantines though they could not keep it. When the Selcuks came, in 1076 after the Battle of Manzikert gave them control of Anatolia, Sultan Süleyman I made Konya his capital. Not that the city had much to commend it; its only real advantage was equal distance from all possible enemies, or, perhaps, the broad, treeless Plain of Konya reminded the Selcuks of their ancestral home on the Asian steppe. For a time the Selcuks, strong as they were, had a hard time holding Konya. During the first Crusade, Godfrey of Bouillon occupied the city for a short while, and Frederick Barbarossa passed through in 1190 on his way to the Holy Land. Neither of these harmed either the city or the Selcuks. Like any of the early Turkish principalities, the Selcuks' Empire of Rum was hardly a modern, centralised state; the real 'capital' was the Sultan's throne, and that moved with him wherever his whims or campaigns took him. Konya, however, was the residence of the Sultans, and the major beneficiary of their building work and philanthropy.

Under their intelligent and tolerant regime, Konya in the twelfth and thirteenth centuries became a refuge for artists and men of learning from all over the Middle East and Moslem Asia, fleeing the depredations of the Mongols and Crusaders. Rulers such as **Alâeddin Keykubad,** who liked to surround themselves with poets and erudite dervishes, endowed a collection of mosques and schools that has made the city the equal of Istanbul and Bursa as a showplace of Turkish architecture. They had hardly begun when the Mongols came in 1243 to spoil the party; they never sacked Konya, but they did put an end to the Selcuk momentum. After the fall of the Empire of Rum, the Karamanoğullari, the Turks from Karaman, filled the vacuum but moved the capital to their own town of Ermenek. Konya declined, and did not recover until the coming of the republic.

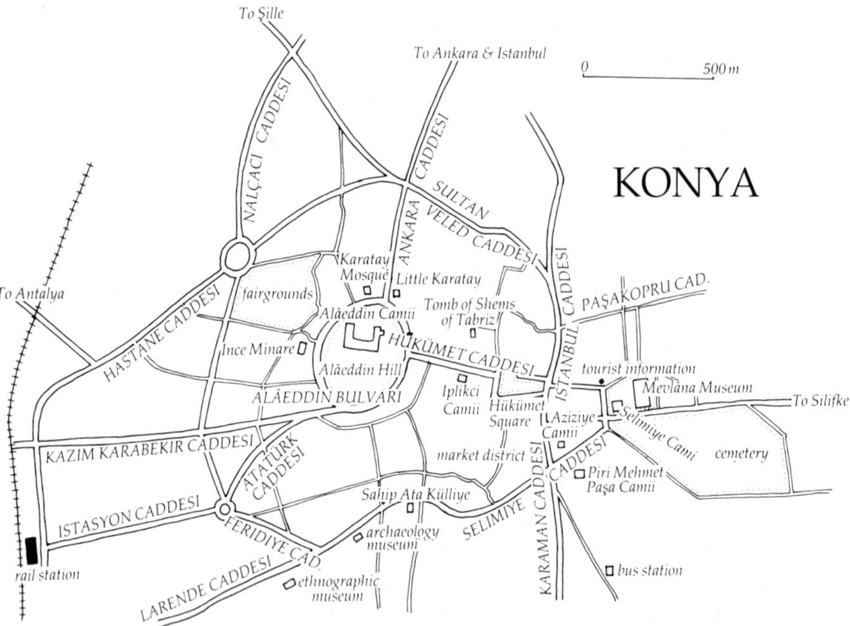

Celâleddin Rumi, the Mevlâna, one of the great mystics of Islam and founder of the 'Whirling' Mevlevi dervishes, was the most famous of all the figures of Konya's golden age (see Turkish Topics) and his spirit continues to animate the city today. Throughout the Ottoman period, Mevlevi sheikhs were often close advisors to the Sultan. Even in 1919, Konya elected the sheikh (the head of the order) to represent it at the first Turkish National Assembly. Today dervishes may be less conspicuous, but the people of Konya like to joke that they're still going around in circles; any trip through the town is likely to lead through the **Alâeddin Bulvari,** the circular road around the Alaeddin Hill in the centre of the city. If you wonder about this little mound, all alone in the broad plain of Konya, you are right to do so; this is a *tell*, the sort of hill that grows up wherever a small town or village occupies a site continuously for thousands of years. Later cultures, including the Selcuks, simply built over the top. The **Alâeddin Kiosk**, the palace of the Selcuk Sultans, or rather the last little bit of it, still stands, lovingly preserved under a modern arched pavilion; interestingly, they built their schools and religious buildings in stone and good brick, but expended only cheap mud brick and conglomerate on themselves.

ALÂEDDIN MOSQUE

Their **Alâeddin Mosque,** begun by Sultan Rukaeddin Mesut in 1130 and finally completed by Alâeddin Keykubad in 1221, has fared somewhat better. Though well built, its position on the northern slope of the unstable mound has made almost constant restoration work a necessity; they're busy on it now. The changes and additions of various Sultans over those 91 years explain the unusual form of the mosque; together with its courtyard behind the great façade, it has the shape of an open book, with a large pillared hall in one corner. The plan of this hall is that of the Selcuk 'great mosques' all over Turkey, but here the neat rows of columns are marble, re-used from Greek and Byzantine buildings. There are more old columns on the façade; the Selcuks apparently found them in different sizes, and cleverly arranged them in a series of arches, slanted to match the slope of the hill. At the centre of the structure are two large *türbes* (tombs). The largest, with a conical roof, contains the bodies of eight Selcuk Sultans, including Alâeddin Keykubad, all in tiled sarcophagi; the adjacent *türbe* stands empty.

KARATAY MEDRESE

The rest of Alâeddin Hill, once all part of the Sultan of Rum's palace grounds, has been rehabilitated and planted with pine trees and flowerbeds among shady cafes. Just across Alâeddin Bulvari from the mosque stands another Selcuk masterpiece, the **Karatay Medrese.** Once famous for its dome of coloured tiles, this former theological school has now fittingly become a museum of Selcuk and Ottoman ceramics. Much of this building complex, like so much else the Selcuks built, has disappeared, but fortunately the portal still stands, echoing the Alâeddin Mosque across the way, with its geometric patterns in white and blue-grey stone. Nothing symbolises the synthesis of cultures the Selcuks tried to create better than this gate. Influences of the Arab and Persian are obvious, and the Greek declares itself in two Corinthian columns flanking the entrances; even the ancient Phrygians seem to be recalled in the geometric lattices of the lower section. This isn't too unlikely; the great Phrygian temple façades aren't very far from Konya, and they must have been known at the time.

The Dome of Stars

Few museum buildings are their own prize exhibit; nothing in the collection of this one, in fact nothing in Turkey, can compare with the Karatay's domed mosque, completely covered in miniature tiles of unsurpassed precision and intensity of colour. These are not the large painted squares of Ottoman Iznik, but a kind of mosaic, in which every colour is fired separately for perfection of colour and glaze. These geometric stars of 24 points, set in neat rows against a deep blue background are meant to represent a firmament of stars. This is a specifically Islamic approach; in many of Turkey's museums there are carefully detailed star charts and almanacs, the legacy of the great Moslem achievement in astronomy, but there are hardly ever actual stars or constellations depicted on them, as if the Islamic prohibition of images extended to the stars themselves. These geometric stars, with a hint of orange fire at the centre, shine like the real thing, and their interconnection demonstrates the divine pattern and meaning in a way that might never occur to a non-Moslem. The equally beautiful panel around the bottom of the dome is an inscription, in a flowering Kufic script, of the words from the Book of the Cow, the first and longest sura of the Koran (and the most tedious stretch of inspired poetry ever written).

Of the other tiles collected for the museum, the examples of later Ottoman work look almost primitive compared to the fine Selcuk fancy; the strict avoidance of living forms was fine for theological schools, but the Selcuk princes enjoyed nothing in their art so much as the kind of birds and fantasy animals and crowned angels displayed here. One plate portrays a *simurgh*, the mythical king of the birds, the object of the mystical search in the great Persian poem *Parliament of the Birds*, which was a favourite among princes and dervishes alike in Selcuk times (and the source of Chaucer's *Parliament of the Fowles*.) Across the street, sheltered under a pavilion like the Alâeddin Kiosk, you can see the portal and sparse remains of another Selcuk school, the **Little Karatay Medrese.**

INCE MINARE MEDRESE

If any film director ever needed a backdrop for the palace of a science-fiction Emperor of Mars, he would do well to study the portal of the **Ince Minare Medrese,** three blocks down Alâeddin Bulvari. This is no insult either to the architect Keluk or to Fahreddin Ali, the Selcuk vezir who paid for it; the unique design and skilful carving of this gate can only be described as utterly bizarre. This complex too has suffered much during centuries of neglect; most of the outbuildings are gone, and the 'slender minaret' that gave the place its name, decorated in patterns of brick and blue tile like other Selcuk works in Sivas and Erzurum, was swatted down to stubbiness by a lightning bolt in 1901. The remains are now the **Museum of Selcuk Stone and Woodcarving.** As with the ceramics, many of the artefacts are from the Selcuk palace on Alâeddin Hill, and the same fantastical forms are represented. Continuing your whirl around Alâeddin Bulvari, you pass a nineteenth-century French church and then, one block later, come to Hükümet Caddesi, the business street of the modern town and the way to the Mevlâna's tomb; there are relics of the mystic throughout the area. On Hükümet, the many reconstructions of the thirteenth-century **Iplikci Camii** have left only a plain brick barn, but this is the mosque in which the Mevlâna did much of his teaching and practised his meditations. The tomb of his spiritual guide, Shems ed-din of Tabriz, a mysterious dervish from Persia, can be seen on a side street two blocks north. The Mevlâna's own disciples murdered this Shems under strange circumstances.

Further down Hükümet Caddesi skirts the market district, passing through a large square with the sixteenth-century **Şerafettin Mosque,** a distinguished Ottoman-style work that replaced a Selcuk original destroyed by fire. Beyond that the street changes its name to Mevlâna Caddesi, and the famous green tiled dome of Rumi's tomb comes into view.

MEVLANA MUSEUM

It is believed the site of the **Mevlâna Museum,** formerly the central *tekke* (dervish house) of the Mevlevi order and burial place of Celaleddin Rumi, was a garden belonging to the Selcuk Sultans, presented as a gift to the Mevlâna's father, Bahaeddin Veled. He was buried here in 1232, and when the Mevlâna joined him in 1273, work was immediately begun on a cylindrical *türbe.* Over the years, the buildings adjacent to the *tekke* were enlarged and expanded; the whole seems to have been reconstructed in the fifteenth century under the patronage of the Ottoman Sultans, particularly Beyazit II. Over the nearly 700 years of the *tekke*'s existence, the çelebis ('inheritors'), the descendants of the Mevlâna onto whom passed the hereditary leadership of the order, were men influential not only in Konya and among the dervishes, but in the affairs of the Empire as well.

By the twentieth century, it seemed to many that such influence, and such easy living, had staled the original spiritual impulse, and the Mevlevi sheikhs were known to be among the most reactionary and self-serving upholders of the old order. Atatürk's inability to prevent them from interfering in the politics of his new republic was the main cause of his decree dissolving the dervish orders. In 1925, a year later, the Konya *tekke* became the first of Atatürk's new museums, with the title of **Konya Museum of Ancient Works.**

If you thought the Turkish republicans were strongly anti-clerical, just look at the back of a 5000 lire note; Atatürk, of course, is on the front, but on the reverse is the Mevlâna himself, smiling beatifically next to the watermark. Dervishes of the Mevlevi and other orders do still practise semi-openly in modern Turkey, and as long as religion stays out of politics, the authorities are content. Even though this *tekke*, along with the others, has been secularised, most Turks still see it as a holy site; most of the visitors at the museum are not tourists, but Turks from all walks of life, good Moslems come to pray at the tomb of a man they regard almost as a saint.

Through the entrance, incongruously embellished with a ticket window, you pass into a small courtyard. The fountain on the left is the **şadirvan,** where ablutions are performed before prayer, that on the right the **Şeb'i Arus** (wedding night pool), a gift of Yavuz Selim; the Mevlâna, in his later years, always spoke of his coming death as a 'wedding', an event to be celebrated rather than mourned, and on its anniversary every December 17 (a modern adjustment from the Moslem calendar), the dervishes performed their whirling dance, the *sema*, around this fountain in remembrance. Three small *türbes* nearby with shallow domes belong to governors of the sixteenth century, when Konya was subject to the Karamanoğullari emirs, themselves also patrons of the Mevlevis.

The Green Dome

Inside the main building, beyond a hall containing exhibits of Islamic calligraphy, lie the Mevlâna, his father, his son Sultan Veled, and other notables of the order, all in elaborate sarcophagi covered with richly embroidered cloths, with the turbans of the deceased placed at the top; six of the sarcophagi belong to the 'men of Horosan' who accompanied the Mevlâna and his father in their flight to Konya. The famous **green dome,** Konya's most conspicuous landmark, rises over the Mevlâna's sarcophagus. On the outside, the blue band of tiles around the dome has the words of the *bismele*, the formula 'In the name of Allah, the compassionate, the merciful', that begins each book of the Koran. Inside, the dome is covered with a pattern of geometric stars; the Mevlevis called it the 'Dome of the Pole'.

Anyone may feel sceptical seeing how much show and glitter have accumulated around the grave of a saintly and humble man. Rather than being any reflection on the Mevlâna, the vast array of sumptuous carpets, cloths, and other works of art show the favour the Mevlevis always enjoyed with the powerful, for almost everything here came as gifts from Sultans and princes. One of the exceptions to this is the Mevlâna's sarcophagus, a triumph of Turkish woodcarving, done by an artist named Abdulvahid solely as a labour of love. Built entirely without nails, the sarcophagus is completely covered with Mevlâna's poetry, carved in different styles and patterns of calligraphy. The introductory inscription begins: 'Here lies Mevlâna, sultan of scholars ...'.

His prayer carpet, said to be a wedding gift from Alâeddin Keykubad, is a work of art in its own right, but it cannot compare with another on display, a 500-year old silk carpet from Persia, said to be the finest ever woven; it has 144 knots to the square centimetre, 2 197 000 in all—it isn't surprising it took five years to complete. Other treasures include musical instruments and books, among them the illuminated first edition of Mevlâna's great poetical work the *Mathnawi*; another is the April Cup, a huge and beautifully carved crater of gold, silver, and bronze, made in Baghdad and presented to the Mevlevis by Elen Said Bahadir, the last Ilhanli Mongol ruler of Mesopotamia.

The Semahane

The **semahane**, a grand vaulted hall adjacent to the mosque and tombs, was the site of the *sema*, the whirling dance, still performed here every year in December. With its carpets and delicate chandeliers, it is as opulent as the tombs. The great chain suspended from the ceiling to balance the chandeliers was carved from a single piece of marble, link by link. Note also the separate galleries for women spectators at the *sema*; although Mevlâna himself had little use for such foolishness, later dervishes have been notoriously afraid of women, and prefer to keep them out of sight lest they be distracted.

Other parts of the museum that may be viewed are outside the complex of tomb and semahane. The **dervishes' cells** line parts of the compound's walls; some have been restored to their original appearance, as also has the **soup kitchen,** where would-be dervishes served an apprenticeship of 1001 days while learning the manners and precepts of the order. Next to the **sheikh's quarters,** now the museum office, stands the famous library of 5000 old works on the Mevlevis and Islamic mysticism. The southern gate of the outer wall leads to a dervish cemetery, the **Garden of Souls.**

OTHER SIGHTS

Sultan Selim I, Yavuz Selim, of all the Ottoman rulers perhaps the most devoted to the work of Mevlâna, left behind the large **Selimiye Mosque** next to the Mevlevi House. With little of the architectural sophistication Selim could get in Istanbul where the Selimiye is one of the finest Imperial mosques, this ungainly work, in elevation a simple cube, is domed and surrounded by domed arcades. From here, a walk down Selimiye Caddesi through the **bazaar** and Konya's southern districts will reveal some of the city's other monuments.

Selim's reign also saw the construction of the **Piri Mehmet Pasha Camii,** built around the turbe of its founder. Another, more endearing mosque right at the centre of the market district is the **Aziziye Camii,** a seventeenth-century structure rebuilt by Sultan Abdul Aziz in 1867 in the gaudiest style of Turkish Rococo, for in sober grey Konya this confection with its impossible minarets stands out like an uptown whore at a school board meeting. Continuing along Selimiye Caddesi, you pass another of the great Selcuk works, the 1258 **Sahip Ata Külliye,** founded by the famous vezir Fahrettin Ali. Its half-ruined state and out-of-the-way location have conspired to keep this complex obscure, but its brick and stone entrance portal is as fine as any in Konya. Konya's **archaeological museum,** two blocks further down where Selimiye changes its name to Larende Caddesi, has an unremarkable collection, except for three well-preserved Roman sarcophagi from Pamphylia. The best known, the Hercules Sarcophagus from about AD 260, depicts the hero gliding through all twelve of his labours.

The Plain of Konya

Konya province, the largest in Turkey, is also one of its most important agricultural regions. One would hardly guess this from looking at a map on which the region appears a strangely empty space, stretching over a hundred and fifty miles from the lake district to Cappadocia. There's really no anomaly—it looks even emptier when you're in it. Somehow, lonesome flat country is always good for wheat, and this is one of the best. Its farmers have serious faces, rosy children, and shiny new Türk Fiat tractors, and they do a lot to keep Turkey self-sufficient in food.

They were at it with much the same vigour eight thousand years ago, with enough leisure left over to create one of the world's first urban cultures, at least until archaeologists find an even older one. History used to begin with Sumer. Now with the great discoveries by James Mellaart at **Çatal Höyük,** we must say it begins here on the Plain of Konya, where long before nation-states, sky-gods or warrior castes, this town, and probably dozens like it, lived what seems an easy and blessedly peaceful existence in trade and agriculture, and making the beautiful works of art on display in the Ankara museum. Don't bother to visit the site—all you will get there is a lesson in the archaeologist's talent in recreating a culture from the tiniest of clues.

The road that passes Çatal Höyük continues on to the Mediterranean coast at Silifke, crossing the beautiful Taurus after **Karaman,** the Larende of ancient times and capital of the Karamanoğullari Turks after the fall of the Empire of Rum. Karaman has its castle, most noteworthy for being the only one in Turkey with its name in an electric sign on top, a fourteenth-century Mevlevi house called Ak Tekke, and a number of other mosques built by the Karamanoğullari. Further along through the mountains, a once great fifth-century Byzantine monastery may be seen at **Alahan;** there are many others in various states of ruin in the area the Turks, with some exaggeration, call **Binbir Kilise** (1001 churches). Here also was the once-thriving city of Derbe, one of the places St Paul visited on his trip through Asia Minor; nothing of the city remains.

North of Konya, the roads to Ankara and Kayseri pass on either side of **Tuz Gölü,** the Salt Lake, a soberingly dismal corner of the republic. Both these roads were important in Selcuk times, and the Sultans of Rum built a large number of elegant *hans*, or caravanserais, along them, free of charge to merchants and travellers. You see them particularly on the route to Kayseri, mostly in ruins, every nine miles, the distance a caravan could cover in a day. The best preserved is at **Sultanhani,** about 100 kilometres north-east of Konya. Alâeddin Keykubad built it in 1229; lately it has been restored with some modern stonework as good as the Selcuks'; the town plans to convert it into a motel.

West of Konya: The Lakes Region

Two roads lead westward from Konya, not counting the short cul-de-sac to the pretty, bucolic village of **Sille;** here, the **Aya Eleni** church in its original form, may have been as early as the fifth century, but it was rebuilt in the nineteenth. There are paintings to see inside, if the key can be found. Of the two major roads, both travel to towns on mountain lakes. **Akşehir** claims to be the home of Nasreddin Hoca (see **Turkish Topics**); you can buy a postcard of the famous picture of him seated backwards on his donkey, and visit his **tomb** in a little pavilion on the town green. On the gate is a big heavy lock, though it's open on the other three sides. **Beyşehir,** on the lake of the same name, has a mosque and medrese from the Karamanoğullari era; nearby, along the lakeshore, is a Hittite relief at **Eflatun Pinari.**

This region of lakes, famous in Turkey for carpets and attar of roses, has only its mountain scenery to detain travellers on their way to the coasts. **Burdur** and **Isparta,** the two provincial capitals, are pleasant towns, and the lakes, especially **Beyşehir Gölü** and **Eğridir Gölü** are dotted with islands with tiny, isolated fishing villages. Between them, a new national park has been established, the **Kizildağ Milli Parki.**

GETTING AROUND

Konya has no airport, but trains from Istanbul pass through Akşehir, Konya, and Karaman on their way to Adana. Here your best bet is the bus, and as usual, there will be no problem making connections to any of the towns. The train station is on Feritpaşa Caddesi, about 2 kilometres south-west of the Alâeddin Hill.

The bus depot is equally far, but towards the south-west, not far from the Mevlâna museum.

Konya is a rather compact city, and you can easily go everywhere on foot.

TOURIST INFORMATION

Konya 21 Mevlana Caddesi, across from the Mevlâna museum, tel. (331) 12032–10000. In Konya, the city tourism association runs a small bookstore on Mevlana Caddesi with some books in English about the city and the Mevlevis.

Isparta: Gazi Kemal Mohallesi Yeni Hamam Arkasi, tel. (32) 144 38.

WHERE TO STAY

The outstanding establishment in Konya, the **Hotel Konya** (H4) is just off Mevlana Caddesi, a block from the Museum, and one of the best-run hotels in Anatolia, and a good bargain besides. Tel. (331) 210 03–166 77; singles 4000 TL, doubles 5700 TL. There's also the modern **Yeni Sema Oteli** on Yeni Meram Yolu, tel. (331) 132 79–159 92, with TV and refrigerators in the rooms for 5300 TL a single, 7500 TL a double; the only hitch is that it's inconvenient unless you have a car. Less expensive, the quiet **Selcuk Oteli,** off Alaeddin Bulvari, tel. (331) 112 59 is in the centre of town, with doubles for 4000 TL, 5000 TL with private bath. There are other hotels less expensive, serving the many Moslems who come to Konya on pilgrimages; they are all clean and very basic.

In the rest of the province, and in the lake region, accommodation is sparse and simple; there are motels on the lakes at Burdur, like the inexpensive **Plaj Motel** (unlisted) and at Eğridir. In Isparta, the most comfortable hotel is the **Bolat** at Demirel Bul. 71, tel. (327) 189 98–155 06, with a tennis court, and singles for 3000 TL, doubles for 4000 TL.

EATING OUT

Konya's most popular elegant restaurant is the **Fuar Lokanta** in the fairgrounds just off Alaeddin Bulvari, with a pleasant outdoor terrace and entertainment; the sweet *tel kadayif* is their dessert speciality. Meals are about 7000 TL. Less costly, the **Çatal Lokantasi** by the Mevlâna museum, specialising in meat, has meals for around 2000 TL. There are other low priced lokantas around Hükümet Caddesi.

Cappadocia

HISTORY

Although never an identifiable nation like Lydia or Phrygia, Cappadocia was known as a kingdom as early as 600 BC; it was probably a loose confederacy united to keep the Persians out, which didn't always work. Though often reduced to a tributary state of the Persian empire, Cappadocia survived until the Romans came, an obscure state of Asia Minor with kings named either Ariarathres or Ariobarzanes, ruling from the capital first at Nyssa (perhaps the modern Nevşehir), and later at Mazaca (today's Kayseri).

In AD 17, Emperor Tiberius' legions invited themselves in, and Cappadocia became a Roman province. Still a backwater, it never did receive its share of theatres or aqueducts; in fact its only discernible benefit from joining the Mediterranean community was a visit from St Paul, who corralled the inhabitants for Christianity with ease. St Paul never had to rebuke the Cappadocians as he did the Galatians. So fervently did they take to the new creed that Cappadocia replaced Africa as the great stronghold of Christian monasticism, and remained such for well over a thousand years. St Basil, fourth-century prelate who laid down the rules for Orthodox monks, as St Benedict was later to do for the Christians of the west, was bishop of Caesarea (Kayseri) and contributed much to the progress of monasticism.

THE CAPPADOCIAN LANDSCAPE

The real history of Cappadocia though, begins some 30 million years ago. In the Cenozoic era, Erciyes Dağ, Hasan Dağ, and Melendiz Dağ, the three tall peaks that dominate the region, were still active volcanoes. Over millions of years, their eruptions covered the land between them with thick layers of volcanic tufa, a type of stone made of compressed volcanic ash that is soft and easily worked. A few million more years of erosion turned Cappadocia into a dream landscape that attracted the hermits of early Christianity, and now entertains a hundred thousand visitors each year.

Words fail the honest writer attempting to do justice to the Cappadocian landscape; landscape, in fact, does not even seem the right word, for no other corner of the earth can have anything like the twisted, billowing forms found in the rocks of Göreme or Ortahisar. What makes Cappadocia so exceedingly strange is the very domesticity of the place. Somewhere, in wandering through the valley of Göreme you may run across a stack of tufa shaped like a banana sticking out of the ground, white as sugar, with a door and window cut at the base, hollowed out long ago by a hermit or just a local farmer. On the window is a potted geranium, and on the doormat will be a sleeping cat.

Kirşehir and Hacibektaş

If you are travelling from Ankara, to reach Cappadocia you pass through towns that have nothing to do with the Greek–Christian air of the cave cities, but add an Islamic angle to the ambient piety; both were the homes of mystic Moslem sects that gained great popularity in the late Middle Ages. **Kirşehir** was headquarters of the Ahi brotherhood, a sensible, plain-living society, widespread among the artisan guides and workmen of central Anatolia. Following the precepts of their leader, Ahi Evran, who is buried here, the Ahis became renowned less for their mystic accomplishments than for their hospitality and good fellowship. Kirşehir's medieval monuments include the **Cacabey Mosque,** built by the Ilhanli Mongols, and the **Alâeddin Mosque,** of which only the richly ornamented portal remains. 'Alâeddin' stands, of course, for Alâeddin Keykubad, the indefatigable Selcuk sultan who contributed something to every town in central Anatolia.

THE BEKTAŞIS

In the same century, the thirteenth, another dervish named Hacibektaş Veli, preaching a message of moderation and discipline, founded the Bektaşi order. When he became spiritual leader of a newly-founded Janissary Corps, his order began its career as the most influential in the Ottoman state, surpassing even the Mevlevis. His tomb, and the former head Bektaşi tekke, are now a **museum** in the town of **Hacibektaş** renamed in his honour. The tomb lies behind a gilded door; here, also, is the beautiful hall where the dervishes performed their rituals, and where the sarcophagi of other notables of their order are alongside three unknown women, mysteriously known only as the 'Beauties of the World'. Other buildings of the complex you may visit are the soup kitchen, perhaps the most important of all for the complicated symbolism the Bektaşis and their Janissary followers built up around the eating of soup. The great cauldron hanging in the hearth is the famous 'Karakazan', the Black Kettle; the Janissaries paraded it through the streets of Istanbul to show their displeasure with the Sultan whenever they felt like deposing one. A Bektaşi festival is still held in Hacibektaş every August 15th to 18th. From here, another 50 kilometres takes you to **Nevşehir.**

Although the castle on the hill above the city dates from the Selcuks, Nevşehir is not an old city. Damad Ibrahim Paşa, an Ottoman Grand Vezir of the Tulip Period, famous for attempts at reform and for introducing European art and culture into Turkey, was born in the tiny village that was Nevşehir in the 1600s. He re-founded it as a city, and built mosques, schools, and libraries; his statue stands in the centre of the town.

Central Cappadocia

Ancient Cappadocia was a large province, but don't be dismayed; seeing its scenic marvels will not require any long or difficult travel. Most of the rock cities, as well as the valley of Göreme, are located between Nevşehir and

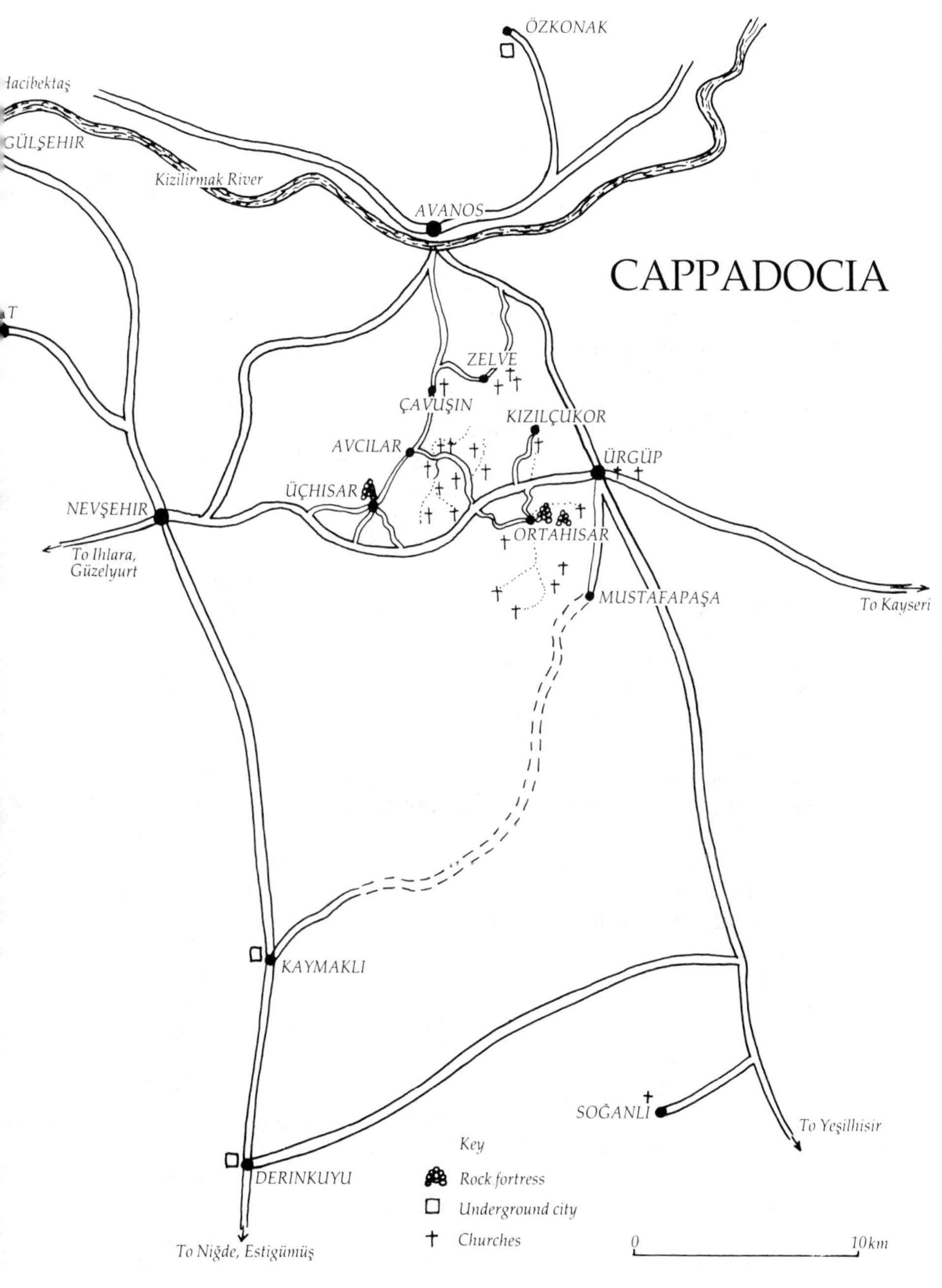

CAPPADOCIA
ÖZKONAK
Hacibektaş
GÜLŞEHIR
Kizilirmak River
AVANOS
ZELVE
ÇAVUŞIN
KIZILÇUKOR
AVCILAR
ÜRGÜP
ÜÇHISAR
NEVŞEHIR
ORTAHISAR
To Ihlara, Güzelyurt
MUSTAFAPAŞA
To Kayseri
KAYMAKLI
SOĞANLI
To Yeşilhisir
DERINKUYU
Key
Rock fortress
Underground city
Churches
0
10km
To Niğde, Estigümüş

Ürgüp, only 18 kilometres to the east. Halfway along this route, the triple rock of **Üçhisar** introduces you to the oddities of the region. Although the villagers of Üçhisar have long ago moved down into more modern lodgings, the peak, the largest in the area, remains laced with the tunnels and chambers they used when it served as their giant apartment house. From the top—a road leads most of the way up—there is a panoramic view of the Göreme valley, just to the east. Come past at night, if you can; the entire rock is illuminated, appearing like some Post-Impressionist skyscraper. If you mean to do any exploring in Üçhisar, *be careful*; some of the floors are weak and could collapse. Keep this caveat in mind for the rest of Cappadocia, too, though there is little danger in seeing the main attractions.

From Üçhisar to Göreme, the road passes more curiosities, including some of the famous **fairy chimneys,** tall needles of stone, often with large rocks balanced on top. Their volcanic origin is not hard to detect. As well as vast quantities of ash, Mt Erciyes would occasionally toss out some boulders of hard basalt. During the periods of erosion, these boulders protected the ash, now hardened into tufa beneath, resulting in a column that grows taller as the land around it is ground away. Also on this road, there is a view point to the right, from which you can see one of the most remarkable corners of Göreme. By now you will certainly have been surprised at the greenness and fertility of this part of Cappadocia; if you saw pictures, you will have come expecting desert rockpiles, only to find instead rolling hills of pretty farms, olive groves and vineyards; the region is famous for its wine. Beneath the good volcanic soil are the rocks, and you must look hard to distinguish the valleys where they have been eroded away. Here, masses of glistening white tufa, blown into shapes of futuristic World's Fair pavilions, fill the valley, dotted here and there with doors and windows, with little gardens and citrus orchards with the spaces between. Some of the outcrops are shaped like lemons, and oddly enough, the farmers use them for storing the lemons and oranges they grow here.

Göreme

The valley of Göreme goes on and on, the scenes changing continuously; many visitors become quite entranced and spend days wandering along its quiet paths. If you haven't the time, at least visit the **Göreme open air museum** where over two dozen churches, some with beautifully painted frescoes, make up the largest monastic complex in the region, all hewn out of the cliffs and crags and joined by stairs, paths, and tunnels. Two very distinct styles of Byzantine painting between them explain something of the Iconoclastic conflict of the eighth and ninth centuries, the bitter struggle over images (and church politics) that sent so many refugees into Cappadocia. Those painted just after the downfall of the Iconoclasts are awkward, almost primitive geometric patterns and symbols—the Greeks had forgotten how to draw. By the tenth century, however, in the surprisingly quick renaissance of art that followed, the monks of Cappadocia contributed some of the finest examples of Byzantine painting.

Most of the churches are called after some feature of the paintings; the **Church with the Apple,** for example. Many of these small churches are carved with arches, pillars, vaults, and domes, distinguishable from an ordinary church only by a lack of windows. In the Church with the Apple, many of the frescoes have peeled away, revealing the simple post-Iconoclastic decoration underneath, like many others, this one has been much defaced by graffiti, the oldest in Greek, the most recent in Turkish, as high up as an adolescent can reach. Only recently has the government spent money to protect and restore them.

Among the other noteworthy churches nearby are the **Church with the Buckle,** with painted scenes from the life of St Basil; the **Church of the Sandal,** where an imprint on the floor is said to be a cast of Jesus' own footstep, brought from Jerusalem; and the **Dark Church** with familiar New Testament scenes, in some of the best work in Cappadocia, recently restored by UNESCO. The **Church with the Snake** shows St George with his dragon, also large figures of Helen and Constantine holding the true cross. There's more fine work at the **Hidden Church,** if you can find it. Further inside the complex the **Jerphanion Church,** named after the French art historian who spent his life uncovering and cataloguing the Göreme paintings, has some of the most interesting primitive frescoes.

Two large, self-contained monasteries can be seen near the valley, the **Firkatan** for men and the **Girls Monastery,** accommodating some 300 nuns, a network of tunnels, cells, and churches on three floors, carved from a large crag. From here, several other attractions of the Göreme valley can be reached on foot, all within a radius of three kilometres: **Avcilar** is a rock city, with a skyline of fairy chimneys around its newer houses. Another is **Çavuşin,** where half the original rock collapsed long ago, leaving the walls and corridors of the ancient rock town open to the sky; in places, the crag is so thin you can see through it. A strairway leads up into the Çavuşin Church, guarded by frescoes of the angels Michael and Gabriel which were exposed by the collapse; inside are more fine paintings, scenes from the life of Christ.

Kizilçukor and Ortahisar

Kizilçukor, a village somewhat further east, has been a wine-making centre since antiquity, and its **Church of the Grapes** has frescoes of scenes of the harvest and wine-making, as well as the usual saints. Five kilometres to the south, the crumbling crag of **Ortahisar** is perhaps the only rock in the world with sash windows; there's an electric sign on top, too. Enough of Ortahisar has been repaired so that you can climb to the top for a view of further religious complexes, fairy chimneys and strange forms. Several churches in the area worth visiting include the **Church with the Hare** and the **Church of the Beet,** both with eleventh-century frescoes.

Zelve

There is yet another canyon full of churches, 6 kilometres northeast of the Göreme museum, at **Zelve** a district where, in some spots, the fairy chimneys grow as thick as trees in a forest. Two old valleys converge at the site of the complex, eroded from the warm, tan rock with, between them, an outcrop shaped like a steamship. Among the many churches is another **Church with the Grape** which has some primitive paintings. Here too, parts of the cliffs have collapsed, exposing, in one spot, a wall lined with neatly cut compartments in rows, just like pigeonholes in a post office.

At the far end of the left-hand valley, you can pick your way through a narrow natural tunnel in the rocks and come out into a beautiful isolated canyon, full of wild flowers around a running stream. Cappadocia is full of surprises like this, both natural and man-made. As times grew worse in the later days of the Byzantine Empire, when the monastic communities began to suffer from raids of marauding Turkish and Arab tribes, defence became a prime consideration. The best defence for the peaceful monks was concealment; and many of the monastic buildings are cleverly hidden in crevices in the cliff faces; undoubtedly some exist that have not yet been discovered.

Avanos

At its northern fringes, Cappadocia touches the southernmost bend of the Kizilirmak River; the red clay along its banks has kept the potters of **Avanos** in business for thousands of years. Avanos is an attractive town, reached from Göreme or Nevşehir by an elaborate old bridge over the Kizilirmak. At the centre, a statue of a potter working testifies to the fame the Avanos work has always had in Antolia. Traditionally painted red with a minimum of decoration, the modern artisans are enjoying something of a revival, selling tons of their work to Cappadocia's tourists. Just east of Avanos, on the old road to Nevşehir, stands another of the caravansarais built by the Selcuk Sultan Alâeddin Keykubad, the **Sarihan,** with an elaborate entrance portal. Avanos and Nevşehir form the two corners of a triangle that bounds most of the sights in the region; the third point would be at **Ürgüp,** the most popular base for visitors to Cappadocia.

Ürgüp

Even more than Avanos, Ürgüp is an exceptionally lovely town, unlike any other in Turkey, with its Belgian-block paved streets and unusual designs carved into the stone of the older buildings. Like Üçhisar and Ortahisar, it has come down from the cliffs in recent decades. Here, however, a few of the cave houses are still occupied; one troglodyte on the edge of the town has recently added a cave-garage for his new car. Ürgüp has most of the region's hotels and restaurants, and also a small **museum** in the city park. Most of the region's vineyards are on the roads just outside Ürgüp. South of the town, the road to Yeşilhisar passes through other towns with cave churches: **Mustafapaşa, Camil,** and the furthest, **Soğanli:** Here, unlike the other sites in which churches are merely cut into the rocks, is a crag that has been sculpted into a church, with even a typical Byzantine cylindrical dome; there are frescoes inside. The locals call it the **Church with the Beret.**

Underground Cities

On top of all this, the most outlandish feature of the Cappadocian fun-house has not yet even been mentioned: the **underground cities.** Six have been discovered so far, and three have been excavated and lit for visitors, at least for a small part of their total extent. Each of them was capable of accommodating several thousand inhabitants, supplied with water by underground springs and air through an elaborate ventilation system.

None have been completely explored—they haven't even found the bottom of one yet. The best known, at Derinkuyu, goes down at least fifteen floors, with air shafts as deep as 400 feet. At Özkonak, the top levels cover some nine square kilometres. Strangest of all, these cities are all interconnected by a network of tunnels, some as much as six miles long. No one knows who built them. Medieval Christians certainly occupied them, but a Roman tomb has also been found on the seventh level of one, and a Hittite-style grain mill deep in another. No one has yet found a mention of them in any history or book of travels, ancient or modern. They must have taken centuries to create; all tunnels and corridors are narrow, and only one man at a time could have worked at digging them. It's most likely that the cities were never continuously occupied, but rather always served the inhabitants of the region as refuges in times of trouble.

The history of warfare has shown that there is no such thing as an invulnerable fortress, but these may be the exception. Storming them would be quite impossible; at all the entrances, and even at many points within the cities, great round 'blocking stones' were set that could seal off the passage in a minute, with no room for the enemy to work at moving them, and with plenty of slits in the walls through which the defenders could thrust in their spears. Secret entrances and hundreds of airshaft openings are scattered over miles of difficult terrain; it would be impossible for an enemy to find them, and wonderfully easy for the people inside to send out forces to harry the attackers, or restock their supplies.

Whoever was responsible for all this, something in it smacks of a bad case of paranoia. Even if built over a period of centuries, the effort to create such prodigies of mole-work could only come from a slave empire with a large economic surplus—of which there is no record here—or an obsession on the part of some petty rulers. There were never many big towns in this part of Anatolia, and it is highly unlikely that any enemy could have been so terrible to country people as to drive them to such extremes.

You may choose which of the three to visit; **Özkonak** is on a dirt road 21 kilometres north of Avanos, and the other two, **Kaymakli** and **Derinkuyu** are south of Nevşehir, 20 and 30 kilometres respectively. None of the three have any special features; the cities are strictly utilitarian, with no embellishment. All have 'blocking stones' and other defensive features, and churches, common dining halls, even tombs marked out in them. All three will wear you out, climbing back up from the lower levels, but the air is surprisingly fresh, and the temperature always cool. In Derinkuyu you can also visit the very unusual **Greek Church** of the last century, with blind arcades, lovely carvings of birds, vines, and floral crosses that hint of an Armenian influence. It has been locked up since the 1920s, and is deteriorating rapidly.

South and West of Göreme

For those not sated with the rupestrian excess of the Göreme area, little bits have spilled over into the lands west and south. On the lowest slopes of **Hasan Dağ,** an extinct volcano, the valley of **Ihlara** has another entire complex of churches in a steep and picturesque valley. Nearby, a side road leads off to the town of **Güzelyurt,** built over and below a cliff full of caves, with another nineteenth-century Greek church and some houses decorated in the same style as in Ürgüp.

Eskigümüş

To the south of Göreme, the road through Derinkuyu continues on to **Eskigümüş** ('old silver'), a former troglodyte colony with yet another Byzantine monastery cut into the cliffs; especially interesting here is the large, open courtyard carved out of the rock, completely hidden from view from the outside. Cells and corridors are carved into the sides on several levels, with sockets from beams and posts that suggest the entire space was once filled with a building of several storeys completely encased in solid rock. Frescoes in the church within, from the seventh to the eleventh centuries, include some particularly well executed figures of Christ, Mary, and the saints. To the left of the narthex, the 600-foot escape tunnel is typical of the precautions medieval monks were forced to take.

Niğde

Niğde, a quiet provincial capital west of Hasan Dağ, marks the southern limits of the land of fairy chimneys and caves. Quiet is the word, for somehow, between Selcuks and Karamanoğullari, Mongols and Ottomans, Niğde has avoided having much history. All the same, it managed to get a good building or two from most of its medieval rulers, and while none are exceptional on their own, together they make a lovely and unified city scape.

Sultan Alâeddin Keykubad is represented here up in the deserted citadel, in the **Alâeddin Mosque** (1223), decorated in unusual geometric flowers and wave designs; its three domes is Niğde's landmark together with an odd minaret that looks more like a lighthouse. In the town below, the **Sungurbey Mosque** of 1335, built by and named after an Ilhanli Mongol emir, has a much more graceful, spirally-fluted minaret, but the decoration of its portal and roofline as in most works begun by the Mongols, are incomplete. Just off Bor Caddesi, the main street, the **Akmedrese** of 1409 is the Karamanoğullari contribution, having the uncommon feature of a loggia built into its façade. Other medieval mosques, as well as schools and fountains, two lovely *türbes* and a sixteenth-century *bedesten* in the bazaar under the citadel walls, combine to make Niğde one of the most architecturally distinguished cities of Anatolia. On the west side of town, the province keeps a small **museum** with a grave stele and handicrafts (but everyone really comes to see the Byzantine mummy).

GETTING AROUND

Cappadocia's attractions may be spread all over the map, but it's not really difficult to see a lot without a car. The very helpful tourist office in Ürgüp prints a timetable of the regular Ürgüp–Nevşehir and Ürgüp–Ortahisar bus services; there's a bus every two hours or so, and using it you can see any of the places like Göreme in between. Also Cappadocia is beautiful; a perfect spot for hiking, or biking. You can get a taxi out of Ürgüp or Nevşehir for a whole day for about 16 000 TL, or less expensively, just use them to get around between the villages.

Nevşehir, Niğde, and less frequently Ürgüp, have regular coach services in all directions.

TOURIST INFORMATION

Lâle Caddesi 22, tel. (4851) 112 28, Nevşehir. In Ürgüp, Kayseri Caddesi, in the park next to the museum, tel. (4868) 59. In Niğde, Vakif Işhani, in the central square, tel. 251.

WHERE TO STAY

As Cappadocia's popularity with tourists increases, the region is beginning to develop establishments that are quite chic by Turkish provincial standards. In Nevşehir the **Hotel Orsan Kapadokya** (H3), on Kayseri Cad., tel. (4851) 1035–2115, fits the bill, with singles for 5500 TL, doubles for 7000. In Ürgüp, there's a pretty, new motel of the Turban chain (M1), tel. (4868) 490–2, just west of town, where rates are 6500 TL a single, 8250 TL a double. Also in Ürgüp is the castle-like **Tepe Oteli** (H4), tel. (4868) 1154 with a swimming pool, at Teslemiye Tepesi, with singles at 4500 TL, doubles at 7000 TL. The Kaya Motel in Üçhisar, with its famous pool overlooking the fairy chimneys, has been taken over by the Club Méditerranée. A new addition to the hotels around Ürgüp, the most expensive one in Cappadocia, is quite possibly the ugliest building in Turkey: the **Boydaş Oteli** on the Ürgüp–Nevşehir road. In Ürgüp, Nevşehir, and Üçhisar you can find cheap pensions—the Ürgüp tourist office publishes a list of these with prices. There are also many campsites around Ürgüp and Nevşehir.

EATING OUT

There are several good restaurants in the centre of Ürgüp, the **Çirağan,** the **Kapadokya,** and the **Köşk,** all with Turkish specialities at around 3000 TL for a dinner. Anywhere else more than a simple lokanta is hard to come by.

Kayseri

Cappadocia's last capital, **Kayseri,** has something of a reputation. If you go there, strolling along the ancient streets around the centre of town looking at the wealth of medieval buildings left by the Selcuks, before long a well dressed young man will turn up, exchanging pleasantries with you in fluent English or French or German. Expressing a heartfelt interest in your well-being, he will offer many interesting sidelights on the city and its people to entertain you. About three minutes into the conversation, you will hear: 'You know, many (Americans, English, Germans, etc.) who come to Kayseri are interested in the fine carpets and kilims made here...' You have met your first commission agent; the further you walk, the more you'll encounter. An old Turkish proverb expresses it best, 'He can't read or write, but he's from Kayseri'. Turkish folklore abounds with tales of the Kayseri Man, the clever fellow who outwits the kadi, or the Jewish merchants, or the devil. He doesn't only sell carpets; Hrozny, the great Czech linguist who deciphered the Hittite hieroglyphics in 1912, found this out to his cost when the Kayseri Man sold him an inscribed tablet from the Hittite city of Kaneş and turned up again regularly over the next few months, each time with another newly 'discovered' tablet to sell; he'd bought them all for a pittance from a farmer, and dangled them before the poor scholar one at a time to get the best price.

HISTORY

Although Kayseri, originally called Mazaca, had already existed for a long time under the Persian-influenced Kingdom of Cappadocia, it was the Romans who first made it into a city; in return, they claimed the privilege of renaming it Caesarea, in honour of Augustus. Under the Byzantines, just as the city was growing into a religious and economic centre of some importance, the first bands of Moslem Arab raiders appeared, wrecking its prosperity, putting it to the sack on several occasions, and mangling its name into Kaisariyeh. Under that name, the city found itself playing a role in one of the stories of the Arabian Nights: the long, sad *Tale of King Umar al-Numan*, has a background of the king's struggle with Afridun, the 'Sultan of Constantinople' for the city. Despite the endless treachery of the Christians, aided by the redoubtable witch 'Mother of Calamity', the soldiers of Allah prevailed. Whatever really happened, in the story Kaisariyeh's defenders to a man converted to Islam and invited the Arabs in for tea.

Getting to Kayseri from fairy chimney-land involves a long detour around **Erciyes Daği,** a formidable snow-clad volcano; at 12 727 feet it is Turkey's highest peak west of Ararat. The mountain was well known in classical times as Mount Argaeus, a word meaning 'bright' or 'white' and on certain days with the sun behind it (the mountain lies south of Kayseri) Erciyes does seem to glow, a wonderful sight wreathed in its entourage of clouds.

THE TOWN

Nobody in Kayseri can explain why there should be two Atatürk monuments, one beside the other, in the chaotic, nameless **square** where the Sivas and Istanbul roads meet at the heart of town. Most of Kayseri's fine medieval monuments are very near, but the old city around them has been bulldozed to make way for new apartment blocks and boulevards. Kayseri wants to be up-to-date, and unlike traditional Konya, all its old districts seem to suffer except the bazaar. Right on the square, the black basalt walls of the **citadel** still watch over Kayseri. Built by the Byzantines, expanded and rebuilt first by the Selcuks and again by Mehmet II, the walls explain at a glance the city's long history of unsuccessful defence. There's no height on which to build a proper fortress here, and Kayseri is the only Turkish city where there is a fortress on level ground. Some stretches of the city's outer walls remain through the old quarter south of the square.

Around the square the **Kurşunlu Cami** of 1584, sometimes attributed to Mimar Sinan, faces a dark grim medical school, the **Sahibiye Medrese,** and the most important of Kayseri's medieval structures, the **Huant Hatun Külliye.** The greater part of this complex has been restored as the city's **Ethnographic Museum,** one of the few really worthwhile examples of the kind to be seen in Anatolia; it goes beyond the usual folk clutter to make a genuine attempt at recreating the life and times of the early Turks. A Turcoman tent is the star exhibit; no simple tepee, but a beautifully functional construction, hung on a stout lattice of canes. Such a home makes the old wandering life of the Turks look quite attractive, though today's Yürüks, the nomadic shepherds of Anatolia, do not make them nearly so well. Some interesting rooms are given over to Selcuk artefacts, ceramic tiles, and coins.

Despite all the attention the Selcuk sultans lavished on Kayseri, the loveliest and best-proportioned structure in the town is not one of theirs. It is a building few tourists or even residents ever notice. The **Zeymel Abidin Türbesi,** next to the tourist information centre, is a mausoleum built only in 1886. Its elegant dome betrays some influence from the city's Christian community, being very similar to that of the 1835 **Meryem Ana Church** of the Armenians; this church, near Talas Caddesi, on the east end of the old town, is worth a visit even in its present sad state, as a much neglected home for a sports club. Almost all of the huge slabs of which it is constructed have strange carvings of what appear to be tools—scissors, knives, carpenter's squares, saws—and other inexplicable symbols carved into them.

Bazaar area

In the old town just behind the citadel, a fine Ottoman house—perhaps the only one you'll see in Kayseri—has been restored as an **Atatürk Museum.** A little further to the west, if you can avoid the carpet sellers, a walk through the truly exotic **bazaar** will reveal the twelfth-century **Ulu Cami;** a fifteenth-century theological school, the **Hatuniye Medrese;** and the **Vezir Han and Bedesten,** built by the Ottomans. Stop inside the Ulu Cami and you'll find most of the people of Kayseri who aren't out selling carpets; with its recycled Corinthian columns, colourful carved mimber and wooden ceiling, is a lovely spot, and like many of the huge 'great Mosques' of central Anatolian cities, people use it as a kind of park in which to sit and reflect.

For whatever reason, Kayseri has by far the most mausolea of any Turkish city. The classical conical roofed *türbeler* are everywhere along the outskirts of town. The famous **Döner Kümbet** ('revolving tomb') carved with tree-of-life motifs, was built for Shah Cihan of the Danişmend Turks, an emirate that held Kayseri through most of the twelfth century, and also constructed the Ulu Cami. It stands just off Talas Caddesi south of the old town, with two other mausolea nearby; the **Emir Ali Kümbeti** and the **Sirçali ('crystal') Kümbet.** To the west, the austere and dignified **Ali Cafer Kümbet** is lost among the apartment buildings of the new town; here the main street is Sivas Caddesi, broad and dismal, a perfect setting for postwar Italian cinema verité. If you follow it long enough, just as anomie sets in you'll run into the thirteenth-century **Çifte Kümbet.**

Near the Sirçali Kümbet, in a large park on the southern edge of the city, is a new **Archaeology Museum** to show off its interesting accumulation of finds; a sympathetic-looking Neolithic goddess from nearby Sarayak, some good geometric-style pots, a Roman sphinx, baby mummies, Hittite reliefs with King Tudhalya's mark, inscribed steles of bragging potentates, cow-shaped pitchers, the best pair of Hittite lions, and the silliest pair of Roman eagles.

OUTSIDE KAYSERI

Outside Kayseri, the road to Sivas will take you to an important Hittite site: **Kültepe** the 'hill of ashes', near the village of Karahöyük. Even before the Hittites, this city was a flourishing commercial centre, lasting well into Roman times. The inscribed tablets found here—those Dr Hrozny bought so dearly—have contributed much to our knowledge of the Hittites and their language. Kaneş was its name, and besides the city upon its mound, where the foundations of the palaces may be seen, there was a lower city just down the hill, a *karum*, or trading colony of the Assyrians. In about 1800 BC, long before the Assyrians became an empire, they were a prosperous trading people who established something like an early model of the Hanseatic league with a network of trading centres across Anatolia and Mesopotamia. Though subject to the local rulers, they lived as closed, self-governing towns; Kaneş, itself overseen directly from Nineveh, was the head town in the system. Both the city and colony were destroyed by fire, and the wealth of objects the fleeting residents left behind constitute one of the greatest Hittite treasures; most are now in Ankara, but a few remain in the small **museum** on the site.

Two other Selcuk caravanserais in this area are in good shape; **Sultan Hani,** built in 1236, is some 30 kilometres past Kültepe on the Sivas road, and **Karatay Han,** 50 kilometres outside Kayseri on the road to Malatya. Celâleddin Karatay, Alâeddin Keykubad's grand vezir who also endowed the Karatay Medrese in Konya, is responsible for both of these.

Twenty kilometres further on you pass the town of **Pinarbaşi,** unremarkable save that most of its inhabitants are Circassians, resettled here by the Ottomans as refugees from enforced Christianisation at the hands of the Russians,who seized their home north of the Black Sea in 1829. Centuries ago the Circassians were famous for the beauty of their women and the fierceness of their soldiers. The early Ottoman sultans, treating them as a favourite nation, made good use of both.

GETTING AROUND

There are daily flights from Ankara to Kayseri, or a long train trip on the way from Ankara to Malatya or Adana. The train station is in the Devlet Yolu, a kilometre north of the centre, and the bus station is on the state road a half kilometre west, both on central dolmuş routes. Any dolmuş or city bus along Talat Cad. can take you out to the archaeological museum.

TOURIST INFORMATION

Kağne Pazari, just off the central square, tel. (351) 261.

WHERE TO STAY

In Kayseri, the best bet is the modern but gracefully declining **Hattat Hotel** (H3), where you can get a refrigerator and TV for 5500 TL a single, 7500 TL a double; tel. (351) 193 31–198 29. It's on Istanbul Cad., just off the square. Less expensive, the **Hotel Sur** on Uğur Sokak 12, tel. (351) 19 545 has clean rooms near the citadel for 3000 TL with bath.

EATING OUT

The **Kristal Lokanta,** next to the Atatürk museum, is a good one in the heart of Kayseri, with Turkish specialities for around 2000 TL. A bit less pricy is the **Kardeşler Lokantasi** on 27 Mayis Cad. Other places are simple and very inexpensive.

Part XII

NORTH-EASTERN ANATOLIA

The Çoban Köprü over the Araxes River between Erzurum and Kars

You may have seen the Dakotas or Saskatchewan, Yakutsk or the endless Gobi; you may have travelled the world over in search of the bleakest and emptiest landscapes, but you can't say you've seen it all until you've been on the lonesome Plain of Erzurum or traversed the featureless black mountains around it.

On the other hand, you might like it. There's a kind of poetry in such a landscape, so grim and still, it shames its people and towns to silence. Every spot of colour—a peasant woman's bright costume, a green irrigated farm, or the blue tiles of an ancient minaret—becomes meaningful. In the very stillness there is a sense of danger. Sudden, fierce blizzards rule this country's winters, and tremendous earthquakes shake its towns to dust with a regularity known in few corners of the earth. The road through Erzurum has been a route for would-be conquerors, marching in either direction, as far back as the chronicles go; just now, no foreign army has camped here for sixty years, perhaps a record in modern times.

People here respond to the precariousness of life as they would anywhere else. When earthquakes wreck their hopes, they rebuild; when invaders come, they resist heroically, and in their lives the bleakness is tranformed to dignity of bearing and a quiet friendliness that matches the landscape perfectly.

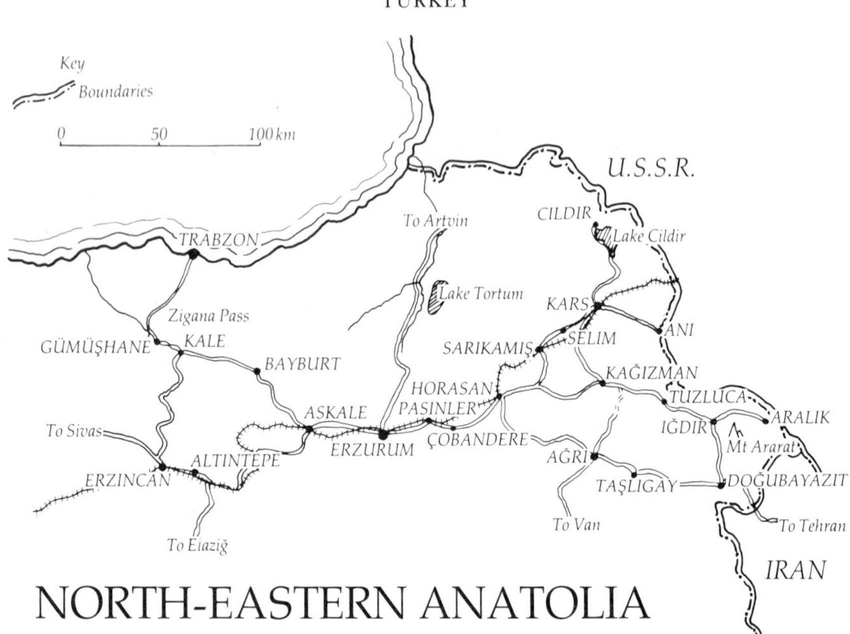

NORTH-EASTERN ANATOLIA

Erzurum

To get there, just take the little trip from **Sivas,** east to **Erzincan.** It's 240 kilometres, and the road passes only four villages the entire trip. Erzincan, called 'Aziris' in ancient times, once was renowned as one of the most beautiful cities in Anatolia. A series of earthquakes, the last in 1939 killing 40 000 people, have left all the Selcuk mosques and medreses in ruins, though the town once again has been rebuilt. The Turks have invented a fancy etymology for the name; from *Ezercan,* meaning 'life crusher'. Once known for metalwork, carpets and, according to Marco Polo who travelled here, buckram, Erzincan today is famous for its earthquakes. Enough of them have so shattered the Urartian fortress of **Altintepe,** 16 kilometres east, that little remains to be seen; the best objects, including two great lions, have been removed to Ankara.

Don't give up here; it's only 180 more kilometres to **Erzurum,** through four other lonely villages. Once in the town, you'll forget some of your misgivings about this trip. Erzurum, if you come from the west, may be the first Turkish city you find as exotic as you expected; it is good and grey, clean and quiet, and, apart from the modern centre, its streetscapes have not changed for centuries.

HISTORY

Erzurum guards the approaches to Anatolia, and consequently has always been an important military prize. As Theodosiopolis, it marked the eastern frontiers of the Romans and Byzantines; the waves of Turks who began battering its ramparts in the ninth century called it Arz-er-Rum, 'land of Rome', and the name stuck when the Selcuks conquered it in 1071. The Selcuks, on their westward path, never looked back, and cared little when the Saltuk Turks took it away from them. Ilhanli Mongols and Ottoman occupations were to follow, and after the 1700s, control of Erzurum became a major goal of the Russian Empire. Battles took place on the plain in most of the Russo-Turkish conflicts, the last in 1916, when the Tzar's troops captured it in one of their few noteworthy feats of arms in World War I. The Turks soon reasserted themselves, however, and one of the congresses that led to Turkish independence took place here in July 1919.

Almost 200,000 people live in Erzurum, but it's a mystery just how they support themselves. The city itself seems to still be living in an age of handicrafts and small shops. A few factories and agricultural installations lie on the outskirts, but the surrounding Plain of Erzurum between the Çoruh Mountains to the north and the Palandöken to the south, seems utterly empty.

It's pleasant strolling around Erzurum, but don't be surprised if you find yourself tiring easily. This is Turkey's highest provincial capital, some 6400 feet above sea level. All the way from the Aegean coast, the Anatolian plateau has been gradually rising, and the eastern end of it, from Erzurum to Mount Ararat, may not be as high as the Himalayas, but the peoples of the Middle East have always thought of it as the roof of the world. Many of the great rivers have their sources here, both the Tigris and Euphrates, flowing down to the Persian Gulf; the **Aras,** ancient 'Araxes', heading for the Caspian; and the rivers of the eastern Black Sea, the Çoruh and the Yeşilirmak. At this height, Erzurum and all the lands east of it stay in the deep freeze all winter; the snow piles up and transit becomes difficult.

Cumhuriyet Caddesi, the modern main street of Erzurum, chops its way right through the old town, and, behind its glass and concrete banks and shops, are fine narrow cobbled streets full of children and cats, lined with the city's typical grey stone houses. Cumhuriyet, though broad and straight, roughly follows the course of an older thoroughfare, and most of Erzurum's sights are located on or near it. Near the town hall, at the corner of Mumcu Caddesi, a small park contains the **Yakutiye Mosque and Medrese,** built by the Mongols in the fourteenth century.

To the east, the next mosque down is the **Ulu Cami,** built in 1179 by the Saltuk emir Abdul Muhammad. Like most 'great mosques' in Turkish cities, this one is huge and plain. Until the conquest of Istanbul, the Turkish idea of architecture was, in respect to where the artistic effort should be made, just the opposite of Christian Europe. The biggest central mosques, submitting to the puritanical streak Islam has always had, are usually little more than utilitarian prayer-halls, Islam has no cathedrals. Adornments, in stone and glazed tile, were saved for the smaller mosques and, above all, the schools, most of them endowed by a single patron anxious to be remembered.

ÇIFTE MINARE MEDRESE

A thirteenth-century Mongol princess named Hatun was one of these, and her gift to Erzurum, the **Çifte Minare Medrese,** remains one of the masterpieces of Turkish architecture. Behind the massive portal, one of the best examples of the style begun by the Selcuks, the gateway arches open to a spacious courtyard, enclosed by a two-storey gallery with a free-standing arch at its centre. From the opposite end, a vaulted hall leads to a very large and beautiful unoccupied *türbe,* with a shallow dome under the usual conical roof. The strange device on the entrance of the medrese is worthy of note, a symbol seen in various forms on the religious buildings of Eastern Anatolia. It's a palm tree, representing the tree of life; its roots have become snakes, and an eagle perches on its topmost branch. This is an Ilhanli symbol, adapted from the eagle and tree the Selcuks used before them.

Restoration of the Çifte Minare is fitfully underway. It's usually left open during the daytime when workmen are around, so see it if you can.

Just two blocks behind the Çifte Minare, in one of the most picturesque corners of old Erzurum, a fenced garden encloses the **Üç Kümbet,** literally 'three tombs'. *Kümbet* is just another name for *türbe*—a round or octagonal mausoleum with a conical roof; these three, with the remains of Saltuk emirs of the thirteenth century inside them, are especially splendid examples. More than most *türbes,* they show the Armenian influence; under Roman and Byzantine rule, Erzurum had been a predominantly Armenian town.

On the other side of Cumhuriyet Caddesi the old lanes wander crazily upwards to the **castle,** well preserved since its last, Ottoman, rebuilding. The **clock tower,** looking out over the city from inside the castle began life as a minaret, but apart from the Ramazan cannon, there's nothing to see here save Turks sneaking off the job for a snooze, and little boys pretending to be Kiliç Aslan (the legendary selcukemir). The **market district** occupies most of the streets north of here. With more donkeys and fewer plastic buckets, it's one of the most old-fashioned and interesting bazaars in Turkey. The old *bedesten* at its heart, the **Rüstem Paşa Çarşisi** bristles with a host of pyramidal chimneys that seem to be the skyline of a strange city in miniature.

THE ÇORUH MOUNTAINS

The black mountains that surround the Plain of Erzurum seem to close it off like a castle wall, and in fact, getting out by any road except the main east–west highway can be difficult three seasons of the year. Almost no traffic braves the unpaved mountain roads to the south and southwest. The road to Artvin and the Black Sea is decent, but a wilder and more interesting route would be to retrace your steps to Askale and take the mainly asphalted route through the Çoruh Mountains to Trabzon, passing two Turkish castles that would put the imagination of a Hollywood director to shame.

At **Bayburt,** the town that has defended this route since the days of the Kingdom of Trebizond, the castle, with its dozens of towers, dwarfs the little village in its shadow. Stouter souls may try the one at **Kale,** perched like a beret atop a needle-thin peak. From here, the road passes through **Gümüşhane;** the name, 'silver house' denotes a mint, a reminder of the ancient mines between here and Bayburt. The town is another new creation, rebuilt from ruins of another earthquake. This is the route Xenophon and his ten thousand took at the end of their epic journey across Eastern Anatolia. Before they could reach Trebizond and the sea, they had to cross over Turkey's highest pass, the **Zigana Geçiti,** where snow may be blowing across the road in any month of the year.

GOING EAST

If you proceed east from Erzurum, the route is equally scenic, following the boisterously rushing Aras River, through green meadows and steep canyons on its way to the Soviet Union. At **Pasinler,** you see a joke of a castle, a modern restoration, of which only one side of the walls remain. It looks like a stage prop, they can't have done it up to impress tourists, and we can only wonder what the idea was. Better, at **Çobandere** ('shepherd's valley') there's a well-preserved **Ottoman bridge,** one of their best, with six graceful arches over the stream. It's attributed to Mimar Sinan, but then so is every other old bridge in Turkey.

East towards Kars

Heading east of Erzurum, the villages become rougher and poorer, the amenities fewer, and the stares directed at tourists longer. **Horasan** and **Sarikamiş,** built around army bases, are two of these villages. The former is named for the great city of Turkish Central Asia, Khorasan, and probably got its start with the waves of Turkish migration that followed the Mongol destructions in that region. Near Sarikamiş the government is constructing a ski resort, and why not? The chief distinction of Sarikamiş is its mean annual temperature of 35°, the lowest in Turkey and equal to that of the northernmost town in Norway. Here the road rejoins the railway line, bending around a fair sized patch of mountains calld **Aladağ,** headed for Kars.

GETTING AROUND

Bus connections to Erzurum are regular from Sivas, Malatya, and Trabzon, the latter a spectacular route over the Eastern Black Sea Mountains. The railroad from Ankara passes through on the way to Kars, though trains are not frequent.

Erzurum's bus station lies a couple of kilometres out of town, and the rail station a kilometre. Outside of those, you'll probably not require public transport for anything within the city. As in other cities where the bus station is far from the centre, it may be worth your while to check at the bus company offices in town for times, and for the possibility of a connecting minibus (some companies provide this service).

TOURIST INFORMATION

Cemal Gürsel Caddesi, tel. (011) 15 697, 19127.

WHERE TO STAY

Outside of the **Oral Oteli** (H2), 3 Terminal Caddesi, tel. (011) 19 740 (single 4500 TL, double 6000), Erzurum's new hotel in an out-of-the-way location, most of the city's middle range and cheap lodgings may be found in a quiet area between the train station and centre, around Kazim Karabekir Cadd. Some of the buses from other cities stop here **after** they arrive at the station. The **Polat** (H4), tel. (011) 11 623 and the **Buhara Oteli** (H4), tel. (011) 15 096, both on Kazim Karabekir Caddesi are comfortable but nothing special, and charge around 4000 TL for a double.

EATING OUT

Just off Cumhuriyet Cad. in Erzurum the **Tufan Restaurant** would be a disappointment anywhere outside Eastern Anatolia. Here it looks good; serving alcohol, in a part of the country where few places do, is its special virtue. Expect to pay around 3000 TL a meal with wine. There are kebab places on Cumhuriyet, but nothing special. The **Mesud Restaurant,** on Tahtacilar Cad. in the hotel district, is a popular spot with the locals (around 2000 TL a meal).

Kars and Ani

Kars

Sarikamiş may be a little colder, but Kars gets more snow. The word itself means 'snow' in Turkish, and here it means about 40 feet in the worst winters. Most people come here only because it's the nearest town to the ruined city of Ani. Few writers have had anything good to say about it; they come by

Tenth-century Armenian Cathedral of the Apostles, Kars

bus or train, see the shacks and mud around the stations, and bolt. It's a pity, for outside the squalid market area where the stations are, Kars is one of the prettier towns in the east. It's secret is it's really a Russian town, most of it built between 1878–1922 when the region was part of the Russian Empire; most citizens of Kars don't know this, nor are they aware that their town was founded by the Armenians. As capital of the Bagratuni dynasty before Ani, it flourished in the ninth and tenth centuries.

THE RUSSIAN OCCUPATION

The Selcuks destroyed Kars in the eleventh century, and attempts at rebuilding were foiled by the Mongols and later Tamerlane, both of whom decimated the town in their invasions. Just as Erzurum protects Anatolia, Kars protects Erzurum, and there has always been a garrison up in Kars castle. There's one in it now. Like Erzurum, Kars was a prize the Russians wanted badly, and they spent much of the nineteenth century trying to get it; in 1807 their siege failed but both in 1828 and 1855, during the Crimean War, they wrested it from the Sultan only to find the European powers forcing them to give it back. On the latter occasion, Kars was defended by a Turkish force led by British officers under General Williams. Their heroic defence against great odds was one of the famous events of the Crimean War: the English public held its breath for weeks as reports and rumours dribbled in over the telegraph line. In 1877 the Russians took Kars again and got to keep it, by the good will of Bismarck at the Treaty of Berlin.

Lenin and Trotsky, in a rare lapse of judgement, gave it back with the rest of the province in 1921. Atatürk and the Turkish assembly had been playing a little game with the Bolsheviks, issuing communiques about the evils of capital and the eternal solidarity of the Russian and Turkish workers. The Soviets fell for it, and gave up their border claims to earn Turkey's friendship. They probably couldn't have held Kars in any case, with the Red Army busy elsewhere and General Kazim Karabakir's Turkish nationalist army knocking on the door.

NEW TOWN

However, during their forty year occupation, the Russians laid out the new town south of the citadel with broad, tree-lined streets. On the business streets, Atatürk Caddesi and Karadağ Caddesi, you'll see blocks of attractive neo-classical façades. Some, like the old government buildings on Ordu Caddesi, and one semi-ruined palace that may once have served as an opera house, are wonderfully grandiose, and seem even more so in this incongruous setting. On one old Russian house, you can admire what must be the best Art Nouveau balcony in all Anatolia. Near the river, the little Kars Çayi, a few Russian cottages with nicely carved porches and window frames moulder away under the plane trees.

The Kars Çayi marks the boundary between the Russian town and the older village under the walls of the **castle.** Sultan Murat III built this fortress over the ruined Armenian foundation in the 1590s. The Turkish Army still uses it, not surprisingly as it is so close to the Russian border, and you can walk around it but not in. Murad also built the **stone bridge** over the stream.

CATHEDRAL OF THE APOSTLES

All that remains from the days when Kars was home to the kings of Armenia is its **Cathedral of the Apostles,** built by King Abbas in 937. The church has led a hard life. Only a century after its construction, Alp Arslan's Selcuks converted it into a mosque, but the Russians made it a church once again in 1878. After the recapture of the town and the dispersal of the Armenian community, the city made it a museum for a while. Now it stands empty, with an enormous rusting diesel motor, property of the machine shop next door, set up like a monument in front of the entrance. Just the same, the cathedral has managed to survive somehow in reasonably good repair; impressive in its own right, it provides a good introduction to the wealth of Armenian architecture you see at Ani.

Few builders ever piled up so much stone to cover so little space as the Armenians did. Like the Cathedral of the Apostles, most of their religious buildings are quite small, with centralised plans, and a space under the dome usually no more than thirty feet in diameter, surrounded by three apses and the entrance where the fourth would be, in the form of a cross. The tip of the dome, however, may be as much as 150 feet high. We don't know whether the medieval Armenians stayed at home on Sundays or squeezed themselves into their churches like sardines, but buildings like this are a kind of 'pure architecture', in which function is subordinated to form for the glory of God. The familiar outline of Armenian churches, a cylinder carved with blind arcades—pillars and arches sculpted in relief—covered with a cone-shaped dome, is a style you've probably seen in enough places already; the Selcuks and other Turkish states copied it for their mausolea.

Here, the cylinder is really a twelve-sided figure, carved with mysterious figures, lions, and whorls in high relief, somewhat like the most famous Armenian church on Akhamar Island in Lake Van. Eight semidomes, the roof of the body of the church, support the central dome and drum, and inside some of the sculpture on the pendentives can still be seen, though most has fallen victim to time or iconoclasts. Note also the altar screen, carved from a single block of marble; here, and elsewhere in the cathedral, geometric patterns are used in a way that seems Islamic in inspiration.

The cathedral doors, with a bell, and other artefacts sent as a gift from Tsar Nicholas II can be seen at the **Kars Museum,** on Cumhuriyet Caddesi, on the outskirts of the town, along with the usual ethnographic exhibits.

Ani

To visit **Ani,** you need permission from the provincial government, a formality the city's tourist office will take care of. The site lies 45 kilometres west of Kars, right on the Soviet border where two streams meet—the usually dry Alaca Çay and the Arpa, a tributary of the Aras. Across the Arpa, Russian sentries will watch you through binoculars from their towers. You can wave to them, but they don't wave back.

THE ARMENIAN KINGDOM

Ani's citadel, on the steep peninsula between the two streams, owes its beginnings to a local prince named Karisarkan in the fifth century, though the site had already been occupied for centuries. The name came from Anahit, an ancient Persian goddess who the Greek mythographers identified with Aphrodite; before Gregory the Illuminator, she was one of the chief deities of the Armenians. Located on a major east–west caravan route, the town grew steadily through the following centuries. At the height of medieval Armenia's golden age in the mid-tenth century, King Ashot III transferred the capital here from Kars, and in the century that followed,

Ashot and his successors endowed the city with the array of sumptuous churches that attract visitors here today.

At that time, according to the chroniclers, Ani was a metropolis of some 100 000 people. Nothing in Europe at the time could rival it, and in the Middle East, only Constantinople, Cairo, and Baghdad were as large and well built. The great wealth of the Bagratuni kings that made it all possible, unfortunately, was soon dissipated in increasing warfare against the Byzantines, their old enemies, and the Selcuk Turks, newly arrived out of Asia. The Byzantines held the independent minded Armenians to be schismatics, and therefore thought nothing of breaking a treaty and attacking them just at the moment when their resources were concentrated against the Selcuks. Greek subversion had been undermining Armenia for a century, and Emperor Constantine IX was finally able to annexe most of Armenia in 1040. By doing so, the Byzantines had foolishly destroyed their own best ally, and when Ani fell to the Turks in 1064, the disaster at Manzikert that lost Anatolia to the Empire forever was only seven years away.

As the Selcuks continued west, Armenian nobles were able to reassert their independence, though as isolated feudal lords, not as a united nation. Ani prospered nevertheless, until an earthquake in 1319 completely levelled the city. Now, with the eastern trade routes circumvented by the merchant adventurers of Italy, and the royal patronage gone, there was nothing to stop Ani from a long and irresistible decline. Today the city is a ruin, abandoned save for the tiny shepherd village outside its walls. The **walls** still stand, along with the citadel and the churches; together they make up the greatest achievement of medieval architecture to be seen anywhere in Turkey, the inspiration for Selcuk architecture and everything else in this corner of the world that is well made.

WALLS

Even before you see the churches, the attention given to even the defence walls gives an indication of the talent of the Armenian builders. The rounded, covered towers are unusual, more reminiscent of bunkers on the Maginot Line than anything from the Middle Ages. The Armenians took the time to beautify them, laying the sandstone blocks of two colours in simple designs. Near the parking lot, the **Lion Gate** provides an entrance to the town; the sculpted lion that occasioned the name is said to have been added by Alp Aslan. Once inside, you will find two paths through the weeds that roughly follow the route of two of Ani's principal streets. The path to the left leads to the cathedral and citadel; the right hand path to the most conspicuous monument near the gate, the **Church of Our Saviour.**

CHURCHES

Trdat, architect of the cathedral, rebuilt this church in the twelfth century after an earthquake; originally, it was constructed in 1036 by the Pahvaluni family. The location must be bad for building, for today exactly half of the church remains, standing as if the rest had been sheared off by a monstrous axe. Don't go in, there's some concern that the rest could soon follow. Admire the frescoes of the **Last Supper** near the remaining half of the dome from the outside.

Many visitors overlook the **Church of Surp Gregor** (St Gregory the Illuminator), hidden on the cliffs above the Arpa, but below the level of the city. This is only one of three churches of St Gregory in Ani, and it's easy to get confused. Another prominent noble, Tigran Honetz, built this one in 1215, both in design and ornamentation the most complex of Ani's surviving churches. Though some 300 years younger than the church at Akhtamar, which it resembles, this one shows the same love of naturalistic detail in the finely carved animal motifs around the blind arcades. Note the sundial on the south wall, a common feature of the Armenian churches. Inside, well preserved frescoes depict some of the oddest scenes in Christendom. For those of us accustomed to the Western European or Greek tradition of religious art, these subjects are difficult to identify. The old Armenians kept some of the books of the Apocrypha in their Bible, which may explain some of them.

The twelve apostles are easy enough, and a series of pictures from the life of St Anne, mother of the Virgin Mary—a popular saint here, perhaps simply the spiritual descendant of old Anihit. Some of the others defy description. In two places along the walls, you see a man suspended upside down from a tree with his legs crossed—the very picture of the Hanged Man from the Tarot cards. One series of paintings has an urban background of arches and gables; medieval Ani must have looked like this.

Cathedral of the Apostles

Surp Gregor Church stands at the easternmost corner of Ani, where a dry stream bed is lined with man-made caves, like those of Cappadocia. Nearby, there's another of the city gates, with a relief, crucifix and long inscription in Armenian. From here, you may either retrace your steps back along the path or cut through the jumble of mounds and ruined foundations westwards to the largest of Ani's buildings, the **Cathedral of the Apostles,** which Trdat built for Gagik I in 1010. Here, to accommodate large crowds, the centralised plan has grown into a broad rectangular nave where the dome, now collapsed, covered only the centre. Unlike European churches, oriented towards monumental west entrances, this cathedral is oriented north–south, with the entrance at the centre of the nave; on the southern wall a tall slit of a window along the meridian was designed to flood the Church with light only at high noon. Some frescoes still exist, but under

Allah's whitewash, awaiting a restoration that may never come. Beyond these, the cathedral's modest decorative scheme hints at the same pious simplicity of a Turkish Ulu Cami; of all Ani's churches, it's the most austere; a single whimsical adornment is allowed in a kind of crypt entrance at the rear, built at a later date and half hidden by weeds. In the same two-tone sandstone of the city walls, this addition is built of great stones masterfully cut into pentagons and five-pointed stars.

MENUÇEHIR MOSQUE

Back towards the palisade of the Arpa Çay, a lonely minaret protrudes from a ruined structure on the edge of the cliff. This building that the sign calls **Menuçehir Mosque** is actually something of a mystery. Believed to date from the year 1072, eight years after the Selcuk conquest, it seems nevertheless to have originally been an Armenian work, not a church, but perhaps with its colonnaded terraces and wonderful view over the Arpa, a palace. The slopes of the valley below are full of sculptural fragments obviously Armenian in style, but the small domes in the colonnades, with their inlaid stonework in geometric and stalactite patterns, suggests a Moslem hand. Whether mosque or palace, here Armenian and Islamic styles harmonise nicely, and suggest that Selcuk rule may not have been such a disaster as historians make it out to be. The minaret has been closed since a German tourist committed suicide by leaping from the top of the minaret; like many others in the Islamic world, it has 99 steps, one for each of the Names of God.

Perhaps the German had suffered an attack of melancholy. This part of Ani is certainly conducive to it. Look down into the river and you'll see the ruins of an exquisite bridge with stone towers, and another, unreachable chapel poised gracefully on a little hill on the Russian side. With no effort, you find yourself imagining colourful royal processions, columns of victorious soldiers, or caravans from Persia climbing the road from the bridge up to the city gates. Turn around, and see the city's skyline of churches still intact, with only the houses between them missing. As corpses of cities go, Ani is still warm. If it were not so beautiful, it would not be so sad.

ALONG THE ALACA ÇAY

Crossing over to the Alaca Çay side of town, another bridge, more troglodyte caves, and a gate and several surviving towers of the fortifications become visible. The narrow strip of land you stand on connects the city proper with the **citadel**. The Jandarmas won't let you visit it; apparently it makes the Russians nervous. Instead, follow the cliffs to the next St Gregory, the **Little St Gregory of Abighaurentz**, an especially tall church with an exceptionally small floor space. Built during the reign of **Gagik I**, in 998, it features six domed apses forming a circle around the central drum and dome, all supported by columns bearing the distinctive Armenian style of capital, a variant on the Ionic form but with three scrolls instead of two. The ruin nearby called the *kervanseray* was really a church rebuilt as a mosque by the Selcuks, with the same coalescence of two styles as that seen in the Menuçehir Mosque. Yet another mosque, the **Ebul Mu'Ammerei Cami** with its fallen minaret, stands as the only monument to the short-lived Ani-Shehhad Kingdom, a state formed in the confusion of the Selcuks' move westward.

The first King Gagik also gets the credit for the other **St Gregory Church,** built in 1001 near the northwestern edge of the city. The church has been victimised by earthquakes, but even in its derelict state it is clear that it was one of the grandest of all, comparable in size to the cathedral. The circular form, with an interior circle of columns and four mighty piers that must have carried an enormous dome, is probably unique in Armenian architecture. The hole in the floor you almost fall into is not a baptismal font, but a well, cut right through the centre of the church. The original religion of the Armenians had much to do with sacred trees and springs, and Gregory the Illuminator made many concessions to the old order in his conversion of the nation; he kept on the old hereditary caste of priests, for example, and it would be interesting to learn what else survived as well.

Returning to the Lion Gate, you pass a single wall remaining from the oldest church in Ani, a relic of the family that founded the city; the three-tiered arches of the seventh century **Karisarkan Church** are carved with a scene of the Annunciation.

GETTING AROUND

The daily **train** from Istanbul passes through Erzincan, Erzurum, and Kars on its way to the Soviet Unon—a brief excursion into the Soviet Caucausus may not be as difficult as you think, but you must have your visa in advance—in your home country. Bus connections into the region from Sivas, Trabzon, or the cities of the southeast are no problem, but all routes are long and usually dreary. The same is true of course if you're driving, and keep in mind that distances in this section are often very great, with few services and no accommodation along the way.

If you're not driving, a taxi is the only way to see Ani (43 kilometres of good road, about 6300 TL for a half day trip). The tourist office in Kars can arrange it, as well as take care of the police formalities.

TOURIST INFORMATION

Faikbey Caddesi, across from the Inönü police station, tel. (0211) 2724.

WHERE TO STAY

A decent hotel in Kars has not yet been discovered—if anyone finds one, drop us a line. Avoid the Yilmaz (H4) invitingly located close to the bus station, and take your chances with any of the unlisted holes-in-the-wall around Faikbey Caddesi.

EATING OUT

Almost any city in Eastern Anatolia has a least one real restaurant—panelled walls and table cloths—that serves drinks and has a slightly wider choice of dishes than the *lokantas*. These aren't really much more expensive, but neither is the quality that much higher. In Kars, such a place is the **Grand Manolya,** on Atatürk Caddesi (about 2000 TL.) Here some of the lokantas are actually better; try the **Imren Lokanta,** on Tenyifat Caddesi.

Mount Ararat

If you think you've reached the end of the world here, you haven't yet seen Mt Ararat. From Kars, or for that matter from anywhere, there's no easy route; whether you drive or take the untamed mountain buses, you pick your way between the peaks, sometimes on long stretches of unpaved road, and eventually arrive. The shortcut to **Kağizman** will spare you another trip to Sarikamiş, and the red, tan, and green Arizona landscape between Aladağ and its shorter cousin Yağlica Dağ may or may not be worth the damage the road does to your nerves. Among the dirty and disorganised villages of this region, Kağizman stands out; the government has put a lot of money into agriculture here and it shows.

Don't bother with the next shortcut to **Ağri,** Turkey's most woebegone provincial capital. The east road for Iğdir follows a narrow plain, and with no little mountains crowding it, it affords a view of the big ones, mostly far off in the Soviet Union, with iridescent peaks catching the sun. Clouds cling to the slopes, but the winds hardly ever permit them to stay still, and the swirling mountain panorama changes by the minute. In many places along this road, the Soviet border is only a few kilometres to the north, across the Aras. To be precise, it is the Armenian S.S.R. over there, but from this road it looks more like Tolkien's land of Mordor, with grey cliffs wreathed in smoke, squat factories, and even a nuclear power plant belching steam.

Doğubayazit

On the Turkish side, you'll see more troglodyte caves at **Tuzluca.** At **Iğdir,** an awful place, take the right turn for **Doğubayazit;** the entire 55 kilometres of this road follows the western flank of Ararat. Doğubayazit, with its streets full of tractors and sheep, is a rough and ready town, with few amenities and plenty of bad smells. Being on one of the main roads from

The Ishak Paşa Palace, Doğubayazit

Iran, it's usually full of Iranian tourists; you see them standing about on the corners, trying to get rid of some of their worthless currency.

Palace of Ishak Paşa

Nothing in the town is very old. A century ago, this was all a lake bordered with marshes; travellers since ancient times have remarked on how the tremendous flow off Ararat turns all the surrounding country to a bog in the spring, though many parts have lately been drained for farming. The original settlement, **Beyazit,** was up in the hills 5 kilometres east, near one of the most unusual attractions in eastern Turkey, the half ruined **Palace of Ishak Paşa**. The Turks like putting this pleasure dome on their travel posters. With its pointed dome and striped minaret, made in two shades of sandstone, Armenia-style, it matches its romantic setting under Ararat, and whispers to the gaping tourist of caravans laden with spices and silk, or eunuchs with scimitars and dark-eyed houris in pointed slippers, with jinns and afrits and the rest of the Arabian nights paraphernalia just offstage. The joke is, it's no older than the 1800s. Ishak Paşa, like his father before him and his son afterwards, held the title of Governor in these parts from the Sultan, but the Sultan was a thousand miles away; conferring the office was only a polite oriental gesture acknowledging the power these feudal lords held over the area. According to whom you ask, you will hear that Isak was an Armenian, a Kurd, or a Jew, and no doubt a man of refinement, too. He built his barely fortified *saray* in the eclectic style, just at the time his counterparts in Europe were beginning to construct Greek or Gothic hotels and railway stations.

Don't let that detract from your enjoyment of this lovely place. The sculpture of the entrance, like an old fashioned medrese gate, and the tree of life motifs on the fountain in the inner courtyard are fine works, as is the mosque, built over the parapets of the castle; inside, note the odd *mimber,* hidden inside the wall, where the *imam* would have to climb up and reappear in a little window like a character in a puppet show. The upper galleries of course are for the ladies; Ihsak Paşa always had plenty on hand—the harem apartment makes up half of his palace. What are ruins of his garden and another mosque, may be seen on the opposite hillside; the ruins lower down belong to old Beyazit.

NOAH'S ARK AND ARARAT

As well as Iranians, you may also find the streets of Doğubayazit full of lost Americans. Since the latest book about a sighting of Noah's Ark on **Mount Ararat,** hosts of divinity professors and evangelists have descended on the unsuspecting town; recently, a retired astronaut joined the crowd, drawing a great deal of publicity. Medieval travellers like Mandeville report that the remains of the Ark were there for all to see, and we can guess the business of peddling old planks to Christians sprang up here at an early date.

It is no disgrace if these seekers go home empty-handed. Even with aircraft and satellites to help, 600 square miles of mountain makes for quite a job. Somewhere on Ararat, a holy place the Armenians called Jacob's Well has been lost for centuries. If there were any literal truth in the story of Noah, it would be a disappointment; finding the original impulse for the myth would be much more significant. Battalions of scholars have already spent careers tracking down and sorting out stories of the flood: those of Noah's, of the Sumerian Utnapishtim, the Deucalion and Pyrrha myth of the Greeks and dozen of other variants from Uganda to Wales. Innumerable theories have been propounded; the school of thought that believes that myths often stem from misrepresentations of pictures in ancient religious icons, for example, sees the story of Noah deriving from a painted scene in which a ship, representing the sun in its passage through the year, carries a sacred king and animals representing the signs of the zodiac.

Other scholars find in the tale a confusion of myth with real floods; tidal waves from the disaster that overtook Minoan Crete, perhaps, or a great flood in the valleys of the Tigris and Euphrates in Mesopotamia. The Utnapishtim story, from that part of the world, describes the ark as a perfect cube; intriguing, though highly unseaworthy. The Knights Templars, who knew all these old stories, used a cubic 'ark' as the altar for their secret observances.

For the moment, the last word must go to Hertha von Dechend, a renowned and remarkable scholar who has spent her life reinterpreting ancient stories as a kind of scientific shorthand for astronomical events. To her, all flood stories denote the passing of a World Age, in a vast cosmic clock measured by the procession of the equinoxes. Briefly, just as the North Pole moves around the sky every 26 000 years, so does the equinoctial colure, the point the sun occupies at the spring equinox. When it passes from one constellation of the zodiac to another (say, from Pisces to Aquarius), a new age begins and the old one, with the old constellation, is 'drowned' beneath the celestial equator. The ancients did love to water their heavens with constellations of rivers and seas, and in the astronomy of the Mesopotamians, there is not only a boat (now Argo), but even a star they call Mount Ararat.

ARARAT ITSELF

When you see Ararat, you won't be surprised that so many stories have grown up around it, or that so many peoples thought of it as the centre of the world. From the plain of Doğubayazit, it rears itself startlingly heavenwards, as if out of the sea. As an extinct volcano, its mass rises as neatly symmetrical as Etna or Mt Fuji. The summit, now visible, now hidden in clouds, is three and a half miles up; of its entourage of smaller peaks, those on the right are all Iranian, those to the left in the Soviet Union.

GETTING AROUND

Getting to Doğubayazit on the bus can be difficult. Buses from Kars that claim to be going all the way may leave you stranded in Iğdir, and those from Van could leave you at Ağri. Connecting minibuses do exist, but the connections sometimes aren't made. However you travel in this area, long detours around big patches of mountains will be the rule. Large sections around Ağri are unpaved, and there's simply no easy route across the mountains to Van or Diyarbakir. Fortunately, the government tourist offices map is quite accurate for this region.

WHERE TO STAY

In Doğubayazit, enough foreigners pass through to scrutinise Mt Ararat for the **Ararat Hotel** (H3) 48 Emniyet Caddesi to do a good business. It has a restaurant and Turkish bath, and it's the fanciest in town for 3500 TL a single, 5000 TL for a double. The **Gül** (unlisted) on the main street is cheaper and acceptable.

EATING OUT

The only place with any pretentions in Doğubayazit is in the Ararat Hotel, popular with Western travellers, with dinner for about 3500 TL. Two acceptable places popular with the locals are the **Karadeniz,** across the street from the Ararat, and even better the **Istanbul Lokanta** on the main street.

Part XII

SOUTH-EASTERN ANATOLIA

Jumbled headstones at Nemrut Daği (Mount Nimrod)

Travellers and vacationers are just beginning to find their way here, mostly adventurous Germans without much luggage. It isn't a part of the world that calls to mind any particular associations, unless you are a scholar familiar with names like Edessa, Harran, and Carchemish and few people ever think of it as a place in which to spend their free time. Approach it in the right frame of mind, however, and it could be a trip to remember. This quarter of Turkey lies just outside the boundary of the known and familiar, where mere geography evaporates into myth along the banks of the Tigris and Euphrates, the mile-high shores of Lake Van, and the ghosts of numberless dead civilisations rise up to spook you from their mouldering ruins.

This is the Middle East, make no mistake about it; for those who have always wanted to see the region but have let the headlines in the papers talk them out of it, this end of Turkey may be the ideal spot to dip into it. Long ago, the climate was much less dry, and the plains of the southeast marked the north edge of the Fertile Crescent, fought over by the Egyptians, Assyrians, and Hittites. Biblical sites and early Christian centres abound, and the present population of Kurds, Turks, and Arabs each have stories of their own. Today, the area strikes a happy medium rare in the Middle East; it is neither grindingly poor, nor rich with petrodollars, and while the summer heat can be as daunting as in Libya or the empty Quarter of Arabia, politically the temperature is much lower. In travelling Turkey's slice of the Middle East you can avoid the religious and political clashes that beset the rest of the region.

Coming from the west, from Adana or the Hatay, your first encounter in this area will be three cities whose names were changed by Atatürk. Maraş, Antep and Urfa, all as old as the Hittites, performed such service in the War of Independence when their local defence committees beat off the invading French armies, that they now bear the titles, respectively, of hero, warrior, and glorious: Kahramanmaraş, Gaziantep, and Şanliurfa. You may see them on maps in either their new or old forms.

Kahramanmaraş

Kahramanmaraş, long as it's been around, basically isn't much; its oldest buildings are mosques from the fifteenth century. The same could be said of **Gaziantep,** but, as Turkey's sixth city, bestriding the two main roads into the south-east, it will probably either introduce you to the region or help you rest at the end of the trip. It's a good place for that, a thoroughly up-to-date town with good hotels and a reputation for good food. Kebab houses all over Turkey proclaim 'Gaziantep style' on their signs.

Gaziantep

Gaziantep owes its recent growth to a burgeoning textile industry; along with prosperity, this has brought the city an expanse of *gecekondu* neighbourhoods spreading over the surrounding hills. The city's ancient fame, the pistachio nut, is still in evidence; any sweet shop in the town will sell you a box at astoundingly cheap prices. Like any busy, lively city, Gaziantep has its share of peculiarities: the giant soda pop bottles for advertising that stand in the centre of all traffic circles, or the motorcycles with sidecars like big wagons, used as informal taxis and delivery trucks in the poorer sections. From the past, the city retains an unusual fashion in minarets, some with spiral fluting and others topped with ornate wooden crows-nests for the muezzin. In the older, eastern parts of the town, these stand side by side with asymmetrical grey stone houses, whose interior stairways project over the sidewalk to form a kind of bay window, a style unique to Gaziantep. The major thoroughfare here begins at the central square as **Suburcu Caddesi,** and changes its name several times on its way through the old town and the **bazaar.** No amount of modernity can kill off a Turkish market and Gaziantep's is as colourful as any. North of this street, the Selcuk era **castle** rises over the city on a hill formed not by nature, but the accumulated debris of

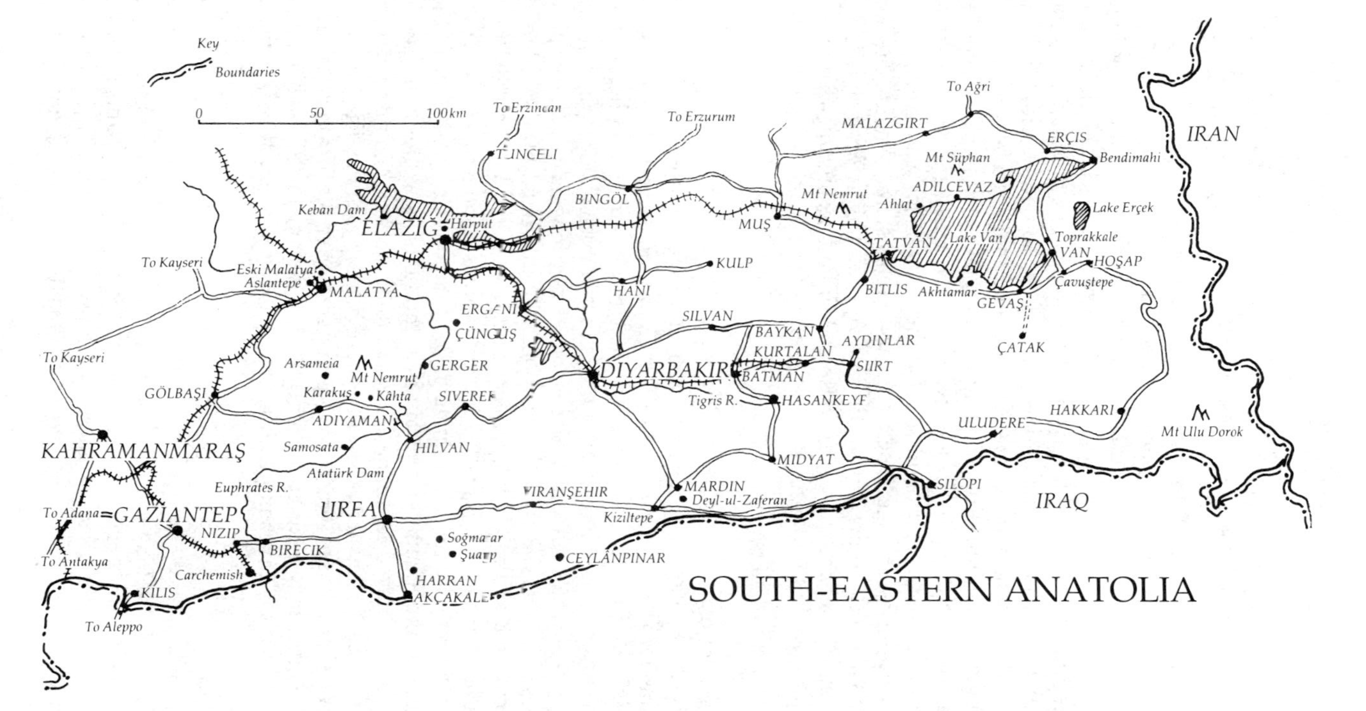
SOUTH-EASTERN ANATOLIA
Key
Boundaries
0
50
100km
IRAN
IRAQ
To Ağri
MALAZGIRT
ERÇIS
Bendimahi
Mt Süphan
ADILCEVAZ
Ahlat
Lake Erçek
Lake Van
Toprakkale
VAN
HOŞAP
Çavuştepe
GEVAŞ
Akhtamar
ÇATAK
TATVAN
Mt Nemrut
MUŞ
BITLIS
To Erzincan
TUNCELI
To Erzurum
BINGÖL
KULP
HANI
Keban Dam
ELAZIĞ
Harput
To Kayseri
Eski Malatya
Aslantepe
MALATYA
ERGANI
ÇÜNGÜŞ
GERGER
Arsameia
Mt Nemrut
Karakuş
Kâhta
SIVEREK
DIYARBAKIR
SILVAN
BAYKAN
KURTALAN
AYDINLAR
SIIRT
BATMAN
Tigris R.
HASANKEYF
MIDYAT
HAKKARI
Mt Ulu Dorok
ULUDERE
SILOPI
MARDIN
Deyl-ul-Zaferan
Kiziltepe
VIRANŞEHIR
GÖLBAŞI
ADIYAMAN
Samosata
Atatürk Dam
HILVAN
KAHRAMANMARAŞ
Euphrates R.
URFA
To Adana
GAZIANTEP
NIZIP
BIRECIK
To Antakya
Carchemish
KILIS
To Aleppo
HARRAN
AKÇAKALE
CEYLÂNPINAR

thousands of years of occupation. There are mounds like this—an archaeologist would call it a *tell*—all over the region.

ARCHAEOLOGY MUSEUM

Enough of them have been excavated for Gaziantep's **Archaeology Museum** to be worth a visit; it lies on the north fringe of the town on Istasyon Caddesi, past the stadium and the garden cafes of the city park, where narghile-smoking is still very much the thing. The museum, in its modern building, claims the largest collection in the southeast, with Hittite reliefs (one depicts the god Tesup with an axe and a fork as if he were marching to dinner), some fine Roman sculpture on grave steles from as far away as Palmyra in Syria, mosaics and cylinder seals, even some recently unearthed mastodon bones to remind you that these hot plains were cool pine forests during the last Ice Age. One finely carved relief shows a smiling Hellenistic-era king shaking hands with the god Apollo. This is Antiochus I, King of Commagene, and if both the pose and subject seem somewhat presumptuous, just wait until you've seen the rest of this man's work up on Nemrut Dağ.

Carchemish

Like Gaziantep itself, most of the ancient cities in its province have little to show for their long histories. Of them, the most important was **Carchemish,** *Kargamiş* in Turkish, a city along major trade routes between Mesopotamia and the Mediterranean, that first flourished under the Hittites, but only really took off when that empire was extinguished. Carchemish was sacked around the same time as Boğazköy, in around 1180 BC, but it soon recovered, and as an independent Hittite kingdom surviving on trade and clever diplomacy, it lasted until the Assyrians razed it in 717 BC.

British excavations beginning in the 1880s, contributed some of the first clues to the identity of the Hittites; the finds, now mostly in London or Ankara, attracted a great deal of attention at the time, and many of the grand Edwardian dilettantes spent time here helping with the dig. Nowadays you have a hard time getting here, as permission from the provincial government in Gaziantep is required. Carchemish lies right on the Syrian border, and as the Syrians are even more difficult neighbours than the Russians the Turks keep security tight.

Birecik

Turkey doesn't have many oil deposits, but the oil isn't far away; right now the Turks are keeping Iraq afloat with the big pipeline that carries their oil through to the Mediterranean. The road from the east into Gaziantep seems a sort of pipeline as well; more often than not, its narrow two lanes are packed solid with tank trucks going in both directions, making the ride east a thrill you'll remember, especially if you take the bus. The road crosses the Euphrates at **Birecik,** a sorry little town on white cliffs, but well liked by the bald ibis, an almost extinct crane, now a special project of the World Wildlife Fund.

Birecik's ruined castle was built or rebuilt by the Franks of the First Crusade as a border outpost for their County of Edessa. Whatever made Count Baldwin and his merry men try to set up a state so far east—the furthest penetration into the Islamic world that the Crusaders ever made—is not clear. Founded in 1092, the County of Edessa was hardly defensible, and the Selcuks destroyed it less than fifty years later. In the First Crusade, at least, we can give the knights some credit for pious motivation, and the ancient city of Edessa, now known as **Urfa,** is holy ground for Christians, much as Palestine was.

Urfa (Edessa)

Abraham, according to traditions of both the Christians and Moslems, received his summons to prophecy while living in the city. The Urfans will show you Job's cave as well, and the belief is widely current among them that Adam and Eve lived here, and that these parched hills were once the Garden of Eden. The stories must stand on their own; we cannot guess how many levels of religious meaning and historical significance lie beneath them. All the evidence we have is this city of Urfa, a holy place for millennia upon millennia. No ground could store up spiritual energy for so long without becoming at least a bit strange and otherworldly, but Urfa, and its hinterlands, goes too far. It is the vortex of Turkey, not a Canterbury but a Salisbury Plain, full of mystery. The city, with its scholarly legacies will seem reasonable enough, but once outside it, anything can happen.

HISTORY

The name Urfa may be a very ancient corruption of Hurri; archaeologists speculate that it was an important town of the Hurri-Mitani confederation, the state that pushed the Hittites around until the successful reign of Hittite King Suppiluliumas I about 1400 BC ended the Hurri ascendancy. As Orhoe, or Orhai, the town continued quietly until Alexander the Great's Seleucid successors renamed it Edessa and helped it grow into its new role as clearinghouse of goods, gods, and ideas, between the Greek world and the East. Under the Byzantines, Urfa found itself attacked repeatedly by the first waves of the expanding Moslem Arabs in the seventh century, changing hands back and forth. While the soldiers were out banging their swords, Christian and Moslem scholars inside the walls and in the nearby city,

Harran, were beginning the great work of translation and teaching that made Greek science and philosophy available to the Moslem world. Centuries later, under the county of Edessa, the learned men of Islam were to return the favour. Books that had long been lost to the West, including important works of Aristotle, were regained by contacts made here and in the other crusader states. Along with them came the fruits of the golden era of Arabic science, works of mathematics and astronomy that were to have an incalculable influence on the West.

POOL OF ABRAHAM

Still striving to maintain something of its old distinction, Urfa today is one of the loveliest cities of Anatolia. Its economy is still based more on the pilgrimages and religious institutions than on commerce, and though it seems as prosperous as Gaziantep, its air of pleasant tranquillity has not suffered. Urfa is a compact city, strung out along the mile and a half length of Atatürk's Caddesi. Most of its sights can be seen in a day but before you go out walking in this ferocious climate—Urfa is on the edge of the Syrian desert—we will at least mention the best place in town for a cold drink and a spot of shade. In the large park around the Pool of Ayn Zeliha, on the southern edge of Urfa, are cafes, pavilions, garden paths and perhaps half the trees in Urfa province. In any of the cafés, you may take a seat by the water and almost instantly a few sleek grey fish will poke their noses out expectantly. Next, a small boy will appear with a plate of seeds or chick peas to sell; you will earn at least a little grace for contributing to the upkeep of Urfa's sacred carp, whose tribe has inhabited this pool for thousands of years. No one knows exactly how long: local stories associate the fish with the story of Abraham. Ancient religions from Ireland to China have had the like, often carp or salmon at holy springs, but it would be hard to find many examples that have survived up to our own day. The carp may not be caught or even disturbed by anyone—in Urfa they will tell you about the drunken soldier who went fishing one night recently and ended up with a stiff prison sentence. Everyone feeds them; with such a soft life it's no wonder there are so many of them, or that they look so fat and serene as they glide through the cool waters. This pond actually serves only for the carp to make little excursions; their true abode is the nearby **Pool of Abraham,** joined by a small canal. No one knows exactly how long this has been here, or to whom it was originally sacred, though it has been associated with the goddess Astarte. The Greeks called the spring that fills the two pools *callirhoe* 'fair flowing', but that name doesn't offer any clues.

In the Moslem tradition, Abraham began his career as the first prophet of monotheism in Urfa. His refusal of idolatry so outraged Nimrod, the legendary Assyrian king oddly associated with so many places in Anatolia, that he determined to have the troublesome prophet burned. An immense pyre was constructed under the walls of Urfa's citadel, but just as Abraham was being tossed onto it, God, or rather Allah, turned the fire into a flowing spring and landed him safely on his feet. On the edge of the Pool of Abraham, reflected in its waters, is an exceptionally lovely mosque, the **Halil Rahman Cami,** its three pointed domes something of an architectural anachronism, since it was only built in the seventeenth century.

CITADEL

The oldest parts of Urfa's **citadel** are Roman and Byzantine, but it became the impressive castle you see today through the energy of the Frankish crusaders, who built the towers and bastions, the donjon inside and the ditch around, cut in some places out of bare rock. The prominent landmark on top, two lone Corinthian columns, has acquired the name the **Throne of Nimrod,** but who actually erected them, no one knows. The spur on which the citadel rises is a part of a long cliff that bounds Urfa on its southern and eastern edges. Of the dozens of man-made and natural caves along the cliff, two are of great importance to Moslems: the **Cave of Abraham** and the **Cave of Job** (the names come out as *Ibrahim* and *Eyyüb* in Turkish). Both of these are religious sites of immeasurable antiquity, and were associated with the two Biblical figures before Moslems ever came here, but now they have become one of the most important places of pilgrimage in the Islamic world. Non-Moslems may also visit, except during the month of Ramazan.

Beneath the cliffs, adjoining the gardens and two pools, a complex of mosques and schools has grown up that is worthy of this holy city. None are very old—one mosque at the very base of the cliff with a huge dome is still under construction—but all are in the elegant style of the Halil Rahman Camii. **Hasan Paşa Camii** and the **Mevlidi Halil Camii** make the greatest impression, but taken all together this complex, with its arches, colonnades and cloisters, gardens and fountains is a masterpiece of urban design, electing praise for Allah and the city in one breath.

OLD NEIGHBOURHOODS

In the old neighbourhoods, along twisting, narrow unusually clean streets, fine old homes with balconies harmonise well with the design of the mosques. One motif you see everywhere, the zigzag line, always appears as if it were a symbol—on the balustrades of the Halil Rahman, on the arches above private doors, and in the metal grillwork. Like the homes in many Middle eastern cities, Urfa's face inwards, turning their backs on the street. Beside the balconies, the doorways are the only decoration, but the citizens have made it a point of pride to beautify them; many have miniatures of the kaa'ba or other religious subjects painted over the arch. If you can find the way through this maze of streets to the east, you'll see the last remaining section of the old city wall, the **Mahmetoğlu Tower** and the gate for the Mardin road beside it.

Urfa's **bazaar** seems to have selected the very narrowest streets in which to ply its trades, just to the north of the religious complex. **Atatürk Caddesi** skirts its edge, and continues northwards from there into the modern quarters of the town, passing several mosques with squat Persian-style minarets. One, the **Husayn Cami** stands right in the middle of the avenue. Its three-domed porch gives it away as an early Ottoman work. The **Ulu Cami,** a bit further north, dates from the twelfth century; the Selcuks built it immediately after their conquest of the city in commemoration of the event. Unique among the mosques of Turkey, if not the rest of the Islamic world, its minaret has a clock on top. The backstreets here have some of the best of Urfa's old houses.

In the modern end of Urfa, the **Archaeological Museum** has increased its collections so much in recent years that a new section is under construction; exhibits go as far back as the Assyrian colonies recently unearthed in the vicinity, and plenty of peculiar stone carvings may be seen in the sculpture garden outside. There aren't any of the customary stone lions here—but several stone pussycats.

Around Urfa to the Southeast

One biblical site this area doesn't claim, surprisingly, is the Valley of Dry Bones. Don't go lightly into any trip into the empty spaces around Urfa. In winter and early spring it's almost green, but during the hot months days of 110° are common, and shade and water are rare. Without a drop of humidity, the air scorches the soil with arid blasts, and the sparse grass left over from spring crackles underfoot like broken glass. If you've always wanted to see a genuine mirage, come in July or August, though after a few hours on the plains, you may not be able to distinguish them from the hallucinations.

It isn't the heat that bewilders, nor the uncanny landscape, wrinkled and ugly and covered with rocks. Both of these add much to the ambience, but the unfathomable strangeness of the place comes from the works of man. All around Urfa, the countryside is littered with caves and mounds, standing stones and cairns, ruins and inscriptions, along with such exotica as the little city, dug down several levels, right into flat ground, visible along the road from Urfa to Gaziantep. Nobody tries to explain who built any of these, or where they all come from; few scholars ever visit.

The best places to see lie among the awful **Tek Tek Mountains** east of the town. With proper directions from the Urfa tourist office, you will know where to leave the Mardin road. Along the passable dirt track south, the first sight to greet your eyes is a blue man painted on a cliff next to a small cave. It's somewhat disconcerting; it can't be too old. Every height in the Tek Tek bears some sort of marker on its summit, such as a large stone or cairn. They stand like sentinels, overlooking the valleys with their dry stream beds that once ran down to the Euphrates. The villages are hard to see, low on the ground or buried in it, with mud-walled huts and stables the same colour as the earth. Livestock grazing, and even agriculture, amazingly still go on; there's just enough rain in the spring to sprout a few crops. The semi-nomadic inhabitants, of uncertain nationality, are just as invisible. Not even they can stay out in the summer oven for long.

Soğmatar

Some 20 kilometres south of the highway, you reach the ruins of **Soğmatar**. The origin of this religious centre has evaporated in history, but the Near East's last pagans, a star and planet worshipping cult called the Sabaeans occupied it well into the Middle Ages. The site has never been thoroughly examined or explained, but enough remains to guess a little of what went on. At the centre of the modern Soğmatar village, the largest of several natural and artificial hills bears a large ruin believed to be the **Temple of the Sun**. Around it, the other heights have caves or buildings dedicated to the planetary deities, all oriented towards the sun temple; this is arranged, oddly enough, as if it were an up-to-date model of our heliocentric system. One of the hilltops for instance, contains a cave decorated with trident shapes or pitchforks, a common symbol throughout the Mediterranean, and the hole bored through its front wall is sighted directly on the sun temple. On the cliffs above, an apparently Greek or Roman era relief depicts a man and a woman—the villagers claim they are **Adam and Eve**—and a long inscription in Syriac. Another summit has a well preserved round tower; other remains are difficult to guess, but no doubt a complete investigation would turn up many other things of interest.

Someone from the village will be around to let you into the stable where another **shrine** can be seen. When your eyes become used to the darkness, a procession of eleven figures, badly eroded, and other Syriac inscriptions come into view, carved into the rock around which the stable is built. Around a central altar, looking down at the real bulls resting in front of them, are two relief bulls with crescent-moon horns.

Şuayp

Some 15 kilometres further on, the same road finds the lost city of **Şuayp**. Prosperous under the Assyrians and Romans, Şuayp was abandoned in the Middle Ages. The largest structure still standing amid its extensive ruins is a three-storey building with, not arches, but lintels over its windows—

difficult to ascribe to any architectural period. Crosses are carved into the walls in some places. Much of Şuayp seems to have been built underground, or into the hillsides. The present village occupies many of these holes, and you may be invited in for a subterranean glass of tea. Many of these caves and warrens were carved out of the soft rock with considerable care, adorned with arches and pilasters, niches and decorative entrances.

Harran

The next stop, only fifteen kilometres from the Syrian border, is **Harran,** more easily accessible by a paved road from Urfa for those who wish to avoid the Tek Tek. Here is a chance to see a city in its last stages before abandonment; Harran has been a city for perhaps 6000 years, at times reaching prominence in trade and culture. Today, its ruins shelter a small village of semi-nomadic Arabs in beehive-shaped desert style houses; these may be the most colourful community in Turkey, with unusually pretty children and women who wear all their jewellery all the time.

To guess at the founding of Harran is impossible—it's always been there—but only after the ninth century BC does it take its place among the big towns of the Near East. Somehow, Harran managed the neat trick of prospering under the Assyrians without being annihilated in a revolt or during the series of wars that followed the Assyrian decline. According to the *Book of Genesis*, Abraham and his family lived here for several years on their way from Ur to Canaan. In Roman times the town had come to be known as Carrhae, and its one appearance in history was a disaster the Romans would long remember. The first Roman triumvirate, you may recall from history or Shakespeare, consisted of Julius Caesar, Pompey, and a useless fool named Crassus that the two great generals kept around to appease the Senate. To prove his mettle while Caesar worked over the Gauls and Pompey cleared up the Cilician pirates, Crassus led an army against the Parthian (Persian) Empire. At Carrhae, in 53 BC, he walked right into a trap; his men were surrounded and cut down by the Parthians' Scythian allies—the first serious Roman defeat since Hannibal.

Later, under the Romans and Byzantines, the city became renowned as a centre of learning, and its reputation continued after the Arab conquest, as the home of the first great Islamic university. When the Mongols wrecked it in the thirteenth century, it stayed wrecked, harbouring intermittent Arab settlements ever since.

Harran's **fortress,** with unusual ten-sided towers, still remains in good condition, as do sections of the **walls,** including the **Aleppo Gate** on the southern edge. Of the rest, little survives. Most of the space within the walls serves as the Arabs' vegetable gardens and grazing lands. Of the famous **university,** only enough is there to hint at the opulence of the buildings, with fountains, paved walks, and the walls and minaret of a once-elegant mosque.

Perhaps it is too early to write Harran's obituary. Currently Turkish planners and engineers are hard at work on the most ambitious development project ever attempted in the Middle East, and the region around Harran and Urfa stands to be the major beneficiary. Consisting of a series of dams along the upper Euphrates, the **Southeast Anatolia Project** means to make this wasteland into the breadbasket of the region, and at the same time produce enough electricity to make Turkey self-sufficient, and end a dangerous addiction to Russian amperage. In its scope, the SAP rivals America's Tennessee Valley Authority. Not only is the land to be transformed, but the people also. They are among Turkey's poorest, and after the failed land reforms of the 1970s they remain at the mercy of feudal landlords, a situation the government wants to change.

ATATÜRK DAM

Sixty kilometres north of Urfa, near the ancient city of Samosata, the engineers are rushing to complete **Atatürk Dam.** When finished, it will be the third largest in the world, almost 600 feet high, and the lake it backs up behind it along the Euphrates will cover thousands of square miles. In front of the dam, a 26-mile tunnel is being drilled through the Urfa Yaylasi (highlands), to bring this water into the south. Construction has been slowed down by the difficulties of financing it and the objections of the Syrians, but when they turn the tap on, some time around 1993, people in Urfa expect their town to become the metropolis of Anatolia.

GETTING AROUND

Be advised that buses in the region, and indeed all of Eastern Anatolia, are not always up to the standard that obtains in the rest of the country— lots of cracked windows are the rule, and they travel at hair-raising speeds when they have a mind to. Still, there's no problem getting anywhere you want to go. If driving, there are no special precautions except to make sure you've got plenty of extra water and a good spare—and be especially careful on the bizarre E24 speed tunnel around Urfa. You'll have to rely on the locals for directions, quite often if you're trying to find the sights in the countryside—they aren't well signposted.

Don't take your car to Soğmatar or Şuayp; especially in the summer, it won't be worth the risk, and you probably won't find them anyway. The standard price for a complete taxi trip from Urfa is about 8400 TL including Harran, 3200 TL if you want to see Harran alone (undependable village minibuses also go there). The tourist office in Urfa can arrange it. Urfa itself can only be reached by bus or car; Gaziantep is connected by THY flights from Ankara; by rail it's linked with Sivas and Malatya.

TOURIST INFORMATION

3 Asfaltyol, right in the centre of the hotel district, two doors off Atatürk Caddesi, tel. (8711) 2467, in Urfa.

WHERE TO STAY

The best in Urfa is the **Turban Urfa Oteli** (H3) on Atatürk Caddesi, tel. (8711) 3520, where singles are 4000 TL and doubles 5000 TL with bath. Many clean, cheaper hotels like the **Güven** are on the same street within a block of the Turban, and charge around 3000 TL for a double. In Gaziantep, the **Murat** (H4) at 83 Inönü Cad. is about the best, with singles for 3000 TL, doubles 5000 TL.

EATING OUT

Urfa's restaurants, though modest, are also good, like the **Lale Lokanta** and the **Çiftlik Restoran,** both around the corner from city hall (Belediye). Food here is cheap: in both establishments expect to pay around 3000 TL for a meal.

You'll see things sold on the streets that aren't found elsewhere in Turkey; some are utterly mysterious and beyond the range of adventurousness of most travel writers, but if you come across dangerous looking black liquids in Urfa, it will be *murra*, a kind of over-boiled fermented coffee or homebrewed Turkish root beer. Drinking either one could change your life.

Gaziantep is famous for its restaurants (in Eastern Anatolia anyhow) and you'll dine well at well known, fancy establishments like the **Keyvanbey** on Hürriyet Caddesi, with an outdoor terrace above street level (complete meal for around 5000 TL) or good cheap lokantas like the **Efes,** just across the square from Keyvanbey.

The Commagenes

In the upheavals and confusions that attended the collapse of Alexander's short-lived empire, adventurers among his generals and their successors were often able to seize the main chance and carve out little tax farms to keep them in spending money. Some of the larger ones, like the Ptolemaic Kingdom in Egypt, and the Seleucid Kingdom in Persia and Anatolia, were able to survive as well-organised states for a long time; others, after a brief career, have been gathering dust in history's curiosity shop ever since.

KINGS OF COMMAGENE

To take the prize of being the most curious, we offer Mithradates Kallinikos and his son Antiochus, Kings of **Commagene,** a small, but rich and fertile, state that appeared in the first century BC along the Euphrates, in what is now the province of Adiyaman. For all the monuments those two left behind, you might think them rulers of a vast empire instead of the Roman puppets they really were, with a kingdom hardly more than a hundred miles wide at its greatest extent. Pompey, in his campaign to bring some kind of order to Anatolia—the Senate didn't want to annexe it yet—propped Antiochus on his throne in 61 BC. For almost a century, as long as the Romans found it expedient to keep them in business, the Commagene kings did their masters' bidding and spent the resources of their kingdom in self-glorification. From their subjects, they asked little more than to be treated as gods made manifest, and that the subjects spend most of their free time carrying rocks up mountains to build them tombs.

NEMRUT DAĞ

Nemrut Dağ, the mountain where Antiochus I is buried, has become one of the most popular tourist sights of Turkey, and the high seriousness of the deified Commagenes has at last got its just deserts. The tourists come in group buses to Adiyaman or the dismal village of Kahta, much closer, and at two in the morning they are dragged out of bed and tossed into minibuses for the long drive to Nemrut. Just as the first signs of dawn appear in the east, the long procession of headlights begins to snake up the mountain, and when the sun finally peeks over the horizon it finds the assemblage huddled together for warmth atop the stepped altar where Commagene hierophants once made dawn sacrifices to their defunct despot; blinking and mumbling, some trying to explain to the children what they're doing here, they gasp like people who have never seen a sunrise before, then grapple to get out their cameras and go to work.

In Kahta, they don't mention the stiff twenty-minute walk from the car park and refreshment stand up to the summit. When you come to the end of the path, it joins the Processional Way, leading to the **East Terrace,** where five colossal statues face the dawn. The heads have toppled to the ground, though as Nemrut's popularity increases the Turks are considering replacing them. It would be quite a job; they weigh several tons each.

Explaining just who these five were will be difficult. The Commagene kings traced their lineage back to Alexander the Great on one side and the Persian king Darius on the other. In their little cosmopolitan state halfway between Greece and Persia, they tried to keep up the Alexandrian principle of syncretism—combining similar gods from different cultures into a single figure, and creating out of the synthesis a new cult, with room in it for the likes of Antiochus and Mithradates. Thus the aesthetic looking fellow on the left is not only **Apollo,** but Mithra and Helios at the same time. **Tyche,** the only lady present, is the 'good spirit' of the Greeks, magnified into a figure that includes all the region's myriad of goddesses.

Zeus, or Ahuramazda, takes pride of place in the centre, with a pointed cap and bushy whiskers. Next comes **Antiochus,** looking completely at home in such company, and finally **Heracles,** or Artagnes or Ares. These five are flanked by pairs of equally colossal staring eagles and lions, looking perhaps for an empire to symbolise. The **altar,** a massive square of stone, is now used as a helicopter platform, with a big H painted on it. All around, and particularly on the backs of the statues, the Commagenes have left us the longest Greek inscription ever found, detailing their royal descent, their births, careers, and the rites with which they desired to be worshipped.

With all this to take in, it may escape your notice that the neat symmetrical peak of this mountain is a fake. Though the highest in the area, Nemrut isn't much of a mountain, and Antiochus found it necessary to add another 150 feet of loose stones to get the desired silhouette. On the ground, it would make a fair-sized pyramid. Somewhere underneath, Antiochus lies buried, but the team of archaeologists who cleaned up Nemrut were unable to find his tomb; they feared any attempt at tunnelling would bring down the entire tumulus.

Another path leads around the north side of the summit to the **West Terrace**. But for the lack of an altar, this is a carbon copy of the East Terrace, where the same five gods enjoy the sunset. Here, though, the statues are in better shape, and some of the **sculptural reliefs** have survived. Three of these portray Antiochus shaking hands with gods—Apollo, Zeus, and Heracles. Such scenes, with the same smiles and poses as the publicity photos in Communist newspapers, were the favourite subject for Commagene art.

Another relief shows a lion with a backdrop of a crescent moon and stars. From the stars' pattern, it has been decided that this represents a conjunction of planets that occurred near the date of Antiochus' accession to the throne. A word needs to be said about all these sculptures. Not only is the work of high artistic merit, but something about these thoughtful, expressive faces seems eerily modern. The Commagenes for all their nonsense, were sophisticated rulers living at the height of the Greek world's achievements. We give the Greeks credit for the invention of the free man, the individual, but if these reliefs of Commagene symbolise anything, it is the decay of that man, and his submission to the statist mysticisms of the East, a process that in later centuries reached its culmination in the palaces of Constantinople.

The other Commagene sites are in the valleys of the **Cendere** and **Nymphaion,** tributaries of the Euphrates, and can be seen, along with Nemrut, in a day. You may mourn for this countryside, once celebrated for its beauty and fertility; something here has gone very wrong. You will not see such poverty, or such blank, twisted faces elsewhere in Turkey. Most of the hills have eroded into slag heaps, but here and there, in a cared-for field or lonely grove of trees, you can see how the grandeur of the mountain scenery was once complemented by greenery. No doubt Commagene had more rain in ancient times, but that doesn't account for all the change. Ambitious kings have a way of making their lands waste, and we should not be surprised if what we see before us is Antiochus' true memorial. Ironically, even where nothing else grows, lovely pink oleanders line the roads.

Arsameia

Arsameia, on the Nymphaion river, served Antiochus for a capital, of which whatever endured into medieval times was incorporated into the Turkish castle called **Yeni Kale.** On the opposite hillside, the **Eski Kale,** despite its name, isn't really a castle at all, but the *hierothesion* or temple tomb Antiochus built for his father **Mithradates,** not quite as grand as his own. At the entrance, a large upright slab bears a relief of **Mithra,** looking towards a large cave in the side of the mountain. It may be the only image of this god you will ever see; in spite of the widespread popularity of this Persian cult, which as late as the third century AD, could claim more followers than Christianity, it seldom penetrated the upper classes deeply enough to be expressed in art.

Where Mithra directs, in the cave, another relief depicts King Mithradates with Helios-Apollo. A large cistern opens from the cave. From here, another path leads across the mountainside to the centrepiece of the hierothesion, where an even larger relief has Mithradates shaking hands with a clumsily-sculpted Hercules. The king, portrayed as the taller and more impressive of the two, wears a tunic decorated with eight-pointed stars, the dynastic emblem of the Commagenes. Next to this, a Greek inscription, similar to those on Nemrut, was carved over the entrance to a tunnel, leading over 300 feet down on stairs through the bare rock. What the purpose of this was, and where Mithradates may be buried, no one knows

Karakuş

Leaving Arsameia for the third Commagene hierothesion, on a hill called **Karakuş,** you pass an **Ottoman bridge** over the Nymphaion and at the point where that stream, now called Kahta Çay, empties into the Cendere, a **Roman bridge** stands, strong enough to carry the modern road. Septimus Severus, who had it built, added two columns at each end, honouring himself and his family in Latin inscriptions. Karakuş, a tumulus of small stones similar to Nemrut but smaller, holds the remains of Antiochus' wife. The tumulus was surrounded by tall columns surmounted by the tiresome Commagene familiars—eagles, lions, and hand-shaking kings, of which onlyl three remain erect. The eagle may have contributed the modern Turkish name; *Karakuş* means 'black bird'. From here it's only a short way back to Kahta.

Adiyaman, the provincial capital and a town of no great antiquity, offers little to see; neither now does **Samosata,** an important town thousands of years ago, where the Roman poet Lucian was born. Some bits of Samosata remain around its castle, but the entire area may soon be underwater when Atatürk Dam, just a few miles down the Euphrates, is completed.

Malatya and Elaziğ

Just north of ancient Commagene, a long chain of mountains, the **Anti-Taurus,** stretches the entire length of South-eastern Anatolia from the Hatay to Lake Van. On the opposite, northern, slopes, the central highway from Kayseri to Van passes through difficult mountain terrain into the valley of the Murat River, climbing gradually upwards through yaylas (highlands) crowded during the summer with nomadic herdsmen and their flocks. **Malatya,** the first and most interesting of the towns along this route, simply cannot stand still. Although its history has been continuous since the Hittities, it has occupied three different sites.

The modern city was founded only in the early nineteenth century, but already has grown to a population of 150 000 supporting themselves by modern industry and ancient crafts; the city has had a reputation for its copper works since the Middle Ages. **Eski Malatya,** the town gradually abandoned since the new foundation was begun, flourished in the thirteenth century as an eastern outpost of the Selcuk sultanate. Parts of the walls remain, along with some of the **Ulu Cami,** built in 1247 by the famous Selcuk architect Hüsrev: its outstanding feature, the entrance portal, is a unique work with tiny faience tiles set into the stone almost like mosaics for the geometric patterns.

If Malatya has not stayed on one site, it does have the distinction of holding on to its name as long as any city in Turkey. Records of both the Hittites and Assyrians speak of a town kingdom of Milid, or Milidia, that made a name for itself after the Hittite collapse, and lasted until the Cimmerians sacked it in the eighth century BC, only to reappear in Roman times as Melitene. The site of ancient Malatya, where ruins of the palace can be seen, are at a spot the Turks call **Aslantepe** because of the reliefs of lions that guarded its gate, and now adorn the Ankara Museum. Aslantepe lies seven miles north of modern Malatya, and Eski Malatya nine miles north along the same road.

Elaziğ, 101 kilometres north-east, is another prospering modern town that tells much the same story. It, too, began in the last century, named after its founder Abdül el-Aziz, and the ancient city it succeeded, **Harput,** which was wrecked by earthquakes, lies 6 kilometres to the north with the ruins of a Turkish castle and mosques. Elaziğ owed its modern good fortune to the giant **Keban Dam,** built in the 1970s as the first stage of the

South-east Anatolia Project. Beyond Elaziğ, the country becomes steeper and less populated. **Bingöl** means 'a thousand lakes', and if 'thousand' in Turkish may really mean 'quite a few', the mountain scenery is still nice. Glaciers gouged out the lake beds two ice ages ago.

GETTING AROUND

THY flights connect Ankara with Malatya and Elaziğ. The major east–west railroad line to Lake Van passes through Elaziğ and Malatya, and the one north–south line through the Eastern provinces, connects Sivas with Malatya.

You can visit all the Commagene sites by car, but it's a long trip with few road signs and service stations along the backroads. You might wait until the tour buses go and follow them. Because it's popular with tourists, prices for these are a bit higher—about 16 800 TL for a minibus from Kahta to Nemrut, etc., and considerably more from Adiyaman. You'll probably find some people in your hotel waiting to make the trip—the more you get together, the cheaper it will be. Ask at your hotel and they'll set you up.

TOURIST INFORMATION

In Adiyaman, Hükümet Caddesi, tel. (8781) 1008; in Malatya, 5 Sivas Caddesi, in the centre of the new city, tel. (821) 177 33; in Elaziğ, 35 Istasyon Cad., tel. (811) 16 572.

WHERE TO STAY

Malatya, and Elaziğ all have good hotels with showers at very reasonable rates. Malatya's best, the **Kent** (H4), Atatürk Cad. 151, tel. (821) 121 75–128 13 and the **Sinan Oteli** (H4) Atatürk Cad. 14, tel. (821) 129 07–130 07 are about the same and charge the same prices: 3000 TL a single, 4000 a double.

In Adiyaman and Kahta, there isn't much to say. Adiyaman has one motel, the **Arsemia** (M2) on the Nemrut road 146, tel. (8781) 2112–3131, with a swimming pool for 3000 TL a single, 5000 TL a double. If you want to stay in Kahta, more convenient to Nemrut Dağ, your choice between the **Merhaba** and the **Kommagene Pansiyon** is no choice at all; prices for both are around 2400 TL for a double.

Diyarbakir

From Kahramanmaraş to **Bitlis** and beyond, the **Anti–Taurus** marks the southern limits of the Anatolian plateau. To the south of it, the land descends in a broad, broken plain towards the deserts of Syria. The Tigris and the Euphrates flow here, and by the time they reach this plain they've gathered enough tributaries to rank as important rivers, impressive enough

Malabadi Bridge

in their spring floods; by June they slow down to trickles, and the assiduous Turkish farmers come down from the villages to sow whatever stretches of good land they can find among the network of streams and rocky shoals these great rivers have become. The country is fertile, and best for wheat. In spite of its cheerless sameness, these tan and treeless plains have supported large populations for millennia.

HISTORY

The natural capital of this region is now and always has been **Diyarbakir,** on the Tigris' banks. Few cities in the world are older. Though its beginnings are so long lost that not even legends survive, Diyarbakir has been a town at least since the time of the Hurrians, some five thousand years ago. A record from Assyria's archives from a later age makes first the mention of the city by its ancient name **Amida.**

Since antiquity, from the northern hills the city has brought dark, heavy basalt to build and rebuild its walls. Even today, these walls are the city's pride and its symbol, and, over the centuries, they have made such an impression on the succession of travellers and conquerors who have passed beneath them that the city is renowned as **Amid the Black.**

Whoever built here first, a glance at the town plan shows Diyarbakir, in its present form, to be a child of the Romans. The city, like so many from Britain to Iraq, is a classic Roman *castrum*, roughly rectangular with two broad streets connecting the four gates at the cardinal points. The Romans under

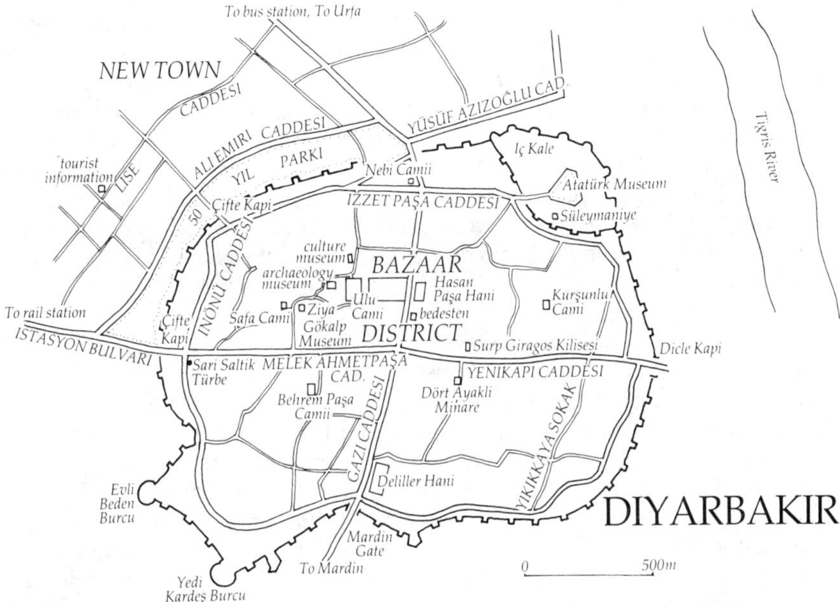

Constantinus II also built the oldest surviving sections of Diyarbakir's walls, and beneath the later façades of black basalt arches and vaults, the characteristic Roman thin brick can be seen in many places. For the Romans, the city was a crucial bastion in the defence against the Sassanid Persians. It changed hands more than once, and later Roman emperors mounted campaigns here whenever they could, including Julian the Apostate, whose success against the Sassanids was negated by his untimely death near Amida in AD 363.

For the next 300 years, Amida remained a Christian town, often brimming with refugees from the surrounding settlements that fell to the Persians. Amida's own turn came in 639, when the new Moslem Arab army made the city its first important conquest within the present-day borders of Turkey; from this, Diyarbakir today likes to claim Turkey's oldest mosque, the Ulu Cami, and its oldest Arabic inscriptions.

Curiously, despite its formidable walls, Diyarbakir was never especially successful in keeping out conquerors. The centuries that followed the decline of the Abbasid caliphate saw dozens of them check their turbans at Diyabakir's gate. Nearly every warrior clan, great or obscure, that clutters the pages of Turkish history came to rule Black Amid for a time: Marvanids,

Selcuks, Damascus Selcuks, Nishanli, Artukid, White Sheep and Black, and more. Ottoman control, in the person of Sultan Selim the Grim, came early in the sixteenth century, and Diyarbakir has been quiet ever since.

Today, besides its walls, Diyarbakir is most proud of watermelons. They say their farmers grow the world's biggest, weighing up to 160 pounds when the rains are good. The best-selling postcards in the town show hollowed-out melons with grinning children peeking out from inside. Like all these surprisingly large cities of south-eastern Anatolia, Diyarbakir is modern, pleasant, and booming; its centre, colourful and lively day and night, forms a neutral zone between the bland newer districts and the exotic old city within the walls.

OLD DIYARBAKIR

Old Diyarbakir can be entered through two gates in the northern walls. In this area, some of the walls were demolished in favour of automobile traffic, while other parts have been included in the **50 Yil Parki** (Fiftieth Anniversary Park), which separates the new city from the old. Near the park's centre, **Çifte Kapi,** the 'twin gates', are a more modern incision in the walls, and near them stands a small thirteenth-century tomb, the **Sari Saltik Türbe** that can serve as an introduction to the city's unique and excellent vernacular architecture. Besides basalt, the region also yields a fine pale sandstone. In all their mosques, tombs, and *hans*, Diyarbakir's medieval architects acquired the habit of using the two together, in alternating layers, so that once within the walls, Amid the Black becomes, less formidably, 'the Striped'. The effect is very attractive, and few cities anywhere have managed the trick of evolving such a simple and lovely style to give themselves a sense of place. On many of the buildings, like the Sari Saltik Türbe, what appears at first to be decorative plaques of the same black and white stone turn out to be Arabic inscriptions, in the rectangular Kufic script, adding to the charm of the design.

The second entrance to the old town, only a few blocks east along Inönü Caddesi, is what was the Harput Gate of ancient times. This, the only gap in Diyarbakir's walls, has become the busiest corner of the modern city; the gate and nearby walls were demolished not long ago to make room for traffic. Everyday these streets fill up with every manner of man; peasants from the countryside, street hawkers, soldiers, porters with their packs, smug-looking businessmen in expensive suits. As a backdrop, new hotels and office blocks of seven or eight floors push their way up through the chaos of the older buildings; both new and old are hidden behind an amazing forest of signboards and placards, hanging over the pavements from the first floor to the eaves. Diyarbakir may be 5000 years old, but this busy commercial exuberance must be very much the same as it was in new American cities of a hundred years ago. You can walk down Izzet Paşa Caddesi and pretend you're on Main Street, Kansas City or Denver, c. 1880—until you run into a mosque. In this case, it's the **Nebi (prophet) Camii,** at the corner of Gazi Caddesi. This lovely and thoroughly striped mosque was built by the White Sheep clan around 1530. Its typical minaret, striped also, like a giant ice cream parfait, is tall and square, another peculiarity of the local style.

IÇ KALE

From this corner, Gazi Caddesi, one of two wide cross-streets of the Roman city, leads south towards the centre, while Izzet Paşa heads towards the Tigris and the **Iç Kale,** or Inner Fortress, the oldest part of Diyarbakir. The pointed arch at the entrance is said to be all that remains from the **Palace of the Artukid Turks** who once ruled here; on it can be seen their symbol, a lion attacking a bull. The bull, we understand, represents worldly riches, and the lion, those strong enough to seize them, an altogether fitting symbol for any Turkish warrior caste in the Gazi tradition. There's another lion on a pretty **fountain** just inside the gate.

In the citadel, under venerable trees, there's room enough only for the provincial courts, the inevitable **Atatürk Museum,** one of two in the city, and the **Süleymaniye Cami** (or Kale Cami) of the sixteenth century. Of the city's landmarks, this mosque, with its especially tall minaret, is famous for the deep underground spring that supplies the water to its *şadirvan* in the courtyard. The good-tasting water stays cold all year, which makes this a popular spot during the brutal summer days; it is probably the original spring that has supplied this citadel for 5000 years. Outside the citadel walls, you can hire a horse-drawn carriage for a ride in the city, or else try to find your way through the narrow twisting streets of this quarter back to Gazi Caddesi. It won't be easy; the old sections of Diyarbakir are as exasperating a maze as any medieval town has anywhere. If you're lucky, you may find another fine mosque, the **Fatih Paşa Camii** of 1520, better known here as the *Kurşunlu Cami* (bullet mosque). These ancient residential quarters are charming, though given over to the city's poor, in the modern fad for concrete apartment blocks. If you poke around them you may find yourself an instant celebrity; most of the children have never seen foreigners.

ULU CAMI

However you get back to Gazi Caddesi, look for the **Ulu Cami,** just off the avenue behind a shady square that was the town's centre in the old days. As stated above, this is arguably the oldest mosque in Turkey, reconstructed out of a Byzantine church called the Martoma. Most of what you see, however, was constructed by the Selcuks in the late eleventh century, and many of the other rulers since have had a hand in the various reconstructions. The

Artukids, for example, added parts of the courtyard, as evidenced by the lions and bulls over the main gate.

The main attraction is not the rather austere mosque but its courtyard. Whoever built it, it's clear that almost everything in this spacious court was quarried from older buildings, with fascinating effect, as if old Byzantine and Arab Amida had been taken to pieces and whimsically reassembled. There are colonnades where each capital is different, columns stacked on larger columns, beautiful friezes of Greek designs next to Arabic Kufic script, intertwined with grapevines. Greek inscriptions look out from the walls in the most unlikely places.

While in this courtyard, you may hear a banging and clattering in the distance, as if a whole army of tinkers were near by. They are—in their street in the crowded and colourful **market district** just outside these walls. As usual, every trade has its own part of the market; the ancient *bedesten* may be full of butchers now, but the street called 'Gold Alley' still glitters with scores of shops, and deals are still made in the **Hasan Paşa Hani** of 1572, an excellent striped building that once was a great terminal caravanserai. It stands just across Gazi Caddesi from the Ulu Cami.

There are three museums within a short distance of each other in the streets just behind Ulu Cami. Diyarbakir's **Archaeological Museum,** currently being restored, is in the old Senceriye Medrese and includes items from as far back as the Hittites. The **Ziya Gökalp Museum** was the home of that very influential turn-of-the century Turkish intellectual, the man credited with inventing the idea of Turkish nationalism. The home of one of his near contemporaries, the poet Cahit Sitki Taranci, has become a **Culture Museum** in his honour, with exhibits of local arts and crafts. The house itself, with its typical courtyard decorated with patterns stencilled in whitewash is a lovely example of the local fashion, and the poet's sitting room, with its stone fountain and its rather elegant old radio, may give an insight into the heights of gracious living in the Diyarbakir of the 1930s. In this area, too, is the **Safa Camii,** with its striped porticos and one of the most unusual minarets in Diyarbakir.

South of Melek Ahmet Paşa Caddesi—the long east–west axis of the city (its name becomes Yenikapi Caddesi as it crosses Gazi Caddesi)—stand two other interesting mosques. The **Behrem Paşa Camii** (1572) is claimed by some to be the jewel of Diyarbakir's mosques, and the **Kasim Padişah Camii,** just off Yenikapi Caddesi, is best known for its minaret, the **'Dört Ayakli Minare',** which is very lofty, but mysteriously separated from its mosque; indeed, the minaret is set up right in the middle of the street, suspended in the air on four broad basalt columns. The locals claim that your wish will come true if you pass between the columns seven times. Near this mosque is one of Diyarbakir's two surviving Christian churches still in use, the Armenian **Surp Giragos Kilisesi.**

Another fine *han*, the **Delillar Hani,** stands at the south end of Gazi Caddesi, at the Mardin Gate. An Ottoman work completed in 1527, it was built especially for travellers to Mecca. At present, the city is restoring this *han* from the ground up; when finished, it will once more assume its old function in a new way—as a modern hotel, with shops under the colonnades of the courtyard.

THE WALLS

Mardin Gate, next to an odd, square *türbe* of uncertain origin, is a good place to begin a tour of Diyarbakir's **walls,** an undertaking that could easily swallow up a day or two. Few city walls have so much of interest chiselled into them. Inscriptions in every language, some as old as the Abbasid caliphs of the early tenth century, can be found anywhere—in decorative friezes around the towers, over the gates, in corners where no one ever looks. Almost every gun port has an inscription, perhaps exhorting the defenders to shoot straight. In addition, there are several examples of Selcuk stone work, with their usual fantastical animals and men carved in reliefs about the towers. You can inspect the outside of the wall, walk over the top of it, and, in many places, even walk through it; numerous corridors inside the walls connect the inner chambers of the towers which are completely protected from enemy attack.

The most impressive section is in the southwest, at a naturally weak point in the defences, where the Artukids, in 1208, constructed two mighty bastions expanding outwards from earlier works of the Selcuks. The two round towers, the **Evli Beden Burcu** and the **Yedi Kardeş Burcu** are almost identical, and are elaborately decorated on the outside. Yedi Kardeş (seven brothers) probably takes its name from the seven chambers that radiate from the central hall inside.

There is a story in Diyarbakir that these two towers were built by a master architect and his former student, in a competition to see who could build the strongest and best. The master, seeing that his rival had outdone him when the Evli Beden was completed, threw himself off his Yedi Kardeş Burcu in despair. From these walls, you can see a long and graceful bridge over the Tigris, built probably by the Ottomans; **'Ten Eyes'** the locals call it, from its ten arches, and according to another story, the pasha who built it also caused a large sum of gold to be hidden under one of its piers; no one knows which. When the bridge falls to ruin, it is supposed the money will be found, enough to construct a new one.

AROUND DIYARBAKIR

Most of the countryside of this region is given over to sheep and cattle; though once heavily farmed when the rains were more frequent and the

Fertile Crescent was really fertile, today these bare hills tolerate only a little dry farming. If you look carefully, on many hillsides you can make out the traces of ancient agricultural terraces. More common, though, are the networks of faint lines winding around the lower slopes; the trails left by columns of sheep. In this dry arid climate, it takes decades for them to wear away.

The landscape may be uninviting, especially in the summer, but it contains a good number of religious and antiquarian sites that foreign visitors seldom see. At **Ergani,** for instance, on the road to Elaziğ, a very ancient mosque on the mountain called **Zülküf Daği** dedicated as a shrine to a local prophet, Zülküf, is honoured by Moslems and Christians alike. People of both faiths make pilgrimages here from all over southern Anatolia. Another such site, at **Cüngüs,** is an eleventh-century dervish retreat still in use. To the east, in **Hani,** pilgrims come to wash in the five-sided holy **Pool of Ayn Kebir,** reputed to have great healing powers. Ruins of the Greek city of **Dakyanos** lie near the town of **Lice.** We may be hearing more from Lice in the future; archaeologists are excitedly digging up an extremely ancient town, several thousand years BC, at a site 30 kilometres north of the town. They aren't sure yet what they've found, but it seems to be one of the most important recent discoveries in the Middle East. Finally, in this region near the village of **Birklin** are caves near which is carved a relief of that most insufferable rooster of an Assyrian, King Tiglath-Pileser II, together with the usual long cuneiform inscription boasting of his many conquests.

Mardin

South of Diyarbakir, in the baking plains near the Syrian border, the highway for Mosul and Baghdad reaches a kind of world's end at **Mardin,** perched on the edge of the Syrian Desert. Due south from here, the next towns of any size are Mecca and Medina, far off in Arabia.

Mardin's reason for existence is its strong citadel; the city flows down from it along a broad hillside. Though probably as old as Diyarbakir, Mardin has never been more than a distant outpost of any state that ruled it, with the possible exception of the White Sheep clan, ruins of whose palace can be seen in the citadel; coincidentally, Mardin is often called the 'white city', in counterpoint to black Diyarbakir. The pale sandstone used, as in Urfa, for its homes and monuments gives the city a striking appearance when seen from a distance. Mardin speaks four languages, transacting its business in Turkish, Kurdish, Arabic and sometimes Aramaic, the ancient language of the Holy Land. This is spoken by the large population of Jacobite Christians who have lived here, co-existing peacefully with their Moslem neighbours ever since the Arab conquest.

Of the several Islamic foundations in the city, the most important is the

Isa Bey Medrese near the citadel, an unusual building with beautifully carved friezes and medallions on its gate. Others, towards the newer quarters of the town, are the often-restored eleventh-century **Ulu Cami** originally a Selcuk work, and the fourteenth-century **Lâtifiye Cami.**

Around Mardin, again in regions likely to be explored only by the most adventurous travellers, are inviting towns like **Viranşehir,** literally the 'ruined city' with its remains of Byzantine and Roman fortifications, and **Hasankeyf,** an ancient town on the Tigris with the ruins of a once-great bridge of the twelfth century. Here too, are the picturesque remains of the fifteenth century **Zeyfelbey Türbesi,** with its brick onion dome and patterns in different-coloured stone.

Kiziltepe, just south of Mardin, has the ruins of the thirteenth-century **Ulu Cami,** built when Kiziltepe was the major city of Dunyasir. The region of the Jacobite, or Syrian Christians, is found east of Mardin in and round **Midyat.** Several Christian monasteries here are still occupied, most notably the ancient Syrian patriarchate at **Deyl-ul-Zaferan,** just outside Mardin.

Towards Lake Van

To go any further eastwards, however, you will have to retrace your steps to Diyarbakir. From there, the road to Lake Van passes through **Silvan,** a dusty farm town built in and around the ruins of a sixth-century Byzantine fortress. Some fifteen miles further on, you cross the Batman, a tributary of the Tigris, on a modern bridge built parallel to the majestic single-arched **Malabadi Bridge,** a famous work of the Artukid Turks, currently undergoing restoration.

Somewhere in this region, and no one is sure where, one of the peculiar historical events that followed the collapse of the Seleucid Empire took place; the founding of the now completely vanished city of **Tigranocerta.** King Tigranes, surnamed 'the Great', was an Armenian prince who, through cleverness and good luck, managed to carve out a small empire for himself, with Rome's blessing, in the troubled early years of the first century BC. Like his father-in-law, Mithradates of Pontus, and their other relatives ruling the Kingdom of Commagene, this Tigranes made a lot of noise, depopulated a few cities to build his capital, and managed a few temporary conquests (in his case, much of Syria). And like those other precursors of Shelley's *Ozymandias,* he found himself looking for a new job when expedience made the Romans (Pompey) pull in the puppet strings in 66 BC. The result, if there was any result, was just another of the sad false starts that clutter the chronicles of the Armenians, and the stones of Tigranocerta, wherever it was, have helped construct and rebuild peasant homes and stables for two thousand years.

Just beyond the Malabadi Bridge, the highway begins to climb up into the lovely Bitlis Mountains, an eastern extension of the **Taurus** that serves to seal off **Lake Van** and the hidden valleys of **Siirt** and **Hakkari** provinces, from the rest of Anatolia. Siirt certainly qualifies as one of the more out-of-the-way corners of Turkey; apart from the mountain scenery, the sole reason to take the only paved road in the province would be to visit the **Mausoleum and Museum of Ibrahim Hakki,** a complex from Ottoman times in the town of **Aydinlar,** 6 kilometres from Siirt. Ibrahim Hakki was a famous Moslem astronomer, and his observatory and instruments are here.

On the map you'll notice that the railway line from Diyarbakir ignominously fades out in the little village of **Kurtalan,** some 45 kilometres short of Siirt. This, at least, deserves an explanation, it was the work of none other than Kaiser Wilhelm II, the last of his line, one of Tigranes the Great's modern-day counterparts. It's an obscure chapter in history now, but at the turn of the century, the Germans' plan for a Berlin-to-Baghdad railway was at the heart of the Kaiser's vast geopolitical scheme; he aimed to create a single economic sphere comprising all of Central Europe and the Middle East, dominated by Germany. The World War, of course, intervened, and Kurtalan was as far as the German engineers ever got.

Bitlis, deep in the mountains, is a town that sticks in the memory for the distinctive cool grey stone and rounded windows of the old buildings, which climb up steep streets to a well preserved **citadel** built by the Ottomans. The **Ulu Cami** here, though restored several times, was originally a twelfth century Selcuk work. From here, it's only 22 kilometres to **Tatvan** on Lake Van; Tatvan is the end, or rather the interruption of another railway line, and the terminal of the T. C. Denizyollari ferry that transfers rail passengers over the Lake to Van. Tatvan these days keeps its police very busy; the town is full of suspicious characters and unmarked truckloads of freight heading to and from places like Iran and Iraq.

GETTING AROUND

There are daily **flights** from Ankara to Diyarbakir, and weekly flights connecting Diyarbakir with Van. Otherwise, **buses** are the only way to get around this region. Local minibus services can bring you to most of the rural sights around Diyarbakir and Mardin; just check to make sure there will be a way to get back. Some of the churches and monasteries east of Mardin are close enough for a taxi trip.

For motorists, the same caveats mentioned in the last section apply here—about water and the difficulty in finding the way to the sights. Within Diyarbakir, taxis are plentiful along Inönü Caddesi, but all the things to see are within walking distance in the old town. The bus and train stations are some distance out though. When you're leaving the town on the bus, buy the ticket in town; most companies have a free minibus service to the station.

TOURIST INFORMATION

Diyarbakir: 24 Lise Caddesi, two blocks north of the city walls, tel. (831) 12173, 17840.
Silvan: 90 Gazi Caddesi, tel. 603.

WHERE TO STAY

The centre of Diyarbakir is full of medium range hotels. The **Aslan** (H4) on Inönü Caddesi, tel. (831) 13971 and the Aslan Palace (H3) next door, are among the best inexpensive hotels you'll find in Turkey. Rates are 4000 TL for a double and 2500 TL for a single. None of the others are much more expensive. In Mardin, the **Şirin Hotel** on the main street is good enough; there is also accommodation in Siirt, Bitlis, and Silvan, but nothing beyond the bare essentials.

EATING OUT

In Diyarbakir, there are some excellent inexpensive lokantas around Inönü and Izzet Paşa Cad., like the **Kent** and **Babaman,** with solid Turkish fare for around 2000 TL a filling meal. Elsewhere the lokantas are simple and unremarkable.

Lake Van

Out here in Turkey's south-eastern marches, on the shores of the bottle-green sea, is quite simply another world. The superbly queer lake itself, the mighty volcanoes that add so much to the scenery along its shores, and the exotic landmarks of the Armenians, Urartians, and Kurds, all coalesce to make this unique and fascinating country.

Take the lake for starters. Lake Van is old, even as geological time is measured; since the volcanic upthrusts that isolated this basin, water can flow in, down from the mountains, but not out. With no circulation, the lake is left to stew in its own juice, a thick broth of sulphides and mineral salts, and consequently it has always been biologically dead. One wonders what the large gull population finds to eat; there are no fish, no molluscs, and no seaweed—but no pollution. The water, though the foulest tasting stuff anywhere, is said to be especially good for washing, and you can swim in it without harm. Though not unusually buoyant, it has an unusual viscous appearance, like warm gelatine. It rises in billows and wrinkles, never in ripples or waves.

The region has always been occupied; the mountains circling Lake Van are full of cave paintings, some dated as far back as 15 000 years. The Hurrians, the shadowy late Neolithic people who provided the indigenous stock of so much of Anatolia, arrived some time around the third millennium BC, and the population increased markedly in the second millennium, when a prolonged drought in the plains to the south-west caused many of the semi-nomadic tribes of that area to migrate into the mountains. Today that migration is echoed in the annual spring wanderings of the shepherds, sometimes covering great distances, to their *yayla,* or summer pasture, in these highlands. From late May onwards their tents blossom everywhere in the mountains of Eastern Anatolia, though today, more often than not, the shepherds and sheep make the trip by truck.

HISTORY

The Hurrian Mitanni state that developed at this time, before the Assyrians exterminated it, marks the beginning of recorded history in the region. The Assyrians provide most of the records, detailing the looting and carnage caused by each of their forays. To them, Lake Van was the 'Upper Sea', and a strategic spot on the borders of their Hittite enemies. In their records of the tenth century BC, we see King Shalmaneser I claiming victories over a new nation, the Uratri, or Urartu, the first mention of that name in history, at a time when the Urartians were probably nothing more than a feudal confederation for defence against the Assyrians. The blessed two centuries of Assyrian weakness that followed, however, gave the Urartians the chance to build a nation and a culture for themselves with its heartland around Lake Van and extending at times as far as the Black Sea and the Caspian.

Even if the refined culture of the Urartians can be better seen in the museums of Ankara and Van than at the sites themselves, you can exercise your imagination in trying to recreate this lost culture on its own grounds. First, the accounts of the Assyrian King Sargon II describe the hills around Van as thickly forested, with pines, beech, and oaks; so densely forested, in fact, that Sargon's chronicles noted that their soldiers could only march through them two abreast (there are still some of these oak groves in the mountains near Bitlis). Rising up out of the forests on natural eminences, we would have seen the fortified palaces with their whitewashed and, most likely, elaborately decorated walls, crowned with stepped gables like the tops of Dutch houses. Such scenes are portrayed on Urartian metalwork, which also shows kings in their chariots hunting wild game in the forests, and the priests in their rich costumes, trimmed with gold sashes and jewellery. Ordinary people, not surprisingly, do not appear anywhere in Urartian art; some evidence from the inscriptions has led scholars to believe the Urartians were a slave society as brutal and stupid as that of their Assyrian neighbours. Their art makes it hard to believe, or rather makes us wish to disbelieve this, but probably, in that nest of snakes that was the early Middle East, it could hardly have been otherwise.

Two mighty volcanoes crowd the north shore of Lake Van, creating a centrepiece for the region's postcard scenery. At 13 188 feet, **Süphan Daği** is the third largest peak in Turkey, its summit snow-covered most of the year. Like Ararat, Süphan Daği towers alone over the low hills, and provides a landmark for the entire region. The second peak, **Nemrut Daği,** barely pokes its head above the lofty mountains behind Tatvan. Not to be confused with the Nemrut Daği of Commagene, this Nemrut, instead of having colossi on top, boasts a lake, Nemrut Gölü, rather like the famous Crater Lake in Oregon but without the trees. Still, its odd volcanic formations create a genuine scenic wonder. The road up is bad and no organised transport exists. You have to climb it yourself, or find someone in Tatvan with a jeep.

AHLAT AND ADILCEVAZ

Ahlat, on the lake shore under Nemrut, was an Armenian principality that flourished under the Selcuks, becoming so famous for stonecarving that its artists were in demand throughout Anatolia. Over the centuries, the city was gradually abandoned, and today in this grave of a town, only the graves remain; there are several fine *türbeler* of the thirteenth to fifteenth centuries, and the famous **graveyard** of distinctive Selcuk tombstones. Strangely, these heavy rectangular upright stones of volcanic rock, most taller than a man, have been more painstakingly carved with more elaborate designs than any of the mausolea. No others exist outside the Van region, each carved with a kind of window at its centre, surrounded by calligraphy and geometric designs so densely packed that they resemble some Mayan relief. Near the town of **Adilcevaz,** some 25 kilometres further along the shore, are the remains of an unnamed Urartian town, built by King Rusa II; the Turks call it **Keyfkalesi.** As the fine stone reliefs discovered here have been removed to the Van museum, little remains to be seen except for some finely squared masonry.

AKHTAMAR

Along the south edge of the lake, mountains prevent the road from hugging the shore for over half the distance to Van. When the road finally winds down from the hills, it affords a wonderful prospect of the lake, its surrounding mountains, and its several islands, the largest of which, with its famed Armenian church, is **Akhtamar.**

During the tenth and eleventh centuries, the same period when the Armenian kingdom at Ani was in full flower, a separate Armenian state called Vaspurakan flourished here on the shores of Lake Van. The greatest of the Vaspurakan kings, named Gagik like his contemporary in Ani, constructed a palace for himself on this lovely island around 920, and raised next to it the **Church of the Holy Cross,** a sight no one should miss if they're anywhere near Lake Van.

Only the obscurity of these Armenian kingdoms, perhaps, has denied their sacred structures their rightful place in the history of art. But two hundred years before anything resembling them could be produced in Europe, and three hundred years before the best Selcuk work, this nation, with no greater cultural influence than its tenuous link to Byzantium, had the talent to create a masterpiece like Akhtamar. In those rough times, it is as if the Armenians had pulled it out of a hat.

Architecture and Reliefs

In form, Akhtamar differs very little from the churches of Ani. Its central plan supports the usual drum and conical dome; here, strangely, the drum is 14-sided and irregular. What makes the church such a jewel is the wealth of sculpture in an unusual squarish style of high relief possibly unique to this building. Later additions have defaced the structure somewhat, a low clumsy porch and what might be either a bell tower or a minaret. No one knows who's responsible for these; the porch incorporates stone not only from earlier Armenian works but also some Moslem gravestones very like the ones at Ahlat. The tower has a sundial, like some of the churches at Ani, but on the other hand, it also has Islamic-style stalactite decoration.

The reliefs of the original church nearly cover it from top to bottom. So rich and varied are its subjects, it seems the artists' intention was not only to tell the whole story of the Bible, but to weave in the very fabric of life itself. With infinite care for detail, and who knows how much time, they succeeded, and ground the warm pink sandstone of their church into a mirror for heaven and earth. Akhtamar exhausts the eye before it exhausts the interest, and one could gaze upon it for days on end and still find new scenes, so here is a brief review of the sculptural scheme:

At the top of the drum, a frieze of running animals is interspersed with grave and serious human faces; similar bands line the architrave and the four gables, from which the four evangelists with their books peer out over the points of the compass. The geometric patterns over the windows of the drum have birds perched in them, while below, dozens of gargoyles, large and small, lions, rams, serpents, eagles, and even a guinea fowl, poke out in all directions. Most have suffered some damage; someone once had nothing better to do than use them for target practice.

Near the top of the drum, another frieze, a vineyard, surrounds the entire structure, full of farmers and labourers, monsters and builders, and hunters and women dancing with bears, all peeking out from the vines. Then, below them, come the large religious scenes, spread randomly about the church. Look long enough and you'll see Adam and Eve with the Serpent, saints in circles as if suspended in bubbles, sea monsters and turkeys, David and Goliath, eagles snatching hares, roosters and angels, lions and bulls, the Virgin Mary, St George and his dragon, battling bears, Jonah tumbling into the whale's mouth (the artists did their best to guess what a whale might look like), a lion licking a man's feet, a bird with a ring in its beak, Judith and Holofernes, and finally King Gagik himself offering his church of Akhtamar to Christ.

THE ISLAND

The foundations of Gagik's palace surround the church. The only other building lies on a small islet nearby, the romantic ruin of a chapel that greets you near the pier on your arrival from the mainland; Akhtamar Island is uninhabited, but it's a beautiful spot, a bare cliff rising straight out of the lake and sloping gently down to the east. There's a beach and a picnic grove, and most visitors spend the whole morning or afternoon on the island. When you're through with the church, take time to observe the equally fascinating variety of the island's natural life; besides the many birds and flowers, some of which you'll never see on the mainland, there are innumerable secret kingdoms of insects among the ruins and rocks, droning away in a hundred different voices, displaying a hundred exotic shapes and colours, including some delicate Art Nouveau dragonflies in sky blue and Lake Van green. Separated by a mile of poison water from the rest of the world, the wildlife of Akhtamar Island has evolved into a world of its own.

To get there, you can take any bus or dolmuş from Van to the quay near Gevaş, 30 kilometres from the city. In Gevaş a fourteenth-century Turkish princess lies in an elegant 12-sided *türbe*, and nearby there's a graveyard with some of the same curious stones as at Ahlat. In the mountains above the town, the village of **Çatak** is located in a wooded corner of the region and near it are the **waterfalls of Gahnisipi,** a distant tributary of the Tigris.

City of Van

The city of **Van** goes back to the ninth century BC and the Urartian King Sarduri I, its founder. His capital of Tushpa was erected on a great rock on the lakeshore that has been the heart of the city throughout its existence; or at least until World War I, when old Van was completely destroyed, in battles first with Armenian rebels and later with the Russians. Instead of rebuilding on the spot, the people of Van instead relocated their town to a higher and healthier spot, $1\frac{1}{2}$ km from the lake. Modern Van, not surprisingly, has little of interest, but is making a credible start toward becoming a pleasant town. Like so many of these 'frontier cities' of Eastern Anatolia, Van turns its best face to the world with a thoroughly modern main street,

Cumhuriyet Caddesi, and two fine new mosques, one still under construction; these may well be the largest new mosques in Turkey. Just a block off the main street, though, are sheds and lumberyards, sheep and empty lots—a town waiting to be built.

CITADEL

Very little remains of old Van apart from the **citadel** on the rock. Here, above the serious, neatly cut 30-ton blocks of the Urartian master masons, successions of Armenian and Turkish rulers built Van's castle in rubble wall and mud brick, now just eroded enough to give the whole an outlandish appearance. The foundations of the Urartian castle, called Sardurburcu today, yielded numerous inscriptions that have contributed much to our knowledge of the Urartians. Most concern relations with Assyria, and the older ones are written in Assyrian cuneiforn, the first script used by the Urartians, while later writings appear in their own hieroglyphics.

From the citadel, the second Urartian capital of **Toprakkale** can be seen, built in the last century of the kingdom's existence. Just why, no one knows; Tushpa, though often besieged, was never taken. The foundations of a temple and palace remain, but as the site is located in a military zone, it cannot now be visited.

Van Museum

However, you can see the best of both these sites and many others at the **Van Museum,** one block north of Cumhuriyet Caddesi, with one of the best archaeological collections of any provincial museum. Here the outdoor sculpture garden competes with the works inside for one's attention. The star of the collection is an exquisitely carved relief of the god Teshup, for whom the Urartian capital was named. Teshup stands on the back of a bull, Hittite-fashion, and near him are what appear to be two tridents with their tines shaped like leaves, an unusual attribute for a god of storms. Also from the Urartians are stones that may have been boundary markers, oddly with Assyrian cuneiform on one side and Armenian crosses on the other. The Karakoyunlu and Akkoyunlu, Black Sheep and White, both of whom frequented the region, are represented with some of their gravestones curved as, of course, sheep; one has a maze on it.

Inside, the museum offers the best collection of Urartian artworks, surpassing even Ankara's. There are many examples of the intricately carved jewellery and cylinder seals, an Urartian speciality, and the well known bronze and gold plates and belts, engraved with lions, bulls, sphinxes, hunting scenes, and religious processions. One intriguing subject is a seated god with a head that resembles the famous Hatti cosmos symbols in the Ankara museum. The Urartians were also skilled in casting bronze, shown here by brooches and bells, and standards in the form of antlers. Finally, there's an

Urartian gameboard, for which you have to imagine what the rules might have been (proto-backgammon?).

Also to remind us that the Urartians are really mere latecomers in this ancient land, the museum contains some of the pictographs archaeologists have found carved in rocks all over Hakkari province. Some go as far back as 7000 BC.

NORTH OF THE CITY

To the north of the city, the road once more leaves the lakeshore, passing through a land of bare green hills; where it rejoins the lake at **Bendimahi,** there's another waterfall, on the Muradiye Creek. **Erçek Gölü,** to the south of Bendimahi, is a midget Lake Van, but by no means are these the only lakes. The topography from Ararat down to the Mesopotamian plain was formed by volcanic action, and instead of neatly folded linear mountain ranges, patches and circlets of extinct volcanoes and lava plateaus surround a series of isolated basins, some low enough to be lakes. Other large lakes are nearby in the USSR, and Lake Reza'iyeh in Iran is even bigger than Lake Van. Sheep thrive here; the Turkish government reports that there are six of them for every person; difficulty of access makes this south-eastern corner of Turkey among the quietest and least known parts of the nation.

Also, these mountain fortresses are the heart of Kurdistan, and depending on your outlook you may see them as the last strongholds of the traditional Kurdish mountain culture, or merely as being backward and poor; whichever, the setting, in the mountain streams and woods of Hakkari province, is one of the most scenic in all Turkey. Only one road leads into this province, following the lovely valley of the River Zap as it negotiates its way through the mountains.

SOUTH-EAST OF THE CITY

Some 36 kilometres south-east from Van, this road passes the ruins called **Çavuştepe,** the eighth-century BC Urartian palace-city of **Sardurihinili.** Sarduri II founded it and named it after himself, and here many of the finest art works of the Urartians have been found. At first glance, the long narrow ridge at the centre of a mountain basin seems much too thin for any sort of a city to fit on it. It is; only the fortress and palace stood here; but look closely down at the surrounding fields and faint traces of ancient streets and foundations will become visible, though they've been tilled over for centuries.

Sarduri's palace must have been a work of some architectural sophistication, strung out along an arrow-straight axis from the castle at the highest point of the ridge, down through the upper and lower terraces of the palace. You can follow the long corridor along this axis, past the royal apartments and offices, the cisterns and storerooms with their huge *pithoi*. As always, only the foundations remain, of finely worked masonry, and in the lower terrace a cuneiform inscription states that Sarduri built the palace and city in honour of 'Haldi, the War God'. Sarduri goes on to speak of 'cities and gardens where nothing was before', and if you look down at the southern flank of the ridge you'll see the famous work that made it possible. The **Semiramis canal,** associated with that legendary queen but actually a project of the Urartian King Menua, is an irrigation canal still in use after 2700 years, watering not only this basin but the plains around Van. All together, the canal snakes for 51 kilometres crossing a range of very high hills; even the Assyrians, who mention it in their records, were impressed with it.

During the extensive excavations of Çavuştepe, one particular artefact was found in great abundance—arrowheads. Identified as Scythian in origin, tens of thousands of them were found scattered in and around the fortress and stuck in Sardurihinili's walls, testimony to the violent and sudden end of Urartian civilisation and to the inability of this troubled fulcrum of the civilised world, once so blessed in human talent and natural abundance, to ever produce anything that lasts.

The Hoşap Fortress, Lake Van

HOŞAP

When the great states falter, isolated regions like this naturally revert to the feudal rule of the local strongman. As evidence from another age, take in the wonderful evocative **Castle of Hoşap,** gripping the summit of a tall crag along the main road some 23 kilometres beyond Çavuştepe. Hoşap appears on Turkish maps as *Güzelsu*; the two words mean 'sweet waters' referring to the springs in the village below, but Hoşap is a Kurdish word and this is a Kurdish Castle, built in 1643 by a local despot named Sari Süleyman in the days when Ottoman control over these parts was slipping.

Hoşap could easily be a castle on the Rhine; certainly it's the only substantial fortification in this corner of Turkey since the days of the Urartians. However he came by it, Sari Süleyman had the money to do the job right; his great gate with its carved lions and teardrop arabesques is both impressive and beautiful. Once behind the formidable iron doors, you can see the round council room of Sari Süleyman, directly above the gate, and the baths, gaols, and harem quarters, all more or less ruined. Beyond these rises the great three-storey keep, crowned with watch towers and ports for dispensing boiling oil.

From the castle, it's easy to make out the wall that once enclosed the town, now a mere village, of Hoşap. Like the fortress at Van, this wall is mud brick and half eroded into odd shapes; one part descending a gentle slope looks, for all the world, like the spiney back of some slumbering dinosaur, crouched among the little houses. Also from the castle, you can look over to the mountains of Iran and Iraq. This is about the end of the line; beyond Hoşap, you can take the scenic route as far as Hakkari, but beyond that, there are only mud brick villages, sheep, and *Jandarmas* chasing the occasional Kurdish bandit back over the borders.

GETTING AROUND

Planes to Van from Ankara five times a week, and from Diyarbakir once a week. The daily train from Istanbul ends at Tatvan, where the T.C. Denizyollari steamer awaits to carry its passengers and freight across to Van.

Because of the rugged mountain terrain in this district, the road network is sparse; even around the lake, the stretch between Tatvan and Adilcevaz is not paved yet. Some roads that have been made up, like the southern shore of the lake or part of the dead-end road to Hakkari, are tortuous and rough on your vehicle.

To get to Akhtamar Island, take any bus going west and mention the island; they'll let you off at the boat dock near Gevaş, where you wait at an outdoor cafe until enough people show up to make the trip. Fares are nominally 16 100 TL for a boatload, but in fact they are whatever the ferryman feels like asking (about 700 TL per person or less, round trip). Still, it's in your interest to go when others do to avoid a long wait. If you find anyone in Van going on a group tour, ask when they're leaving and get there first.

If you're without a car, a trip to Hoşap can be done by bus, but the return is chancy, especially if you want to stop at Çavuştepe. The 160 km taxi trip will be about 8400 TL.

The farther you get from Van, the more difficult getting around becomes. And be advised that there is a security problem in the mountain strongholds where the paved roads don't go. In Siirt and Hakkari provinces, and the southern fringes of Van, Kurdish separatists shoot up a police outpost every few months, but no foreigners, as far as we know, have ever been involved. This has been going on for at least 500 years.

TOURIST INFORMATION

Van: 127 Cumhuriyet Caddesi, right behind Büyük Asur Hotel, tel. (0611) 2018 or 3675.
Hakkari: Belediye (city hall), no phone.

WHERE TO STAY

There are two hotels in Van with any pretentions: the brand new Büyük Urartu (not yet rated), 60 Cumhuriyet Caddesi, tel. (0611) 3753, decorated in Urartian Art Deco, with singles for 2500 TL and doubles at 3000 TL; and the **Akdamar Oteli** (H 2), tel. (0611) 3036–2908, at 22 Kazim Karabekir Cad. 22, which for 4000 TL a single, 5100 a double has television, but also mandatory half board. Among the cheaper ones, the pleasant **Beşkardeş Oteli** (H4) 34 Cumhuriyet Cad., tel. (0611) 1116–7 is the best, with singles for 1500 TL, and doubles for 2000. In Hakkari, take what you can find.

EATING OUT

One good lokanta in Van is the **Şafak** on Maraş Caddesi, just off Cumhuriyet, near the tourist office, which has a wide selection of Turkish specialities and outdoor dining, for around 2000 TL a meal. Also in the city, there are several in the small area east of Cumhuriyet; none look very encouraging anywhere else in the province.

CHRONOLOGY

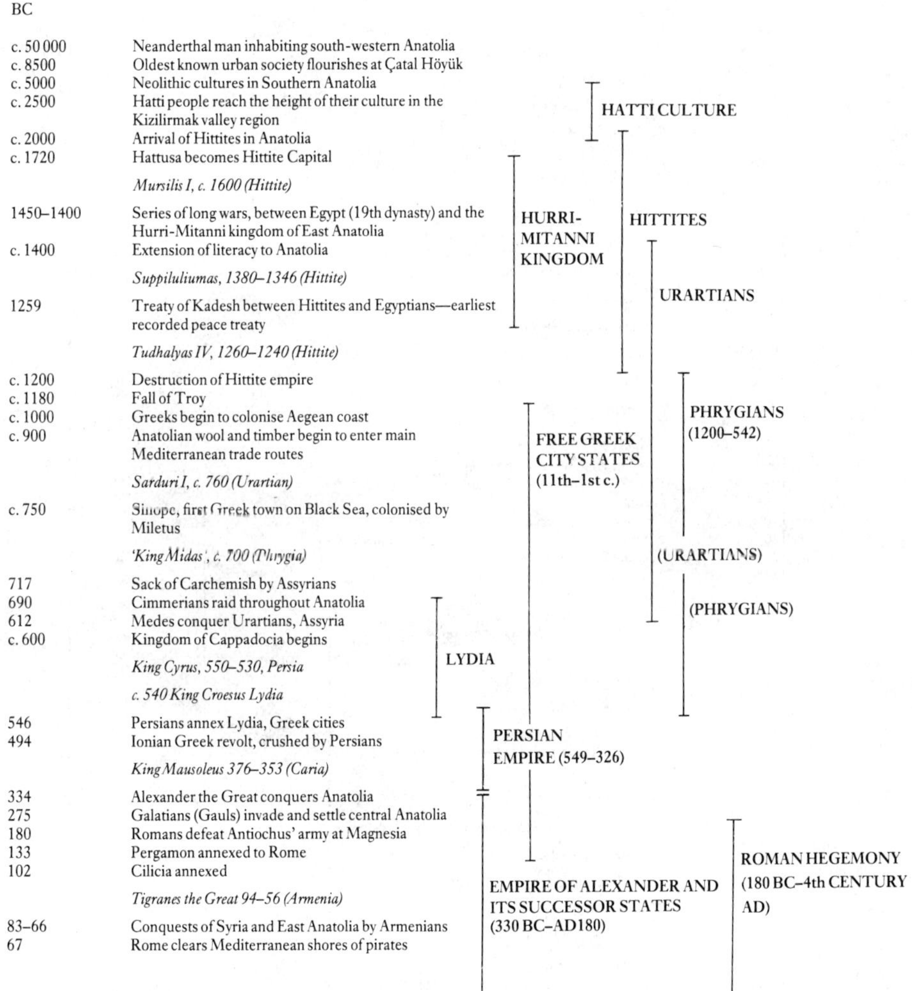

BC

c. 50 000	Neanderthal man inhabiting south-western Anatolia
c. 8500	Oldest known urban society flourishes at Çatal Höyük
c. 5000	Neolithic cultures in Southern Anatolia
c. 2500	Hatti people reach the height of their culture in the Kizilirmak valley region
c. 2000	Arrival of Hittites in Anatolia
c. 1720	Hattusa becomes Hittite Capital
	Mursilis I, c. 1600 (Hittite)
1450–1400	Series of long wars, between Egypt (19th dynasty) and the Hurri-Mitanni kingdom of East Anatolia
c. 1400	Extension of literacy to Anatolia
	Suppiluliumas, 1380–1346 (Hittite)
1259	Treaty of Kadesh between Hittites and Egyptians—earliest recorded peace treaty
	Tudhalyas IV, 1260–1240 (Hittite)
c. 1200	Destruction of Hittite empire
c. 1180	Fall of Troy
c. 1000	Greeks begin to colonise Aegean coast
c. 900	Anatolian wool and timber begin to enter main Mediterranean trade routes
	Sarduri I, c. 760 (Urartian)
c. 750	Sinope, first Greek town on Black Sea, colonised by Miletus
	'King Midas', c. 700 (Phrygia)
717	Sack of Carchemish by Assyrians
690	Cimmerians raid throughout Anatolia
612	Medes conquer Urartians, Assyria
c. 600	Kingdom of Cappadocia begins
	King Cyrus, 550–530, Persia
	c. 540 King Croesus Lydia
546	Persians annex Lydia, Greek cities
494	Ionian Greek revolt, crushed by Persians
	King Mausoleus 376–353 (Caria)
334	Alexander the Great conquers Anatolia
275	Galatians (Gauls) invade and settle central Anatolia
180	Romans defeat Antiochus' army at Magnesia
133	Pergamon annexed to Rome
102	Cilicia annexed
	Tigranes the Great 94–56 (Armenia)
83–66	Conquests of Syria and East Anatolia by Armenians
67	Rome clears Mediterranean shores of pirates

TURKEY

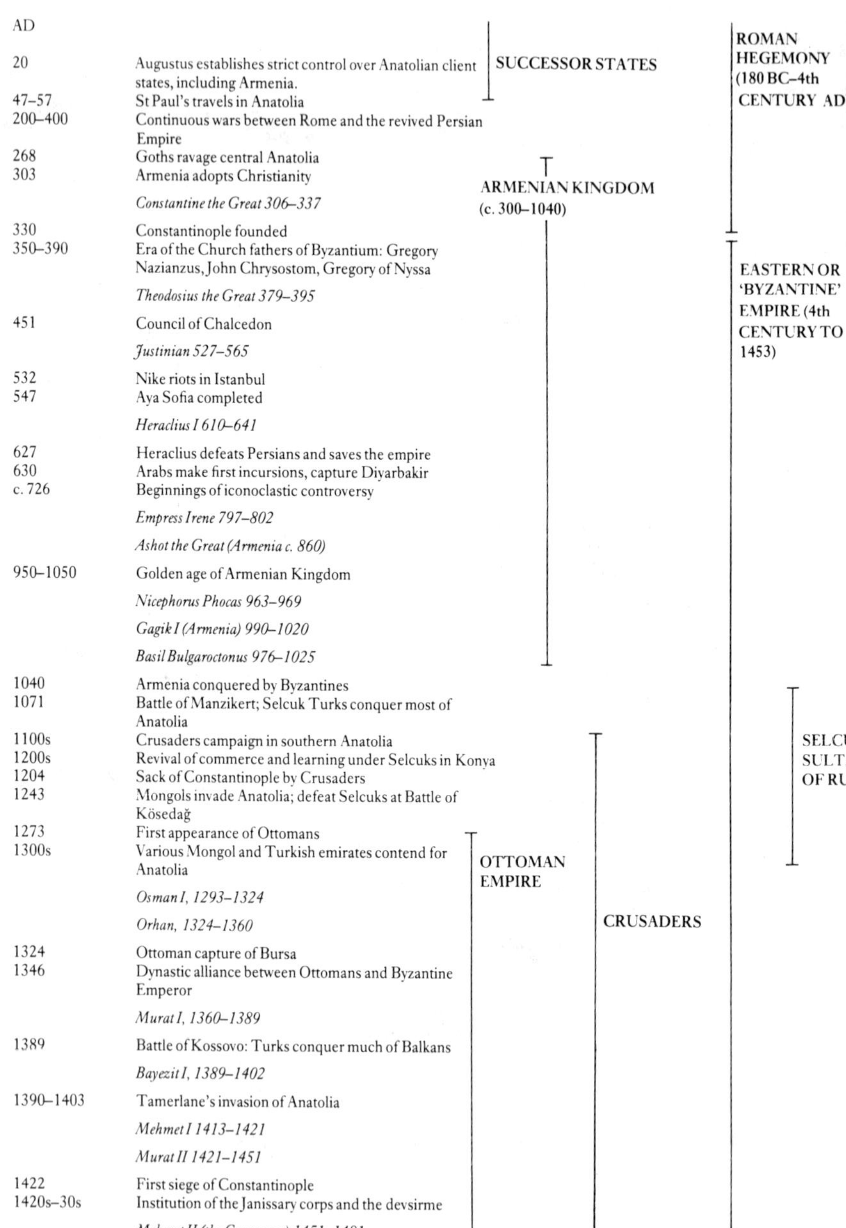

AD	
20	Augustus establishes strict control over Anatolian client states, including Armenia.
47–57	St Paul's travels in Anatolia
200–400	Continuous wars between Rome and the revived Persian Empire
268	Goths ravage central Anatolia
303	Armenia adopts Christianity
	Constantine the Great 306–337
330	Constantinople founded
350–390	Era of the Church fathers of Byzantium: Gregory Nazianzus, John Chrysostom, Gregory of Nyssa
	Theodosius the Great 379–395
451	Council of Chalcedon
	Justinian 527–565
532	Nike riots in Istanbul
547	Aya Sofia completed
	Heraclius I 610–641
627	Heraclius defeats Persians and saves the empire
630	Arabs make first incursions, capture Diyarbakir
c. 726	Beginnings of iconoclastic controversy
	Empress Irene 797–802
	Ashot the Great (Armenia c. 860)
950–1050	Golden age of Armenian Kingdom
	Nicephorus Phocas 963–969
	Gagik I (Armenia) 990–1020
	Basil Bulgaroctonus 976–1025
1040	Armenia conquered by Byzantines
1071	Battle of Manzikert; Selcuk Turks conquer most of Anatolia
1100s	Crusaders campaign in southern Anatolia
1200s	Revival of commerce and learning under Selcuks in Konya
1204	Sack of Constantinople by Crusaders
1243	Mongols invade Anatolia; defeat Selcuks at Battle of Kösedağ
1273	First appearance of Ottomans
1300s	Various Mongol and Turkish emirates contend for Anatolia
	Osman I, 1293–1324
	Orhan, 1324–1360
1324	Ottoman capture of Bursa
1346	Dynastic alliance between Ottomans and Byzantine Emperor
	Murat I, 1360–1389
1389	Battle of Kossovo: Turks conquer much of Balkans
	Bayezit I, 1389–1402
1390–1403	Tamerlane's invasion of Anatolia
	Mehmet I 1413–1421
	Murat II 1421–1451
1422	First siege of Constantinople
1420s–30s	Institution of the Janissary corps and the devsirme
	Mehmet II (the Conqueror) 1451–1481

SUCCESSOR STATES

ARMENIAN KINGDOM (c. 300–1040)

OTTOMAN EMPIRE

CRUSADERS

ROMAN HEGEMONY (180 BC–4th CENTURY AD)

EASTERN OR 'BYZANTINE' EMPIRE (4th CENTURY TO 1453)

SELCU SULTA OF RU

CHRONOLOGY

(CRUSADERS)

(OTTOMAN EMPIRE)

1453	Conquest of Constantinople
1460s	Conquest of Trebizond, Konya
	Bayezit II (the Mystic) 1481–1512
1480s	Civil wars of the pretender Prince Cem.
1490s	Shiite revolts in Anatolia
	Selim I (the Grim) 1512–1520
1510s	Conquest of Egypt and the last surviving Turkish emirates
	Süleyman I (the Magnificent) 1520–1566
1522	Expulsion of Crusaders from Aegean coast
1530–50	New Ottoman Navy controls much of the Mediterranean; high point of Ottoman power
1622	Murder of reforming Sultan Osman II
1683	Second siege of Vienna
	Ahmet III 1703–30
1717–30	The 'Tulip Period'
1727	First books in Turkish published
1770	Battle of Çeşme; total destruction of Ottoman fleet by Russians
	Selim II 1789–1807
1804–21	Greek and Serbian wars of Independence
	Mahmud II 1808–1839
1826	The Auspicious Incident: massacre of the Janissaries
1830	'Tanzimat' reforms; abolition of feudalism
	Abdül Mecit I 1839–61
1853–6	Crimean War
	Abdül Hamid 1876–1909
1876	First constitution
1909	'Young Turk' revolution
1912–13	Balkan Wars
1914–18	World War I
1919–23	Wars of Independence
1920s–30s	Atatürk's era of reforms
1938	Death of Atatürk
1939	The Hatay joins Turkey through plebiscite
1949	First free nationwide elections
1960	First of three military coups; civilian government restored in 1960
1980	Political crisis and terrorism results in third army takeover; civilian government re-established in 1983

TURKISH REPUBLIC

PLACE NAMES

The following is a list of some of the main historical sites mentioned in the guide giving their classical names and the corresponding modern Turkish place names.

Classical name	*Modern name*
Adrianople	Edirne
Antioch	Antakya
Assos	Behramkale
Constantinople	Istanbul
Daphne	Harbiye
Edessa	Urfa
Gallipoli	Gelibolu
Halicarnassus	Bodrum
Magnesia ad Sipylus	Manisa
Myra	Demre
Nicaea	Iznik
Pergamon	Bergama
Phocaea	Foça
Sardis	Sart
Smyrna	Izmir
Trebizond	Trabzon

THE TURKISH LANGUAGE

Linguists say Turkish is a member of the Ural-Altaic group, which makes it related to Finnish, Hungarian, and little else. As well as the 50 million Turks in Turkey, dialects are spoken by perhaps as many as 100 million more Turcomans, Kirghiz, Uzbeks, and others in central Asia; a Turk from Istanbul could make himself understood as far east as Manchuria.

He couldn't get far, though, in Helsinki or Budapest. This is one of the truly grey areas in linguistics, but what proves these languages have a common origin is their use of *agglutination.* Turkish has no prepositions, and most of the difficulties of the language are caused by the subtleties of the infinite number of suffixes that are tacked onto words or replace them. In this book, for instance, words may often be disguised by their endings: *Yeşil Cami*—Green Mosque, but *Rüstem Paşa Camii*—Mosque *of* Rustem Pasha.

The Turks are very proud of their language, with its long and distinguished list of poets and writers, its melodious vowel harmony, and its wealth of expressive colloquialisms. There is even a slang dictionary for Turkish. The Turks love playing word games; there are palindromes like '*Traş niçin şart?*' or 'Why get a haircut?', and long nightmares of agglutination; the longest word yet discovered in Turkish is an entire sentence: '*Çekoslovakyalilaştiramadiklarimizdanmisiniz?*' meaning 'Are you the people whose nationality we cannot change to Czechoslovakian?'.

Like the French, the Turks have a semi-official body concerned with keeping the purity of the language. In the 1930s, this was a hot political issue; reforming the language was one of Atatürk's pet ideas, and he replaced thousands of Arabic, Persian, and Greek words with 'Turkish' equivalents, either invented or found in use in obscure corners of the nation. The drive for reform slowed down when parents began to have trouble understanding their children—and Atatürk's speeches. The 30s was also the decade of the great Alphabet Reform. Previously, Turkish, with its eight vowels had been shoehorned into Arabic characters, which have only three, with results such as the words for 'great' and 'dead' being written the same (*ulu, ölü*). In part for this reason, but also to make European languages accessible to the Turks, Atatürk decreed that the change must be made. Throughout the decade, he travelled to almost every large town in Turkey with chalk and a blackboard. While the people crowded around in thousands to see their nation's hero, they got their first lesson in Roman letters. Amazingly, it all worked, far better, in fact, than Atatürk ever dreamed. The changeover that was supposed to take fifteen years was accomplished in five.

LEARNING TURKISH

If you want to learn some Turkish before you go, the best book is *Colloquial Turkish* by Yusuf Mardin (Routledge & Kegan Paul). Second best is *Teach Yourself Turkish* by G. L. Lewis (Hodder and Stoughton) a more stiff and formal approach with big grammar charts. Don't try to use a phrase book. The difficulties in pronunciation are great, and most of the phrases in such books will either perplex the Turks or make them laugh. If you can learn the numbers, and some of the words listed below, you can communicate almost all your wishes, and make your stay in Turkey infinitely more fun. Literature from the Turkish Travel Office tends to overestimate the number of people you'll find who speak English or German—which also comes in handy. Knowing just a few words will also endear you to the Turks (and probably prevent you from ever getting ripped off).

PRONUNCIATION

This is regular and logical, since the alphabet was designed to fit the language. Get to know these new letters:

â—faint 'y' sound in preceding consonant; lâleli is lyaah-leh-lee
ç—'ch' as in 'chin';
c—is pronounced like the English 'j'
ş—'sh' as in 'ship'
ğ—'silent' as the 'gh' in 'eight'; it sometimes lengthens the preceding vowel
ö—as the 'eu' in French
ü—as the 'u' in French, almost the same as 'eu'

Turkish also has an **undotted 'I'**, hardly a letter at all; its sound is half swallowed, like the English 'e' in 'barrel' or 'packer'. For printing reasons, it is omitted in this book. All the other letters are more or less as in English except **j** which is 'zh' as in 'measure' and 'v' is more like the English 'w'. All vowels are short except 'o', which is sometimes long, and 'g' is always hard.

Note: Turkish syllables almost *always carry equal weight.* If there is any stress, it will usually be at the end. Besides forgetting that 'c' is sounded like English 'j', the most common mistake foreigners make is to put accents where they don't belong. We do it naturally, but it makes Turkish words unintelligible to the Turks.

Turkish plural forms are -ler or -lar added to the end of the word, for example *adam* (man), *adamlar* (men) or *kalem* (pen), *kalemler* (pens).

VOCABULARY

Because it's impossible to represent phonetically the sounds of the Turkish ü and ö, we've represented both as *eu*; they're almost the same. The sound of the Turkish undotted i is represented by (*ital.*). See the chart above for the pronunciation of these difficult vowels.

Remember that all syllables are unstressed—pronounced with equal emphasis.

Directions and Geography

Nerede? as in:	neh-reh-deh	where is?
Karakol nerede?	Kah-rah-kol neh-reh-deh	Where is the police station?
Şehir	sheh-hihr	city
Su, Çay	soo, chahy	stream
Irmak, Nehir	*i*hr-mahk, neh-hihr	river
Kuzey	koo-zay	north
Guney	g*eu*-nay	south
Bati	bah-t*i*h	west
Doğu	doh-oo	east
Sol	sohl	left
Sağ	say	right
Höyük	h*eu*-y*eu*k	mound
Yayla	yay-lah	mountain pastureland
Ada	ah-dah	island
Dere	deh-reh	valley
Körfez	k*eu*r-fehz	bay
Göl	g*eu*l	lake
Kapi	kah-p*i*h	gate
Hisar, Kale	hih-sahr, kah-leh	castle
Saray	sahr-ahy	palace
Geçit	geh-chit	pass
Tepe	teh-peh	hill
Pinar	pih-nahr	spring
Kuyu	koo-yoo	well
Orman	ohr-mahn	forest
Kilise	kih-lih-seh	church
Cami	jah-mee	mosque
Sokak, Caddesi	soh-kahk, jah-deh-sih	street
Yol	yohl	road
Köy	k*eu*y	village
Çiftlik	chihft-lihk	farm
Deniz	deh-nihz	sea
Gümrük	g*eu*m-r*eu*k	customs

Lise	lih-seh	school
Postane	pos-tah-neh	post office
Türbe, kümbet	t*eu*r-beh, k*eu*m-beht	mausoleum
Karakol	kah-rah-kol	police station
Banka	bahn-kah	bank
Lokanta	loh-kahn-tah	restaurant
Gazino	gah-zih-noh	night club
Gar, Istasyon	gahr, ihs-tas-yohn	train station
Otogar	oh-toh-gahr	bus station
Hamam	hah-mahm	Turkish bath
Benzin istasyonu	ben-zihn ihs-tahs-yohn-oo	petrol station
Çeşme	chesh-meh	fountain
Çarşi	chahr-sh*i*h	market, bazaar
Vilayet	vil-ahy-eht	provincial government house
Kisa	k*i*h-sah	short
Uzun	oo-zoon	long
Durak	doo-rahk	stop (noun)
Dur!	door	stop (imperative)
Yakin	yah-k*i*n	near
Uzak	oo-zahk	far
Burada	boo-rah-dah	here
Şurada	shoo-rah-dah	there
Orada	o-rah-dah	over there
Meydan	may-dahn	square
Hava alani	hah-vah ah-lah-nih	airport
Liman	lih-mahn	port
Iskele	ihs-keh-leh	quay
Köprü	k*eu*-pr*eu*	bridge
Türkiye	T*eu*r-kee-yeh	Turkey
Akdeniz	ahk-deh-nihz	Mediterranean ('white sea')
Karadeniz	kah-rah-deh-nihz	Black Sea
Ege Deniz	eg-eh deh-nihz	Aegean Sea
Trakya	trahk-yah	Thrace
Anadolu	ah-nah-doh-loo	Anatolia
Yunanistan	yoo-nan-ih-stan	Greece
Kibris	kih-brihs	Cyprus

Time

Sabah	sah-bah	morning
Akşam	ahk-shahm	evening

Gece	geh-jeh	night
Şimdi	shihm-dee	now
Ay	ahy	month
Hafta	hahf-tah	week
Yil	yihl	year
Mevsim	mev-sihm	season
Bu/Gelecek	boo/gel-eh-jek	this/next
Bugün	boo-g*eu*n	today
Yarin	yahr-*i*hn	tomorrow
Dün	d*eu*n	yesterday
Kaç saat?	kahtch saaht	What time is it?
Kaçta?	kahch-tah	What time (will it occur?)
Ne zaman?	neh zah-mahn	When?

Days

Pazar	pah-zahr	Sunday
Pazartesi	pah-zahr-teh-sih	Monday
Sali	sah-l*i*h	Tuesday
Çarşamba	chahr-shahm-bah	Wednesday
Perşembe	pehr-shem-beh	Thursday
Cuma	joo-mah	Friday
Cumartesi	joo-mar-teh-sih	Saturday

Months

Ocak	o-jahk	January
Şubat	shoo-baht	February
Mart	mahrt	March
Nisan	nih-sahn	April
Mayis	my-*i*hs	May
Haziran	hah-zih-rahn	June
Temmuz	tem-mooz	July
Ağustos	ah-oos-tohs	August
Eylül	ai-l*eu*l	September
Ekim	eh-kihm	October
Kasim	kah-s*i*hm	November
Aralik	ah-rah-l*i*hk	December

Numbers

Bir	bihr	one
Iki	ih-kih	two
Üç	*eu*tch	three
Dört	d*eu*rt	four

Beş	besh	five
Alti	ahl-t*ı*h	six
Yedi	yeh-dih	seven
Sekiz	seh-kihz	eight
Dokuz	doh-kooz	nine
On	ohn	ten
Onbir	ohn-bihr	eleven
Oniki	ohn-ih-kih	twelve
Yirmi	yihr-mih	twenty
Yirmibir	yihr-mihbihr	twenty one
Otuz	oh-tooz	thirty
Kirk	kihrk	forty
Elli	el-lih	fifty
Altmiş	ahlt-m*ı*sh	sixty
Yetmiş	yet-mish	seventy
Seksen	sek-sehn	eighty
Doksan	dohk-sahn	ninety
Yüz	y*euz*	hundred
Iki yüz	ihk-y*euz*	two hundred
Beş yüz altmiş dört	besh-y*euz*-ahlt-mish-d*eur*t	564
Bin	bihn	thousand
Bin bir	bihn-bihr	a thousand and one
Milyon	mil-yoan	million
Milyar	mil-yahr	milliard (billion)

Note: for a number of objects, use the word *tane* (tah-neh) (piece, bit) in all instances after the number, ex.: *iki tane biletler*—two tickets, *not* iki biletler.

Conversation

Evet	eh-veht	yes
Hayir	hy-*ı*hr	no
Var	vahr	there is
Yok	yohk	there's none
Belki	behl-kih	perhaps
Biliyorum	bihl-ih-yohr-oom	I know
Bilmiyorum	bihl-mih-yohr-oom	I don't know
Lütfen	l*eu*t-fehn	please
(Çok) teşekkür ederim	(chohk) tesh-eh-k*eu*r eh-deh-r*ı*hm	thank you (very much)
Bir şey değil	bihr shay dayl	you're welcome, not at all

Affedersiniz	ahf-feh-dehr-sih-niz	pardon, excuse me
Allahaismarladik	ahl-ahs-mahr-lah-d*i*k	good bye ('Allah go with you')
Güle güle	g*eu*-leh g*eu*-leh	good bye ('smiling, smiling')

Allahaismarladik is said by the person leaving, güle güle is said by the person staying behind.

Merhaba	mehr-hah-bah	hello
Salaam aleikum	sahl-aahm-ahl-ahy-kum	hello ('peace be with you')
Günaydin	g*eu*n-ahy-din	good day
Iyi akşamlar	eey ahk-shahm-lahr	good evening
Iyi geceler	eey geh-jeh-lehr	good night
Yavaş yavaş	yah-vahsh yah-vahsh	slow, wait!
Güzel!	g*eu*-zehl	beautiful (all-purpose compliment)
Çok iyi	chohk eey	very good
Nasilsiniz?	nah-s*i*l-s*i*n-*i*z	How are you?
Türkçe bilmiyorum	t*eu*rk-cheh bihl-mih-yohr-um	I don't speak Turkish
Bu nedir? O nedir?	boo/o neh-dihr	What is this/that?
Ne kadar?	neh kah-dahr	How much is it?
. . . istiyorum	ihs-tih-yohr-um	I want . . .
Niçin?	nih-chihn	how?
Bir dakika	bihr dah-kih-kah	wait a minute
Yaramaz	yahr-ah-mahz	good for nothing! useless
Ucuz	oo-jooz	cheap
Pahali	pah-hah-l*i*h	expensive
Para	pah-rah	money
Hasta	hahs-tah	sick, ill
Sicak	sih-jahk	hot
Soğuk	so-ook	cold
Eski	es-kih	old
Yeni	yeh-nih	new

ARCHITECTURAL TERMS

acroterion: acanthus-leaf decoration on the roofline of a Greek temple
acropolis: citadel; usually the original habitation of a Greek city
agora: market-place, public forum
basilica: a rectangular building of three aisles divided by columns: originally a Roman government building, later a form for Byzantine churches
bedesten: an inner chamber of a Turkish market, built to keep safe the merchant's most valuable goods
bouleuterion: council chamber of a Greek city
cami: Turkish for mosque
caravanserai: inn for caravans and merchants
cavea: semicircle of seats in a Greek theatre
cella: inner sanctum of a Greek temple
exedra: semi-circular recess—space contained under a semi-dome
gymnasium: Greek or Roman school
hamam: Turkish bath
han: inn for merchants
heroon: shrine of a hero—demigod or mortal
hisar: a Turkish citadel or castle
kale: a *hisar*
kilise: Turkish for church
külliye: complex of pious foundations (educational or charitable) around a mosque
kümbet: a *türbe* (see below)
medrese: old school of theology
megaron: large house from Mycenaean period
mescid: a place set aside for Moslem prayer; it may be anything from a small mosque in a palace or *han* to a simple room in a bus station
mihrab: niche in a mosque indicating the direction of Mecca
mimber: mosque pulpit
narthex: outer porch of a church
nave: central aisle of basilica form church
nymphaion: sanctuary of nymphs, or public fountain
oculus: a circular opening at the top of a dome
odeion: concert hall
orchestra: the circular space at the centre of an ancient theatre; originally the dancing ground, later the centre of the action in early Greek drama

palaestra: exercise ground of a *gymnasium*
pendentives: (also known as squinches) spherical sections that support a dome over a square space
prytaneion: committee room of a *bouleuterion* (see above) locale of a city's sacred fire
şadirvan: mosque fountain
stoa: large colonnaded porch attached to another building
temenos: sacred enclosure of a temple
türbe: a mausoleum for a ruler, political dignitary or holy man. In Turkey they are usually free-standing structures with six or eight sides, and a round or prismatic dome

FURTHER READING

ANCIENT HISTORY

Mellaart, James, *Earliest Civilizations of the Near East*, Thames and Hudson, 1965 and *Çatal Höyük*, Thames and Hudson, 1967. Two fascinating books by the archaeologist who uncovered the most important site in the Middle East since Schliemann.

Sandars, N. K. *The Sea Peoples: Warriors of the Ancient Mediterranean*, Thames and Hudson, 1978. The true story of the dark age that brought down the curtain on Troy and the Hittites.

Wood, Michael, *In Search of the Trojan War*, BBC, 1985. A good compilation of current thought on Troy, from the popular TV series.

Erzen, Prof. Dr Afif, *Eastern Anatolia and the Urartians*, Türk Tarih Kurumu, Ankara, 1984.

Akurgal, Ekrem, *Ancient Civilizations and Ruins of Turkey*, Türk Tarih Kurumu, Ankara, 1983. The indispensable guide for anyone interested in exploring Turkey's innumerable archaeological sites in detail (though weak on eastern Anatolia).

Bittel, Kurt, *Guide to Boğazköy*, Ankara, 1972. A must for all Hittite fans, by the archaeologists who excavated their capital.

Young, Rodney S., *Gordion*, Ankara, 1975. More about the Phrygians.

Bean, George, *Aegean Turkey*, 1966; *Turkey's Southern Shore*, 1968; *Turkey Beyond the Maeander*, 1971; and *Lycia*, 1978, Ernest Benn. Fine, anecdotal accounts and detailed guides to Turkey's Greek and Roman sites, by a scholar who discovered not a few of them himself.

Apollonius of Rhodes, *The Voyage of Argo*, translated by E. V. Rieu, Penguin, 1971. Jason's journey along the Black Sea coast.

Arrian, *The Campaigns of Alexander*, translated by Aubrey de Sélincourt, Penguin, 1971.

BYZANTINES AND OTTOMANS

Barber, Noel, *The Sultans*, Simon and Schuster, 1973. The inside story.

Lord Kinross, *The Ottoman Centuries*, Morrow, NY/Jonathan Cape, London, 1977. The best known popular history.

Runciman, Steven, *Byzantine Civilization*, Edward Arnold, London, 1933, and *The Fall of Constantinople, 1453*, Cambridge University Press, 1965. Excellent accounts by the foremost scholar in the field, coloured by a dislike of both Muslims and Turks.

Shaw, Stanford and Ezel, Kual, *History of the Ottoman Empire and Modern Turkey*, 2 vols., Cambridge University Press, 1976.

Goodwin, Godfrey, *A History of Ottoman Architecture*, Thames and Hudson, 1971. The best book on the subject.

MODERN TURKEY

Garnett, Lucy M. J., *The Turkish People; their social life, religious beliefs, institutions and domestic life*, Methuen, London AMS Press NY 1909. Hard to find, but very interesting account by a turn-of-the-century traveller.

Hotham, David, *The Turks*, Murray, London, 1972. One of the best books about modern Turkey.

Stewart, Deamond, *Turkey*, Life World Library, NY, 1965.

Kazancagil, Ali and Özbudun, Ergun, eds., *Atatürk, founder of a modern state*, Anchor, Hamden, Conn., 1981.

Volkan, Vamik D., Itzkowitz, Norman, *The Immortal Atatürk, A Psychobiography*. Unintentionally hilarious ('Little Mustafa's grandiose self was his basic character trait').

Lewis, Bernard, *The Emergence of Modern Turkey*, Oxford Library Press, 1968.

RELIGION AND FOLKLORE

Nicholson, Reynold A., trans. *Rumi: Poet and Mystic*, George Allen & Unwin, 1950. An introduction to the great Sufi teacher, the Mevlana.

Önder, Mehmed, *Mevlâna and Mevlâna Museum*, Istanbul, 1985. Story of the Mevlâna's life in Konya.

Walker, Warren S. & Uysal, Ahmet E., *Tales Alive in Turkey*, Harvard University Press, 1966. An absorbing collection of Turkish folk tales and lore.

And, Metin, *Karagoz: Turkish Shadow Theatre*, Dost, Istanbul, 1979. An excellent account of a dying art, readily available in Turkey.

INDEX

INDEX

INDEX

INDEX